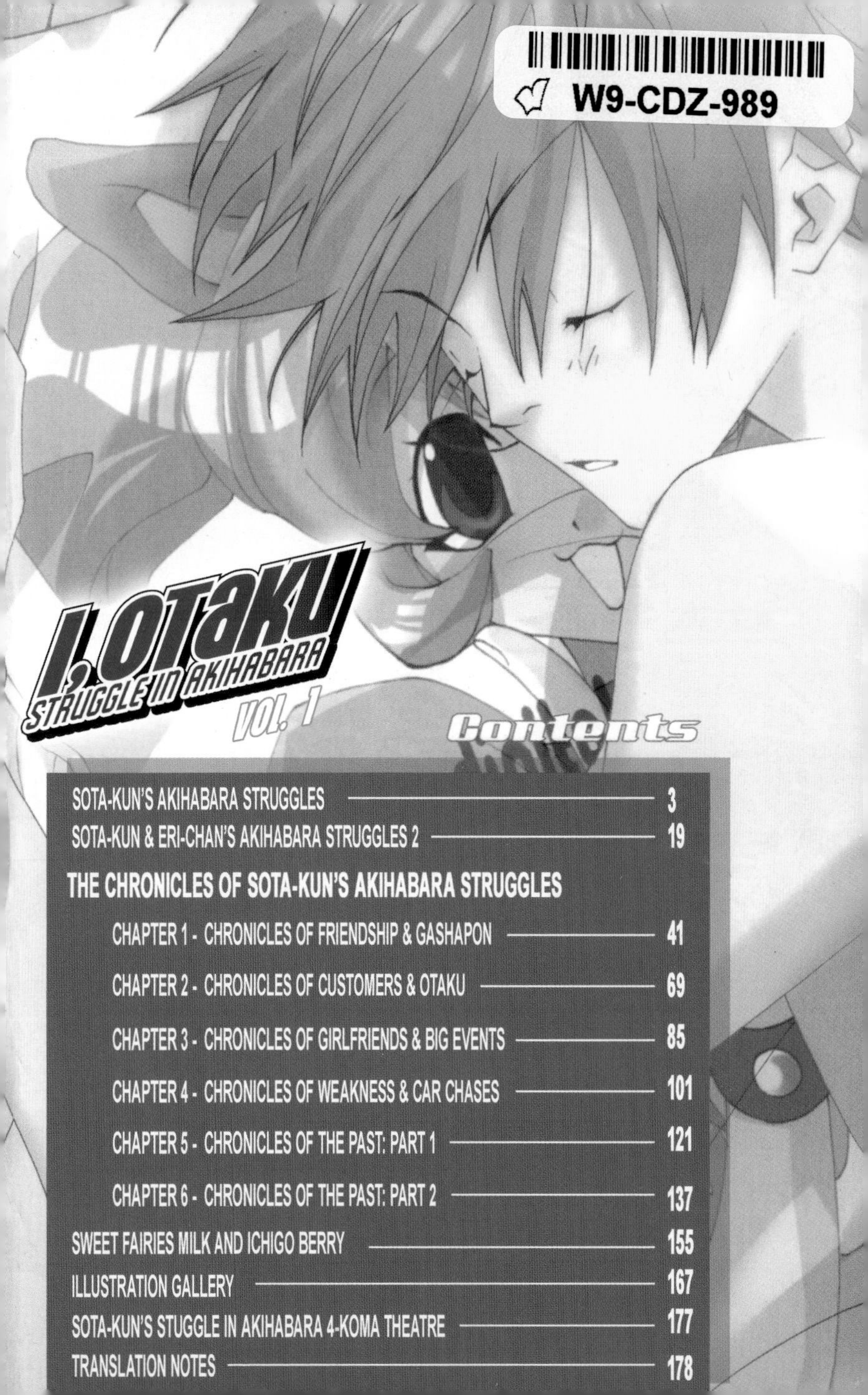
I, OTAKU
STRUGGLE IN AKIHABARA
vol. 1

Contents

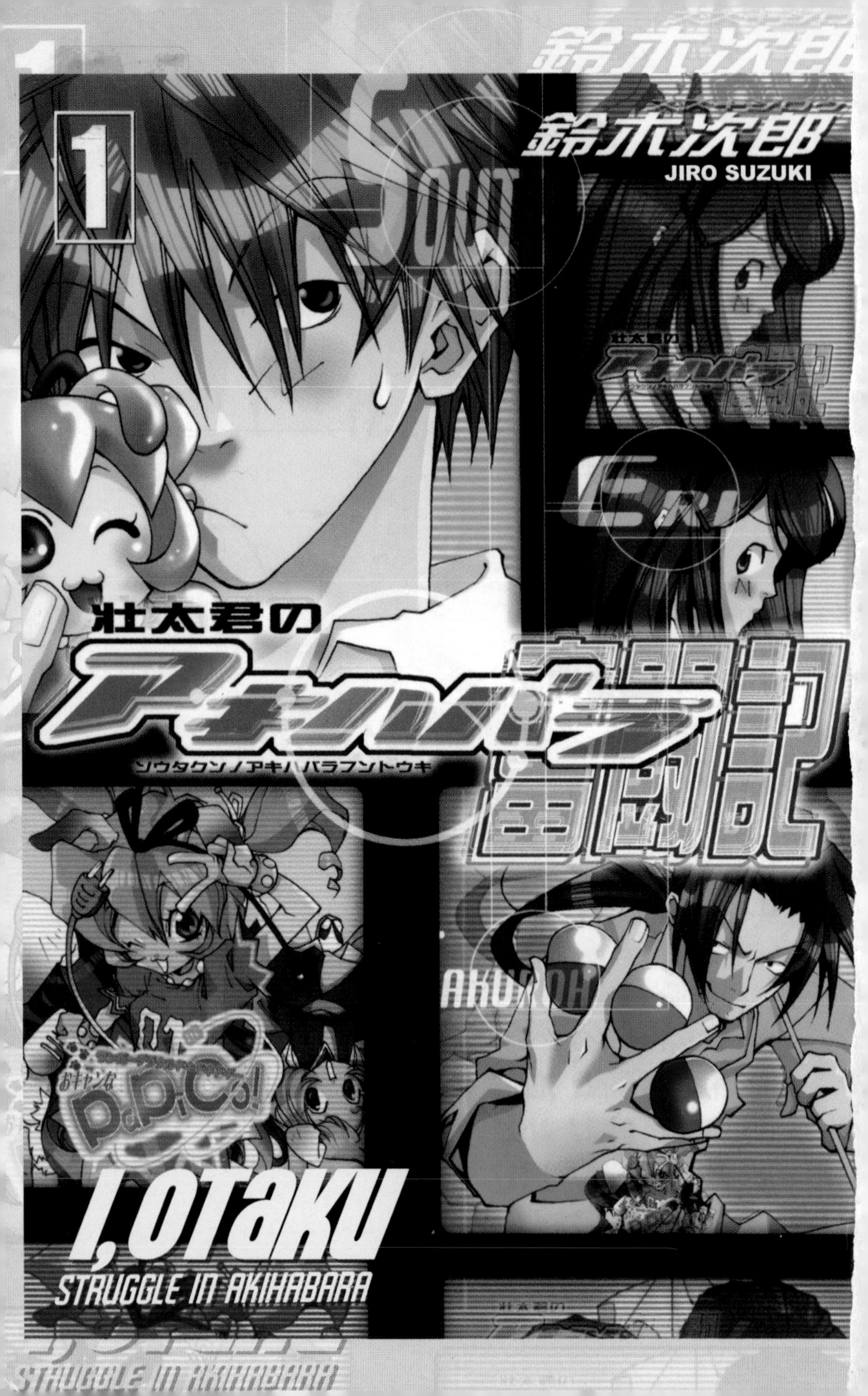
1
鈴木次郎
JIRO SUZUKI
壮太君の
アキハバラ
奮闘記
ソウタクンノアキハバラフントウキ
I, OTAKU
STRUGGLE IN AKIHABARA

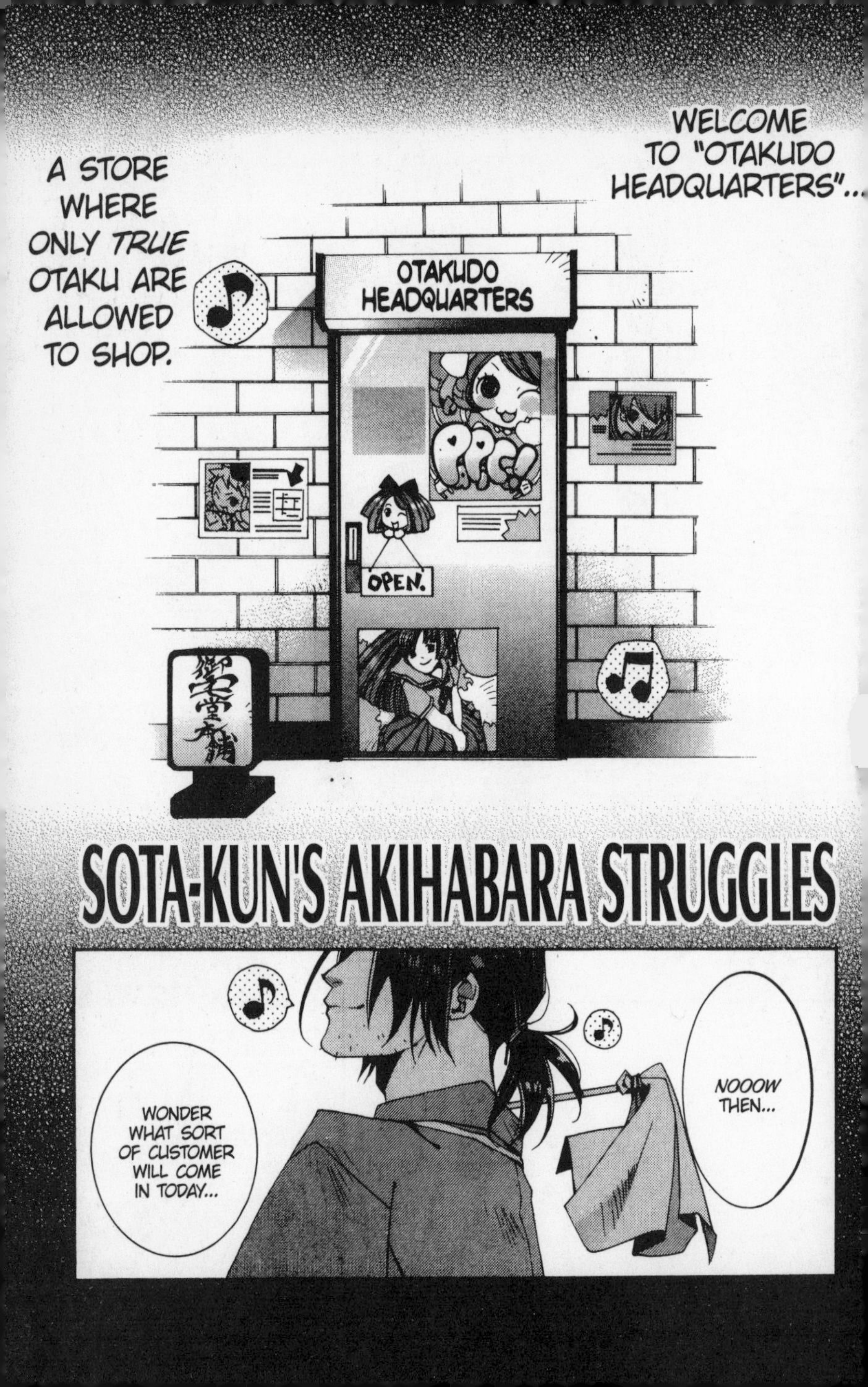
WELCOME TO "OTAKUDO HEADQUARTERS"...
A STORE WHERE ONLY *TRUE* OTAKU ARE ALLOWED TO SHOP.
OTAKUDO HEADQUARTERS
OPEN.
SOTA-KUN'S AKIHABARA STRUGGLES
NOOOW THEN...
WONDER WHAT SORT OF CUSTOMER WILL COME IN TODAY...

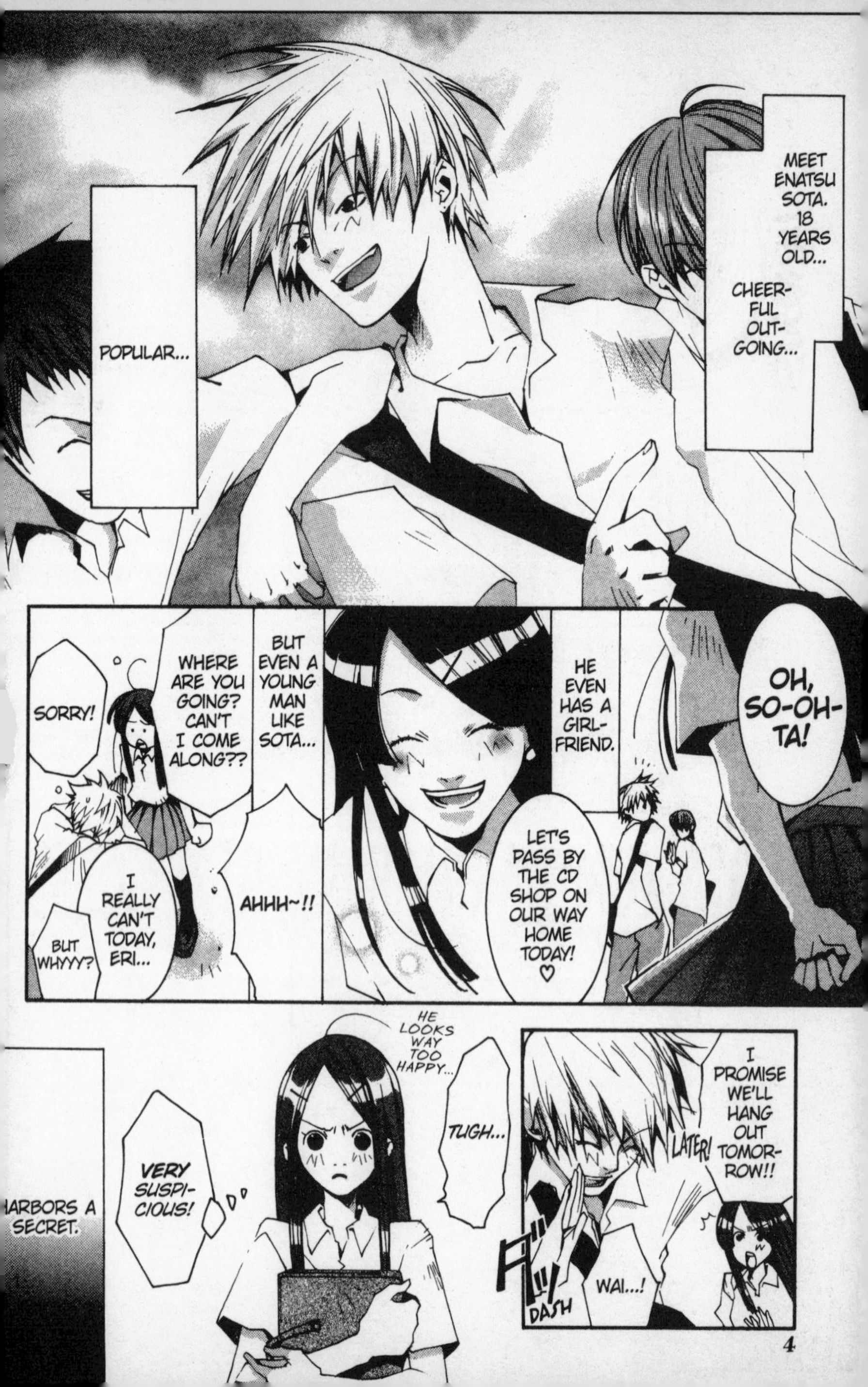
MEET ENATSU SOTA. 18 YEARS OLD...
CHEERFUL OUT-GOING...
POPULAR...
OH, SO-OH-TA!
HE EVEN HAS A GIRL-FRIEND.
LET'S PASS BY THE CD SHOP ON OUR WAY HOME TODAY! ♡
BUT EVEN A YOUNG MAN LIKE SOTA...
AHHH~!!
WHERE ARE YOU GOING? CAN'T I COME ALONG??
SORRY!
I REALLY CAN'T TODAY, ERI...
BUT WHYYY?
I PROMISE WE'LL HANG OUT TOMORROW!!
LATER!
WAI...!
DASH
HE LOOKS WAY TOO HAPPY...
TUGH...
VERY SUSPICIOUS!
HARBORS A SECRET.

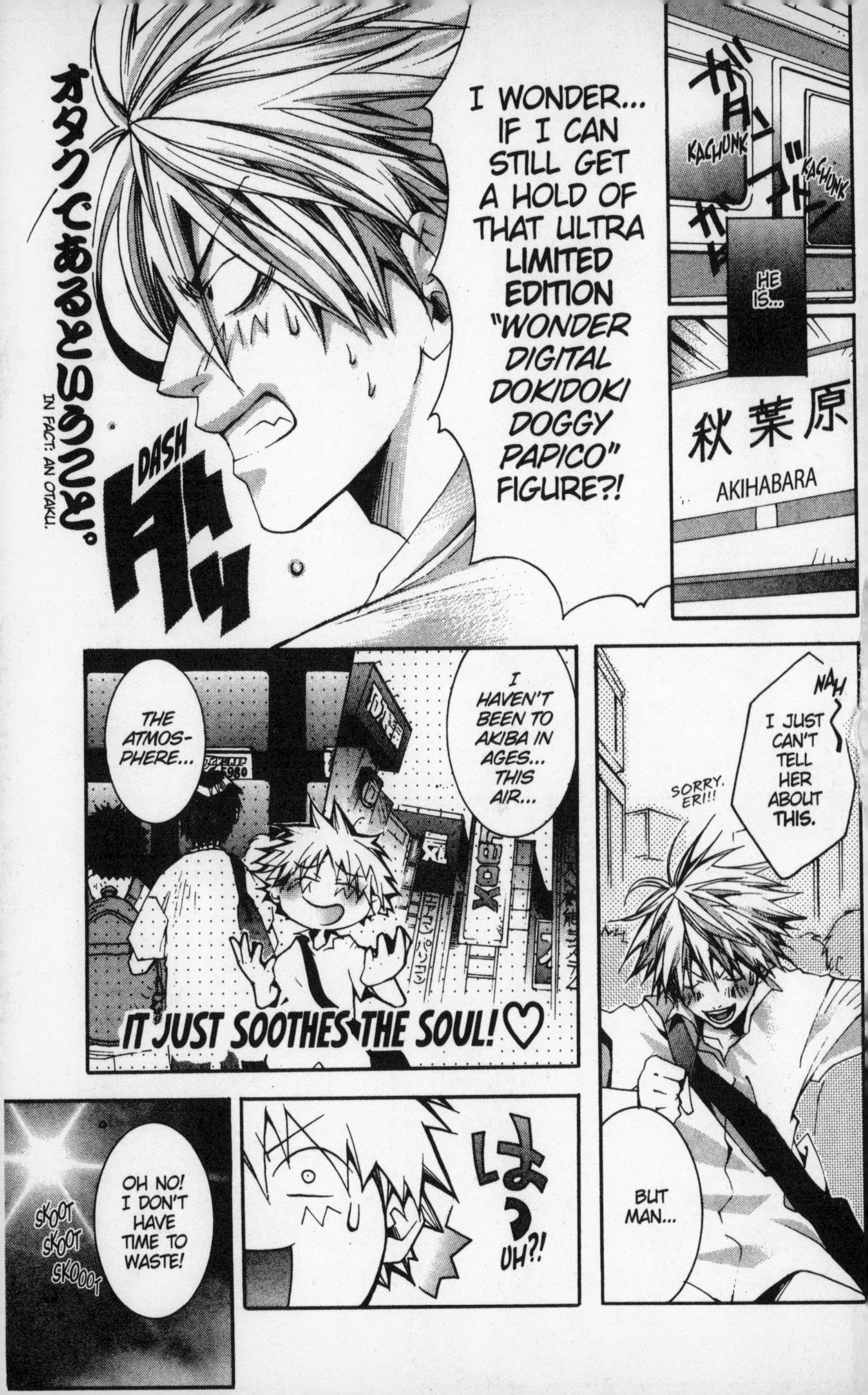

KACHUNK
KACHUNK
HE IS...
秋葉原
AKIHABARA
I WONDER... IF I CAN STILL GET A HOLD OF THAT ULTRA LIMITED EDITION "WONDER DIGITAL DOKIDOKI DOGGY PAPICO" FIGURE?!
DASH
オタクであるということ。
IN FACT: AN OTAKU.
NAH~ I JUST CAN'T TELL HER ABOUT THIS.
SORRY, ERI!!
I HAVEN'T BEEN TO AKIBA IN AGES... THIS AIR...
THE ATMOSPHERE...
IT JUST SOOTHES THE SOUL!♡
BUT MAN...
はっ
UH?!
OH NO! I DON'T HAVE TIME TO WASTE!
SKOOT SKOOT SKOOOT

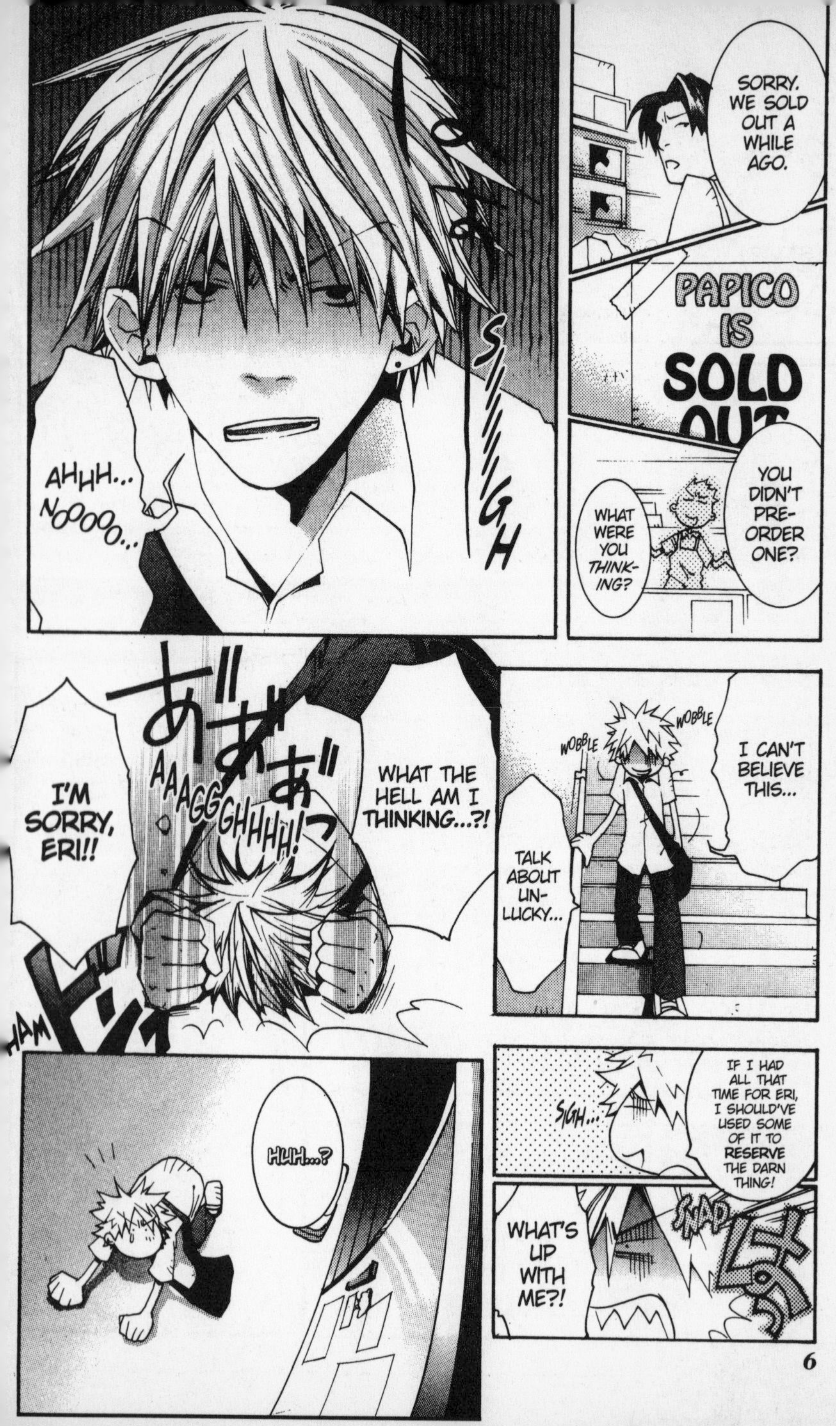
SORRY. WE SOLD OUT A WHILE AGO.
PAPICO IS SOLD OUT
YOU DIDN'T PRE-ORDER ONE?
WHAT WERE YOU THINKING?
SIIIIIGH
AHHH... NOOOOO...
WOBBLE
WOBBLE
I CAN'T BELIEVE THIS...
TALK ABOUT UN-LUCKY...
WHAT THE HELL AM I THINKING...?!
AAAAGGGHHHH!
I'M SORRY, ERI!!
WHAM
IF I HAD ALL THAT TIME FOR ERI, I SHOULD'VE USED SOME OF IT TO RESERVE THE DARN THING!
SIGH...
SNAP
WHAT'S UP WITH ME?!
HUH...?

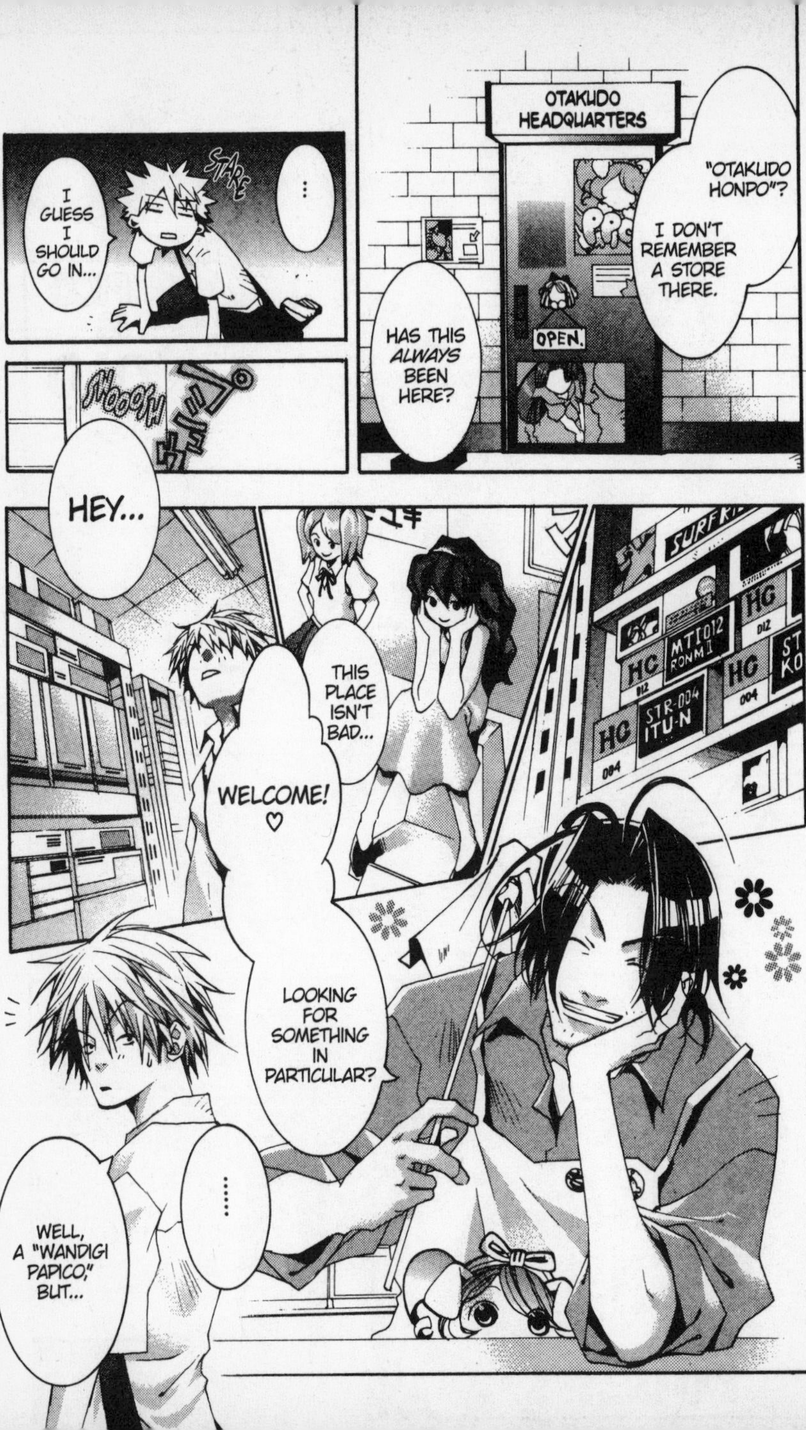
OTAKUDO HEADQUARTERS
"OTAKUDO HONPO"? I DON'T REMEMBER A STORE THERE.
HAS THIS *ALWAYS* BEEN HERE?
OPEN.
...
STARE
I GUESS I SHOULD GO IN...
SHOOOSH
HEY...
THIS PLACE ISN'T BAD...
WELCOME! ♡
LOOKING FOR SOMETHING IN PARTICULAR?
......
WELL, A "WANDIGI PAPICO," BUT...

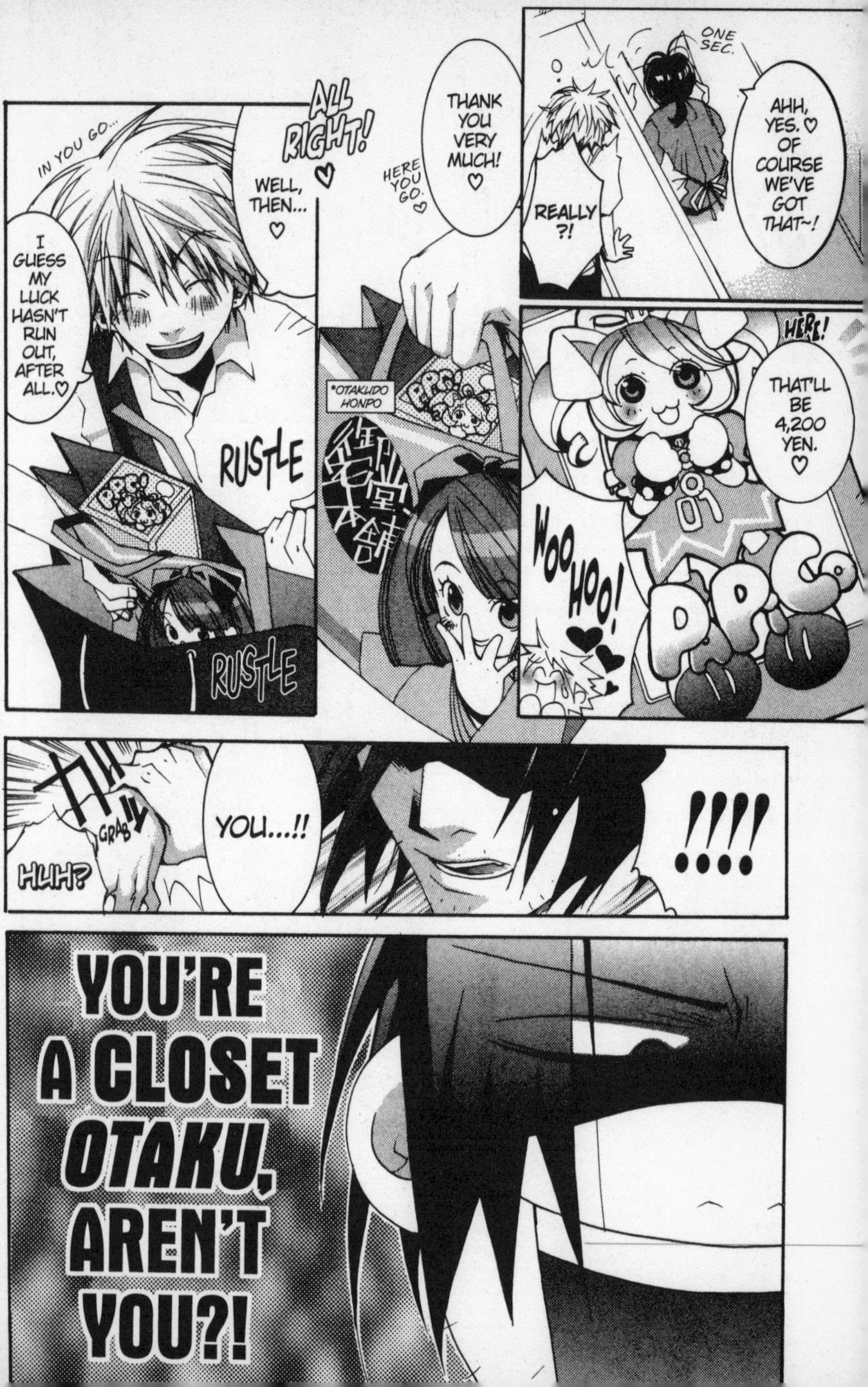
ONE SEC.
AHH, YES. ♡ OF COURSE WE'VE GOT THAT~!
REALLY?!
HERE!
THAT'LL BE 4,200 YEN. ♡
WOO HOO!
THANK YOU VERY MUCH! ♡
HERE YOU GO. ♡
*OTAKUDO HONPO
ALL RIGHT! ♡
WELL, THEN... ♡
IN YOU GO...
I GUESS MY LUCK HASN'T RUN OUT, AFTER ALL. ♡
RUSTLE
RUSTLE
!!!!
YOU...!!
GRAB
HUH?
YOU'RE A CLOSET OTAKU, AREN'T YOU?!

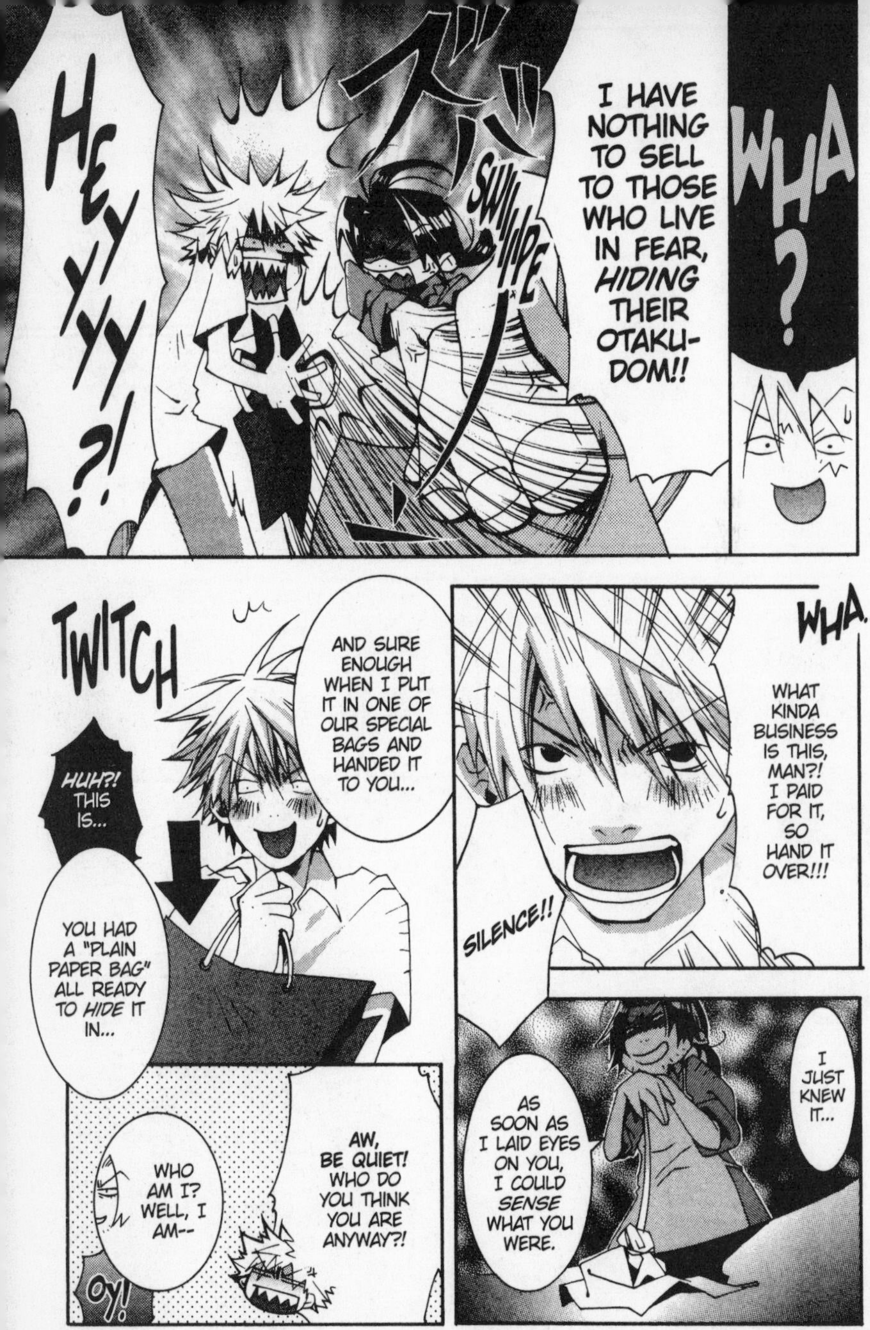
WHA?
I HAVE NOTHING TO SELL TO THOSE WHO LIVE IN FEAR, *HIDING* THEIR OTAKU-DOM!!
SWIIIIPE
HEYYYY?!
WHA...
WHAT KINDA BUSINESS IS THIS, MAN?! I PAID FOR IT, SO HAND IT OVER!!!
SILENCE!!
AND SURE ENOUGH WHEN I PUT IT IN ONE OF OUR SPECIAL BAGS AND HANDED IT TO YOU...
TWITCH
HUH?! THIS IS...
YOU HAD A "PLAIN PAPER BAG" ALL READY TO *HIDE* IT IN...
I JUST KNEW IT...
AS SOON AS I LAID EYES ON YOU, I COULD *SENSE* WHAT YOU WERE.
AW, BE QUIET! WHO DO YOU THINK YOU ARE ANYWAY?!
WHO AM I? WELL, I AM--
Oy!

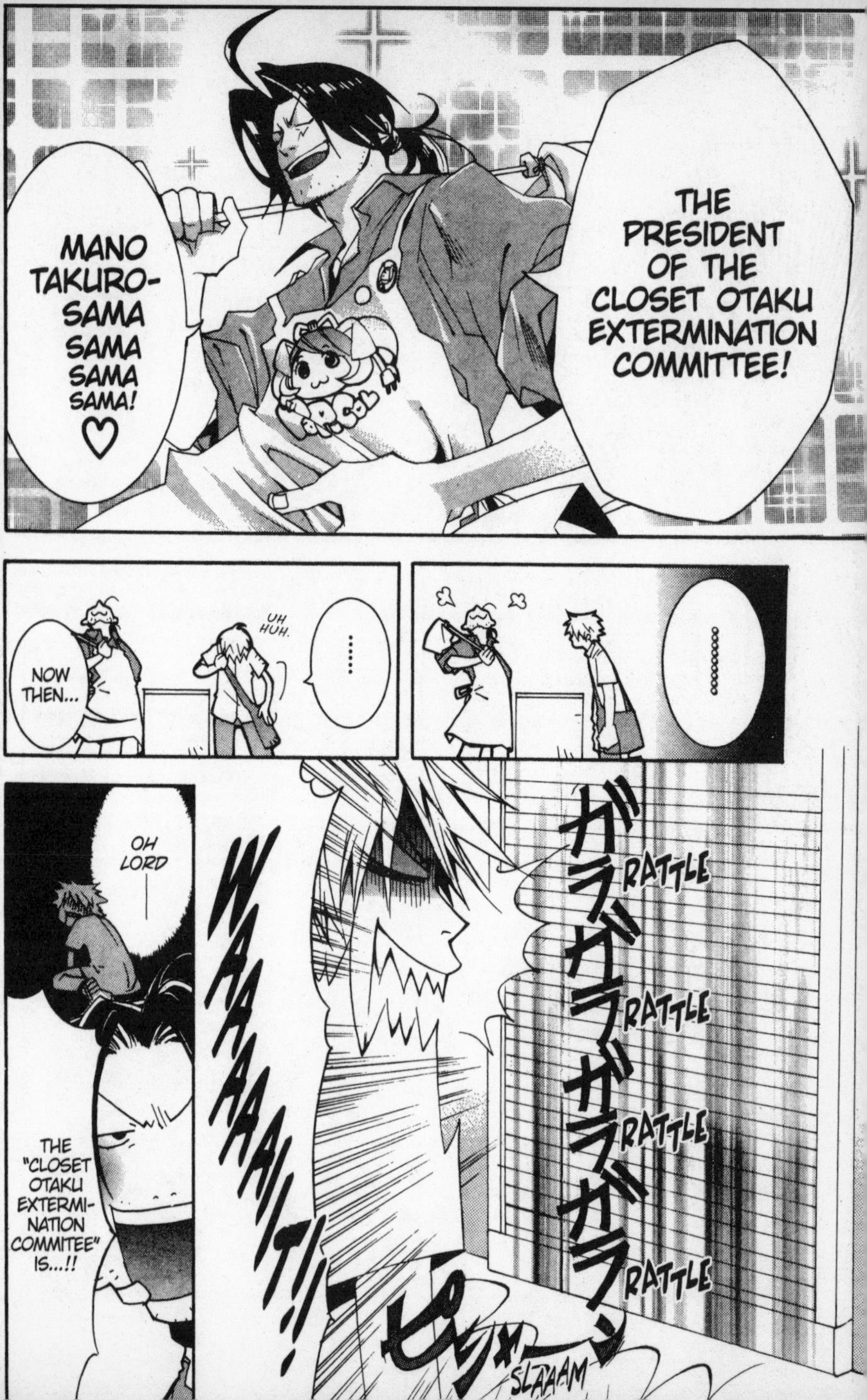
THE PRESIDENT OF THE CLOSET OTAKU EXTERMINATION COMMITTEE!
MANO TAKURO-SAMA SAMA SAMA SAMA! ♡
....
......
UH HUH.
NOW THEN...
ガラガラガラガラ
RATTLE RATTLE RATTLE RATTLE
WAAAAAAAIT!!!
ピシャン
SLAAAM
OH LORD —
THE "CLOSET OTAKU EXTERMINATION COMMITEE" IS...!!

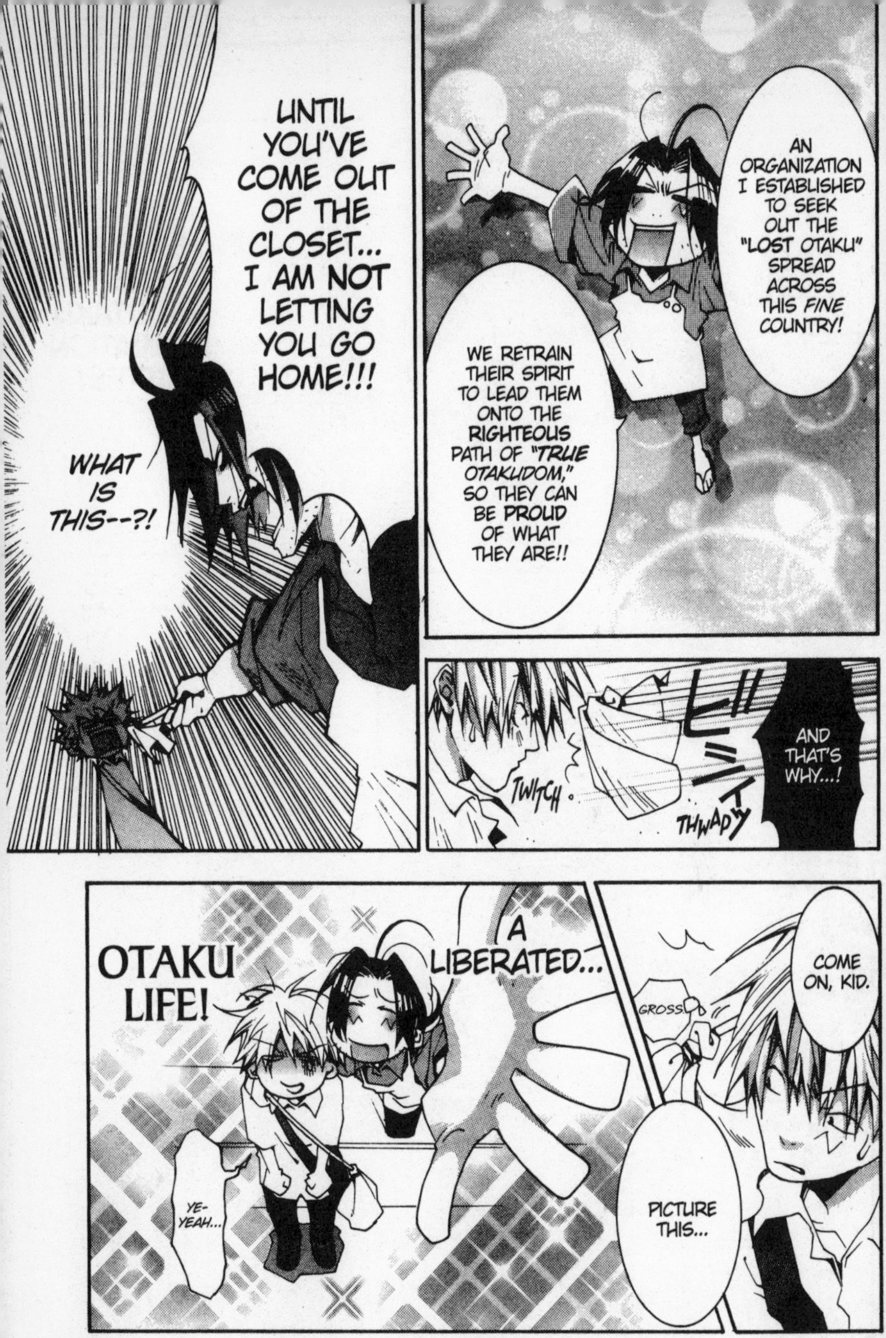
AN ORGANIZATION I ESTABLISHED TO SEEK OUT THE "LOST OTAKU" SPREAD ACROSS THIS *FINE* COUNTRY!
WE RETRAIN THEIR SPIRIT TO LEAD THEM ONTO THE **RIGHTEOUS** PATH OF *"TRUE OTAKUDOM,"* SO THEY CAN BE **PROUD** OF WHAT THEY ARE!!
AND THAT'S WHY...!
TWITCH
THWAP
UNTIL YOU'VE COME OUT OF THE CLOSET... I AM NOT LETTING YOU GO HOME!!!
WHAT IS THIS--?!
COME ON, KID.
GROSS
PICTURE THIS...
A LIBERATED...
OTAKU LIFE!
YE-YEAH...

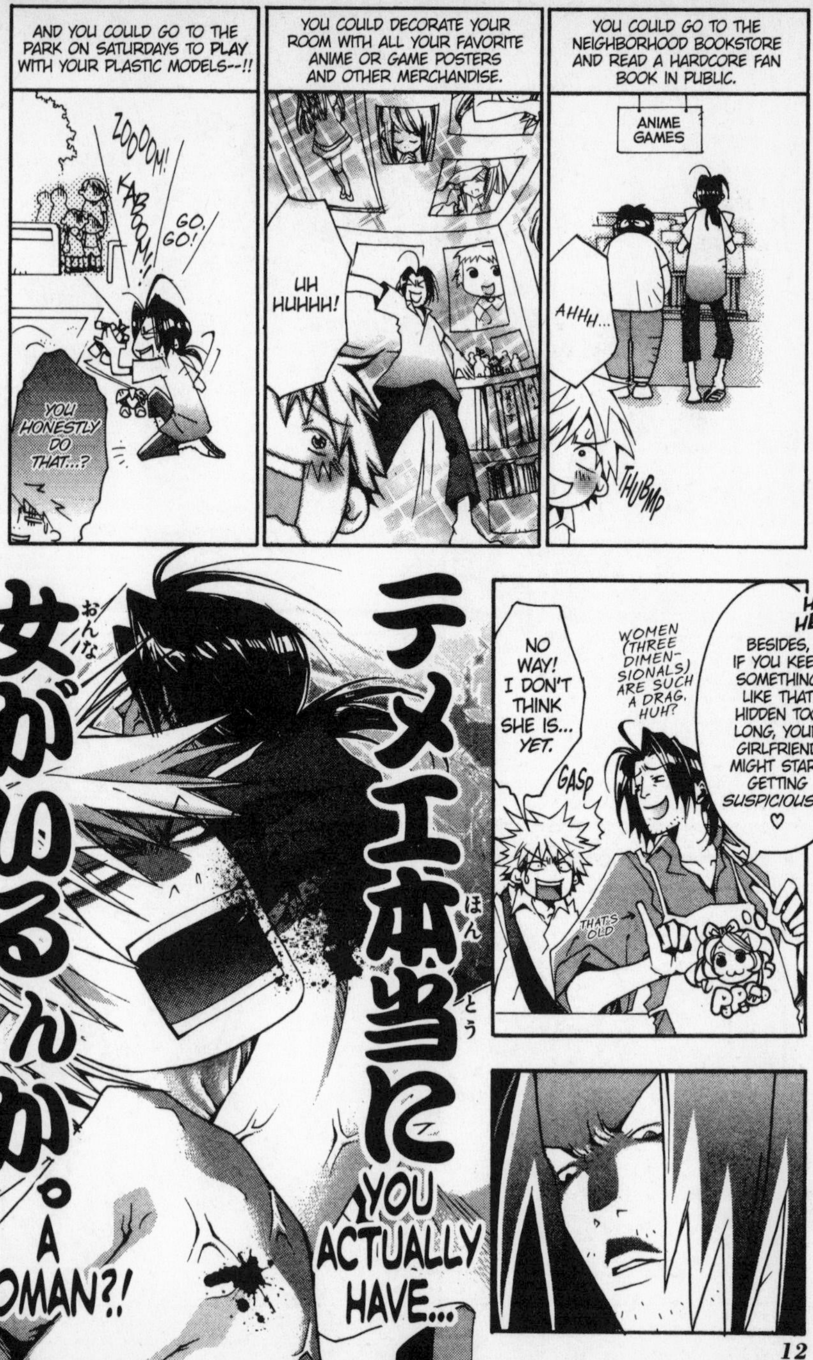
YOU COULD GO TO THE NEIGHBORHOOD BOOKSTORE AND READ A HARDCORE FAN BOOK IN PUBLIC.
ANIME GAMES
AHHH...
THUBMP
YOU COULD DECORATE YOUR ROOM WITH ALL YOUR FAVORITE ANIME OR GAME POSTERS AND OTHER MERCHANDISE.
UH HUHHH!
AND YOU COULD GO TO THE PARK ON SATURDAYS TO PLAY WITH YOUR PLASTIC MODELS--!!
ZOOOOM!
KABOOM!!
GO, GO!
YOU HONESTLY DO THAT...?
HEH HEH...
BESIDES, IF YOU KEEP SOMETHING LIKE THAT HIDDEN TOO LONG, YOUR GIRLFRIEND MIGHT START GETTING SUSPICIOUS~! ♡
WOMEN (THREE DIMENSIONALS) ARE SUCH A DRAG, HUH?
NO WAY! I DON'T THINK SHE IS... YET.
GASP
THAT'S OLD
テメエ本当に
YOU ACTUALLY HAVE...
女がいるんか。
A
OMAN?!

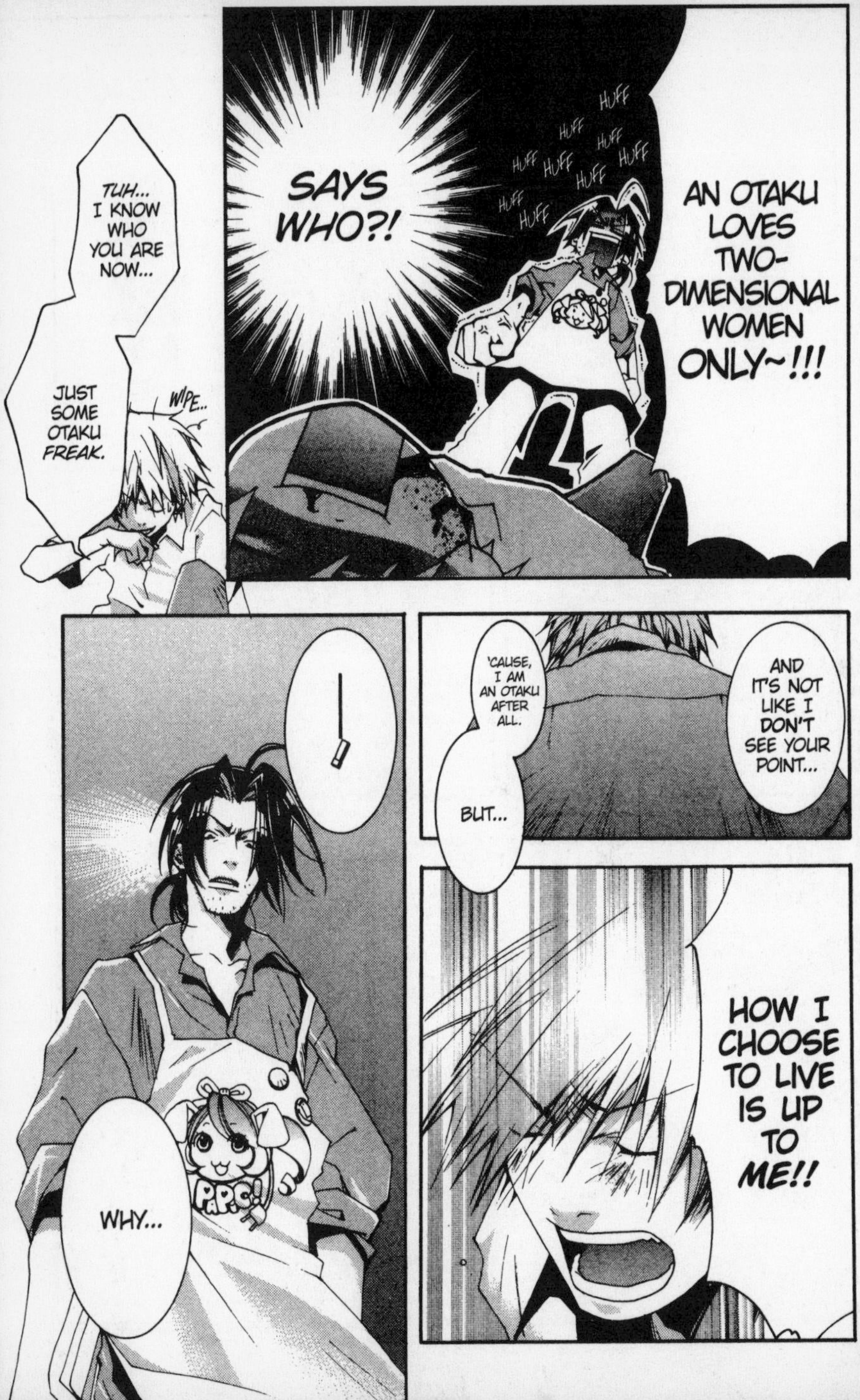
AN OTAKU LOVES TWO-DIMENSIONAL WOMEN ONLY~!!!
HUFF HUFF HUFF HUFF HUFF HUFF HUFF HUFF
SAYS WHO?!
TUH... I KNOW WHO YOU ARE NOW...
JUST SOME OTAKU FREAK.
WIPE...
AND IT'S NOT LIKE I DON'T SEE YOUR POINT...
'CAUSE, I AM AN OTAKU AFTER ALL.
BUT...
HOW I CHOOSE TO LIVE IS UP TO ME!!
!
WHY...
PAPIC!

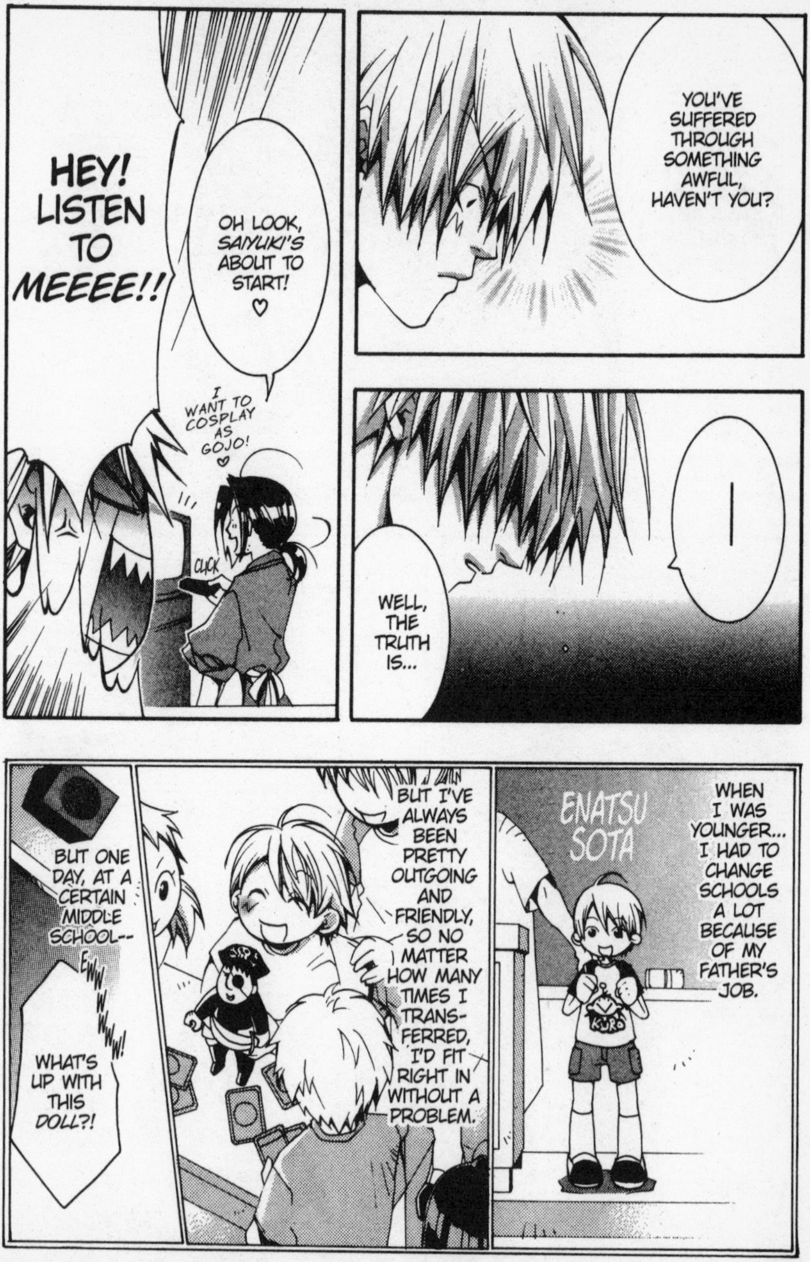
YOU'VE SUFFERED THROUGH SOMETHING AWFUL, HAVEN'T YOU?
I
WELL, THE TRUTH IS...
OH LOOK, SAIYUKI'S ABOUT TO START! ♡
HEY! LISTEN TO MEEEE!!
I WANT TO COSPLAY AS GOJO! ♡
CLICK
WHEN I WAS YOUNGER... I HAD TO CHANGE SCHOOLS A LOT BECAUSE OF MY FATHER'S JOB.
ENATSU SOTA
BUT I'VE ALWAYS BEEN PRETTY OUTGOING AND FRIENDLY, SO NO MATTER HOW MANY TIMES I TRANSFERRED, I'D FIT RIGHT IN WITHOUT A PROBLEM.
BUT ONE DAY, AT A CERTAIN MIDDLE SCHOOL--
EWWWWWWW!
WHAT'S UP WITH THIS DOLL?!

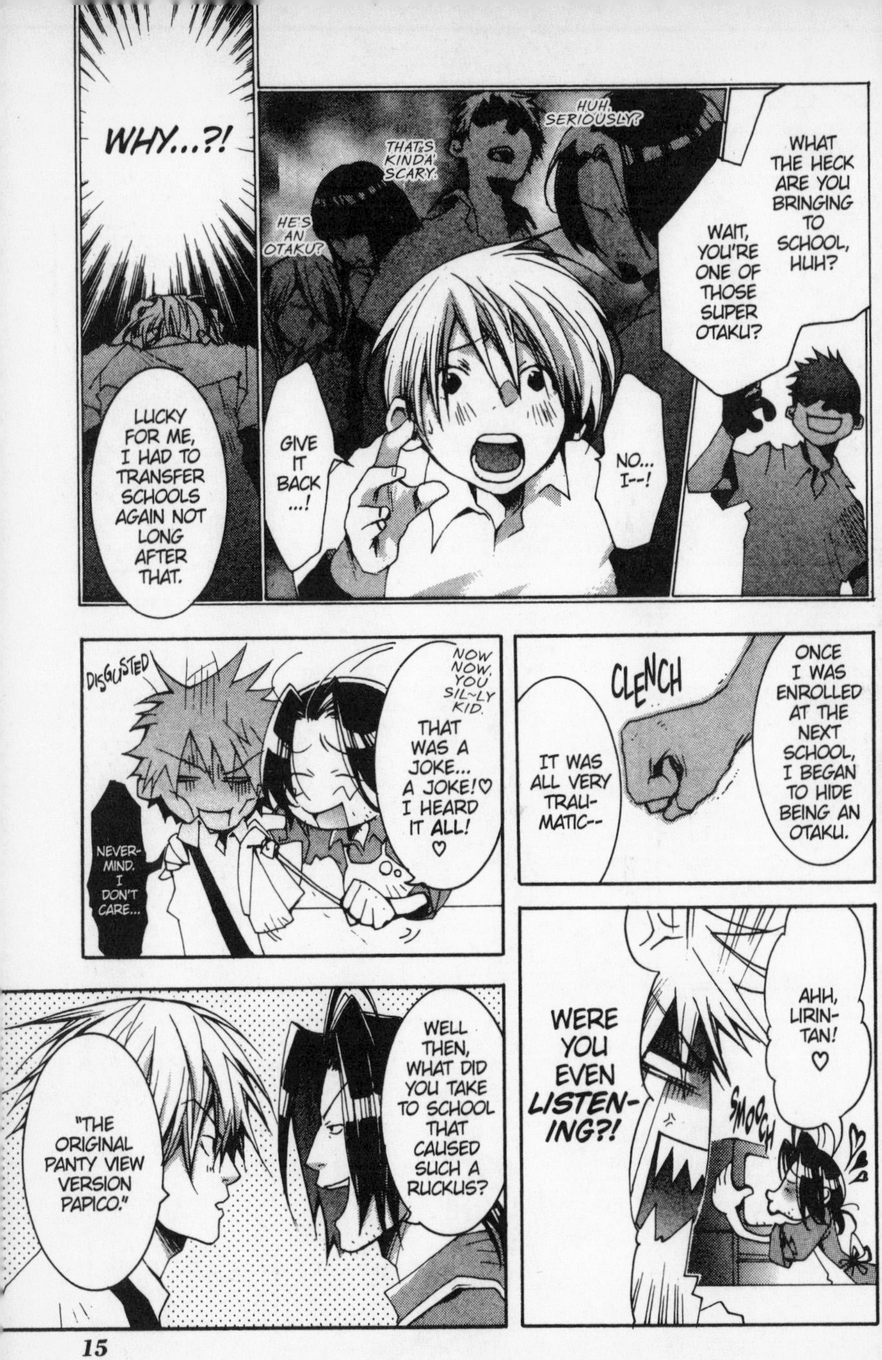
WHAT THE HECK ARE YOU BRINGING TO SCHOOL, HUH?
WAIT, YOU'RE ONE OF THOSE SUPER OTAKU?
HUH, SERIOUSLY?
THAT'S KINDA' SCARY.
HE'S AN OTAKU?
NO... I--!
GIVE IT BACK...!
WHY...?!
LUCKY FOR ME, I HAD TO TRANSFER SCHOOLS AGAIN NOT LONG AFTER THAT.
ONCE I WAS ENROLLED AT THE NEXT SCHOOL, I BEGAN TO HIDE BEING AN OTAKU.
CLENCH
IT WAS ALL VERY TRAUMATIC--
NOW NOW, YOU SIL~LY KID.
THAT WAS A JOKE... A JOKE! ♡ I HEARD IT ALL! ♡
DISGUSTED
NEVER-MIND. I DON'T CARE...
AHH, LIRIN-TAN! ♡
SMOOCH
WERE YOU EVEN LISTEN-ING?!
WELL THEN, WHAT DID YOU TAKE TO SCHOOL THAT CAUSED SUCH A RUCKUS?
"THE ORIGINAL PANTY VIEW VERSION PAPICO."

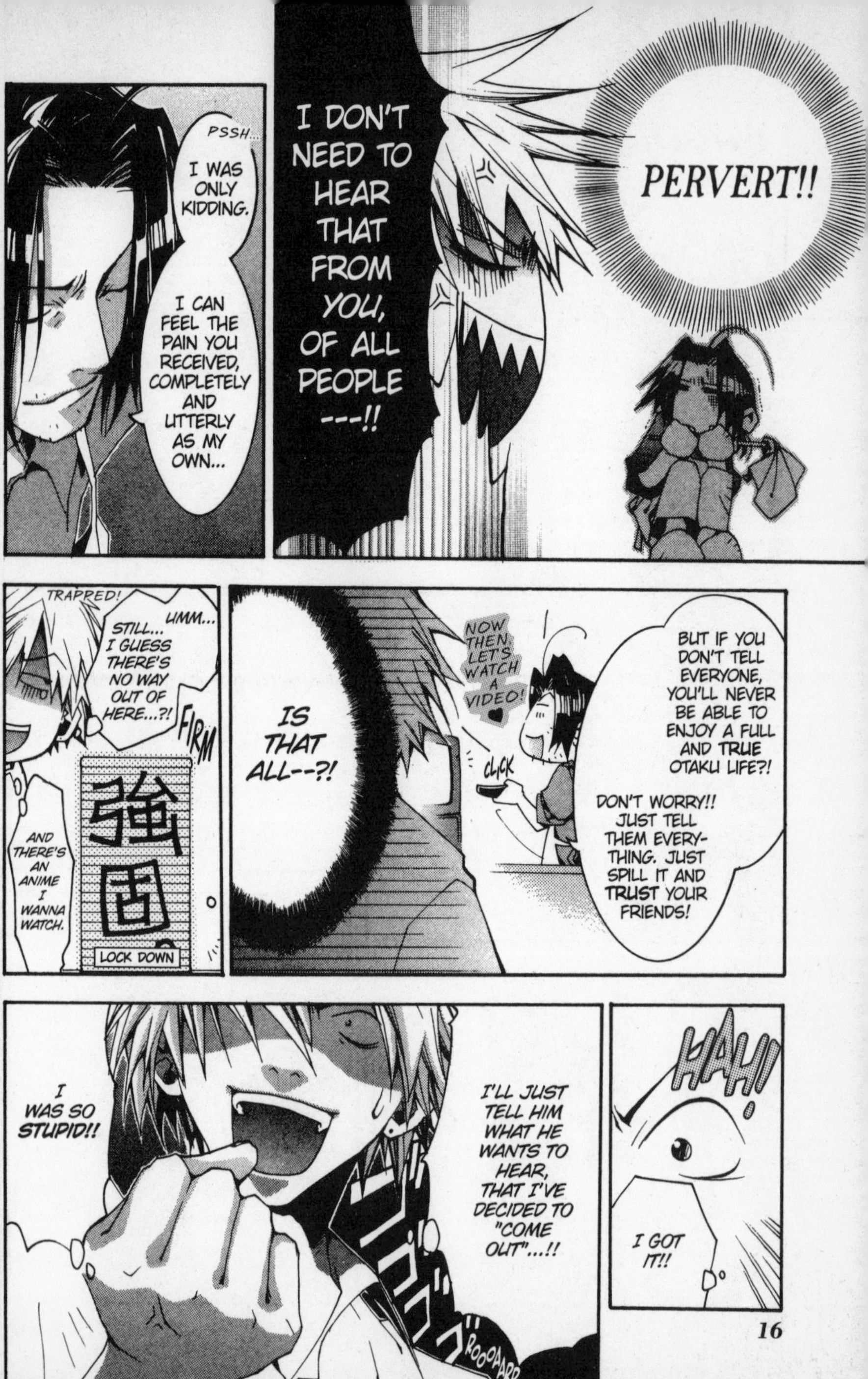
PERVERT!!
I DON'T NEED TO HEAR THAT FROM YOU, OF ALL PEOPLE---!!
PSSH...
I WAS ONLY KIDDING.
I CAN FEEL THE PAIN YOU RECEIVED, COMPLETELY AND UTTERLY AS MY OWN...
BUT IF YOU DON'T TELL EVERYONE, YOU'LL NEVER BE ABLE TO ENJOY A FULL AND TRUE OTAKU LIFE?!
DON'T WORRY!! JUST TELL THEM EVERYTHING. JUST SPILL IT AND TRUST YOUR FRIENDS!
NOW THEN, LET'S WATCH A VIDEO! ♥
CLICK
IS THAT ALL--?!
TRAPPED!
UMM...
STILL... I GUESS THERE'S NO WAY OUT OF HERE...?!
FIRM
強固
LOCK DOWN
AND THERE'S AN ANIME I WANNA WATCH.
HAH!
I GOT IT!!
I'LL JUST TELL HIM WHAT HE WANTS TO HEAR, THAT I'VE DECIDED TO "COME OUT"...!!
I WAS SO STUPID!!
ROOOAARR

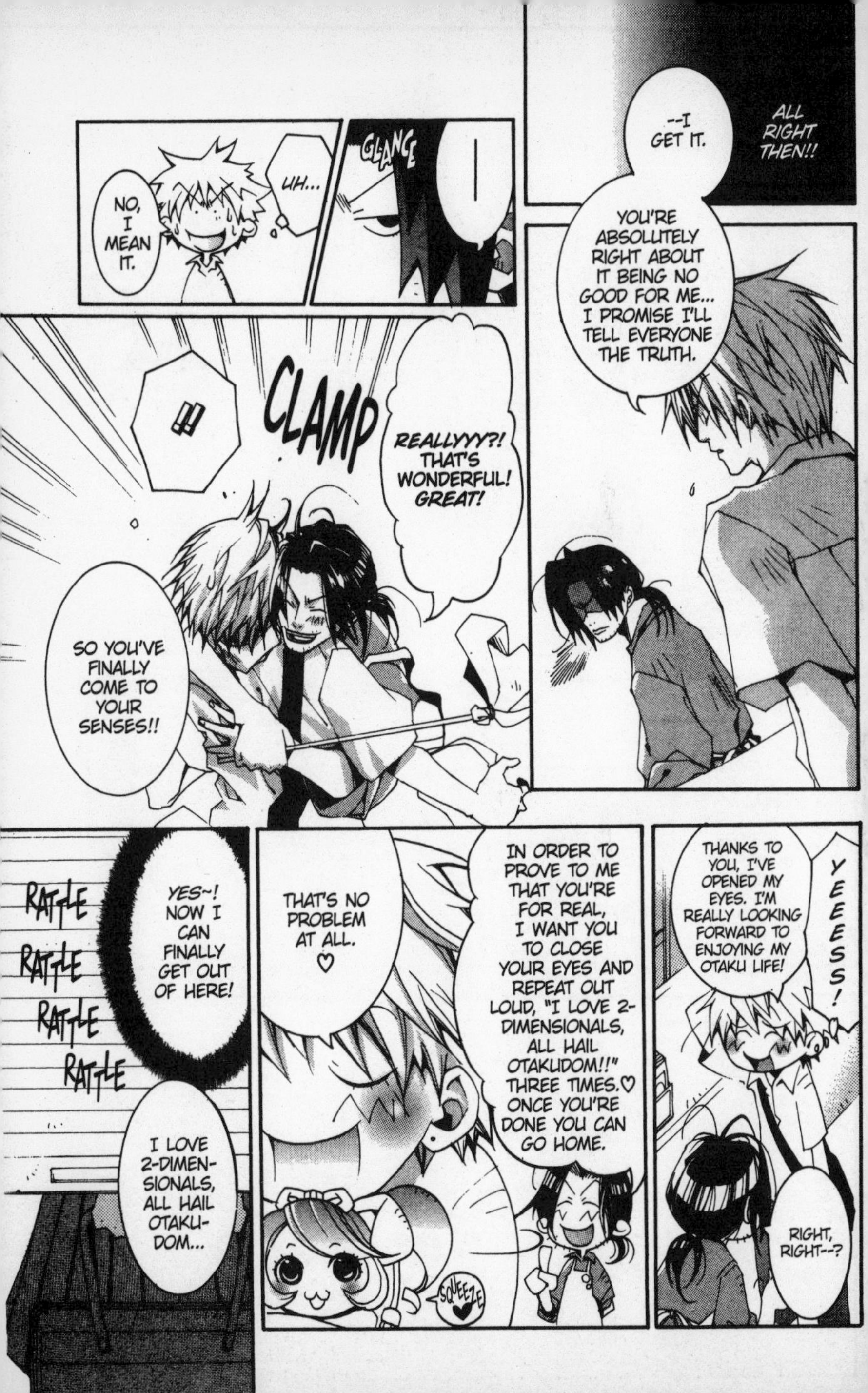

ALL RIGHT THEN!!
--I GET IT.
GLANCE
UH...
NO, I MEAN IT.
YOU'RE ABSOLUTELY RIGHT ABOUT IT BEING NO GOOD FOR ME... I PROMISE I'LL TELL EVERYONE THE TRUTH.
REALLYYY?! THAT'S WONDERFUL! GREAT!
CLAMP
!!
SO YOU'VE FINALLY COME TO YOUR SENSES!!
YEEESS!
THANKS TO YOU, I'VE OPENED MY EYES. I'M REALLY LOOKING FORWARD TO ENJOYING MY OTAKU LIFE!
RIGHT, RIGHT--?
IN ORDER TO PROVE TO ME THAT YOU'RE FOR REAL, I WANT YOU TO CLOSE YOUR EYES AND REPEAT OUT LOUD, "I LOVE 2-DIMENSIONALS, ALL HAIL OTAKUDOM!!" THREE TIMES.♡ ONCE YOU'RE DONE YOU CAN GO HOME.
THAT'S NO PROBLEM AT ALL. ♡
SQUEEZE ♥
RATTLE RATTLE RATTLE RATTLE
YES~! NOW I CAN FINALLY GET OUT OF HERE!
I LOVE 2-DIMENSIONALS, ALL HAIL OTAKUDOM...

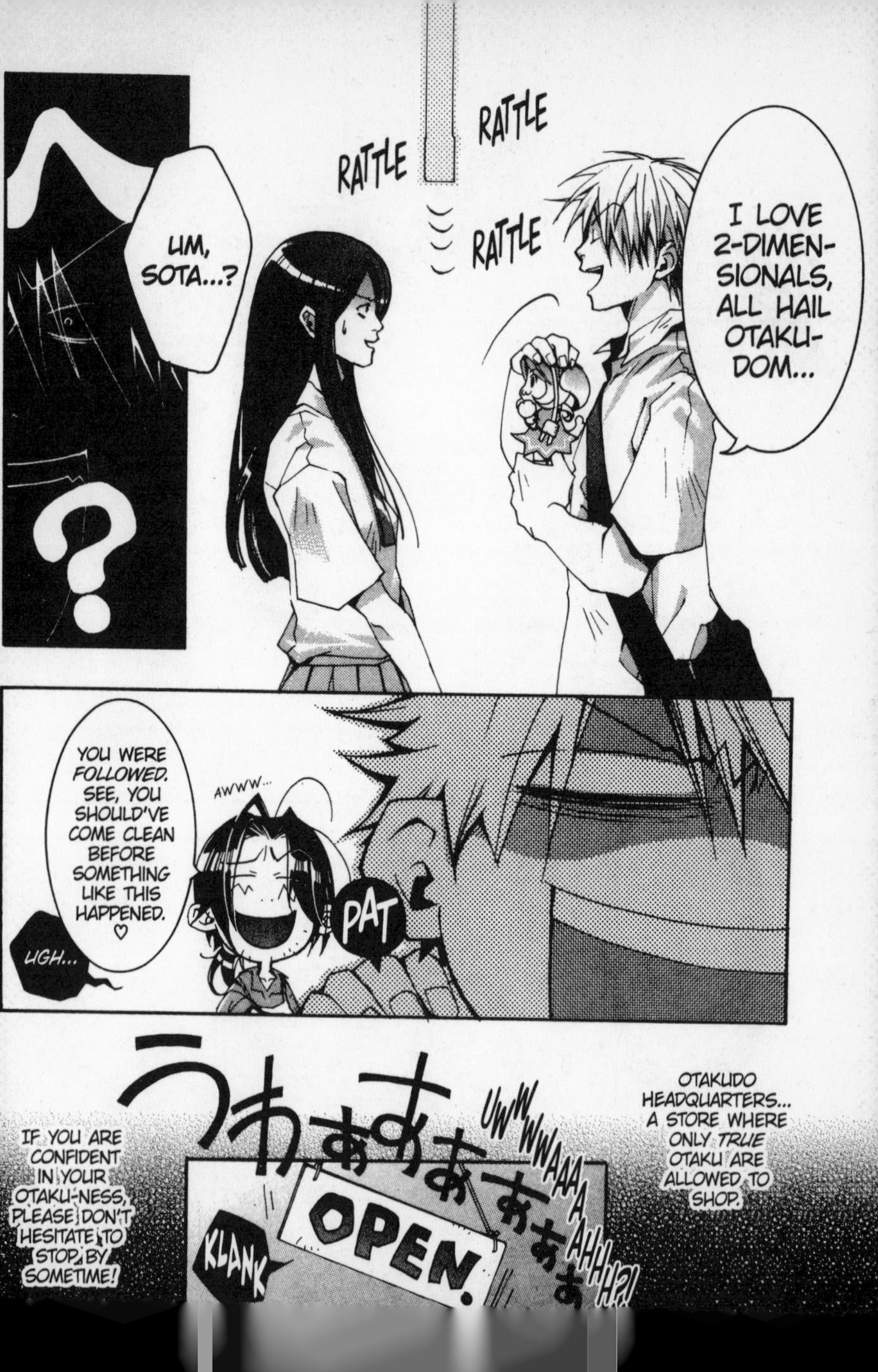
I LOVE 2-DIMENSIONALS, ALL HAIL OTAKUDOM...
RATTLE
RATTLE
RATTLE
UM, SOTA...?
YOU WERE *FOLLOWED.* SEE, YOU SHOULD'VE COME CLEAN BEFORE SOMETHING LIKE THIS HAPPENED. ♡
AWWW...
PAT
UGH...
OTAKUDO HEADQUARTERS... A STORE WHERE ONLY *TRUE* OTAKU ARE ALLOWED TO SHOP.
UWWWWAAAAAHHH?!
うわあああーあああ
OPEN
KLANK
IF YOU ARE CONFIDENT IN YOUR OTAKU-NESS, PLEASE DON'T HESITATE TO STOP BY SOMETIME!

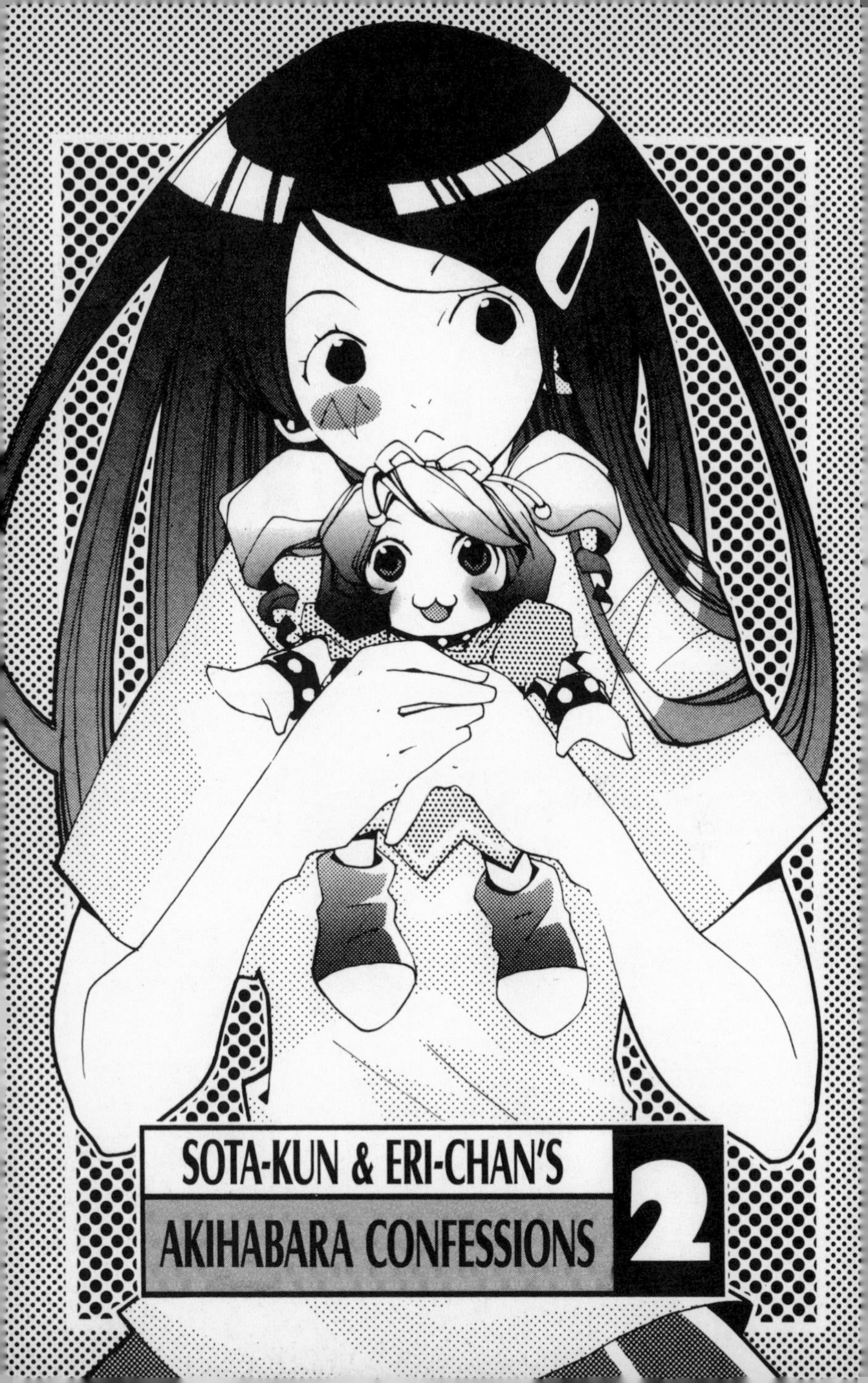

SOTA-KUN & ERI-CHAN'S AKIHABARA CONFESSIONS 2

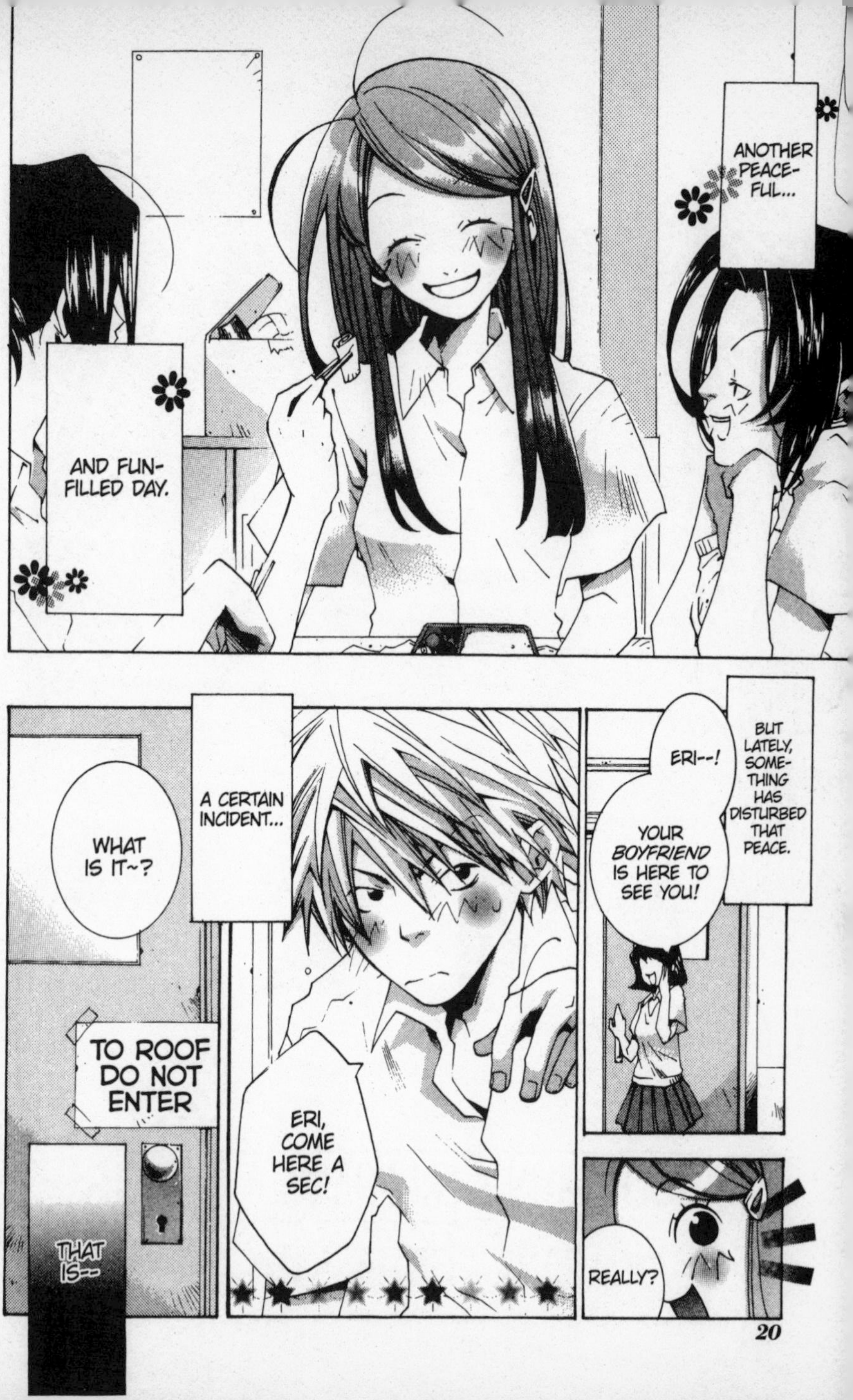
ANOTHER PEACE-FUL...
AND FUN-FILLED DAY.
BUT LATELY, SOME-THING HAS DISTURBED THAT PEACE.
ERI--!
YOUR BOYFRIEND IS HERE TO SEE YOU!
REALLY?
A CERTAIN INCIDENT...
ERI, COME HERE A SEC!
WHAT IS IT~?
TO ROOF DO NOT ENTER
THAT IS--

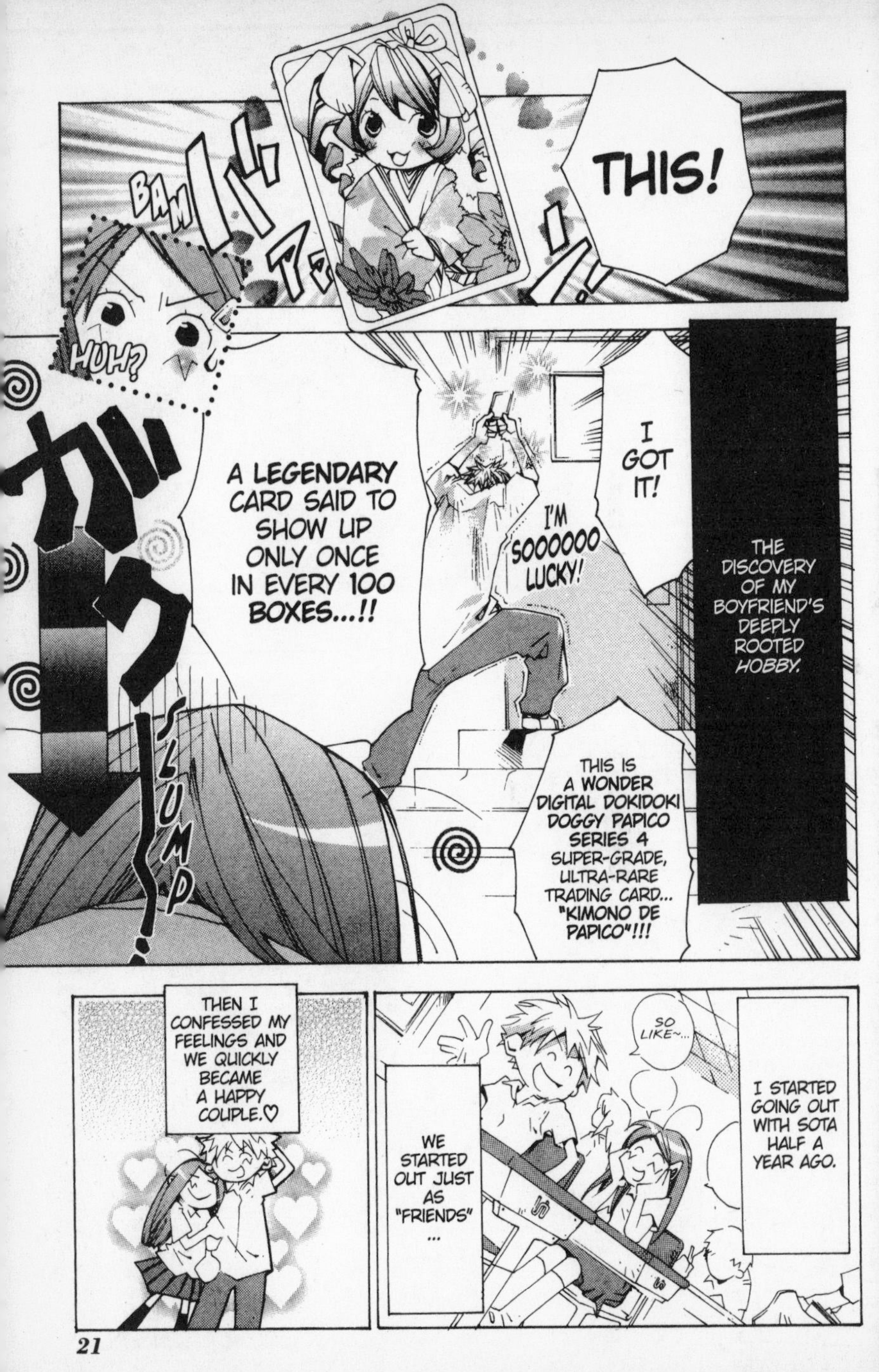
THIS!
BAM
HUH?
THE DISCOVERY OF MY BOYFRIEND'S DEEPLY ROOTED *HOBBY.*
I GOT IT!
I'M SOOOOOO LUCKY!
THIS IS A WONDER DIGITAL DOKIDOKI DOGGY PAPICO SERIES 4 SUPER-GRADE, ULTRA-RARE TRADING CARD... "KIMONO DE PAPICO"!!!
A LEGENDARY CARD SAID TO SHOW UP ONLY ONCE IN EVERY 100 BOXES...!!
SLUMP
I STARTED GOING OUT WITH SOTA HALF A YEAR AGO.
SO LIKE~...
WE STARTED OUT JUST AS "FRIENDS" ...
THEN I CONFESSED MY FEELINGS AND WE QUICKLY BECAME A HAPPY COUPLE.♡

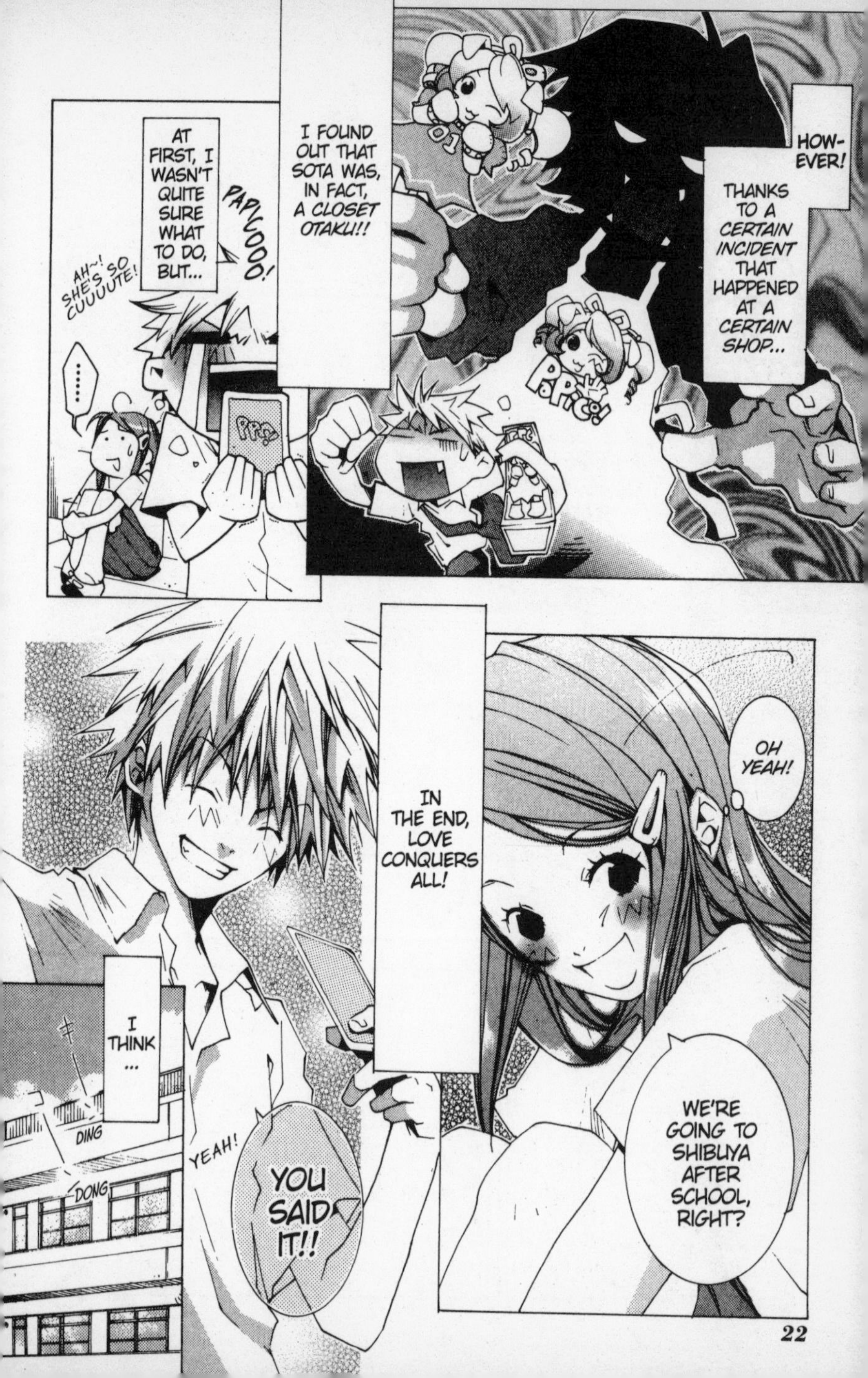
HOW-EVER!
THANKS TO A CERTAIN INCIDENT THAT HAPPENED AT A CERTAIN SHOP...
PAPICO!
I FOUND OUT THAT SOTA WAS, IN FACT, A CLOSET OTAKU!!
AT FIRST, I WASN'T QUITE SURE WHAT TO DO, BUT...
PAPICOOO!
AH~! SHE'S SO CUUUUTE!
......
OH YEAH!
IN THE END, LOVE CONQUERS ALL!
WE'RE GOING TO SHIBUYA AFTER SCHOOL, RIGHT?
YOU SAID IT!!
YEAH!
I THINK...
DING
DONG

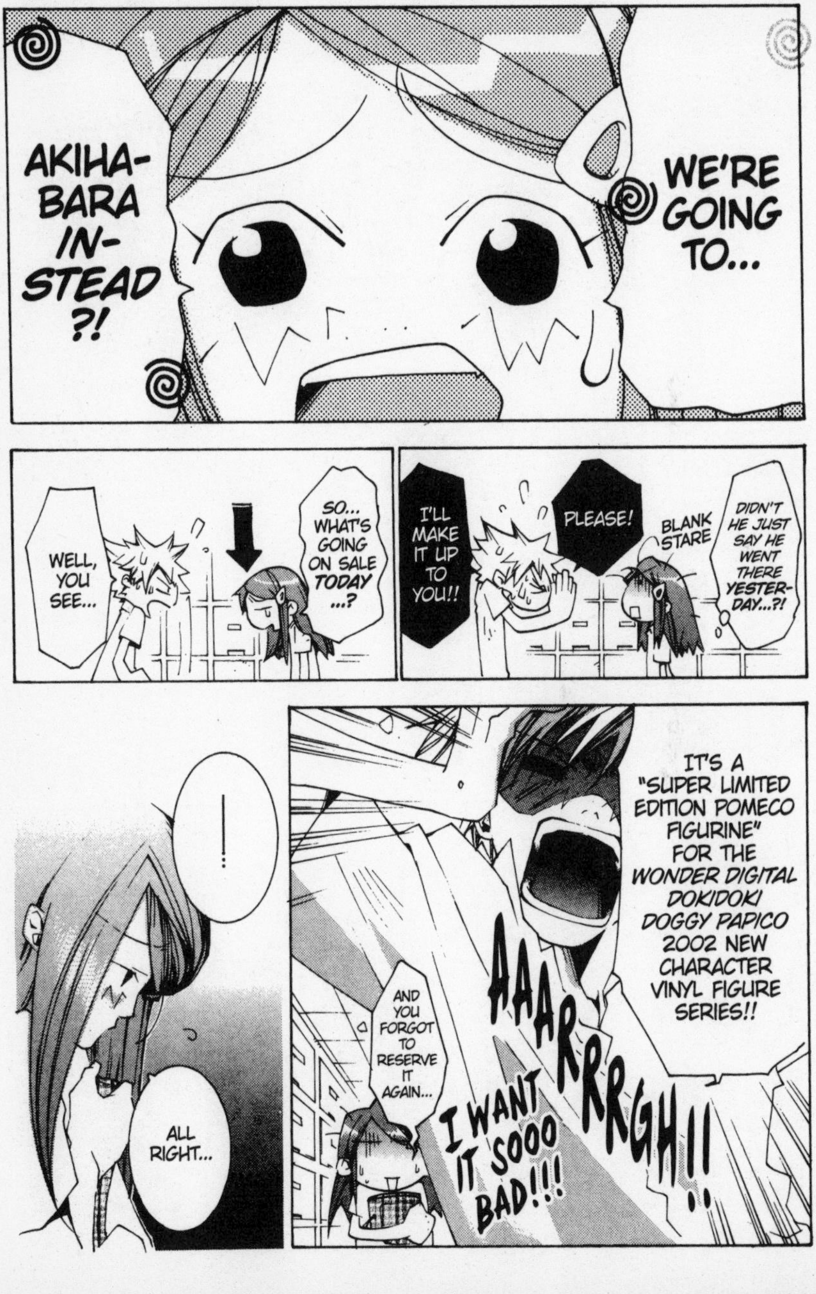
WE'RE GOING TO...
AKIHABARA INSTEAD?!
DIDN'T HE JUST SAY HE WENT THERE YESTERDAY...?!
BLANK STARE
PLEASE!
I'LL MAKE IT UP TO YOU!!
SO... WHAT'S GOING ON SALE TODAY...?
WELL, YOU SEE...
IT'S A "SUPER LIMITED EDITION POMECO FIGURINE" FOR THE WONDER DIGITAL DOKIDOKI DOGGY PAPICO 2002 NEW CHARACTER VINYL FIGURE SERIES!!
AAARRRGH!!
I WANT IT SOOO BAD!!!
AND YOU FORGOT TO RESERVE IT AGAIN...
...!
ALL RIGHT...

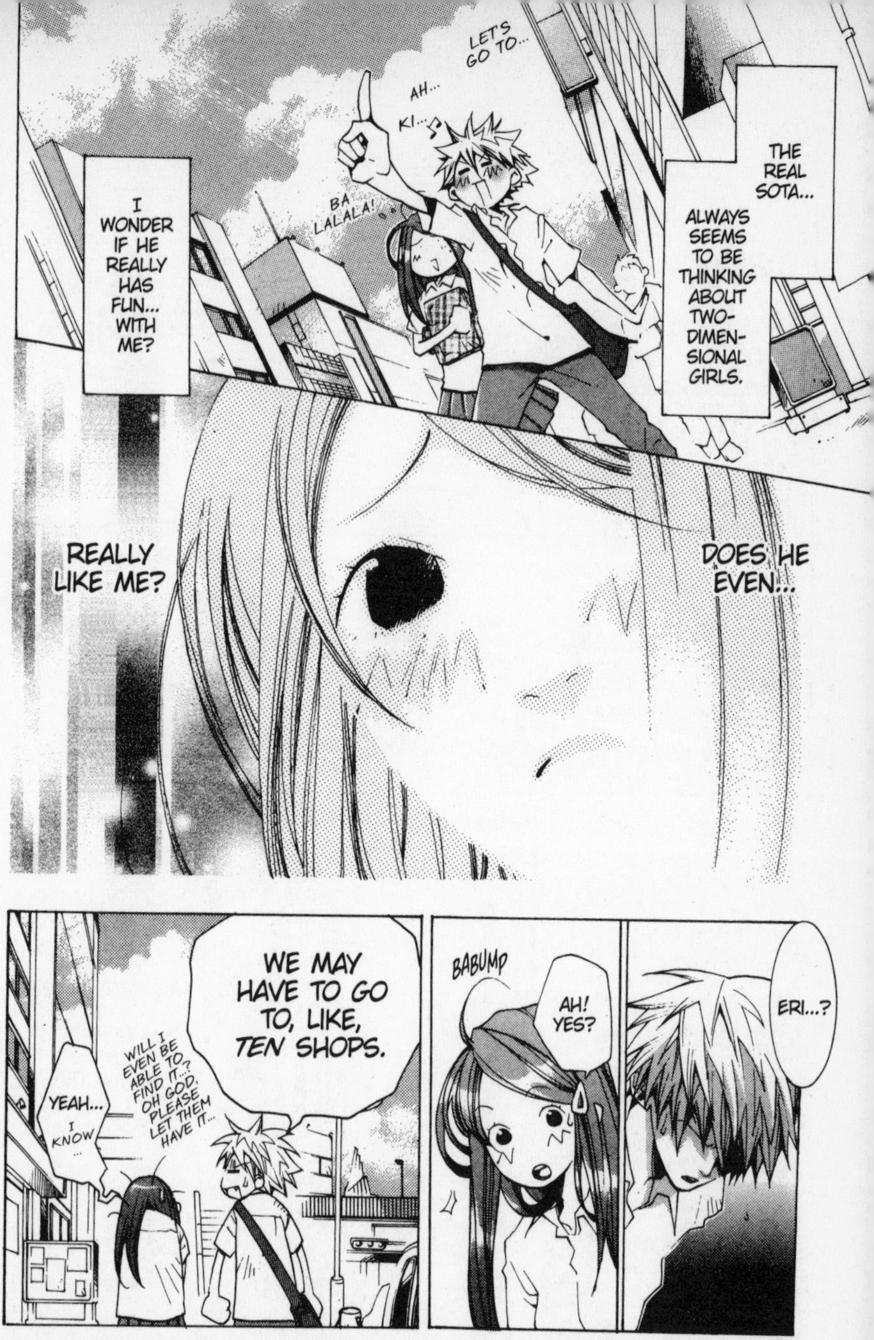
THE REAL SOTA...
ALWAYS SEEMS TO BE THINKING ABOUT TWO-DIMENSIONAL GIRLS.
LET'S GO TO...
AH...
KI...♪
BA LALALA!
I WONDER IF HE REALLY HAS FUN... WITH ME?
DOES HE EVEN...
REALLY LIKE ME?
ERI...?
BABUMP
AH! YES?
WE MAY HAVE TO GO TO, LIKE, *TEN* SHOPS.
WILL I EVEN BE ABLE TO FIND IT...? OH GOD, PLEASE LET THEM HAVE IT...
YEAH... I KNOW...

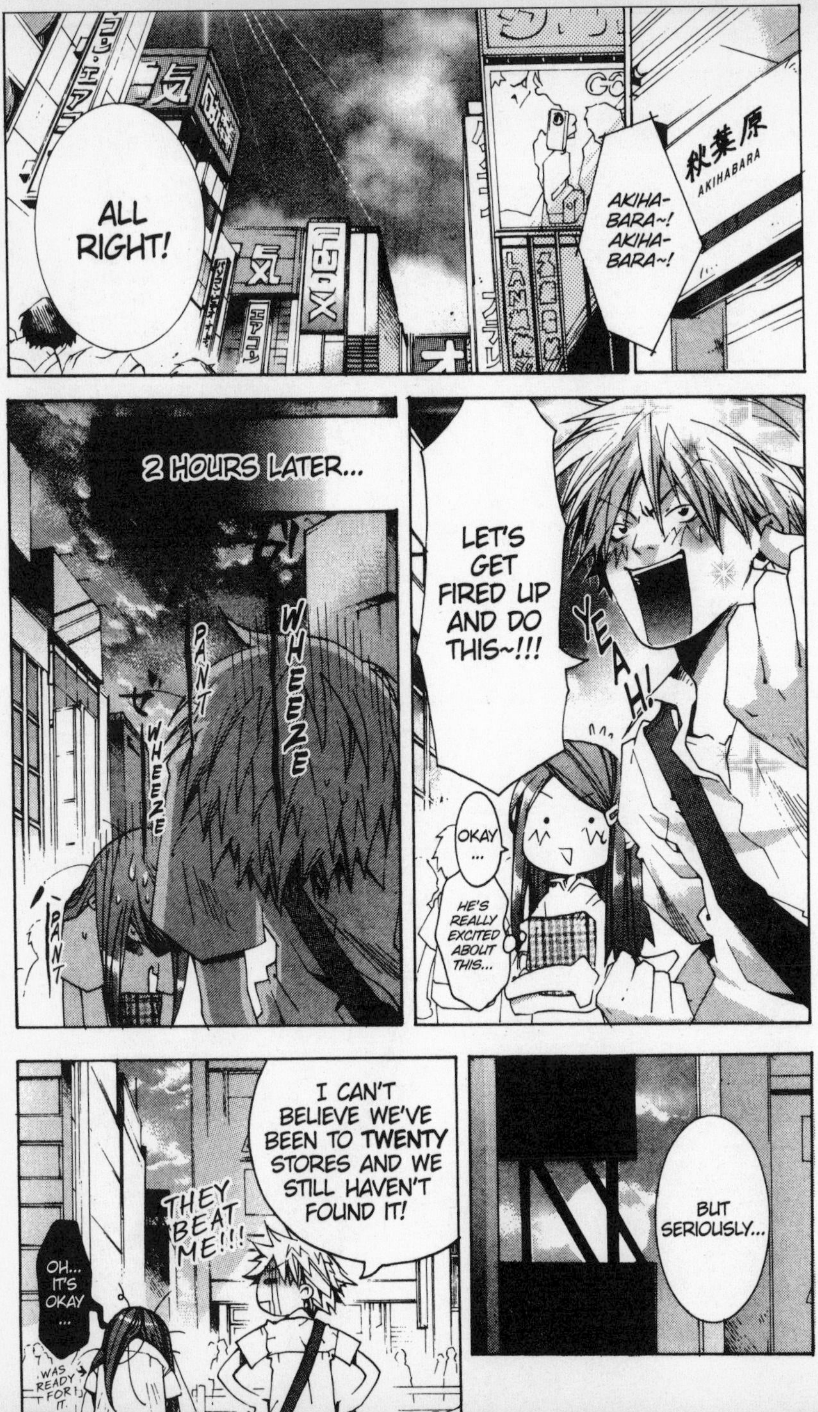
秋葉原
AKIHABARA
AKIHA-BARA~! AKIHA-BARA~!
ALL RIGHT!
LET'S GET FIRED UP AND DO THIS~!!!
YEAH!
OKAY...
HE'S REALLY EXCITED ABOUT THIS...
2 HOURS LATER...
WHEEZE
PANT
WHEEZE
PANT
BUT SERIOUSLY...
I CAN'T BELIEVE WE'VE BEEN TO TWENTY STORES AND WE STILL HAVEN'T FOUND IT!
THEY BEAT ME!!!
OH... IT'S OKAY...
WAS READY FOR IT.

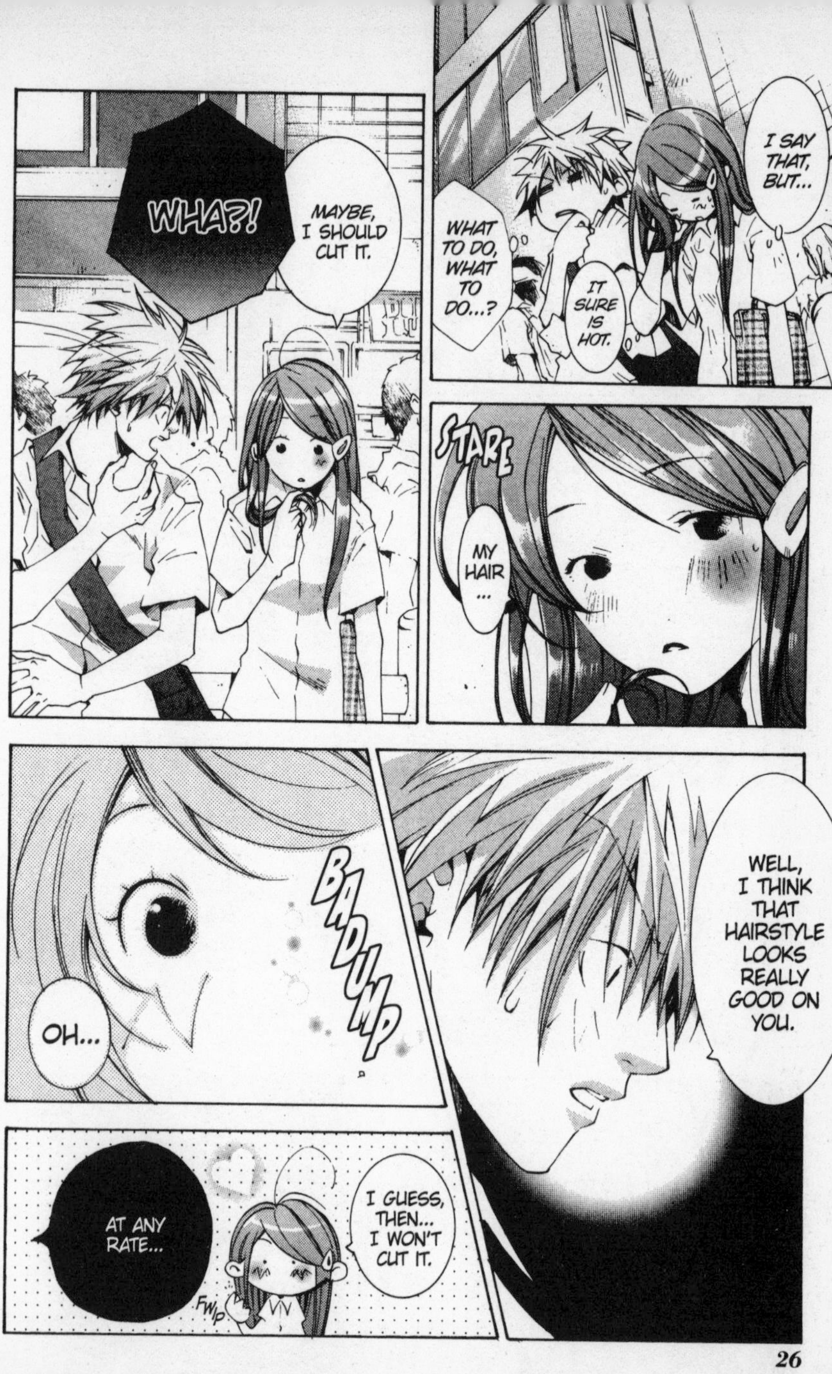
I SAY THAT, BUT...
WHAT TO DO, WHAT TO DO...?
IT SURE IS HOT.
STARE
MY HAIR ...
MAYBE, I SHOULD CUT IT.
WHA?!
WELL, I THINK THAT HAIRSTYLE LOOKS REALLY GOOD ON YOU.
BADUMP
OH...
I GUESS, THEN... I WON'T CUT IT.
FWIP
AT ANY RATE...

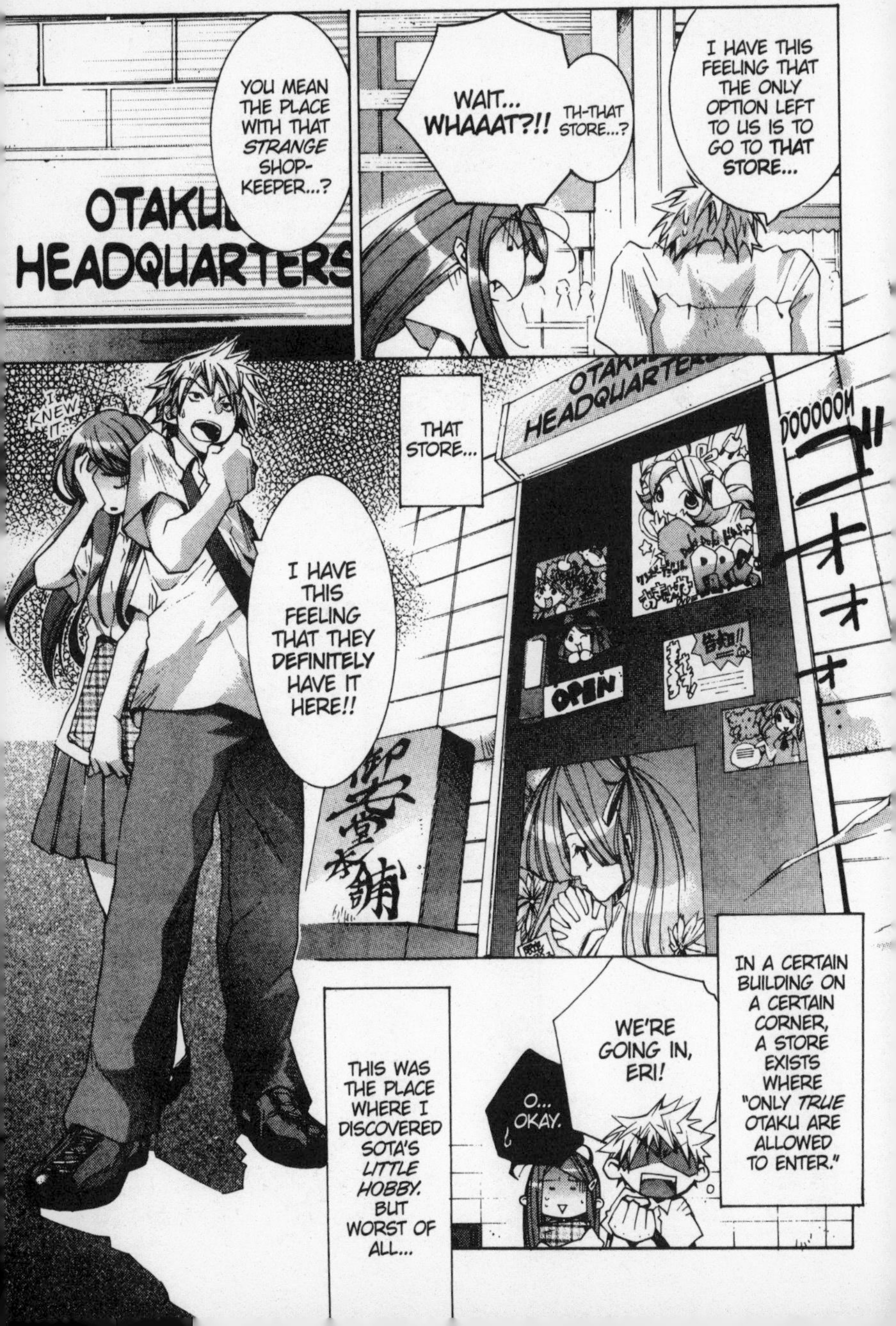
I HAVE THIS FEELING THAT THE ONLY OPTION LEFT TO US IS TO GO TO THAT STORE...
TH-THAT STORE...?
WAIT... WHAAAT?!!
YOU MEAN THE PLACE WITH THAT *STRANGE* SHOP-KEEPER...?
OTAKU HEADQUARTERS
DOOOOOOM
OTAKU HEADQUARTERS
THAT STORE...
OPEN
I HAVE THIS FEELING THAT THEY DEFINITELY HAVE IT HERE!!
I KNEW IT...
IN A CERTAIN BUILDING ON A CERTAIN CORNER, A STORE EXISTS WHERE "ONLY *TRUE* OTAKU ARE ALLOWED TO ENTER."
WE'RE GOING IN, ERI!
O... OKAY.
THIS WAS THE PLACE WHERE I DISCOVERED SOTA'S *LITTLE HOBBY.* BUT WORST OF ALL...

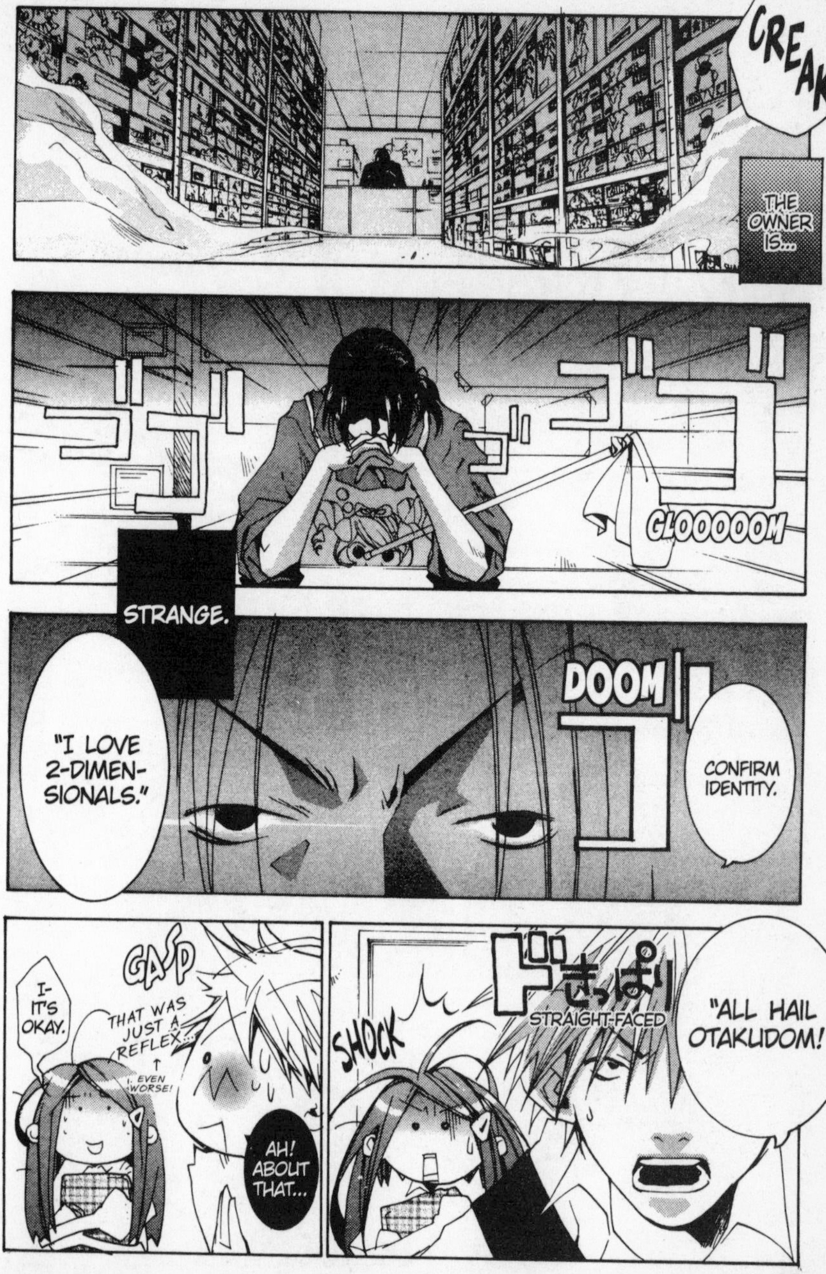
CREAK
THE OWNER IS...
GLOOOOOM
STRANGE.
DOOM
CONFIRM IDENTITY.
"I LOVE 2-DIMEN-SIONALS."
"ALL HAIL OTAKUDOM!"
STRAIGHT-FACED
SHOCK
GASP
THAT WAS JUST A REFLEX...
EVEN WORSE!
AH! ABOUT THAT...
I- IT'S OKAY.

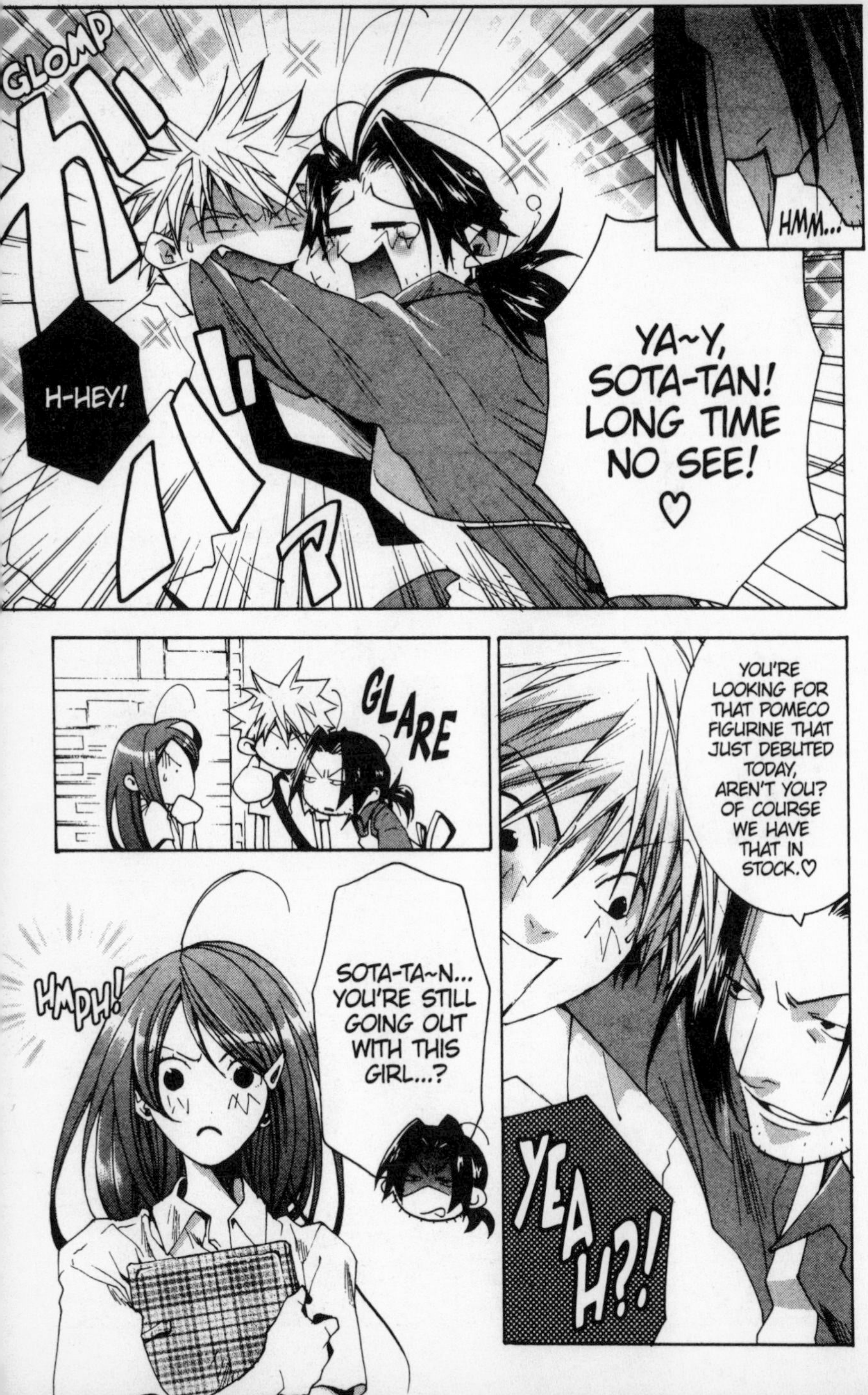
HMM...
YA~Y, SOTA-TAN! LONG TIME NO SEE! ♡
GLOMP
H-HEY!
YOU'RE LOOKING FOR THAT POMECO FIGURINE THAT JUST DEBUTED TODAY, AREN'T YOU? OF COURSE WE HAVE THAT IN STOCK.♡
YEAH?!
GLARE
SOTA-TA~N... YOU'RE STILL GOING OUT WITH THIS GIRL...?
HMPH!

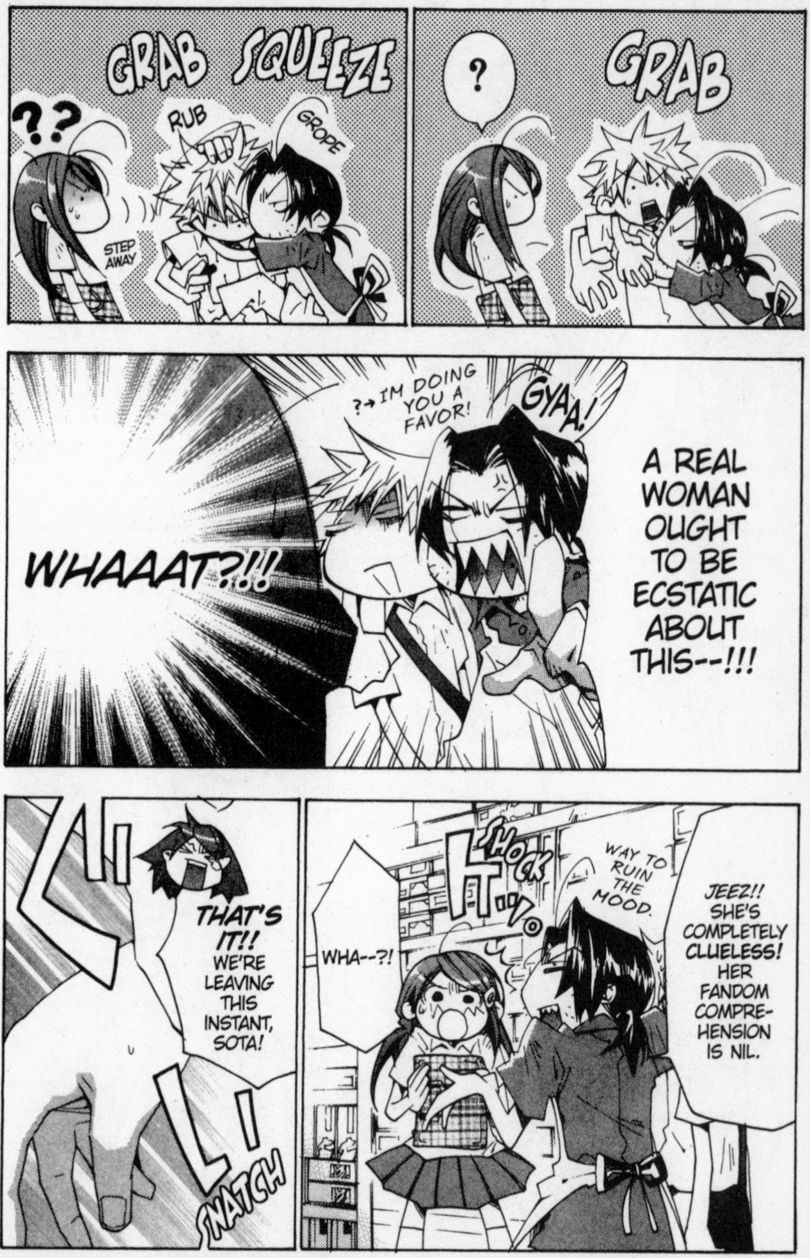
?
GRAB
GRAB SQUEEZE
GROPE
RUB
??
STEP AWAY
GYAA!
?→ IM DOING YOU A FAVOR!
A REAL WOMAN OUGHT TO BE ECSTATIC ABOUT THIS--!!!
WHAAAT?!!
JEEZ!! SHE'S COMPLETELY CLUELESS! HER FANDOM COMPREHENSION IS NIL.
WAY TO RUIN THE MOOD.
SHOCK
WHA--?!
THAT'S IT!! WE'RE LEAVING THIS INSTANT, SOTA!
SNATCH

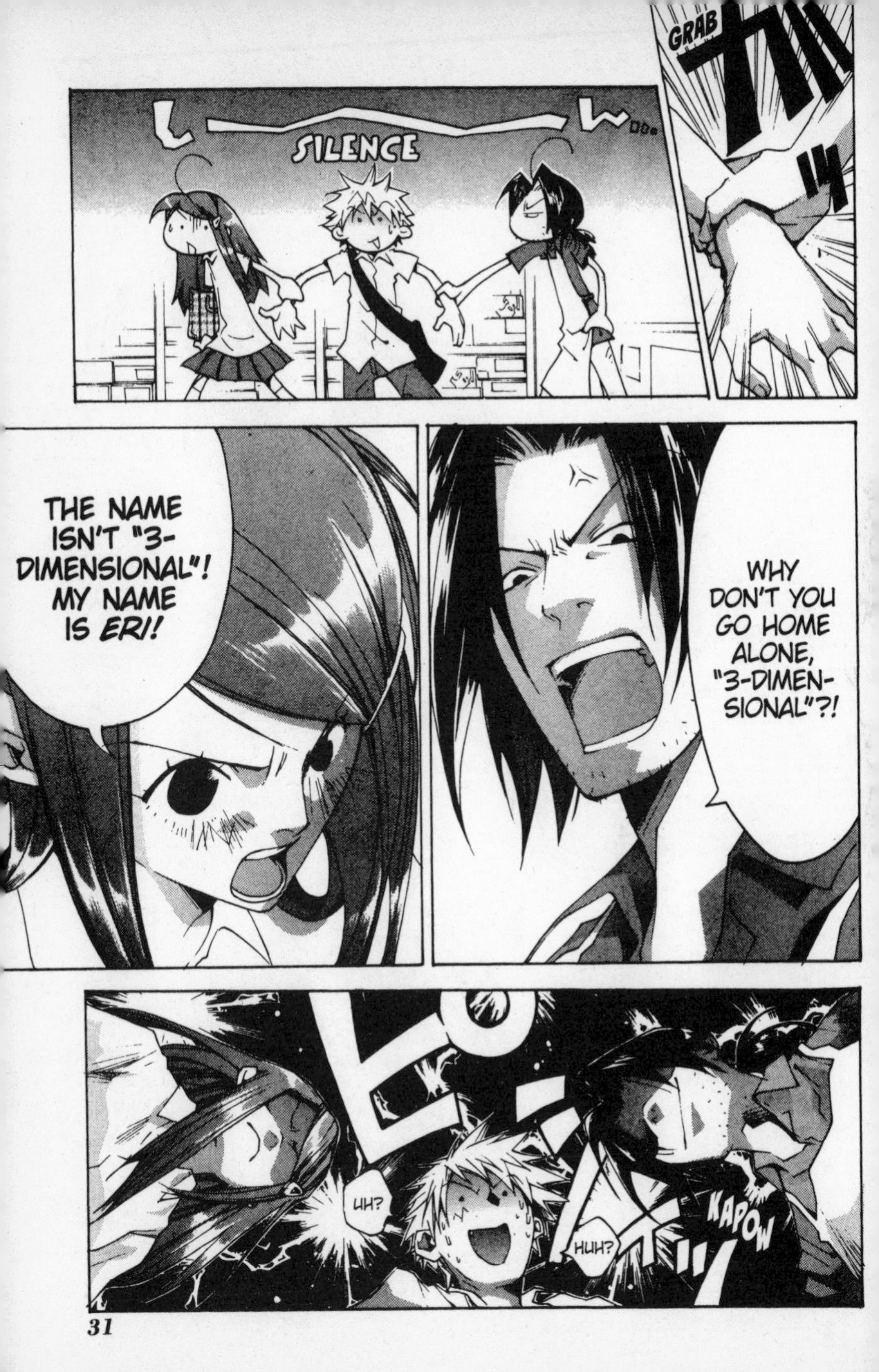
GRAB
SILENCE
WHY DON'T YOU GO HOME ALONE, "3-DIMENSIONAL"?!
THE NAME ISN'T "3-DIMENSIONAL"! MY NAME IS *ERI*!
KAPOW
HUH?
UH?

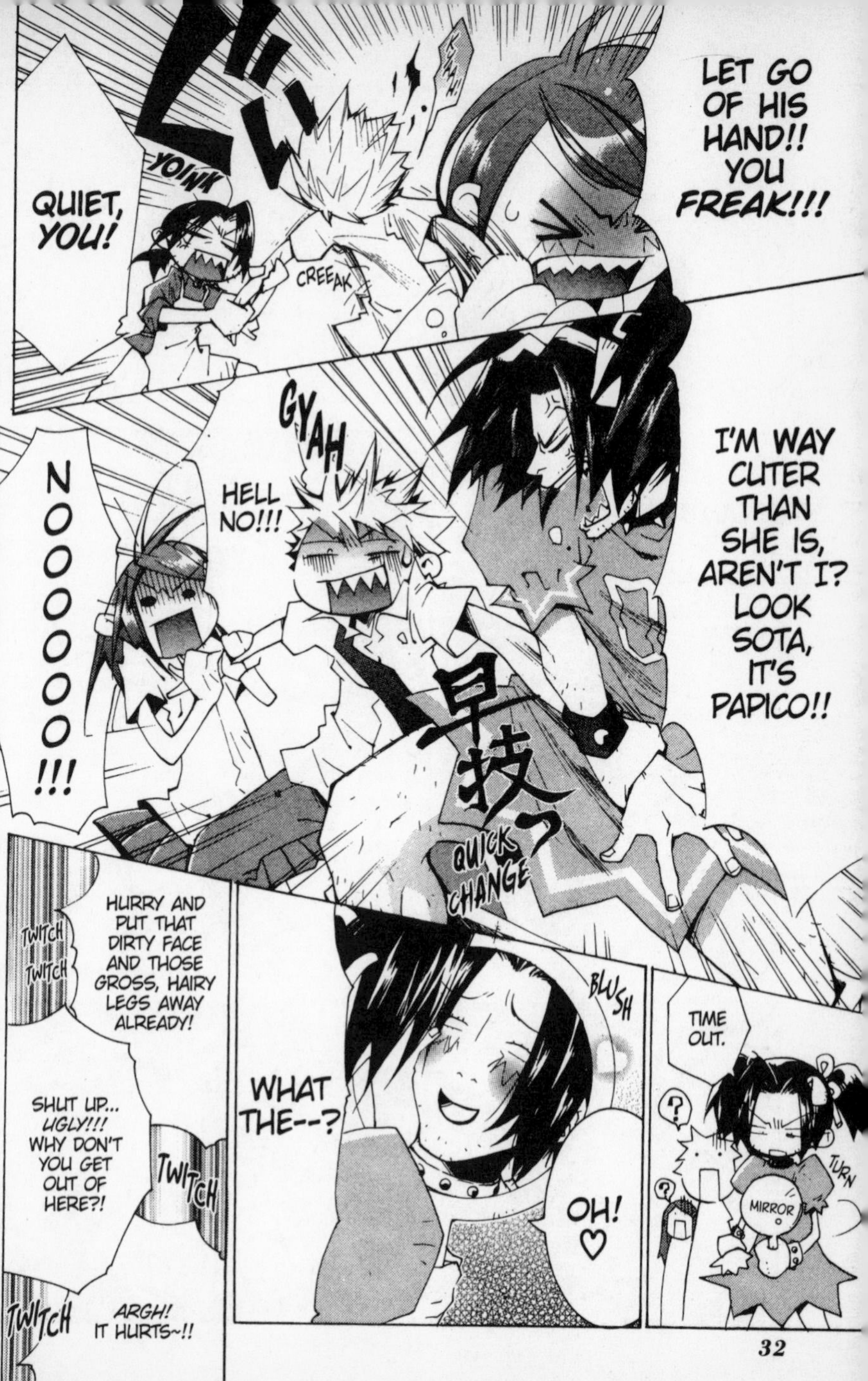
LET GO OF HIS HAND!! YOU FREAK!!!
YOINK
QUIET, YOU!
CREEAK
I'M WAY CUTER THAN SHE IS, AREN'T I? LOOK SOTA, IT'S PAPICO!!
早技
QUICK CHANGE
GYAH
HELL NO!!!
NOOOOOOO!!!
TIME OUT.
TURN
MIRROR
BLUSH
WHAT THE--?
OH! ♡
HURRY AND PUT THAT DIRTY FACE AND THOSE GROSS, HAIRY LEGS AWAY ALREADY!
TWITCH TWITCH
SHUT UP... UGLY!!! WHY DON'T YOU GET OUT OF HERE?!
TWITCH
TWITCH
ARGH! IT HURTS~!!

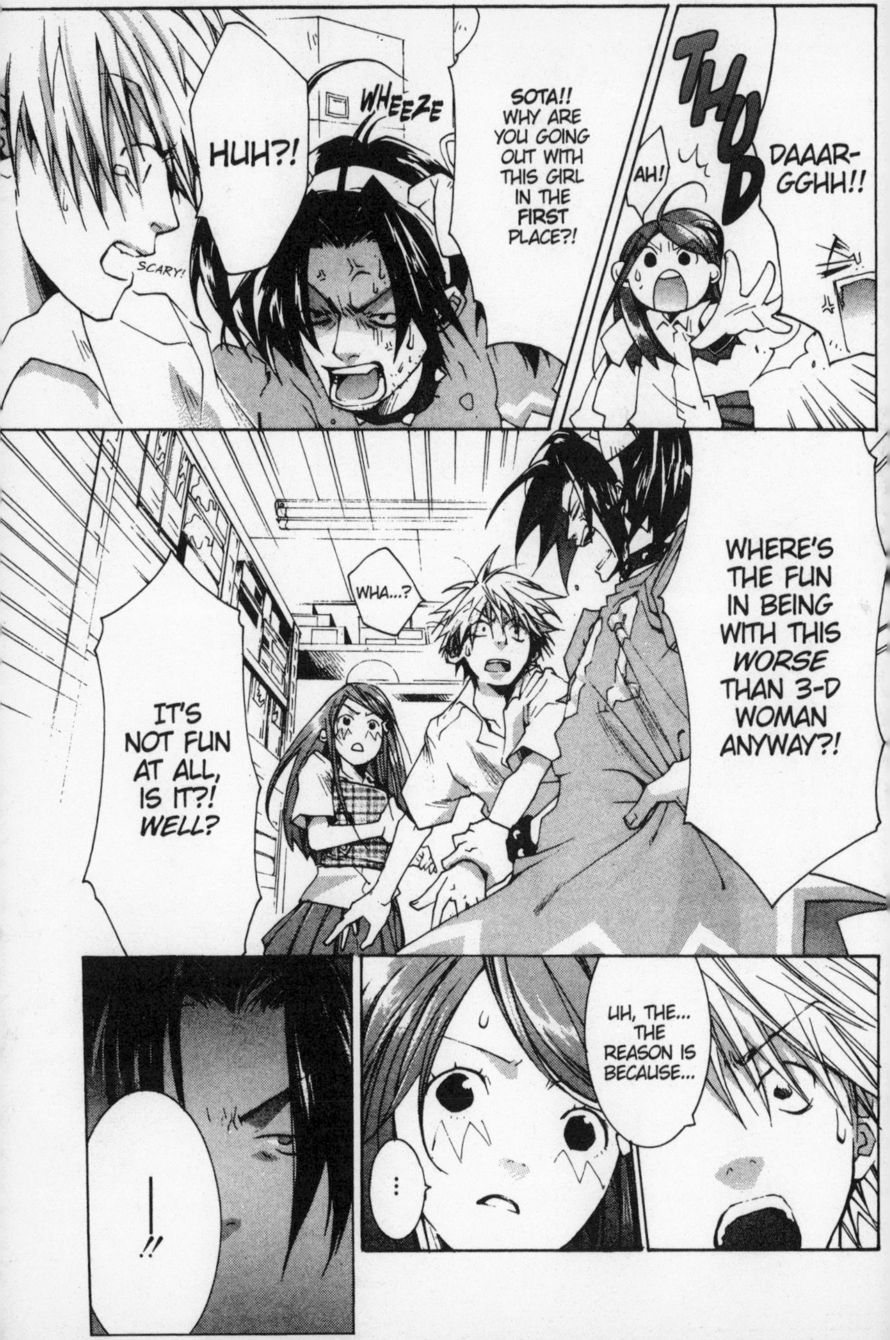
THUD
DAAAR-GGHH!!
AH!
SOTA!! WHY ARE YOU GOING OUT WITH THIS GIRL IN THE FIRST PLACE?!
WHEEZE
HUH?!
SCARY!
WHERE'S THE FUN IN BEING WITH THIS *WORSE* THAN 3-D WOMAN ANYWAY?!
WHA...?
IT'S NOT FUN AT ALL, IS IT?! *WELL?*
UH, THE... THE REASON IS BECAUSE...
...
—!!

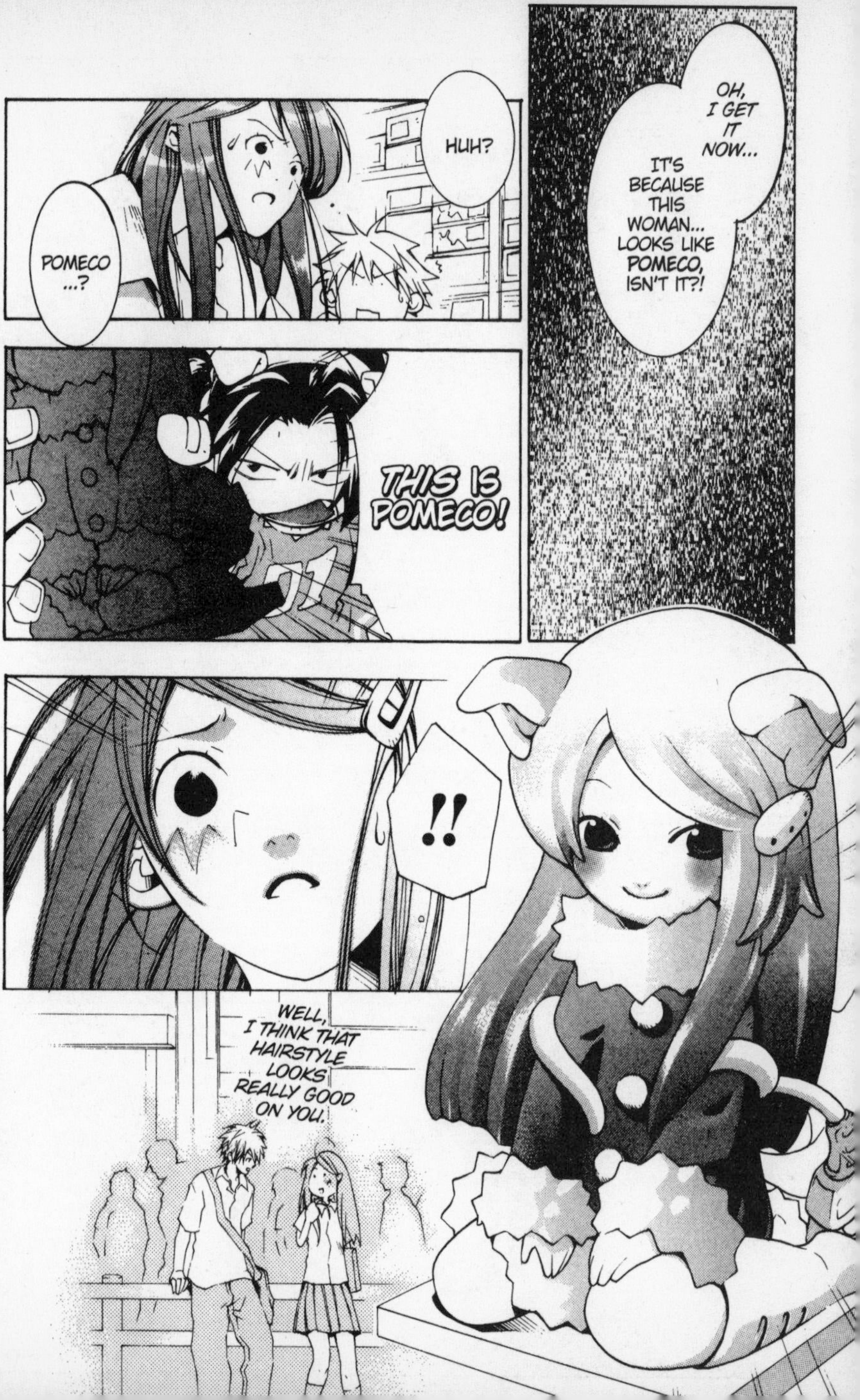
OH, I GET IT NOW... IT'S BECAUSE THIS WOMAN... LOOKS LIKE POMECO, ISN'T IT?!
HUH?
POMECO ...?
THIS IS POMECO!
!!
WELL, I THINK THAT HAIRSTYLE LOOKS REALLY GOOD ON YOU.

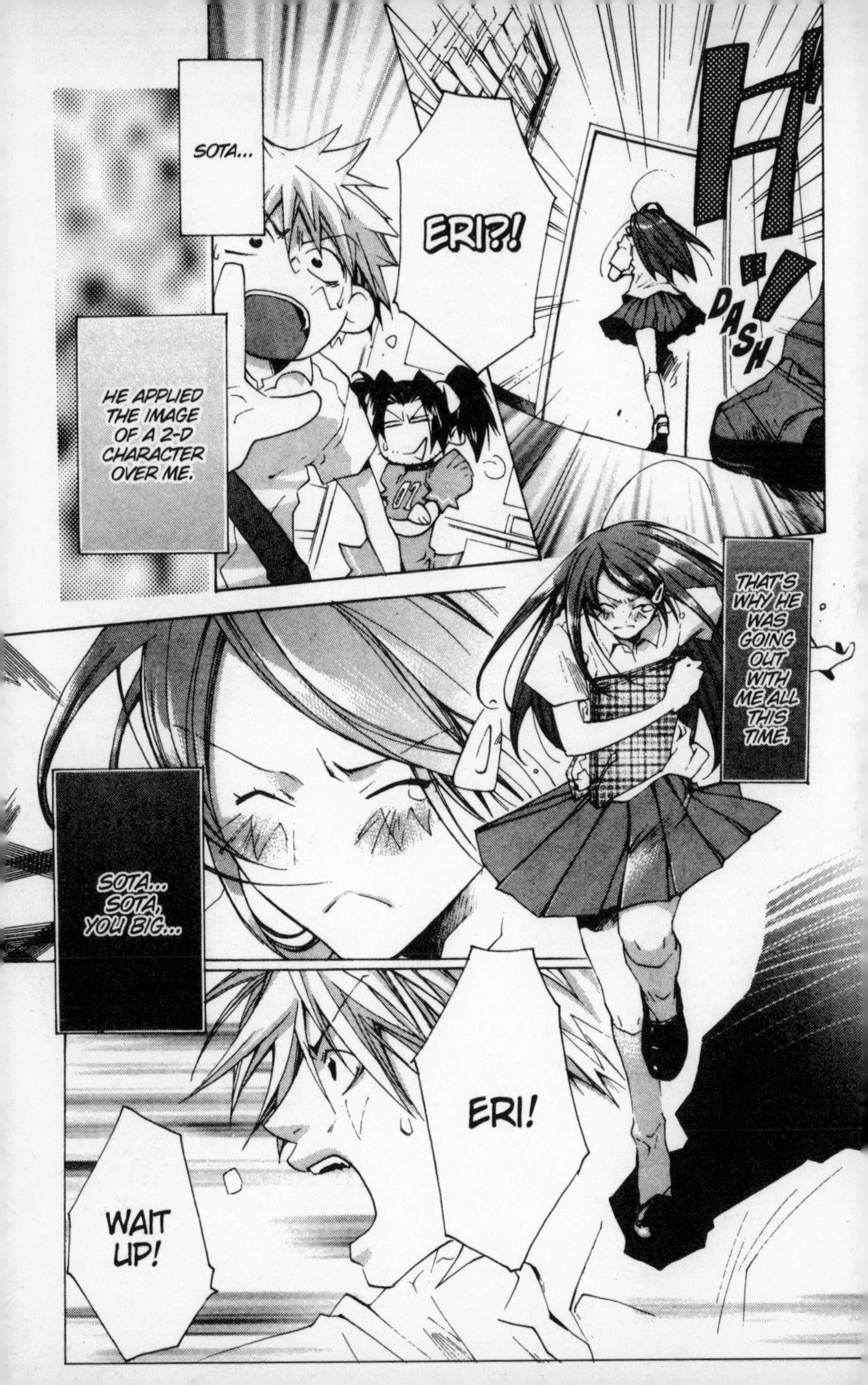
DASH
ERI?!
SOTA...
HE APPLIED THE IMAGE OF A 2-D CHARACTER OVER ME.
THAT'S WHY HE WAS GOING OUT WITH ME ALL THIS TIME.
SOTA... SOTA, YOU BIG...
ERI!
WAIT UP!

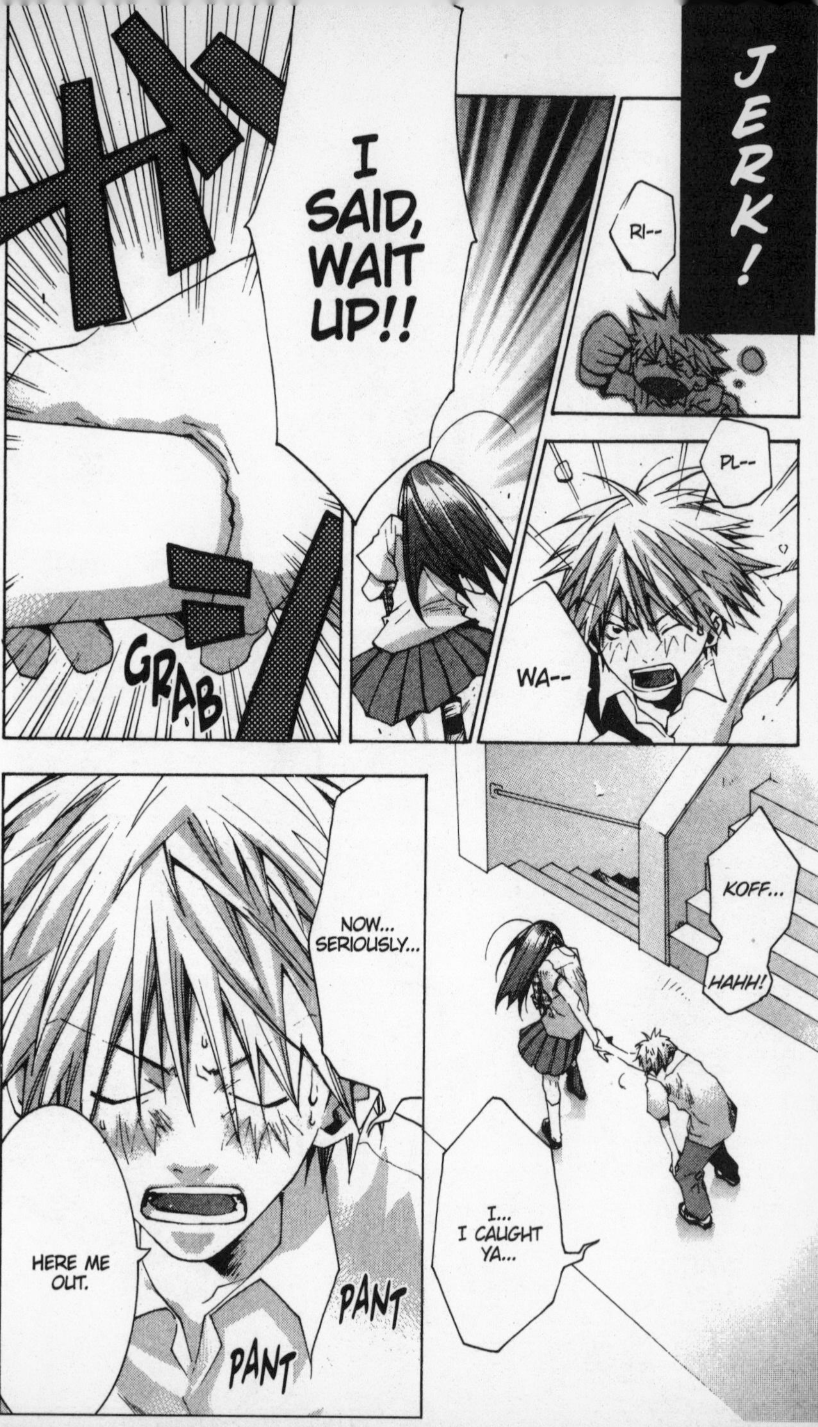
JERK!
RI--
PL--
WA--
I SAID, WAIT UP!!
GRAB
KOFF...
HAHH!
I... I CAUGHT YA...
NOW... SERIOUSLY...
HERE ME OUT.
PANT
PANT

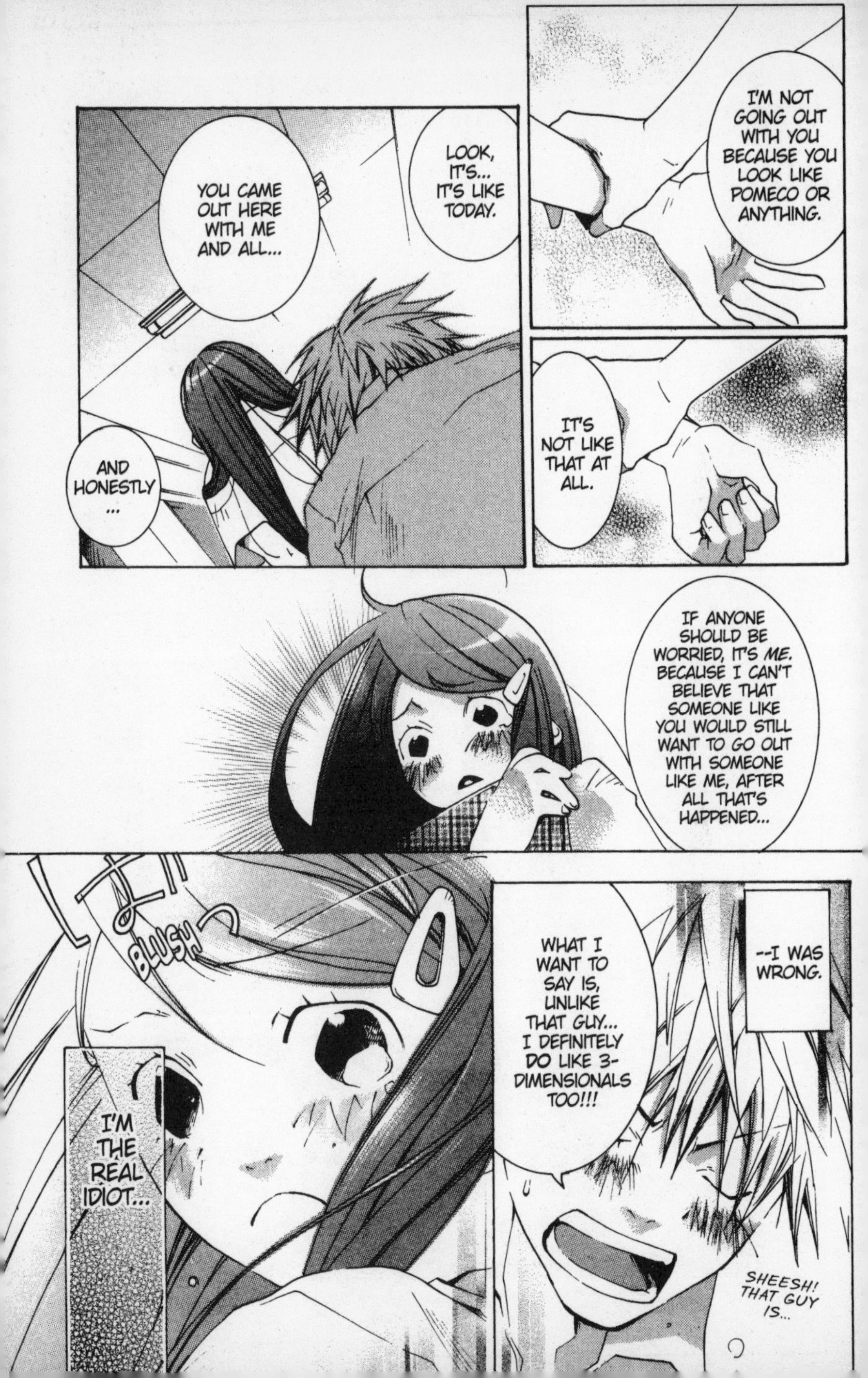
I'M NOT GOING OUT WITH YOU BECAUSE YOU LOOK LIKE POMECO OR ANYTHING.
IT'S NOT LIKE THAT AT ALL.
LOOK, IT'S... IT'S LIKE TODAY.
YOU CAME OUT HERE WITH ME AND ALL...
AND HONESTLY...
IF ANYONE SHOULD BE WORRIED, IT'S *ME*. BECAUSE I CAN'T BELIEVE THAT SOMEONE LIKE YOU WOULD STILL WANT TO GO OUT WITH SOMEONE LIKE ME, AFTER ALL THAT'S HAPPENED...
--I WAS WRONG.
WHAT I WANT TO SAY IS, UNLIKE THAT GUY... I DEFINITELY DO LIKE 3-DIMENSIONALS TOO!!!
SHEESH! THAT GUY IS...
BLUSH
I'M THE REAL IDIOT...

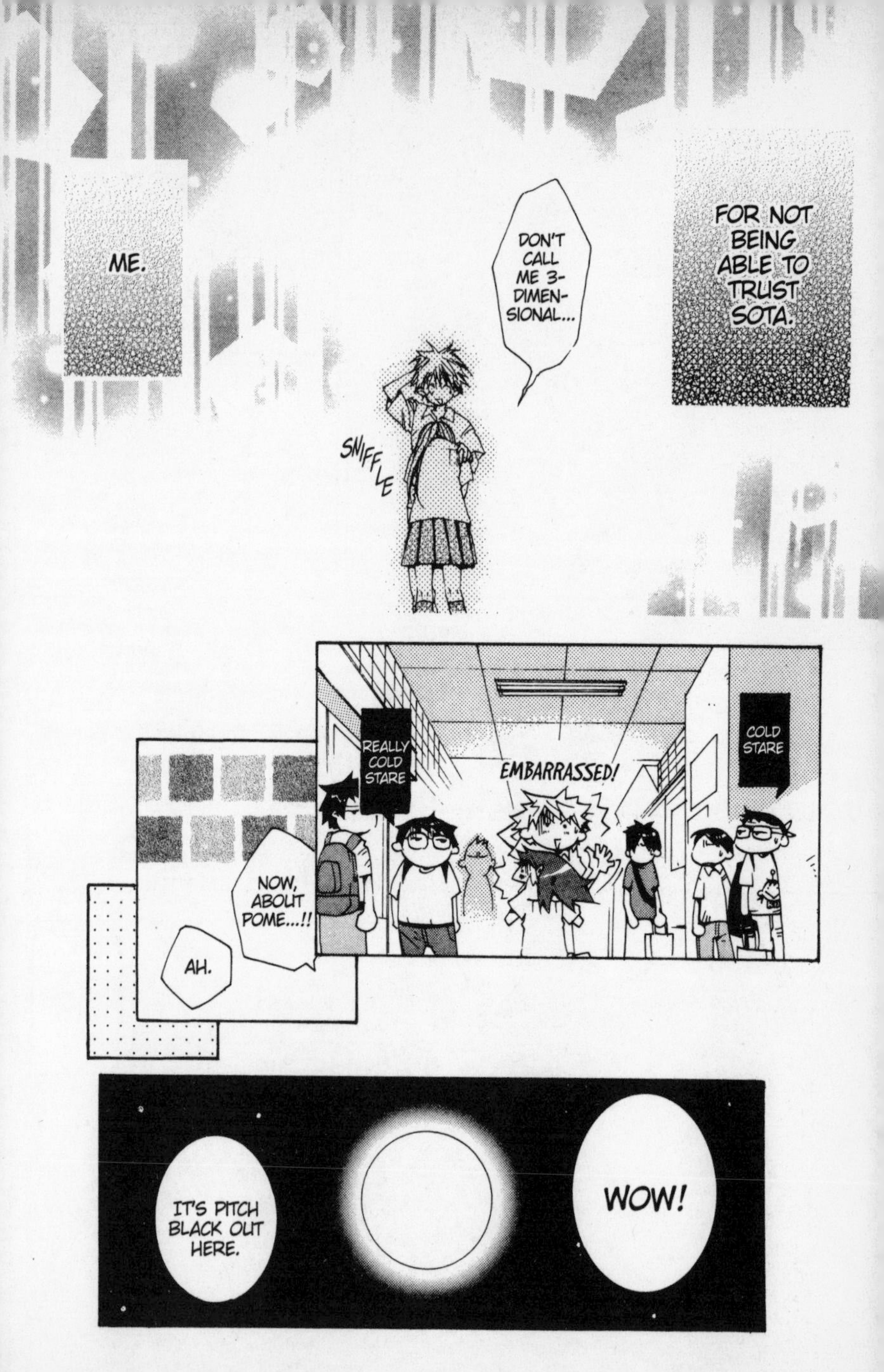
FOR NOT BEING ABLE TO TRUST SOTA.
DON'T CALL ME 3-DIMENSIONAL...
SNIFFLE
ME.
COLD STARE
EMBARRASSED!
REALLY COLD STARE
NOW, ABOUT POME...!!
AH.
WOW!
IT'S PITCH BLACK OUT HERE.

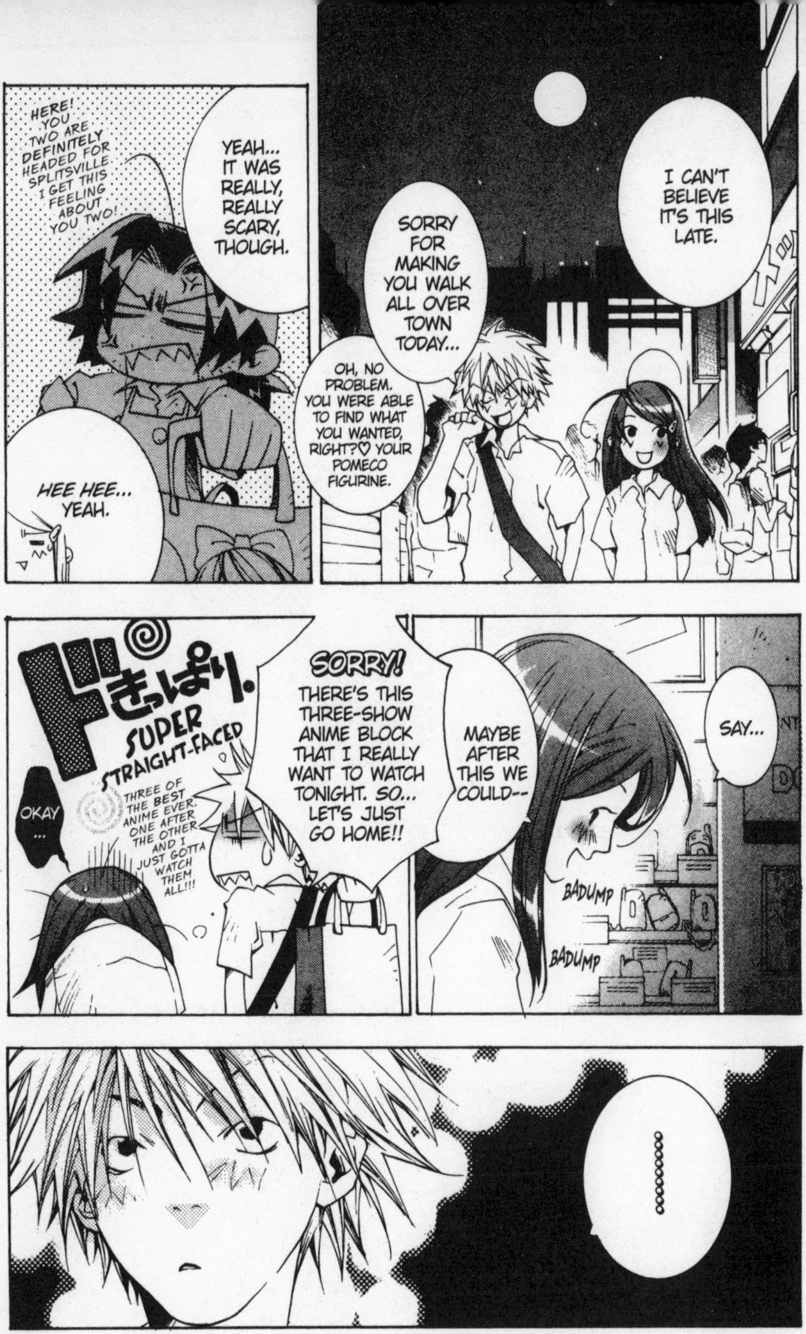
I CAN'T BELIEVE IT'S THIS LATE.
SORRY FOR MAKING YOU WALK ALL OVER TOWN TODAY...
OH, NO PROBLEM. YOU WERE ABLE TO FIND WHAT YOU WANTED, RIGHT?♡ YOUR POMECO FIGURINE.
YEAH... IT WAS REALLY, REALLY SCARY, THOUGH.
HERE! YOU TWO ARE DEFINITELY HEADED FOR SPLITSVILLE. I GET THIS FEELING ABOUT YOU TWO!
HEE HEE... YEAH.
SAY...
MAYBE AFTER THIS WE COULD--
BADUMP
BADUMP
SORRY! THERE'S THIS THREE-SHOW ANIME BLOCK THAT I REALLY WANT TO WATCH TONIGHT. SO... LET'S JUST GO HOME!!
ドきっぱり。
SUPER STRAIGHT-FACED
THREE OF THE BEST ANIME EVER, ONE AFTER THE OTHER AND I JUST GOTTA WATCH THEM ALL!!!
OKAY...
....

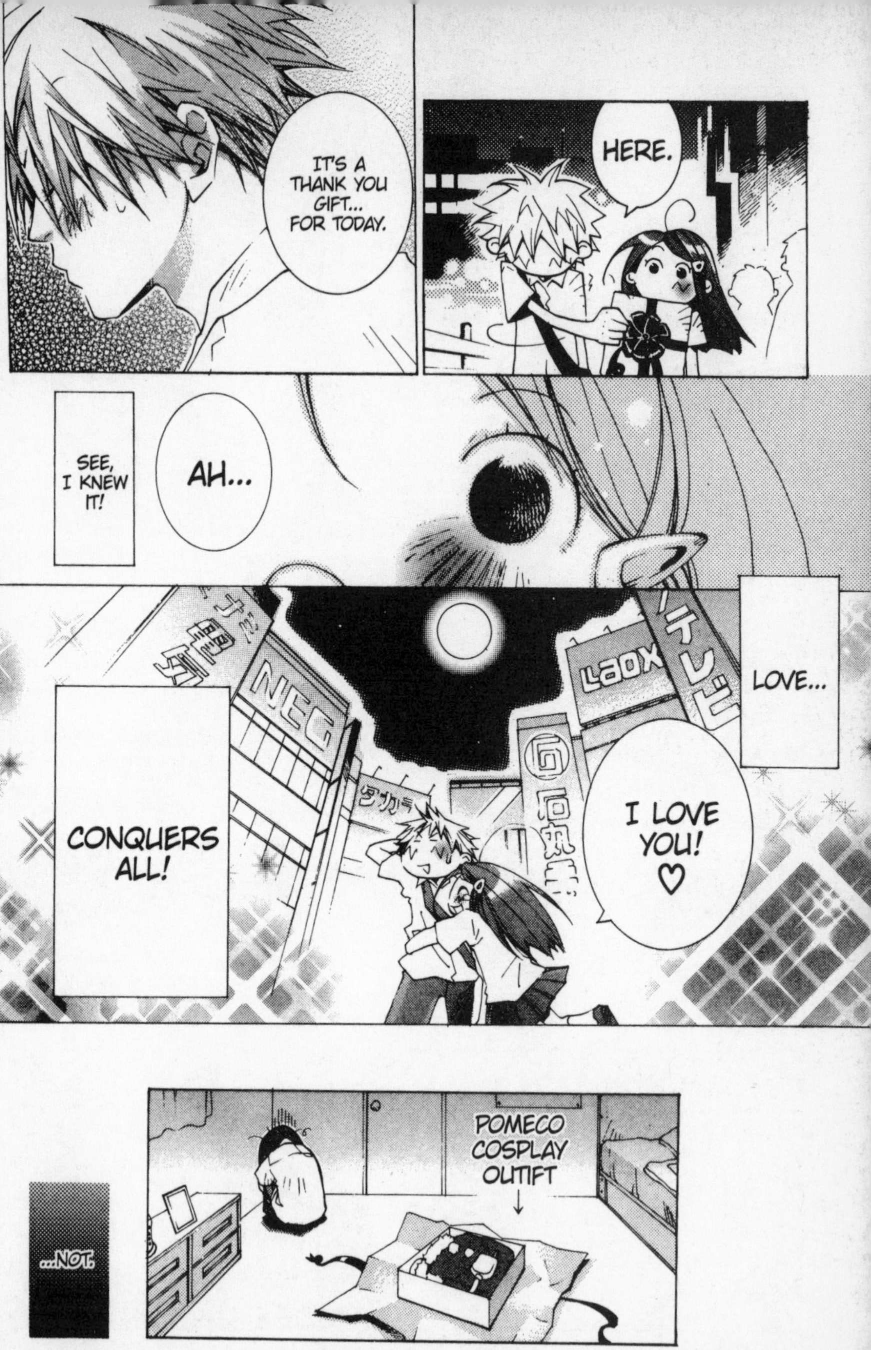
HERE.
IT'S A THANK YOU GIFT... FOR TODAY.
AH...
SEE, I KNEW IT!
LOVE...
LAOX
NEG
I LOVE YOU! ♡
CONQUERS ALL!
POMECO COSPLAY OUTIFT
↓
...NOT.

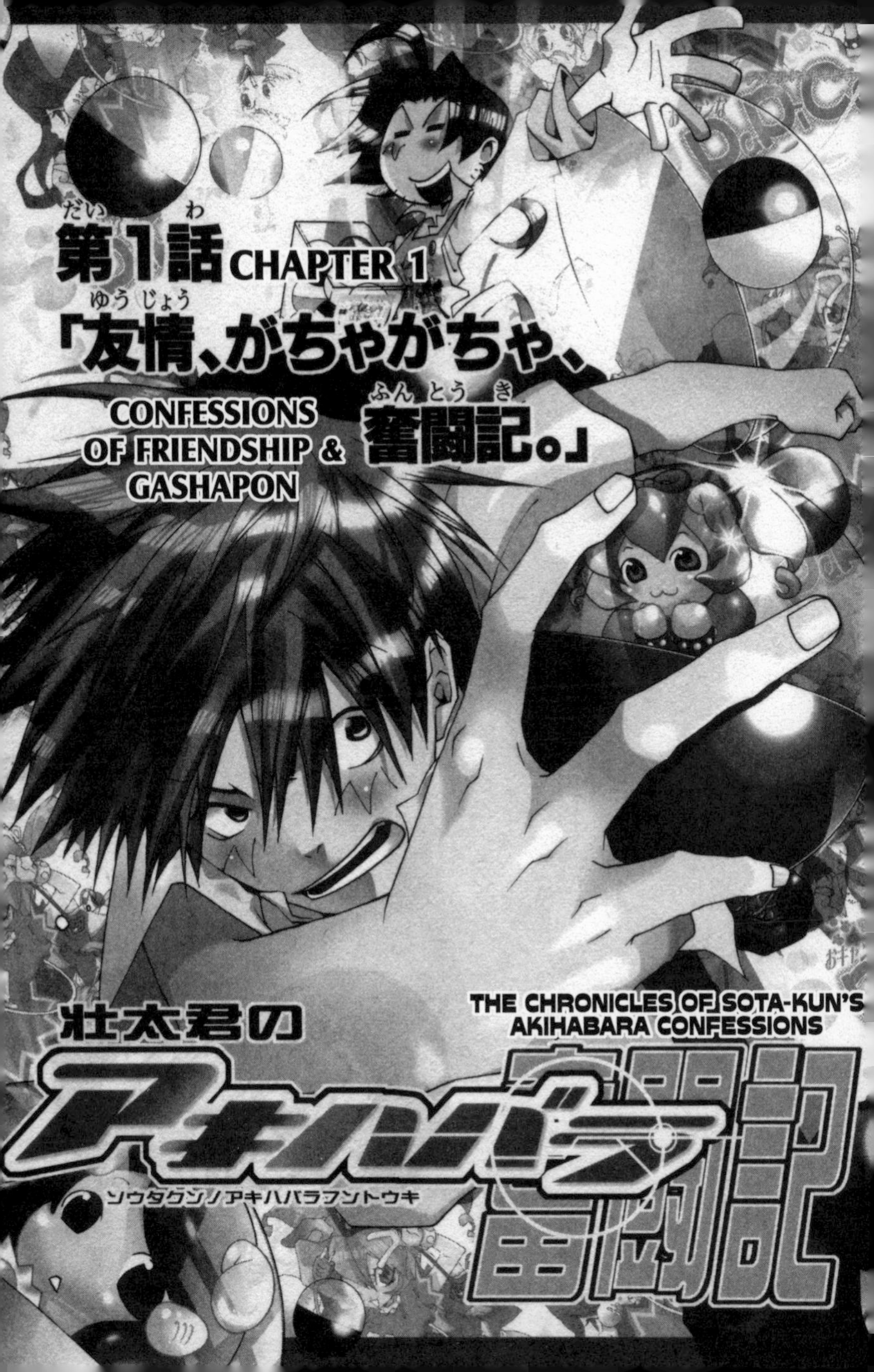
第1話 CHAPTER 1
「友情、がちゃがちゃ、奮闘記。」
CONFESSIONS OF FRIENDSHIP & GASHAPON
壮太君の
THE CHRONICLES OF SOTA-KUN'S AKIHABARA CONFESSIONS
アキハバラ奮闘記
ソウタクンノアキハバラフントウキ

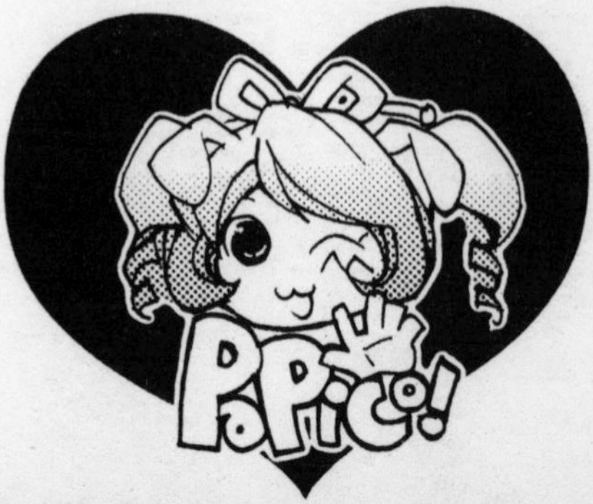
PoPiCo!

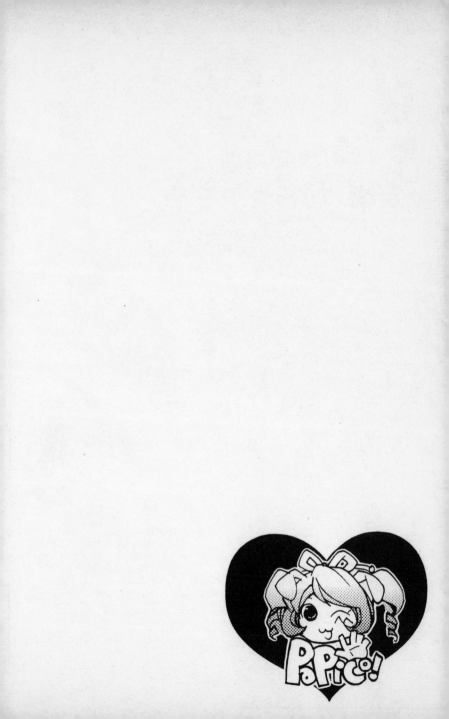

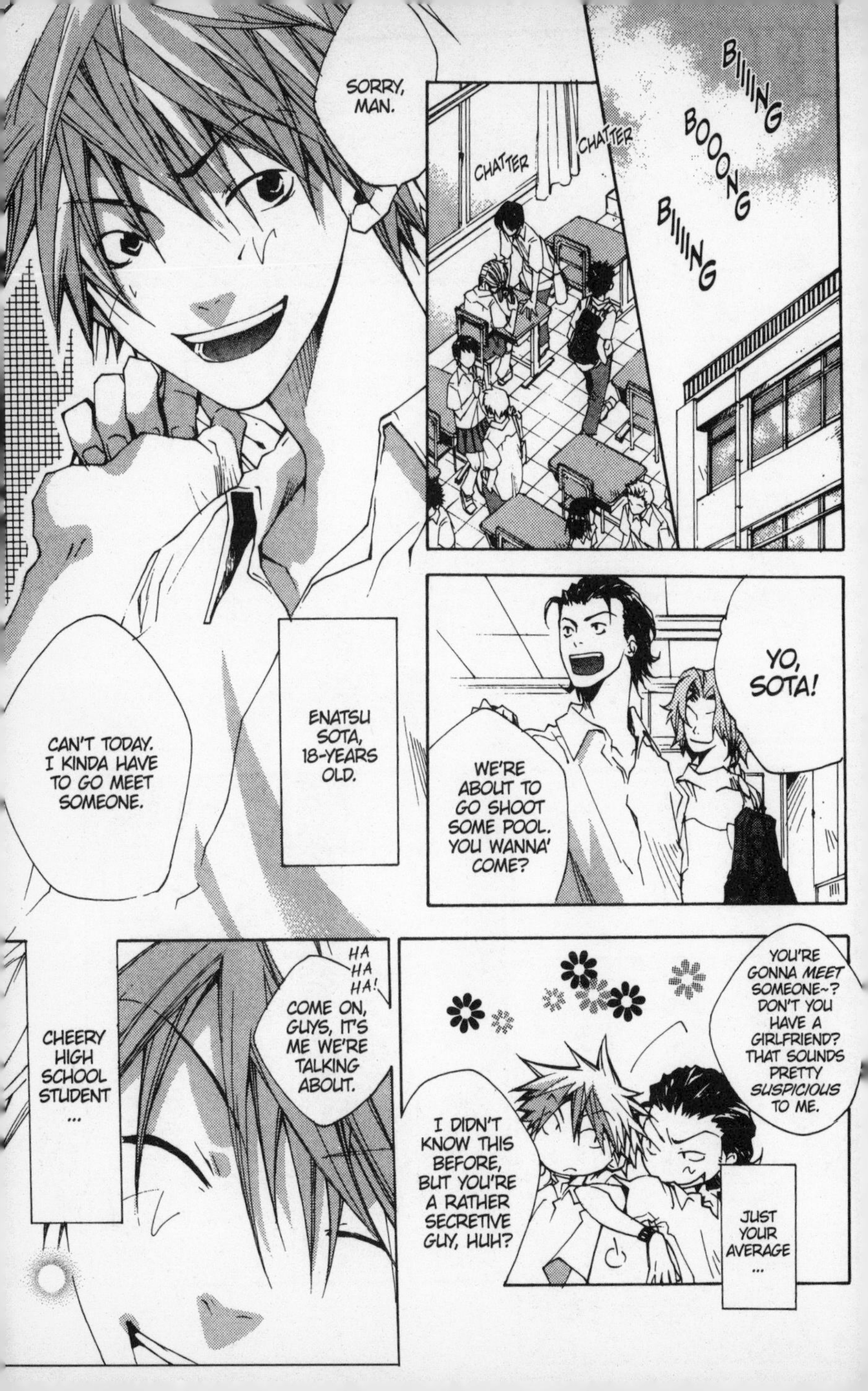
BIIIING
BOOONG
BIIIING
CHATTER
CHATTER
YO, SOTA!
WE'RE ABOUT TO GO SHOOT SOME POOL. YOU WANNA' COME?
SORRY, MAN.
ENATSU SOTA, 18-YEARS OLD.
CAN'T TODAY. I KINDA HAVE TO GO MEET SOMEONE.
YOU'RE GONNA *MEET* SOMEONE~? DON'T YOU HAVE A GIRLFRIEND? THAT SOUNDS PRETTY *SUSPICIOUS* TO ME.
I DIDN'T KNOW THIS BEFORE, BUT YOU'RE A RATHER SECRETIVE GUY, HUH?
JUST YOUR AVERAGE ...
HA HA HA!
COME ON, GUYS, IT'S ME WE'RE TALKING ABOUT.
CHEERY HIGH SCHOOL STUDENT ...

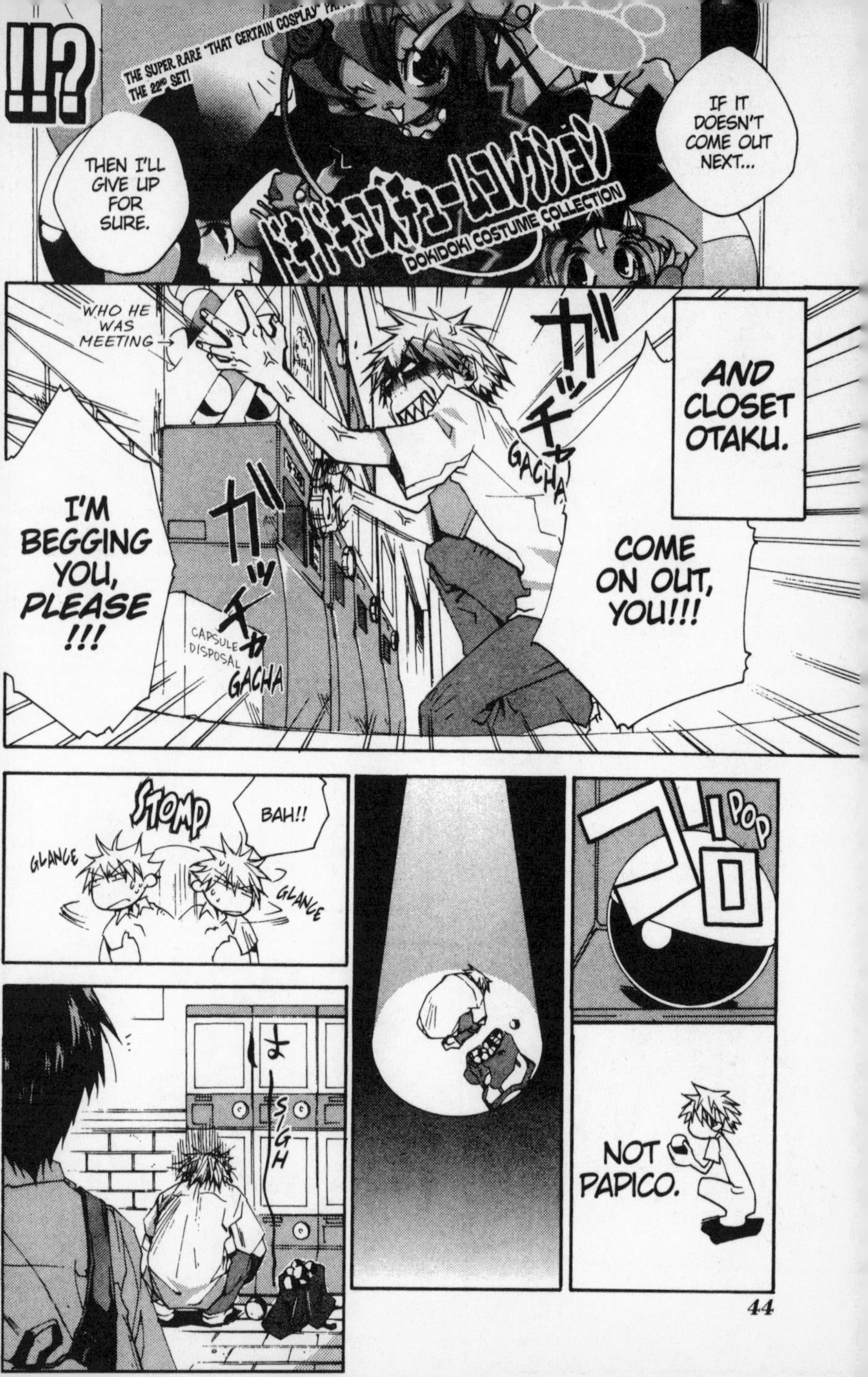
IF IT DOESN'T COME OUT NEXT...
DOKIDOKI COSTUME COLLECTION
THE SUPER RARE "THAT CERTAIN COSPLAY"
THE 22nd SET!
THEN I'LL GIVE UP FOR SURE.
!!?
AND CLOSET OTAKU.
GACHA
COME ON OUT, YOU!!!
WHO HE WAS MEETING →
CAPSULE DISPOSAL
GACHA
I'M BEGGING YOU, PLEASE!!!
POP
NOT PAPICO.
BAH!!
STOMP
GLANCE
GLANCE
SIGH

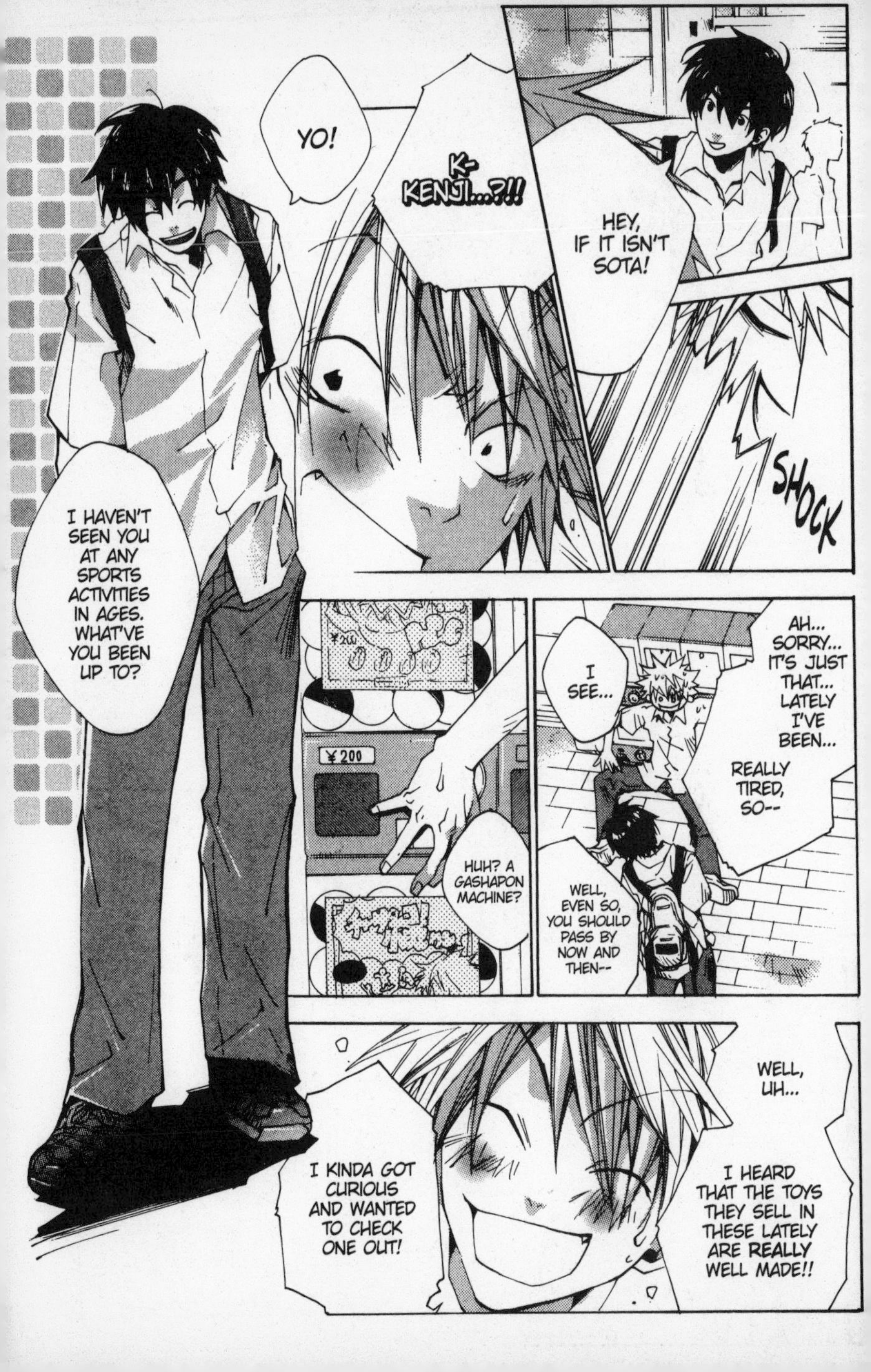
YO!
HEY, IF IT ISN'T SOTA!
SHOCK
K-KENJI...?!!
I HAVEN'T SEEN YOU AT ANY SPORTS ACTIVITIES IN AGES. WHAT'VE YOU BEEN UP TO?
AH... SORRY... IT'S JUST THAT... LATELY I'VE BEEN...
REALLY TIRED, SO--
I SEE...
WELL, EVEN SO, YOU SHOULD PASS BY NOW AND THEN--
HUH? A GASHAPON MACHINE?
WELL, UH...
I HEARD THAT THE TOYS THEY SELL IN THESE LATELY ARE REALLY WELL MADE!!
I KINDA GOT CURIOUS AND WANTED TO CHECK ONE OUT!

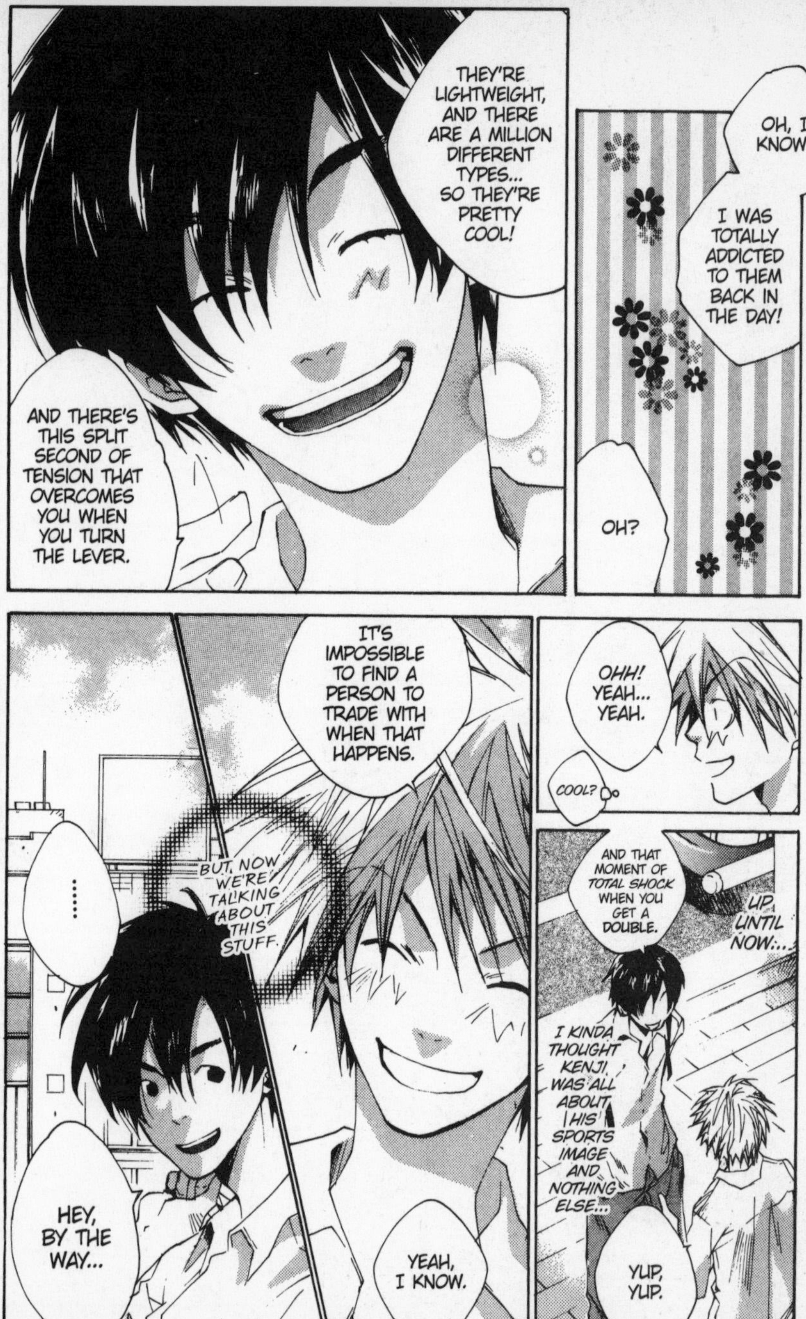
OH, I KNOW!
I WAS TOTALLY ADDICTED TO THEM BACK IN THE DAY!
OH?
THEY'RE LIGHTWEIGHT, AND THERE ARE A MILLION DIFFERENT TYPES... SO THEY'RE PRETTY COOL!
AND THERE'S THIS SPLIT SECOND OF TENSION THAT OVERCOMES YOU WHEN YOU TURN THE LEVER.
OHH! YEAH... YEAH.
COOL?
AND THAT MOMENT OF TOTAL SHOCK WHEN YOU GET A DOUBLE.
UP UNTIL NOW...
I KINDA THOUGHT KENJI WAS ALL ABOUT HIS SPORTS IMAGE AND NOTHING ELSE...
YUP, YUP.
IT'S IMPOSSIBLE TO FIND A PERSON TO TRADE WITH WHEN THAT HAPPENS.
BUT, NOW WE'RE TALKING ABOUT THIS STUFF.
......
YEAH, I KNOW.
HEY, BY THE WAY...

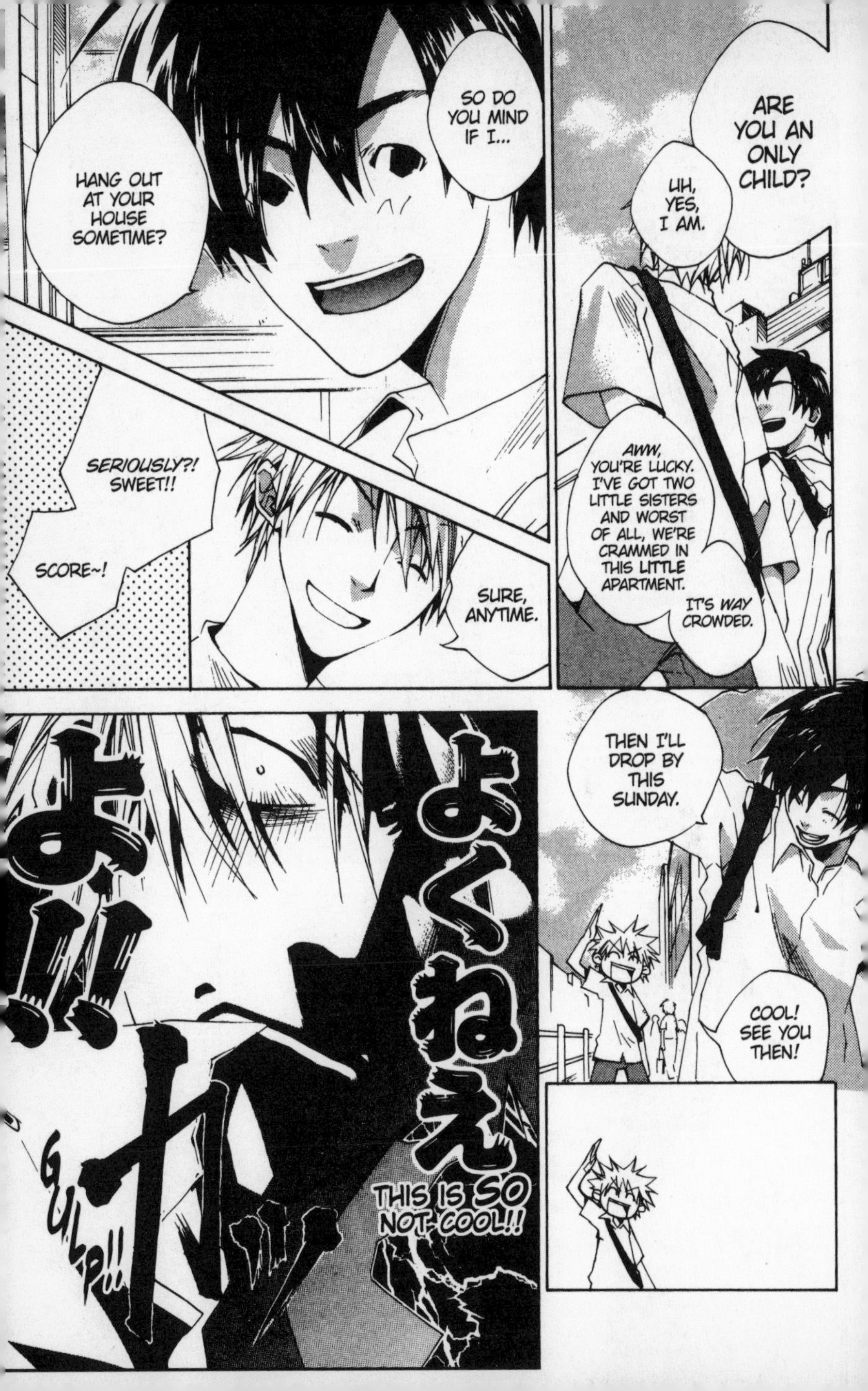
ARE YOU AN ONLY CHILD?
UH, YES, I AM.
AWW, YOU'RE LUCKY. I'VE GOT TWO LITTLE SISTERS AND WORST OF ALL, WE'RE CRAMMED IN THIS LITTLE APARTMENT.
IT'S *WAY* CROWDED.
SO DO YOU MIND IF I...
HANG OUT AT YOUR HOUSE SOMETIME?
SURE, ANYTIME.
SERIOUSLY?! SWEET!!
SCORE~!
THEN I'LL DROP BY THIS SUNDAY.
COOL! SEE YOU THEN!
よくねえ
THIS IS SO NOT COOL!!
G.U.L.p!!

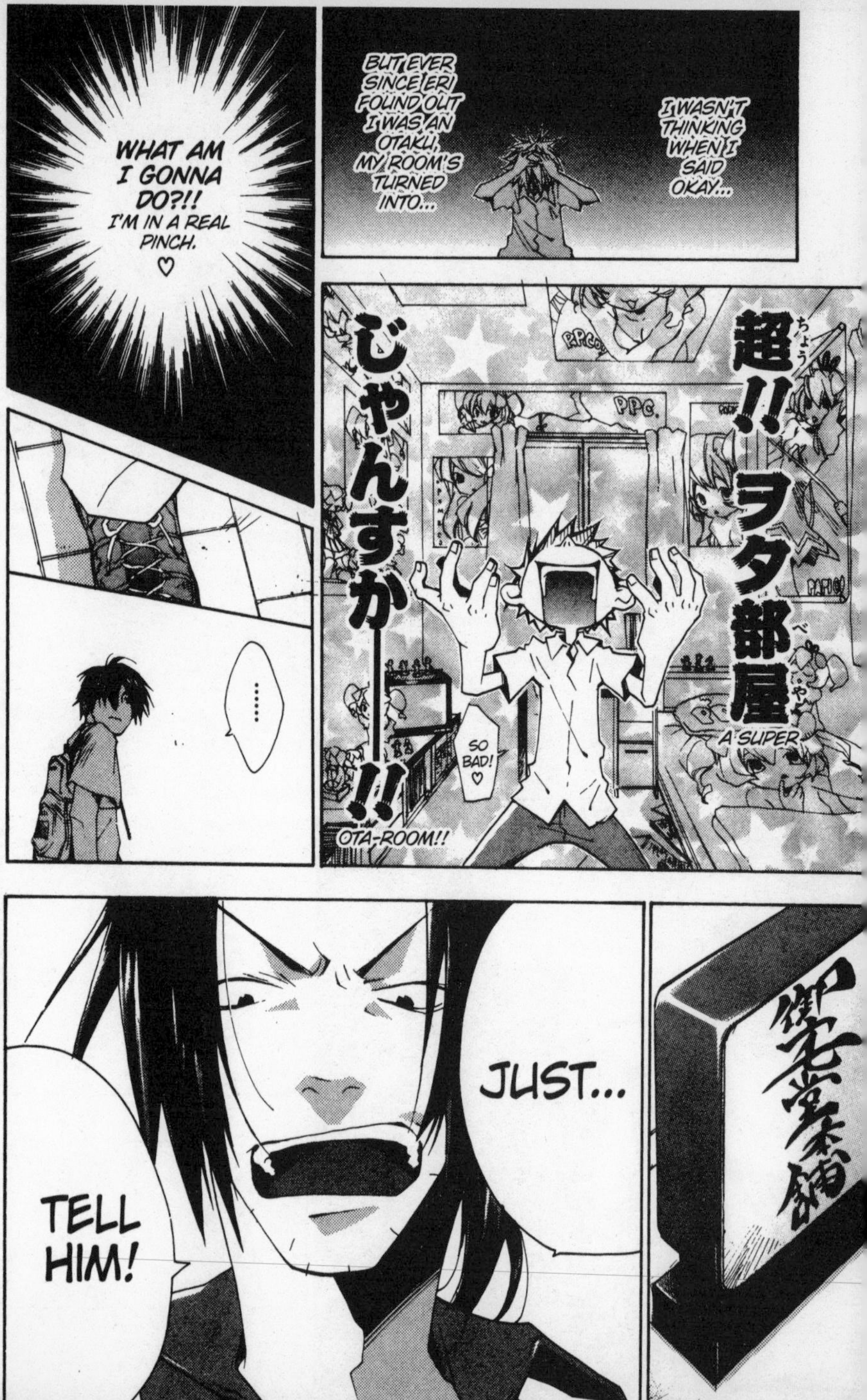
I WASN'T THINKING WHEN I SAID OKAY...
BUT EVER SINCE ERI FOUND OUT I WAS AN OTAKU, MY ROOM'S TURNED INTO...
超!!ヲタ部屋
A SUPER
じゃんすか——!!
OTA-ROOM!!
SO BAD! ♡
WHAT AM I GONNA DO?!! I'M IN A REAL PINCH. ♡
......
JUST...
TELL HIM!

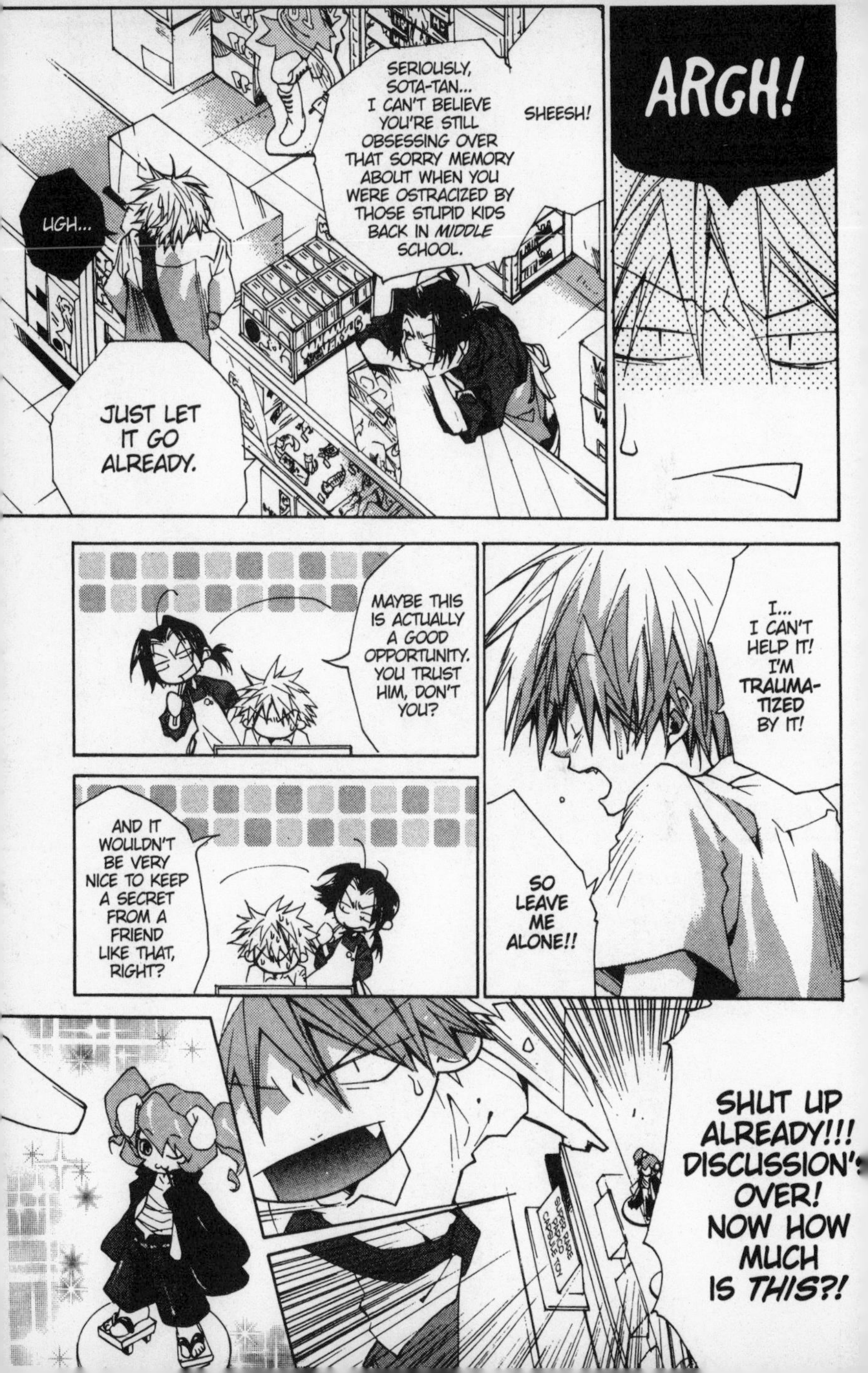
ARGH!
SHEESH!
SERIOUSLY, SOTA-TAN... I CAN'T BELIEVE YOU'RE STILL OBSESSING OVER THAT SORRY MEMORY ABOUT WHEN YOU WERE OSTRACIZED BY THOSE STUPID KIDS BACK IN *MIDDLE* SCHOOL.
UGH...
JUST LET IT GO ALREADY.
I... I CAN'T HELP IT! I'M TRAUMA-TIZED BY IT!
SO LEAVE ME ALONE!!
MAYBE THIS IS ACTUALLY A GOOD OPPORTUNITY. YOU TRUST HIM, DON'T YOU?
AND IT WOULDN'T BE VERY NICE TO KEEP A SECRET FROM A FRIEND LIKE THAT, RIGHT?
SHUT UP ALREADY!!! DISCUSSION' OVER! NOW HOW MUCH IS *THIS*?!

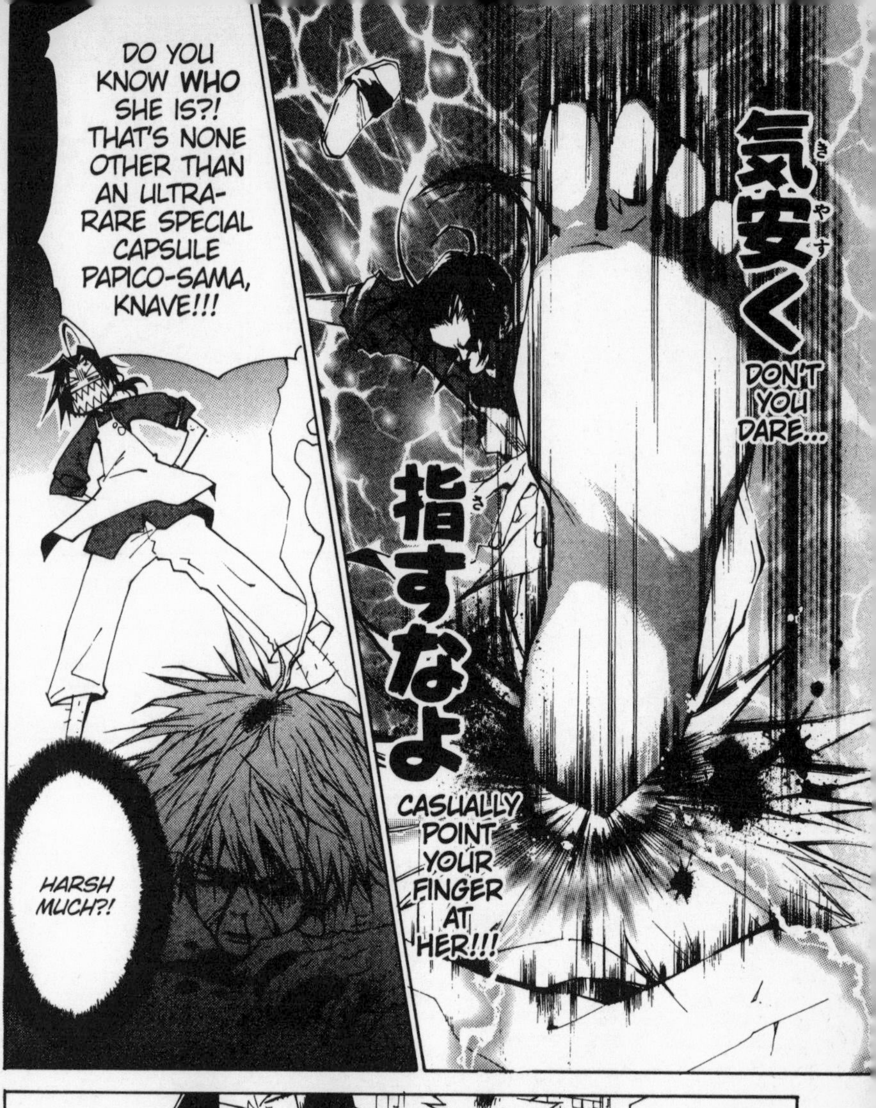
気安(きやす)く
DON'T YOU DARE...
指(さ)すなよ
CASUALLY POINT YOUR FINGER AT HER!!!
DO YOU KNOW WHO SHE IS?! THAT'S NONE OTHER THAN AN ULTRA-RARE SPECIAL CAPSULE PAPICO-SAMA, KNAVE!!!
HARSH MUCH?!
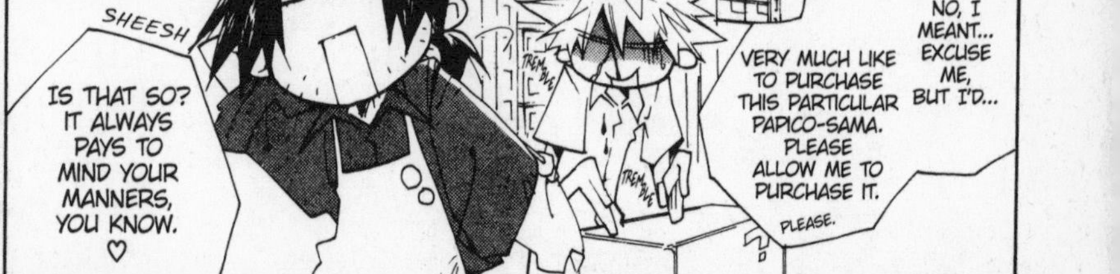
NO, I MEANT... EXCUSE ME, BUT I'D...
VERY MUCH LIKE TO PURCHASE THIS PARTICULAR PAPICO-SAMA. PLEASE ALLOW ME TO PURCHASE IT.
PLEASE.
TREMBLE
TREMBLE
SHEESH
IS THAT SO? IT ALWAYS PAYS TO MIND YOUR MANNERS, YOU KNOW. ♡

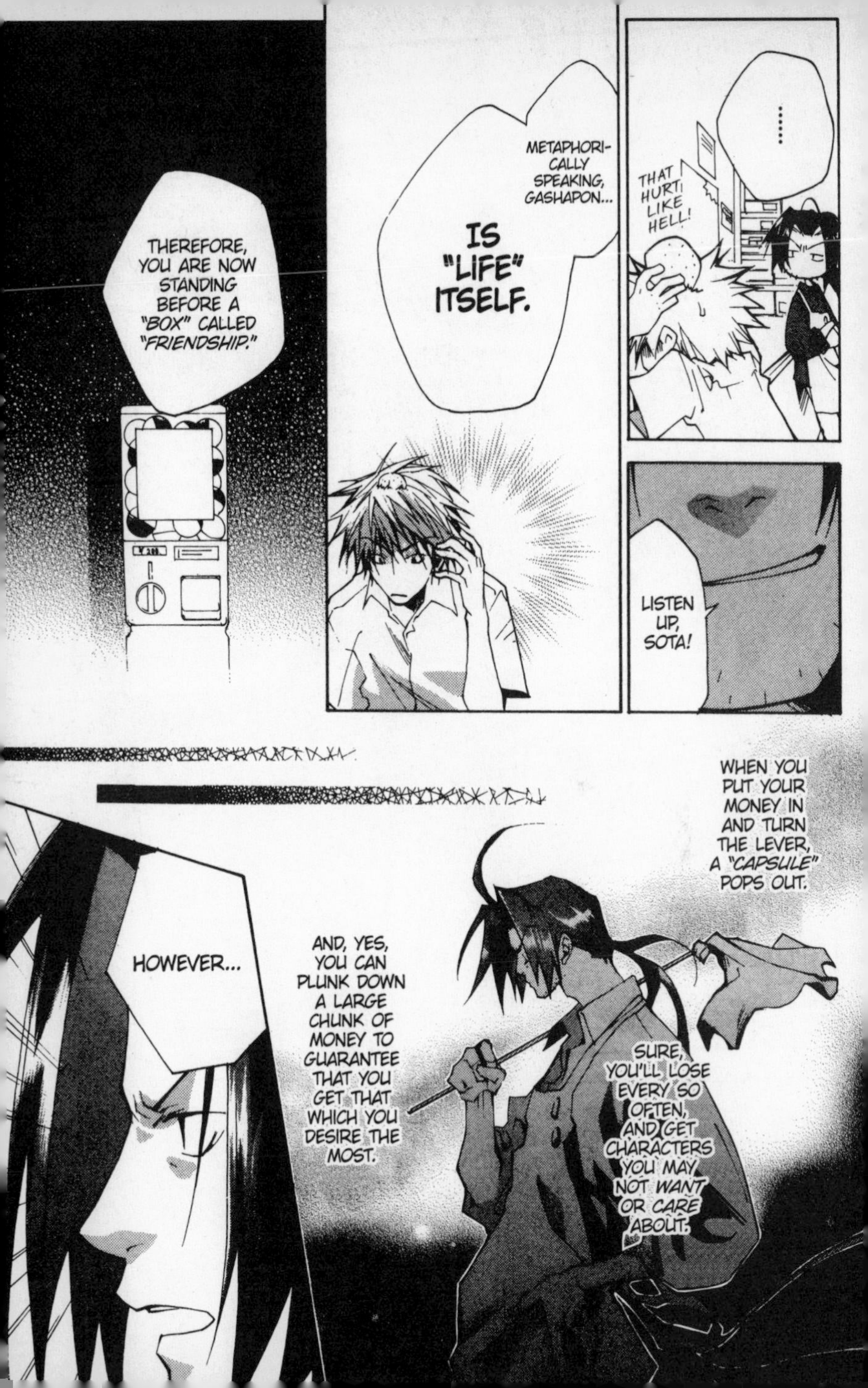
......
THAT HURT LIKE HELL!
LISTEN UP, SOTA!
METAPHORICALLY SPEAKING, GASHAPON...
IS "LIFE" ITSELF.
THEREFORE, YOU ARE NOW STANDING BEFORE A "BOX" CALLED "FRIENDSHIP."
WHEN YOU PUT YOUR MONEY IN AND TURN THE LEVER, A "CAPSULE" POPS OUT.
SURE, YOU'LL LOSE EVERY SO OFTEN, AND GET CHARACTERS YOU MAY NOT WANT OR CARE ABOUT.
AND, YES, YOU CAN PLUNK DOWN A LARGE CHUNK OF MONEY TO GUARANTEE THAT YOU GET THAT WHICH YOU DESIRE THE MOST.
HOWEVER...

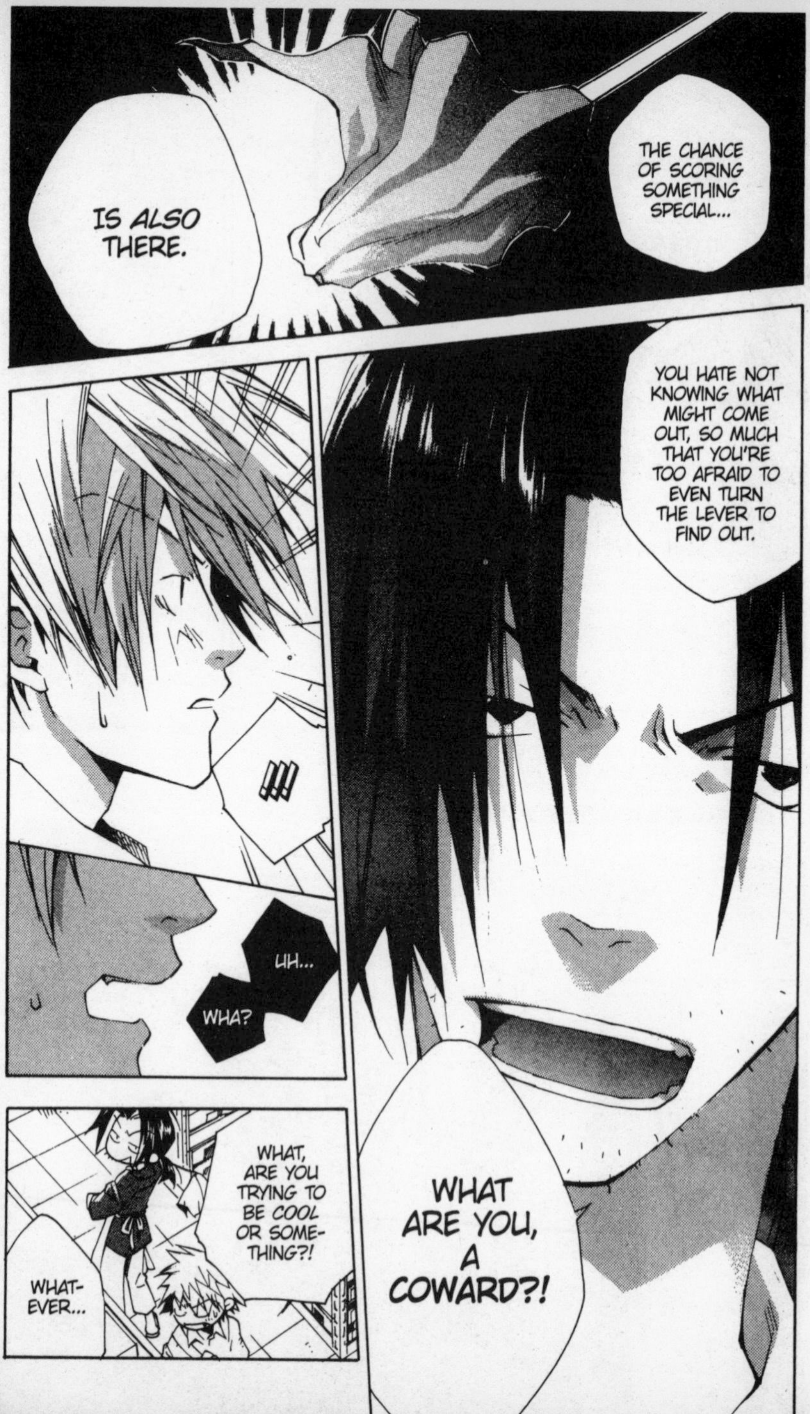
THE CHANCE OF SCORING SOMETHING SPECIAL...
IS ALSO THERE.
YOU HATE NOT KNOWING WHAT MIGHT COME OUT, SO MUCH THAT YOU'RE TOO AFRAID TO EVEN TURN THE LEVER TO FIND OUT.
WHAT ARE YOU, A COWARD?!
!!!!
UH...
WHA?
WHAT, ARE YOU TRYING TO BE COOL OR SOME-THING?!
WHAT-EVER...

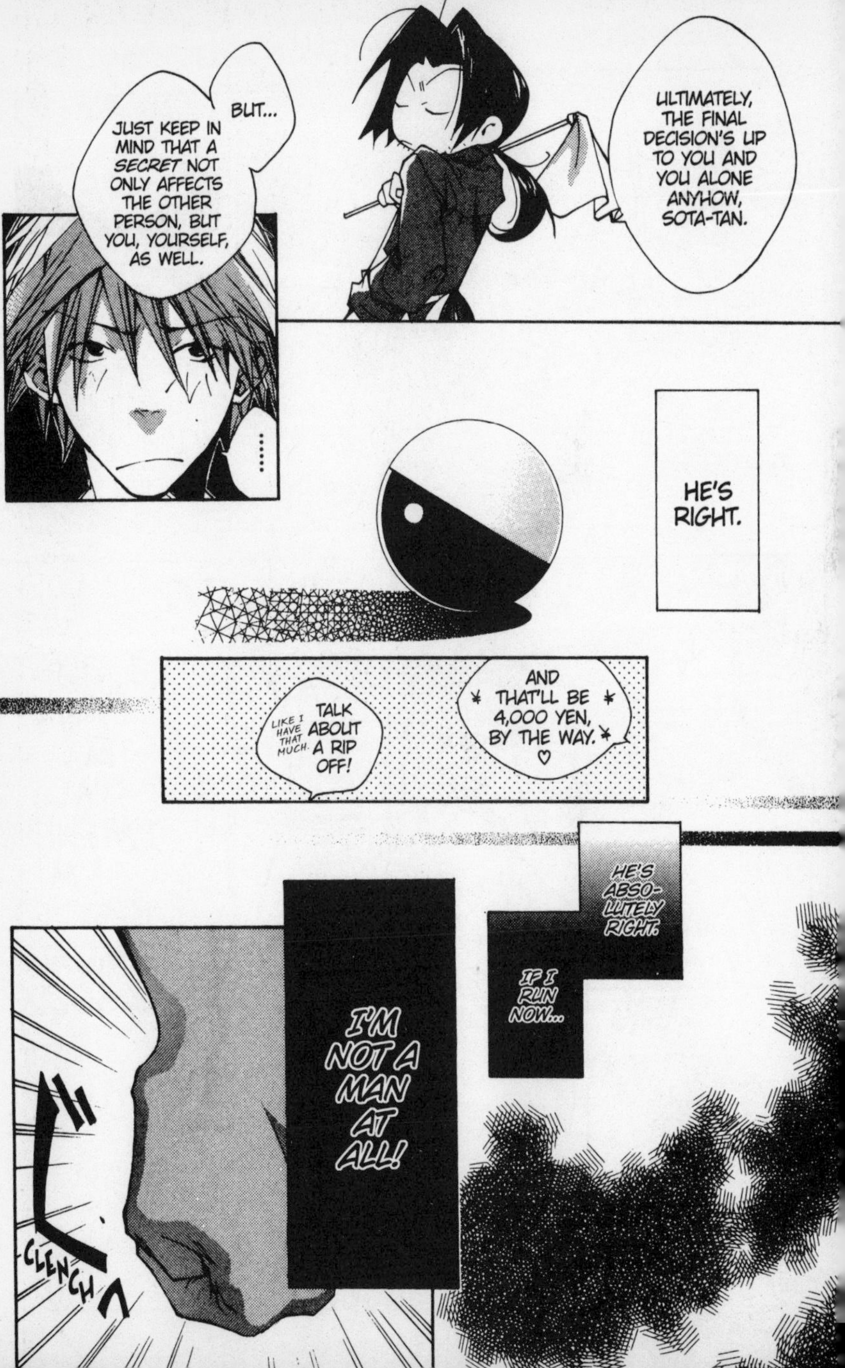
ULTIMATELY, THE FINAL DECISION'S UP TO YOU AND YOU ALONE ANYHOW, SOTA-TAN.
BUT...
JUST KEEP IN MIND THAT A *SECRET* NOT ONLY AFFECTS THE OTHER PERSON, BUT YOU, YOURSELF, AS WELL.
......
HE'S RIGHT.
AND THAT'LL BE 4,000 YEN, BY THE WAY.
TALK ABOUT A RIP OFF!
LIKE I HAVE THAT MUCH.
HE'S ABSO-LUTELY RIGHT.
IF I RUN NOW...
I'M NOT A MAN AT ALL!
CLENCH

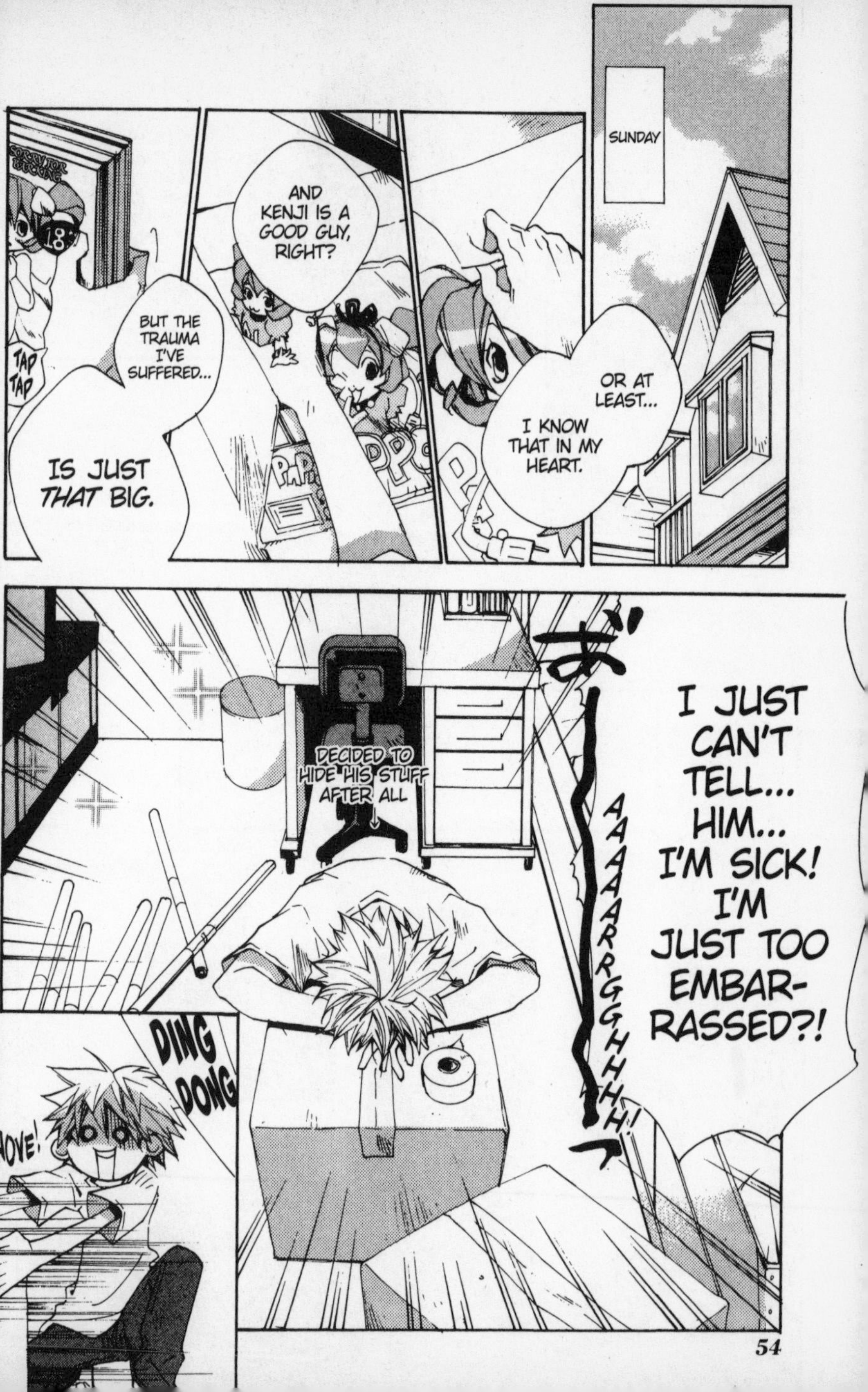
SUNDAY
OR AT LEAST...
I KNOW THAT IN MY HEART.
AND KENJI IS A GOOD GUY, RIGHT?
BUT THE TRAUMA I'VE SUFFERED...
TAP TAP
IS JUST *THAT* BIG.
I JUST CAN'T TELL... HIM... I'M SICK! I'M JUST TOO EMBARRASSED?!
AAAAARRGGHHHH!
DECIDED TO HIDE HIS STUFF AFTER ALL
DING DONG
HOVE!

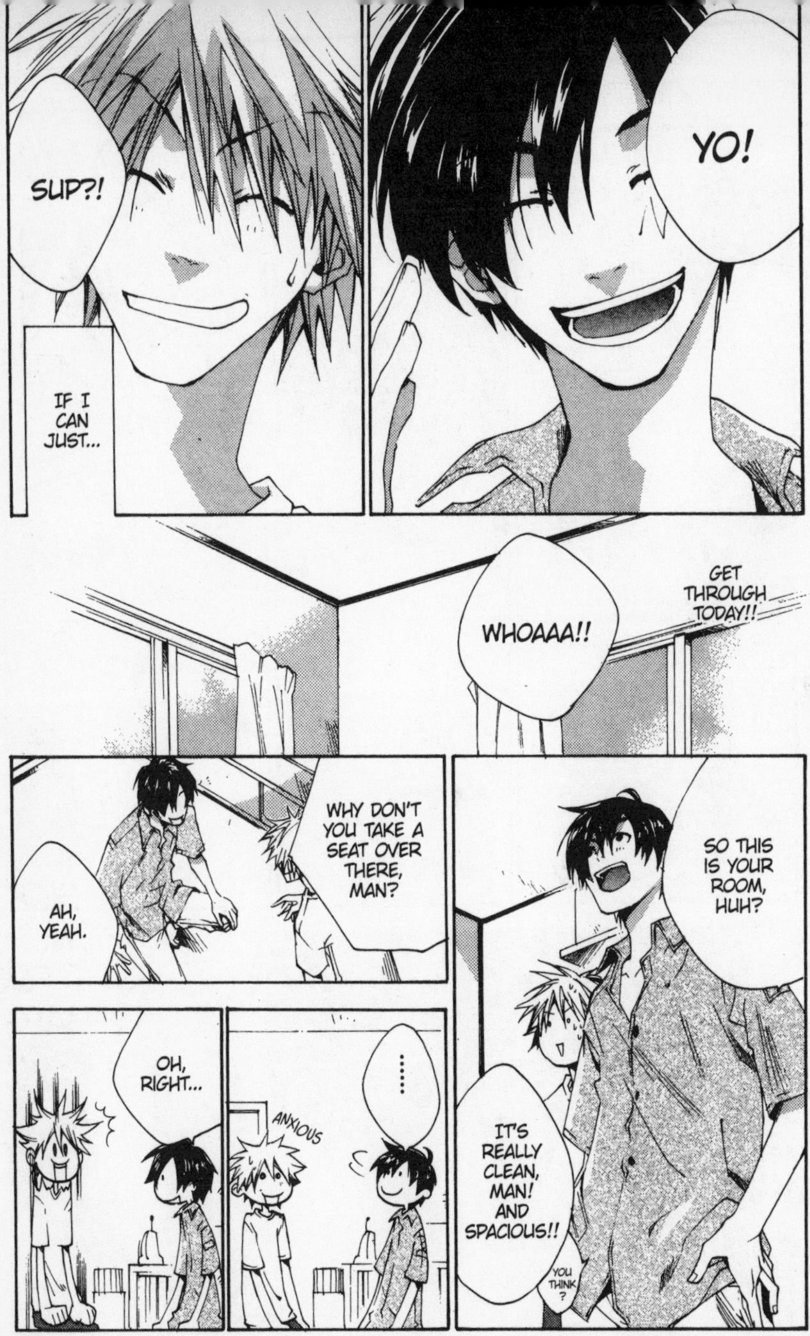

YO!
SUP?!
IF I CAN JUST...
GET THROUGH TODAY!!
WHOAAA!!
SO THIS IS YOUR ROOM, HUH?
IT'S REALLY CLEAN, MAN! AND SPACIOUS!!
YOU THINK?
WHY DON'T YOU TAKE A SEAT OVER THERE, MAN?
AH, YEAH.
......
ANXIOUS
OH, RIGHT...

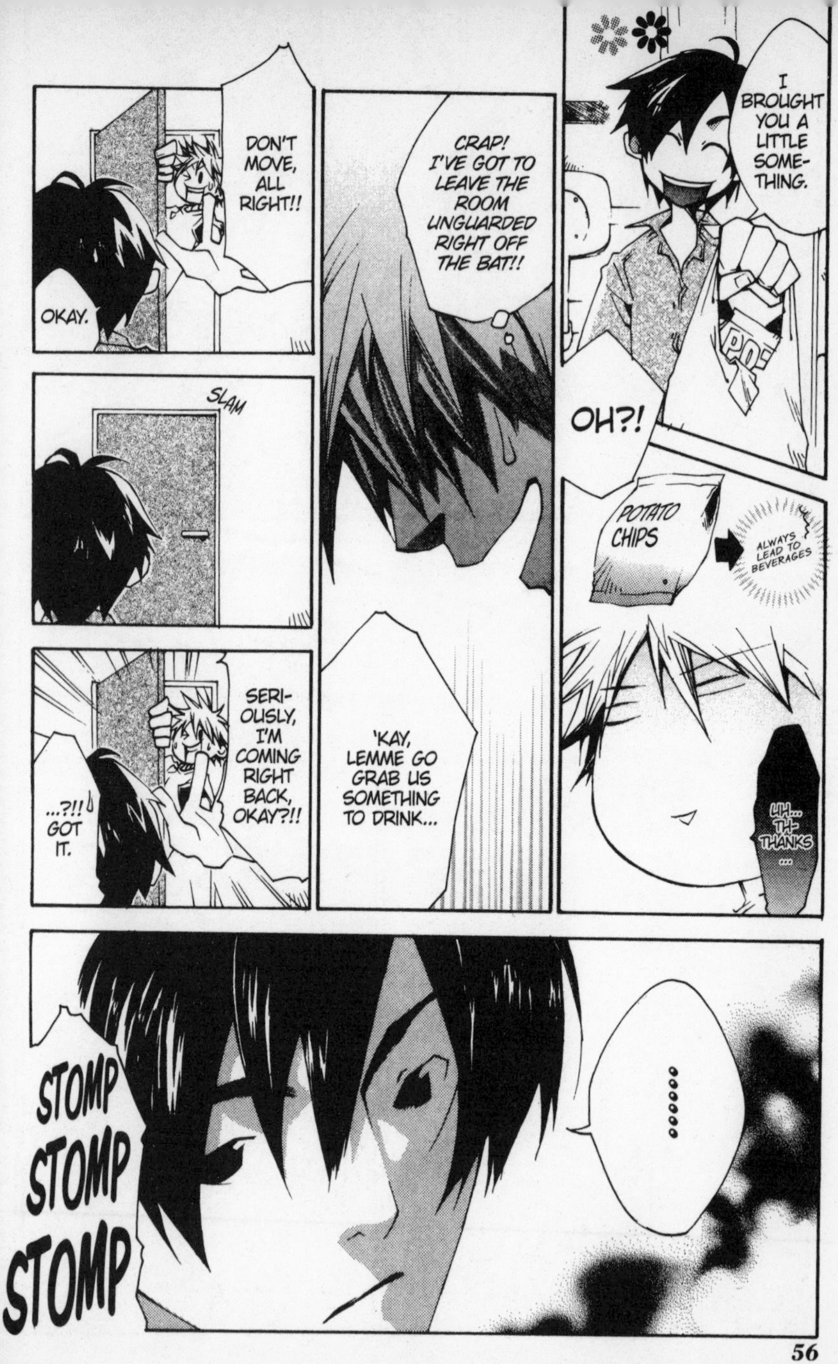
I BROUGHT YOU A LITTLE SOMETHING.
OH?!
POTATO CHIPS
ALWAYS LEAD TO BEVERAGES
UH... TH-THANKS...
CRAP! I'VE GOT TO LEAVE THE ROOM UNGUARDED RIGHT OFF THE BAT!!
'KAY, LEMME GO GRAB US SOMETHING TO DRINK...
DON'T MOVE, ALL RIGHT!!
OKAY.
SLAM
SERIOUSLY, I'M COMING RIGHT BACK, OKAY?!!
...?!! GOT IT.
......
STOMP STOMP STOMP

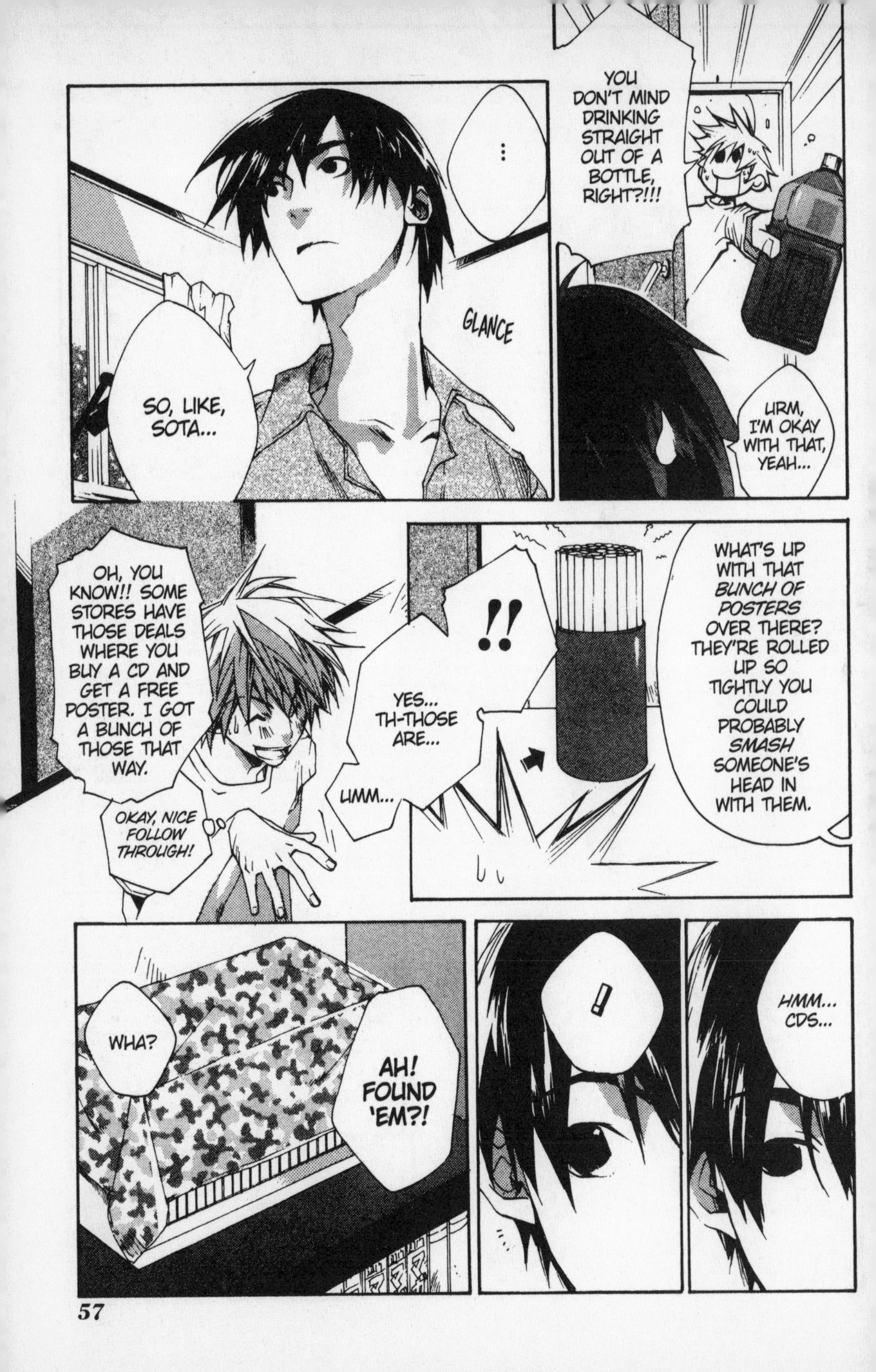
YOU DON'T MIND DRINKING STRAIGHT OUT OF A BOTTLE, RIGHT?!!!
URM, I'M OKAY WITH THAT, YEAH...
...
GLANCE
SO, LIKE, SOTA...
WHAT'S UP WITH THAT BUNCH OF POSTERS OVER THERE? THEY'RE ROLLED UP SO TIGHTLY YOU COULD PROBABLY SMASH SOMEONE'S HEAD IN WITH THEM.
!!
YES... TH-THOSE ARE...
UMM...
OH, YOU KNOW!! SOME STORES HAVE THOSE DEALS WHERE YOU BUY A CD AND GET A FREE POSTER. I GOT A BUNCH OF THOSE THAT WAY.
OKAY, NICE FOLLOW THROUGH!
HMM... CDS...
!
AH! FOUND 'EM?!
WHA?

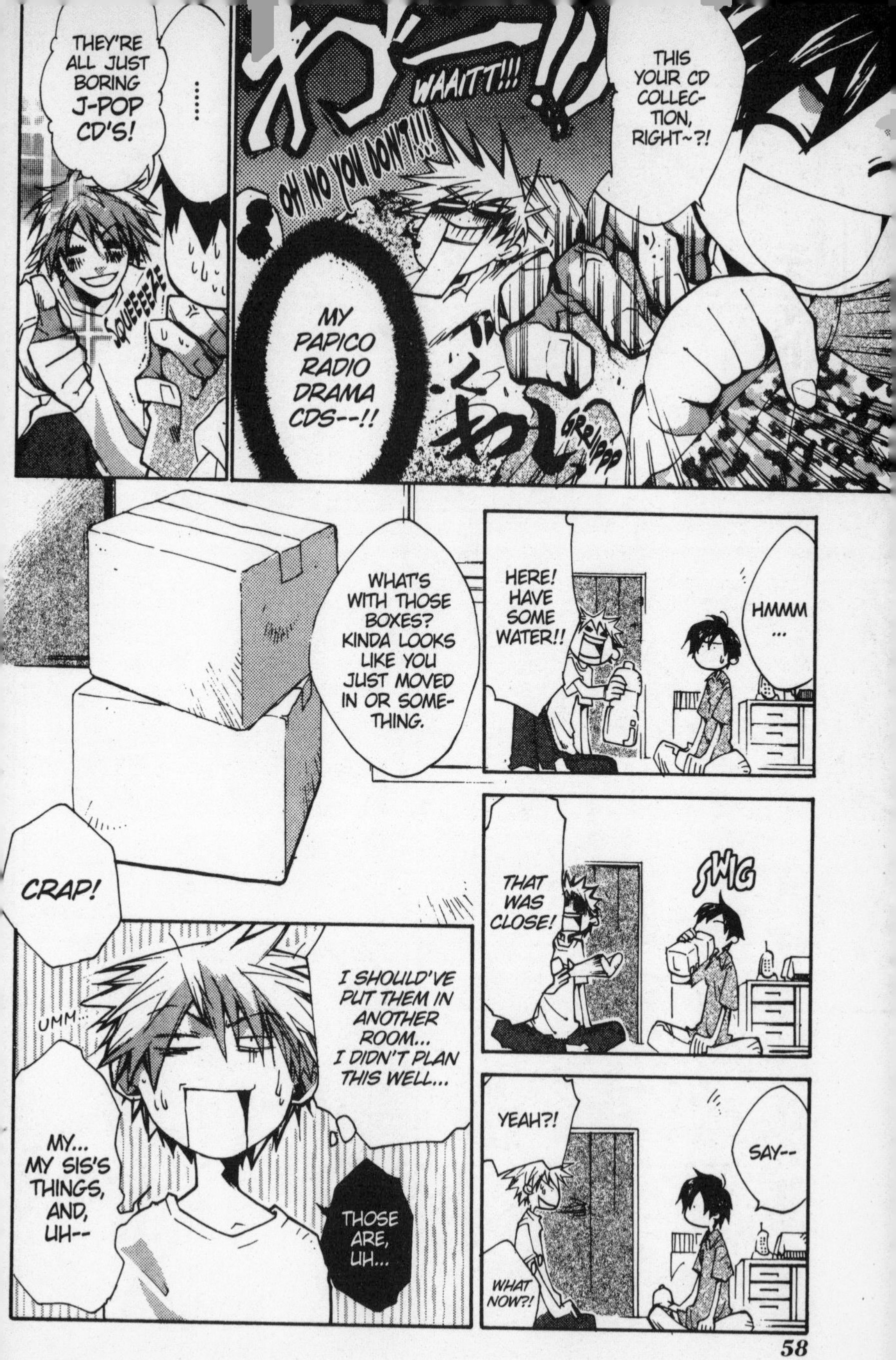
THIS YOUR CD COLLECTION, RIGHT~?!
WAAITT!!!
OH NO YOU DON'T!!!
MY PAPICO RADIO DRAMA CDS--!!
GRRIPPP
THEY'RE ALL JUST BORING J-POP CD'S!
......
SQUEEEEEZE
HMMM...
HERE! HAVE SOME WATER!!
SWIG
THAT WAS CLOSE!
SAY--
YEAH?!
WHAT NOW?!
WHAT'S WITH THOSE BOXES? KINDA LOOKS LIKE YOU JUST MOVED IN OR SOMETHING.
CRAP!
I SHOULD'VE PUT THEM IN ANOTHER ROOM... I DIDN'T PLAN THIS WELL...
UMM...
THOSE ARE, UH...
MY... MY SIS'S THINGS, AND, UH--

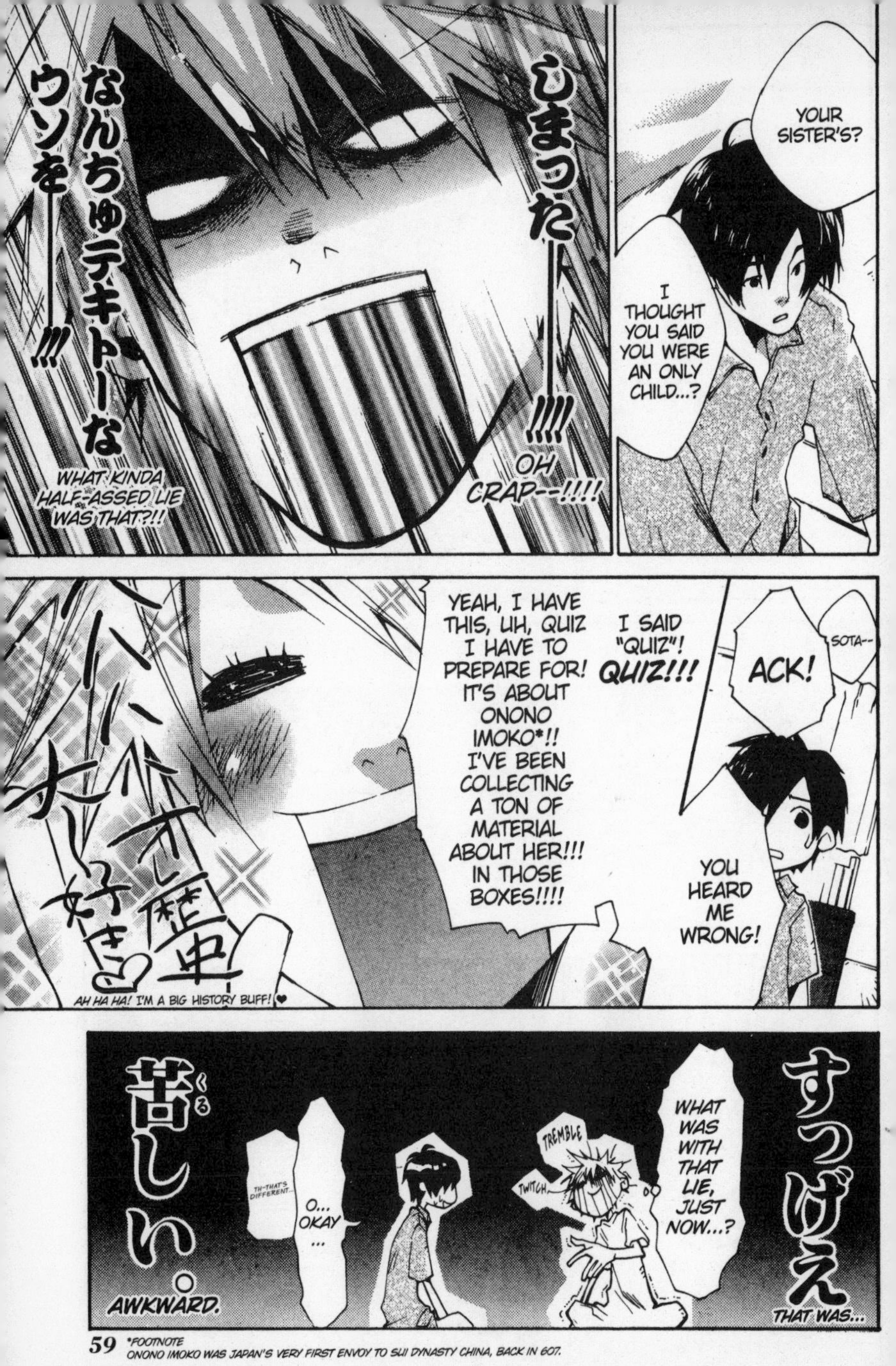
YOUR SISTER'S?
I THOUGHT YOU SAID YOU WERE AN ONLY CHILD...?
しまった!!!!
OH CRAP--!!!!
なんちゅテキトーなウソを!!!
WHAT KINDA HALF-ASSED LIE WAS THAT?!!
SOTA--
ACK!
I SAID "QUIZ"! QUIZ!!!
YEAH, I HAVE THIS, UH, QUIZ I HAVE TO PREPARE FOR! IT'S ABOUT ONONO IMOKO*!! I'VE BEEN COLLECTING A TON OF MATERIAL ABOUT HER!!! IN THOSE BOXES!!!!
YOU HEARD ME WRONG!
AH HA HA! I'M A BIG HISTORY BUFF! ♥
すっげえ
THAT WAS...
WHAT WAS WITH THAT LIE, JUST NOW...?
TREMBLE
TWITCH
O... OKAY ...
TH-THAT'S DIFFERENT...
苦しい。
AWKWARD.

*FOOTNOTE
ONONO IMOKO WAS JAPAN'S VERY FIRST ENVOY TO SUI DYNASTY CHINA, BACK IN 607.

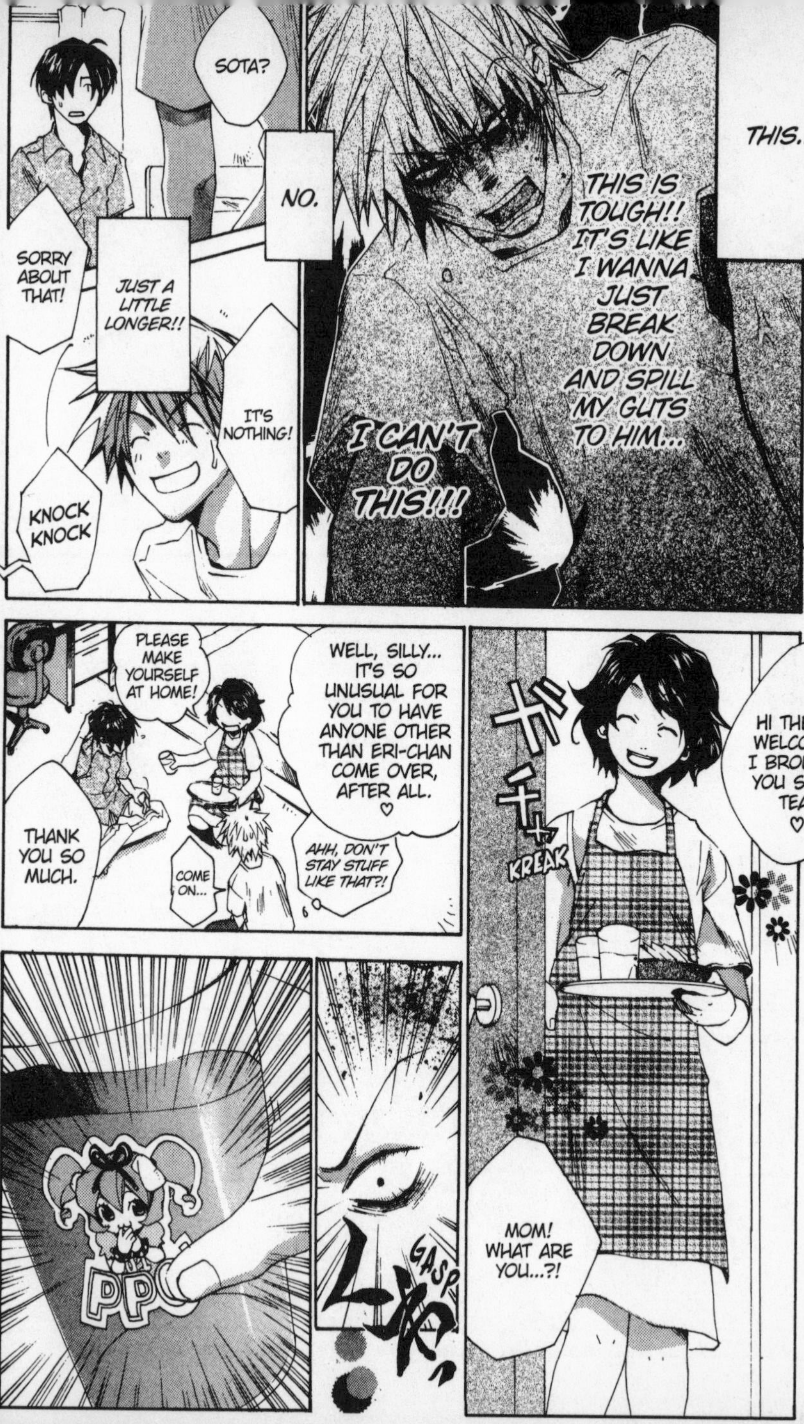
THIS...
THIS IS TOUGH!! IT'S LIKE I WANNA JUST BREAK DOWN AND SPILL MY GUTS TO HIM...
I CAN'T DO THIS!!!
SOTA?
NO.
JUST A LITTLE LONGER!!
SORRY ABOUT THAT!
IT'S NOTHING!
KNOCK KNOCK
KREAK
HI THERE. WELCOME! I BROUGHT YOU SOME TEA. ♡
MOM! WHAT ARE YOU...?!
WELL, SILLY... IT'S SO UNUSUAL FOR YOU TO HAVE ANYONE OTHER THAN ERI-CHAN COME OVER, AFTER ALL. ♡
PLEASE MAKE YOURSELF AT HOME!
AHH, DON'T STAY STUFF LIKE THAT?!
THANK YOU SO MUCH.
COME ON...
GASP

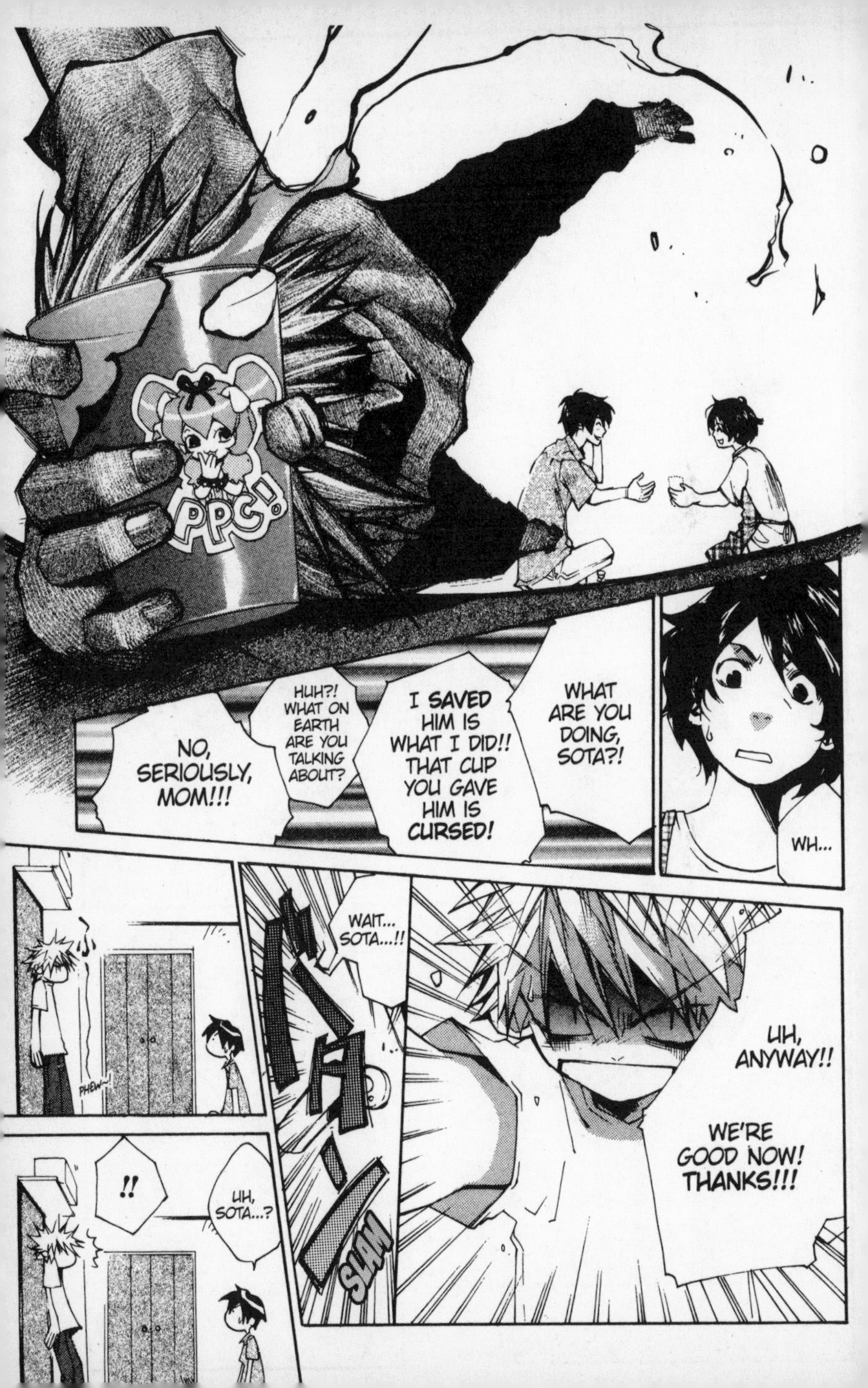

WH...
WHAT ARE YOU DOING, SOTA?!
I SAVED HIM IS WHAT I DID!! THAT CUP YOU GAVE HIM IS CURSED!
HUH?! WHAT ON EARTH ARE YOU TALKING ABOUT?
NO, SERIOUSLY, MOM!!!
UH, ANYWAY!!
WE'RE GOOD NOW! THANKS!!!
WAIT... SOTA...!!
SLAM
PHEW~!
UH, SOTA...?
!!

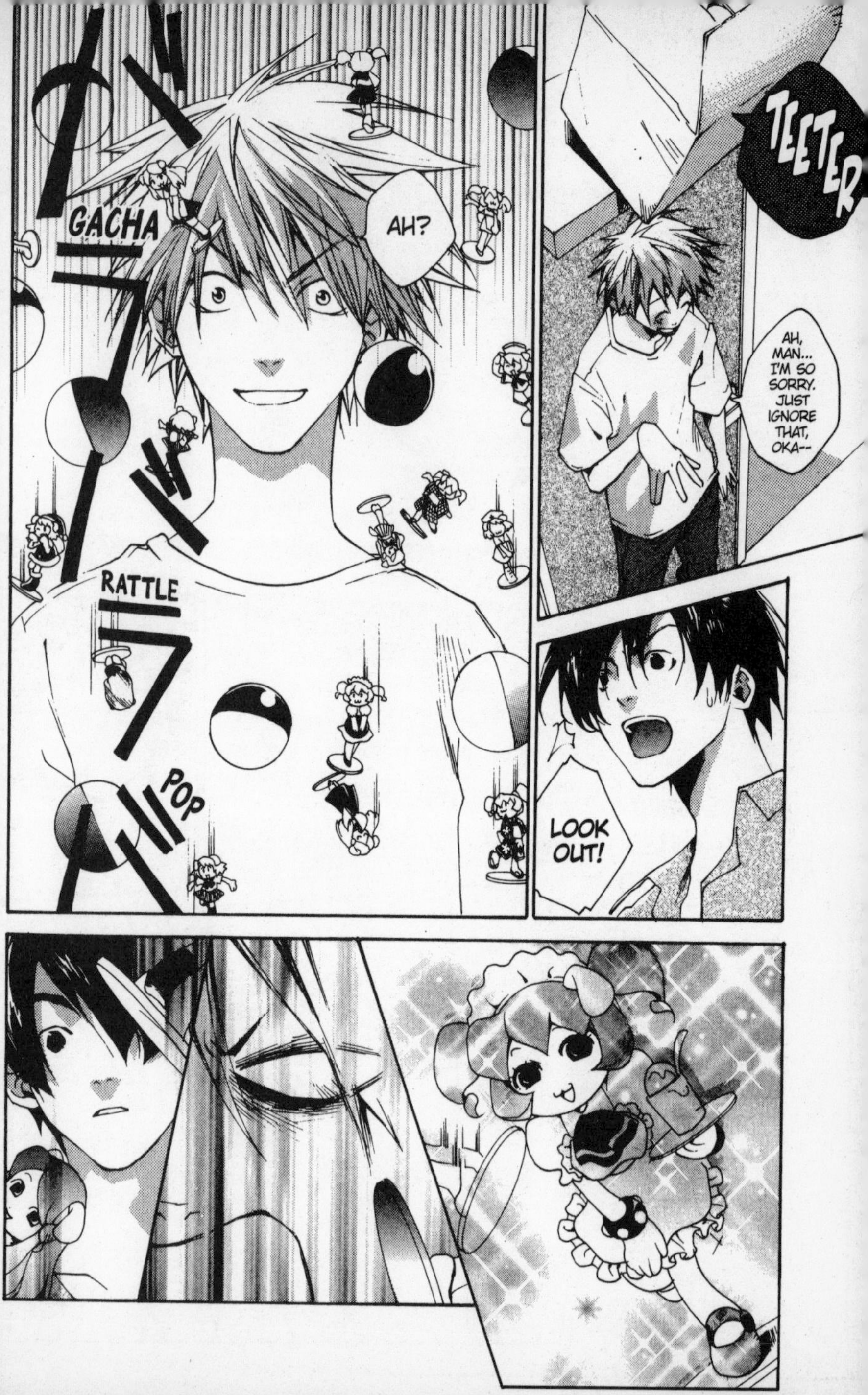
TEETER
AH, MAN... I'M SO SORRY. JUST IGNORE THAT, OKA--
LOOK OUT!
AH?
GACHA
RATTLE
POP

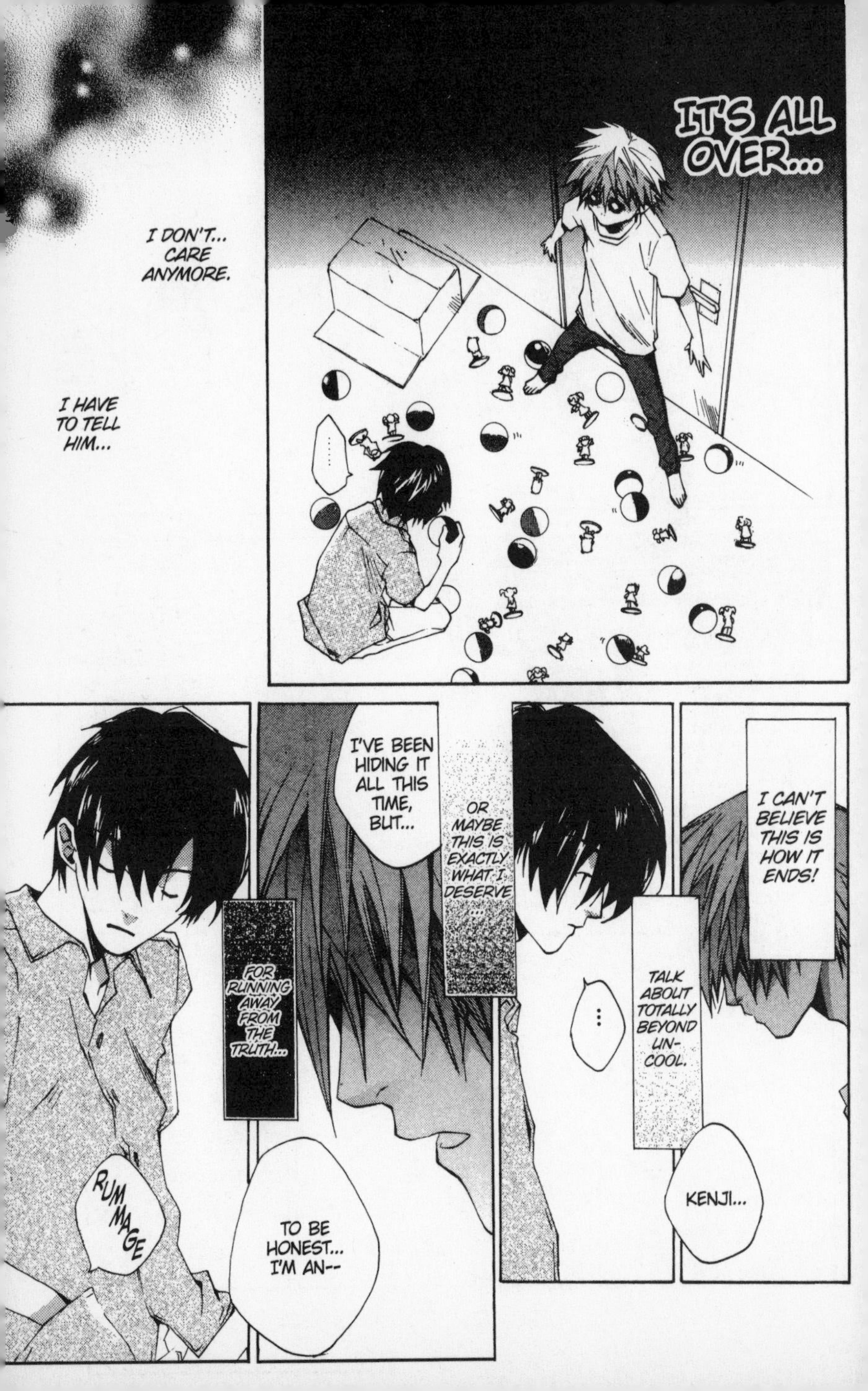
IT'S ALL OVER...
......
I DON'T... CARE ANYMORE.
I HAVE TO TELL HIM...
I CAN'T BELIEVE THIS IS HOW IT ENDS!
KENJI...
TALK ABOUT TOTALLY BEYOND UN-COOL.
...
OR MAYBE THIS IS EXACTLY WHAT I DESERVE...
I'VE BEEN HIDING IT ALL THIS TIME, BUT...
FOR RUNNING AWAY FROM THE TRUTH...
TO BE HONEST... I'M AN--
RUMMAGE

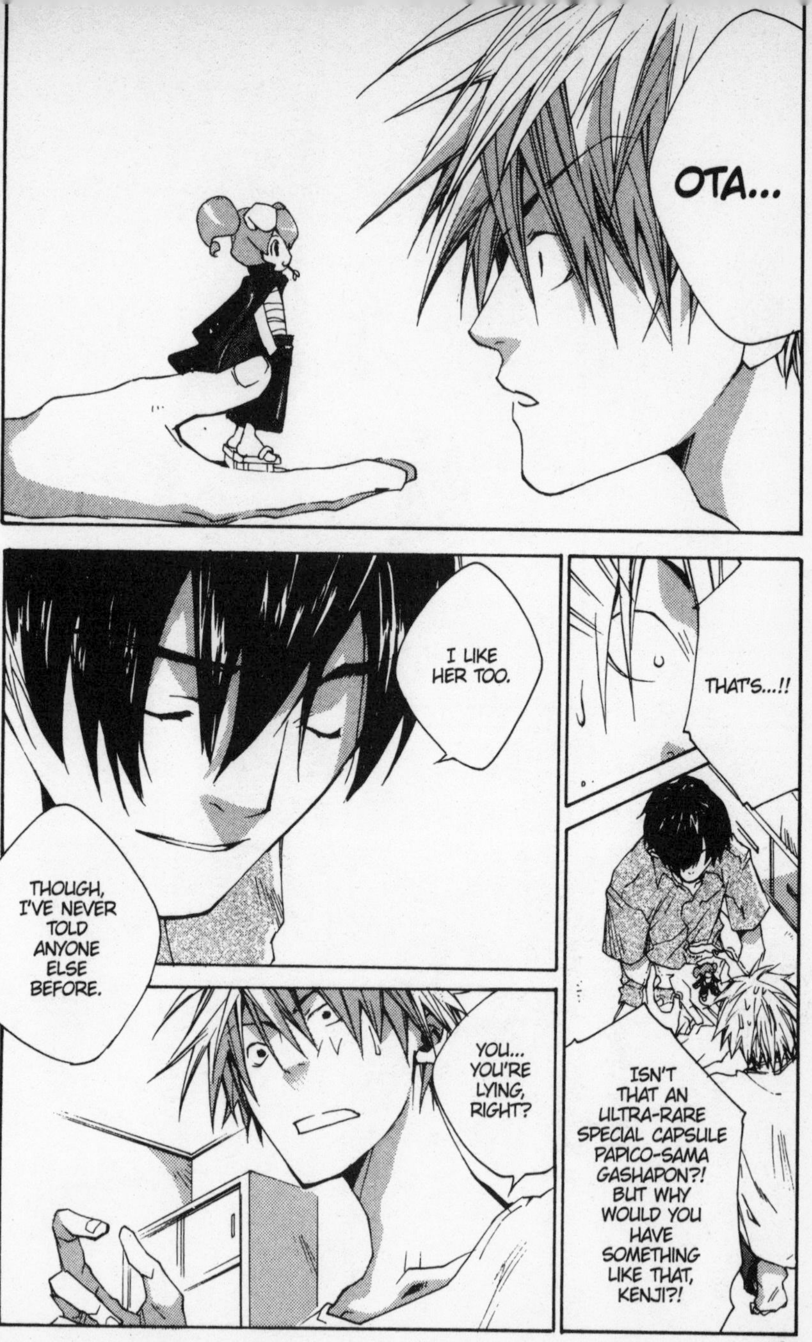
OTA...
THAT'S...!!
ISN'T THAT AN ULTRA-RARE SPECIAL CAPSULE PAPICO-SAMA GASHAPON?! BUT WHY WOULD YOU HAVE SOMETHING LIKE THAT, KENJI?!
I LIKE HER TOO.
THOUGH, I'VE NEVER TOLD ANYONE ELSE BEFORE.
YOU... YOU'RE LYING, RIGHT?

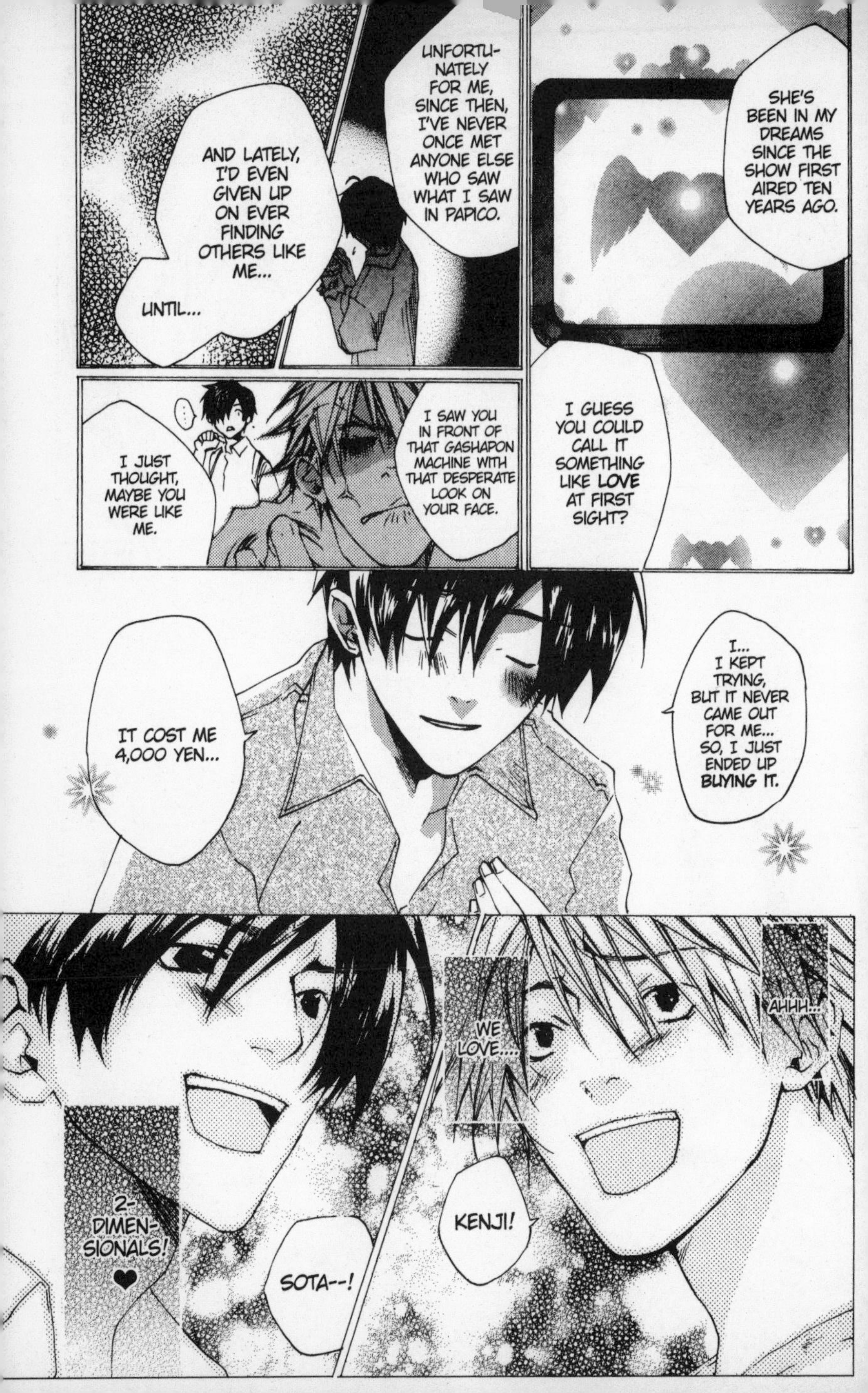
SHE'S BEEN IN MY DREAMS SINCE THE SHOW FIRST AIRED TEN YEARS AGO.
I GUESS YOU COULD CALL IT SOMETHING LIKE LOVE AT FIRST SIGHT?
UNFORTUNATELY FOR ME, SINCE THEN, I'VE NEVER ONCE MET ANYONE ELSE WHO SAW WHAT I SAW IN PAPICO.
AND LATELY, I'D EVEN GIVEN UP ON EVER FINDING OTHERS LIKE ME...
UNTIL...
I SAW YOU IN FRONT OF THAT GASHAPON MACHINE WITH THAT DESPERATE LOOK ON YOUR FACE.
...
I JUST THOUGHT, MAYBE YOU WERE LIKE ME.
I... I KEPT TRYING, BUT IT NEVER CAME OUT FOR ME... SO, I JUST ENDED UP BUYING IT.
IT COST ME 4,000 YEN...
AHHH...
WE LOVE....
KENJI!
2-DIMENSIONALS! ❤
SOTA--!

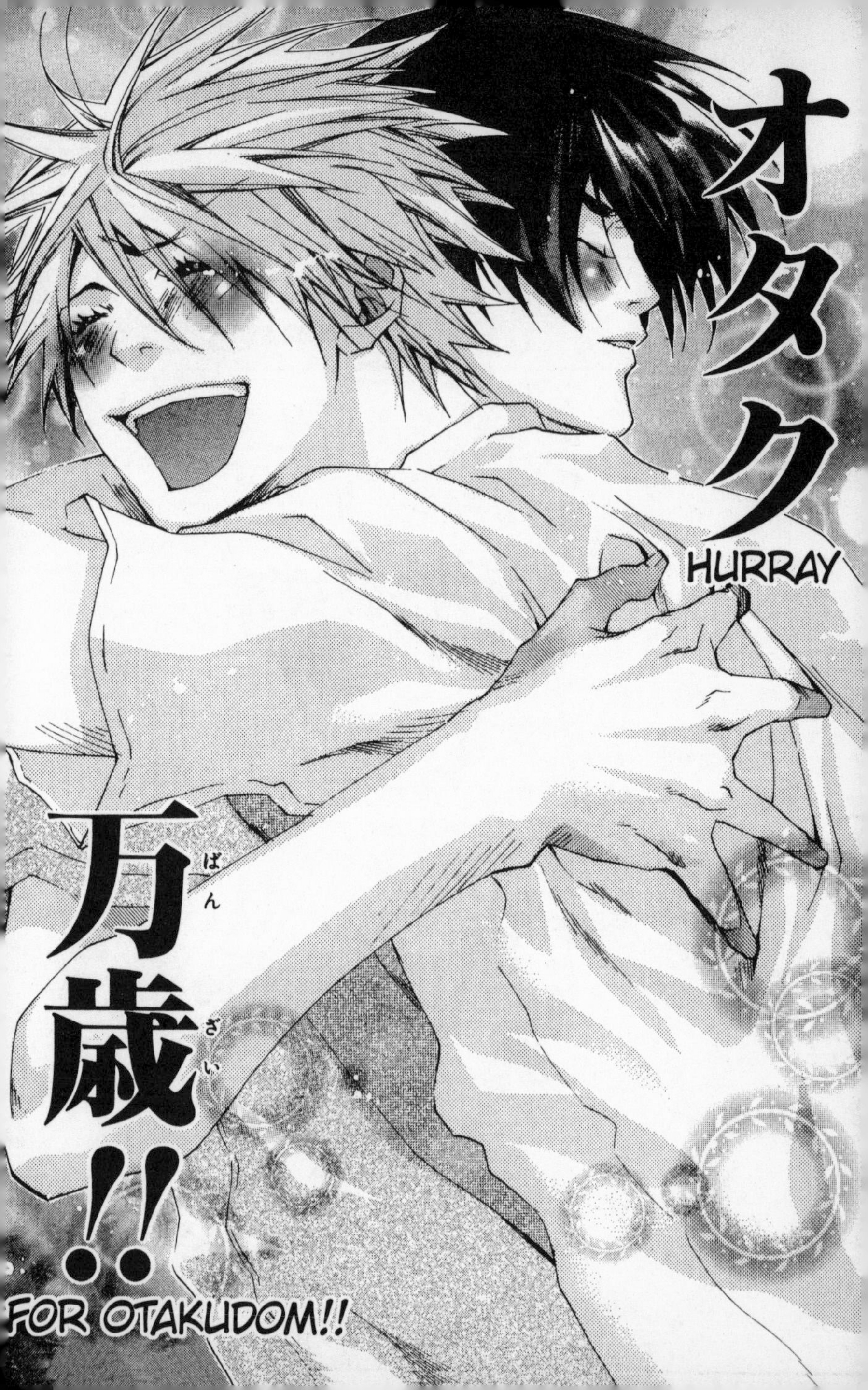
オタク
HURRAY
万歳!!
FOR OTAKUDOM!!

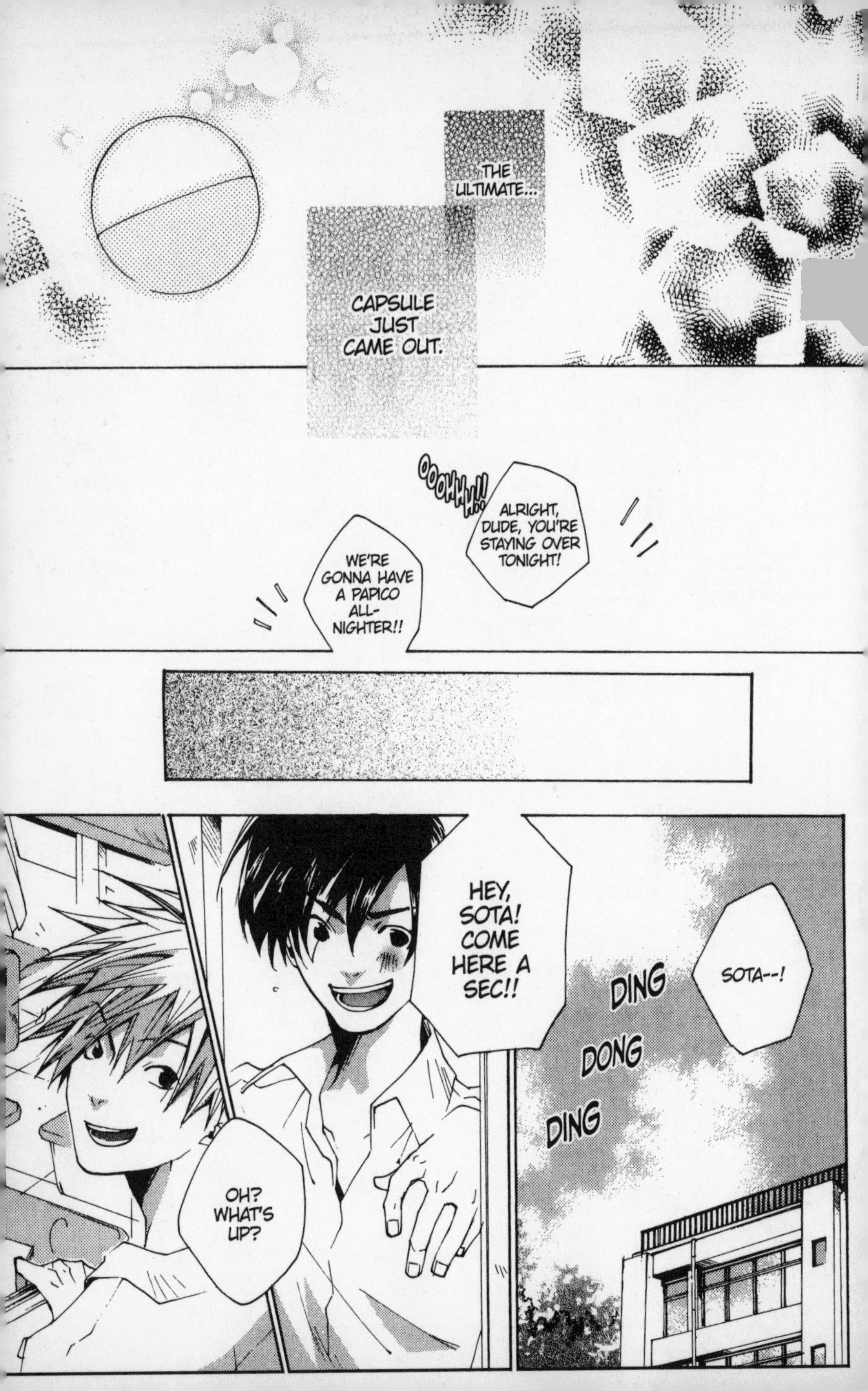
THE ULTIMATE...
CAPSULE JUST CAME OUT.
OOOHHH!!
ALRIGHT, DUDE, YOU'RE STAYING OVER TONIGHT!
WE'RE GONNA HAVE A PAPICO ALL-NIGHTER!!
SOTA--!
DING
DONG
DING
HEY, SOTA! COME HERE A SEC!!
OH? WHAT'S UP?

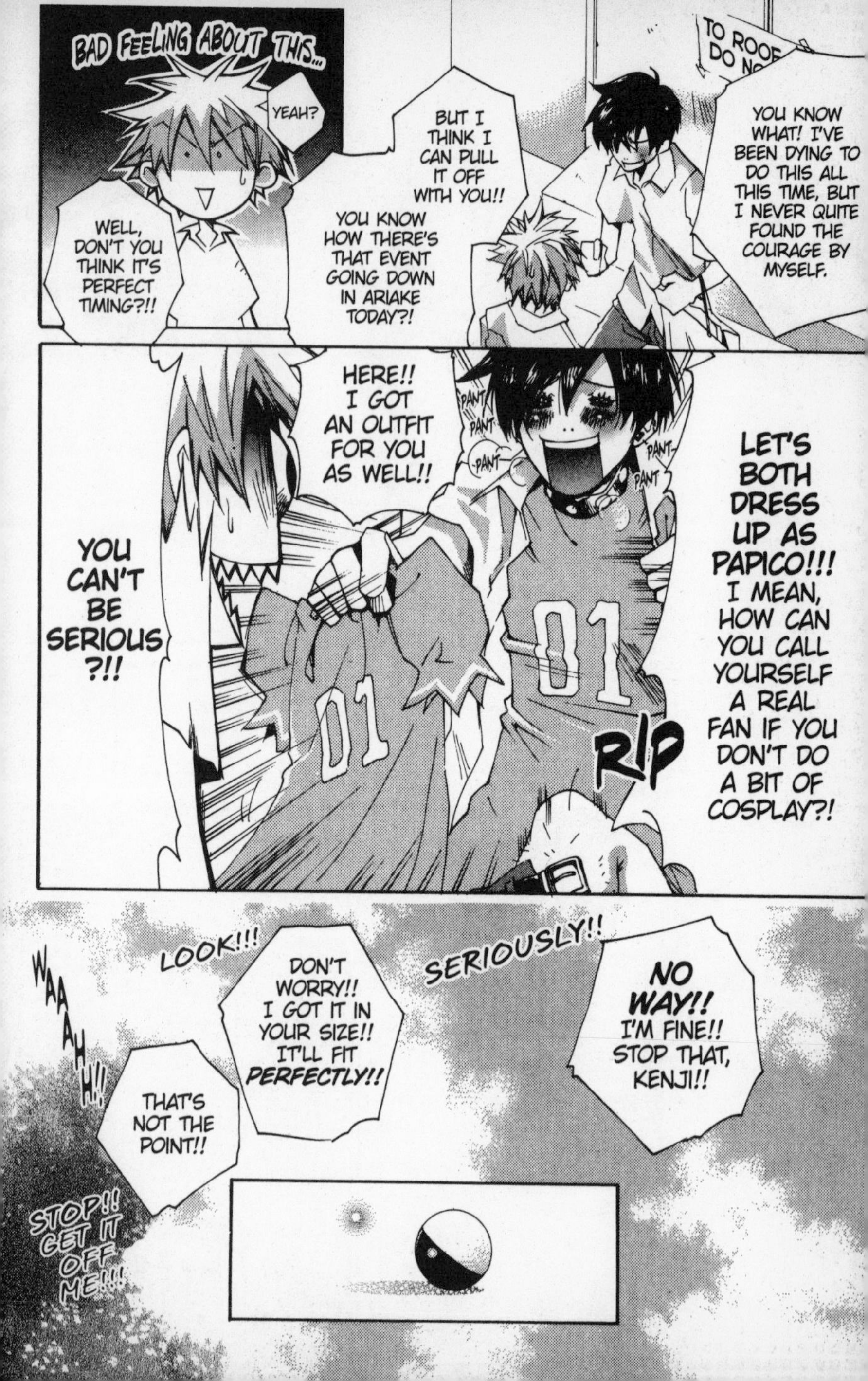

TO ROOF
DO NO
YOU KNOW WHAT! I'VE BEEN DYING TO DO THIS ALL THIS TIME, BUT I NEVER QUITE FOUND THE COURAGE BY MYSELF.
BUT I THINK I CAN PULL IT OFF WITH YOU!!
YOU KNOW HOW THERE'S THAT EVENT GOING DOWN IN ARIAKE TODAY?!
YEAH?
WELL, DON'T YOU THINK IT'S PERFECT TIMING?!!
BAD FEELING ABOUT THIS...
LET'S BOTH DRESS UP AS PAPICO!!! I MEAN, HOW CAN YOU CALL YOURSELF A REAL FAN IF YOU DON'T DO A BIT OF COSPLAY?!
PANT PANT
PANT PANT
PANT PANT
HERE!! I GOT AN OUTFIT FOR YOU AS WELL!!
RIP
YOU CAN'T BE SERIOUS?!!
NO WAY!! I'M FINE!! STOP THAT, KENJI!!
SERIOUSLY!!
DON'T WORRY!! I GOT IT IN YOUR SIZE!! IT'LL FIT PERFECTLY!!
LOOK!!!
THAT'S NOT THE POINT!!
WAAAAHH!!
STOP!! GET IT OFF ME!!!

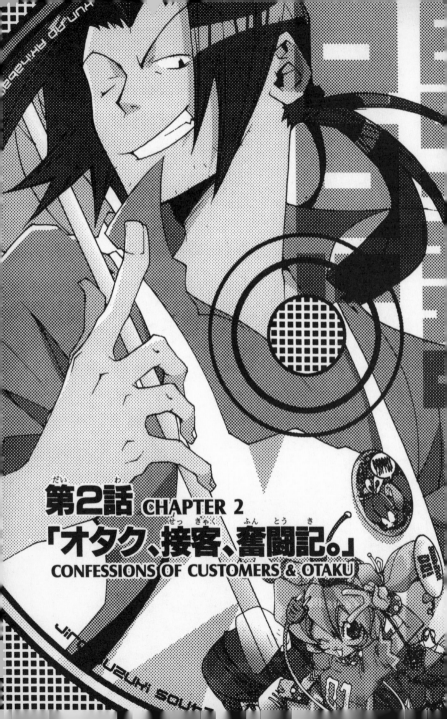

第2話 CHAPTER 2
「オタク、接客、奮闘記。」
CONFESSIONS OF CUSTOMERS & OTAKU

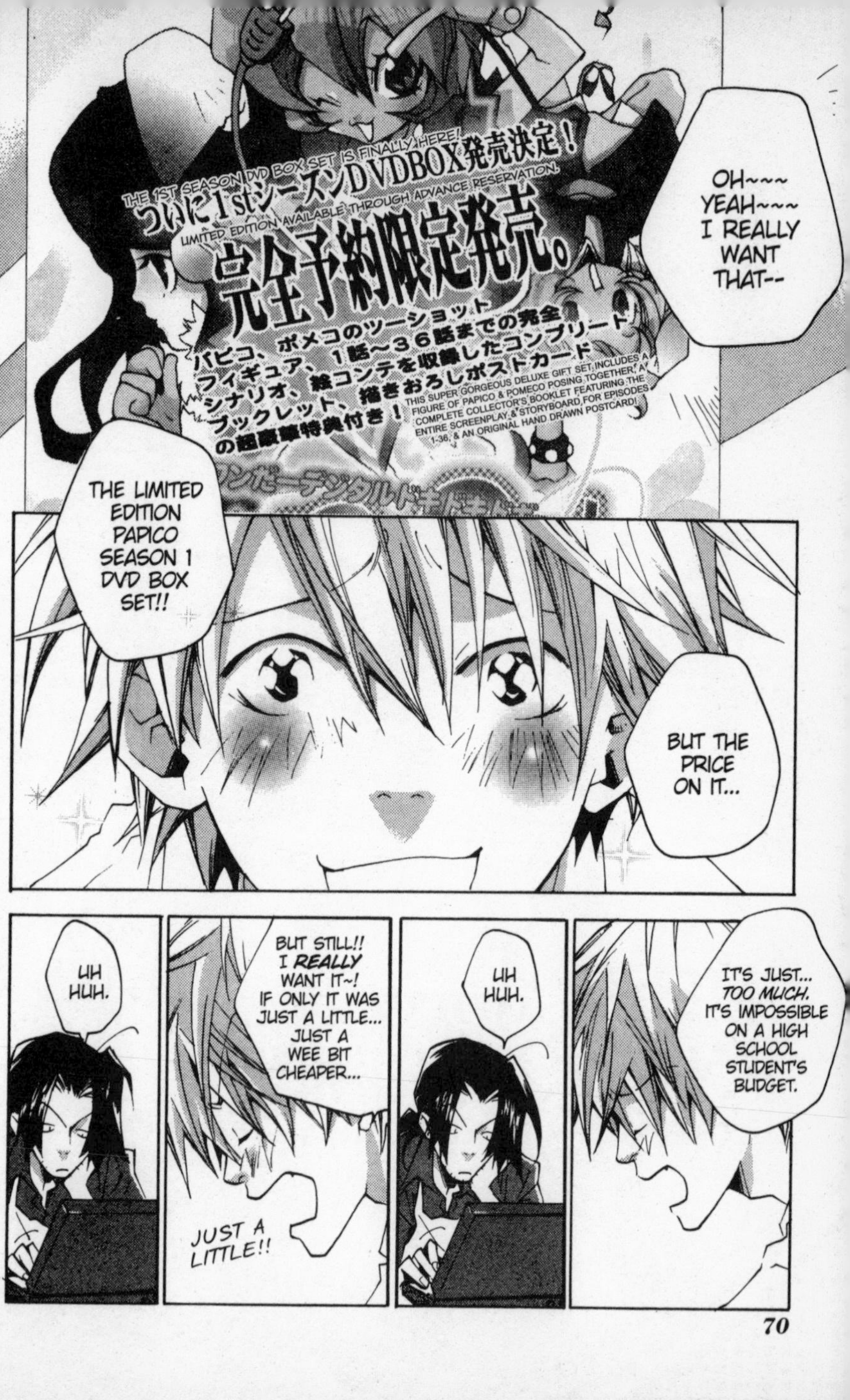
OH~~~ YEAH~~~ I REALLY WANT THAT--
THE 1ST SEASON DVD BOX SET IS FINALLY HERE!
ついに1stシーズンDVDBOX発売決定！
LIMITED EDITION AVAILABLE THROUGH ADVANCE RESERVATION.
完全予約限定発売。
パピコ、ポメコのツーショットフィギュア、1話～36話までの完全シナリオ、絵コンテを収録したコンプリートブックレット、描きおろしポストカードの超豪華特典付き！
THIS SUPER GORGEOUS DELUXE GIFT SET INCLUDES A FIGURE OF PAPICO & POMECO POSING TOGETHER, A COMPLETE COLLECTOR'S BOOKLET FEATURING THE ENTIRE SCREENPLAY & STORYBOARD FOR EPISODES 1-36, & AN ORIGINAL HAND DRAWN POSTCARD!
THE LIMITED EDITION PAPICO SEASON 1 DVD BOX SET!!
BUT THE PRICE ON IT...
IT'S JUST... *TOO MUCH.* IT'S IMPOSSIBLE ON A HIGH SCHOOL STUDENT'S BUDGET.
UH HUH.
BUT STILL!! I *REALLY* WANT IT~! IF ONLY IT WAS JUST A LITTLE... JUST A WEE BIT CHEAPER...
JUST A LITTLE!!
UH HUH.

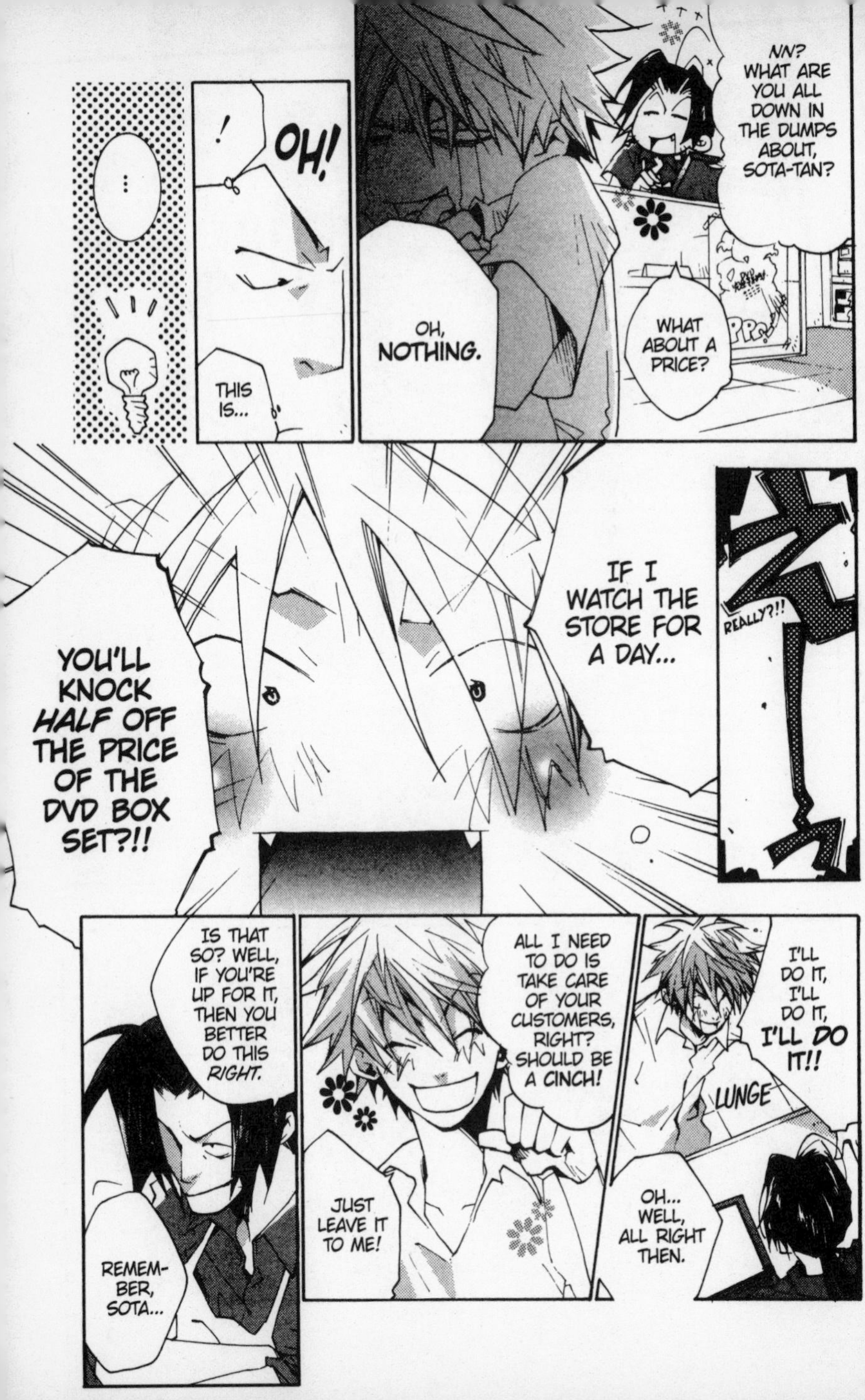
NN? WHAT ARE YOU ALL DOWN IN THE DUMPS ABOUT, SOTA-TAN?
WHAT ABOUT A PRICE?
OH, NOTHING.
!
OH!
THIS IS...
...
REALLY?!!
IF I WATCH THE STORE FOR A DAY...
YOU'LL KNOCK HALF OFF THE PRICE OF THE DVD BOX SET?!!
I'LL DO IT, I'LL DO IT, I'LL DO IT!!
LUNGE
OH... WELL, ALL RIGHT THEN.
ALL I NEED TO DO IS TAKE CARE OF YOUR CUSTOMERS, RIGHT? SHOULD BE A CINCH!
JUST LEAVE IT TO ME!
IS THAT SO? WELL, IF YOU'RE UP FOR IT, THEN YOU BETTER DO THIS RIGHT.
REMEMBER, SOTA...

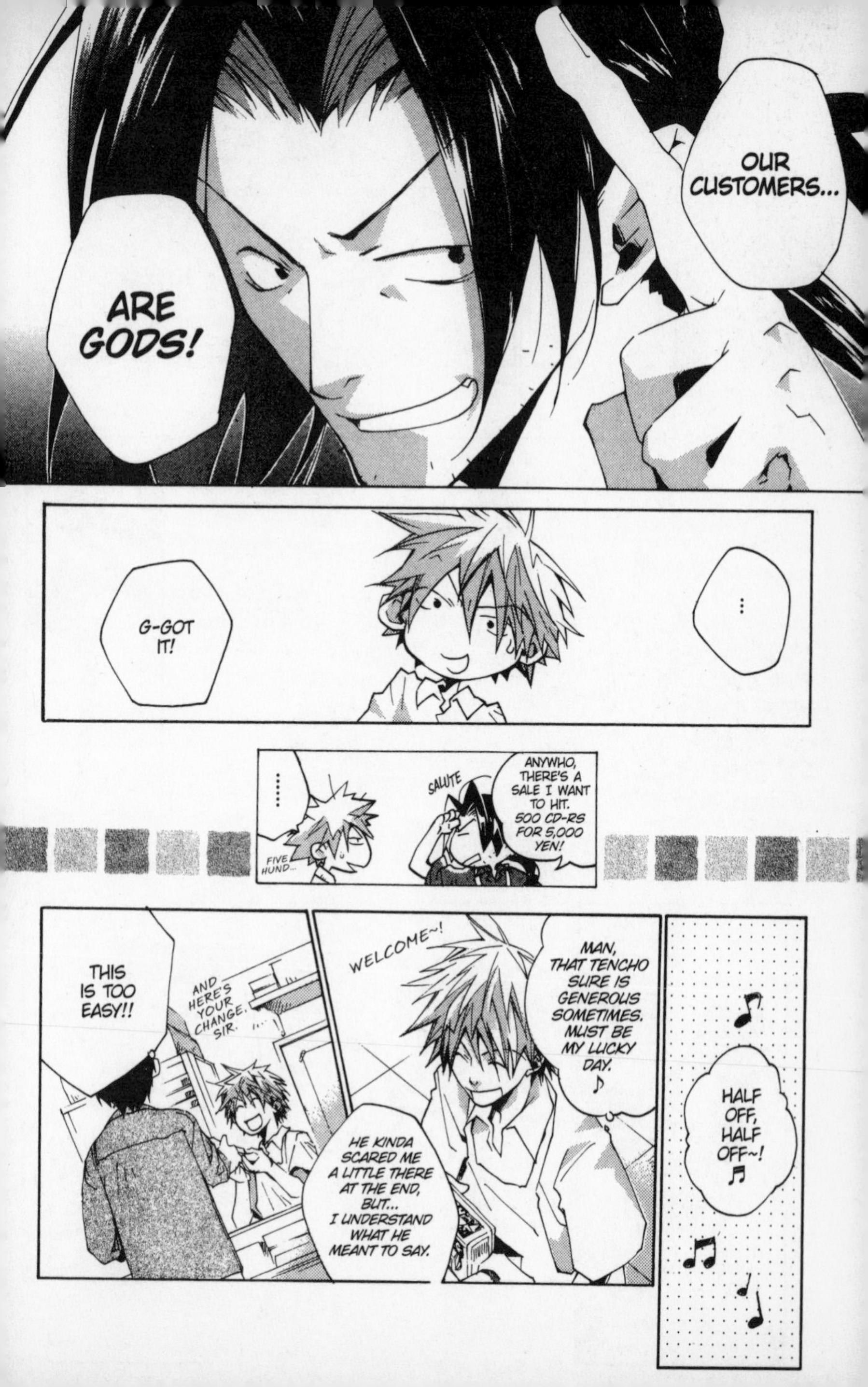
OUR CUSTOMERS...
ARE GODS!
...
G-GOT IT!
ANYWHO, THERE'S A SALE I WANT TO HIT. 500 CD-RS FOR 5,000 YEN!
SALUTE
......
FIVE HUND...
HALF OFF, HALF OFF~! ♬
MAN, THAT TENCHO SURE IS GENEROUS SOMETIMES. MUST BE MY LUCKY DAY. ♪
WELCOME~!
HE KINDA SCARED ME A LITTLE THERE AT THE END, BUT... I UNDERSTAND WHAT HE MEANT TO SAY.
AND HERE'S YOUR CHANGE, SIR.
THIS IS TOO EASY!!

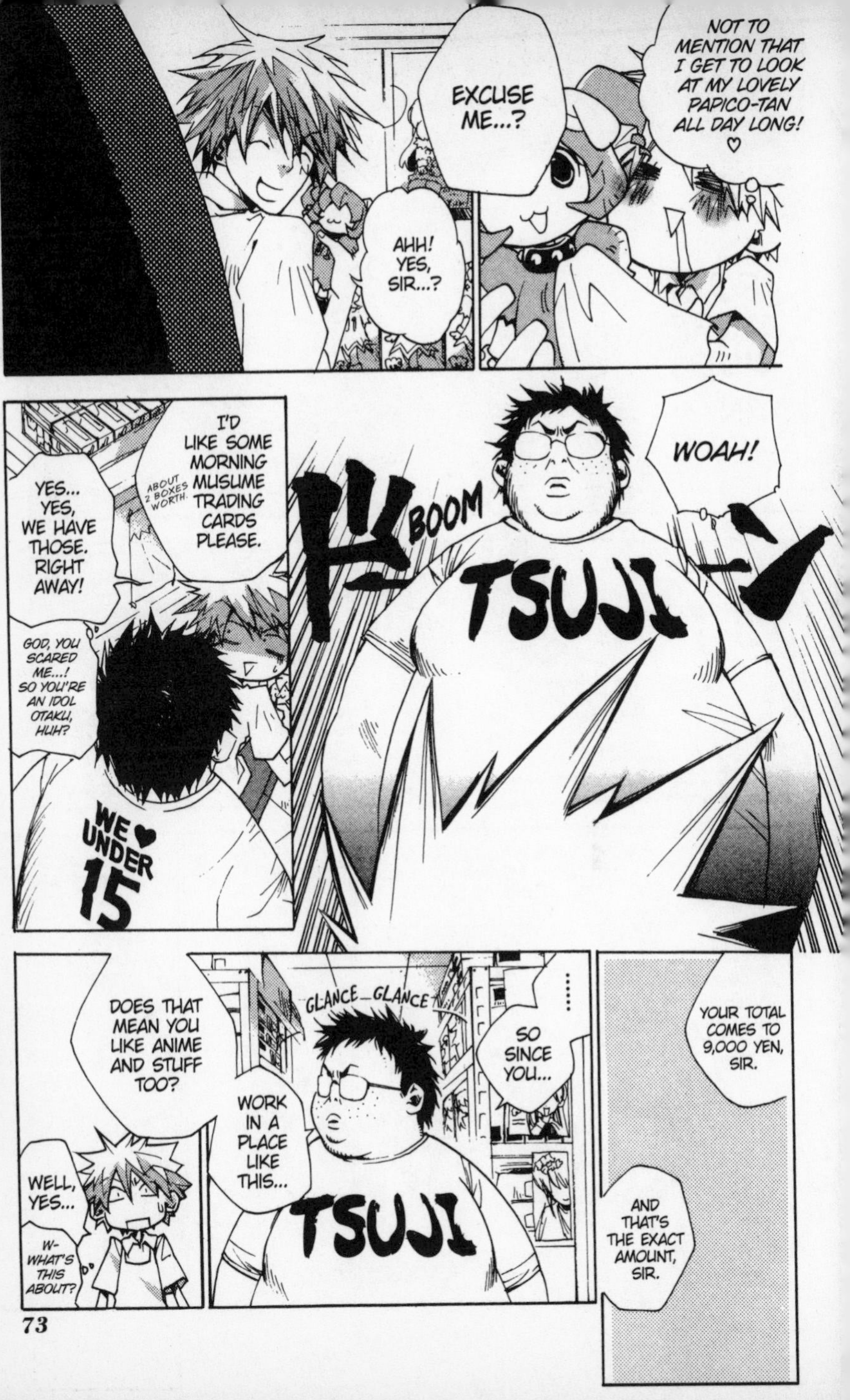
NOT TO MENTION THAT I GET TO LOOK AT MY LOVELY PAPICO-TAN ALL DAY LONG! ♡
EXCUSE ME...?
AHH! YES, SIR...?
WOAH!
BOOM
TSUJI
I'D LIKE SOME MORNING MUSUME TRADING CARDS PLEASE.
ABOUT 2 BOXES WORTH.
YES... YES, WE HAVE THOSE. RIGHT AWAY!
GOD, YOU SCARED ME...! SO YOU'RE AN IDOL OTAKU, HUH?
WE ♥ UNDER 15
YOUR TOTAL COMES TO 9,000 YEN, SIR.
AND THAT'S THE EXACT AMOUNT, SIR.
.....
SO SINCE YOU...
GLANCE GLANCE
WORK IN A PLACE LIKE THIS...
TSUJI
DOES THAT MEAN YOU LIKE ANIME AND STUFF TOO?
WELL, YES...
W-WHAT'S THIS ABOUT?

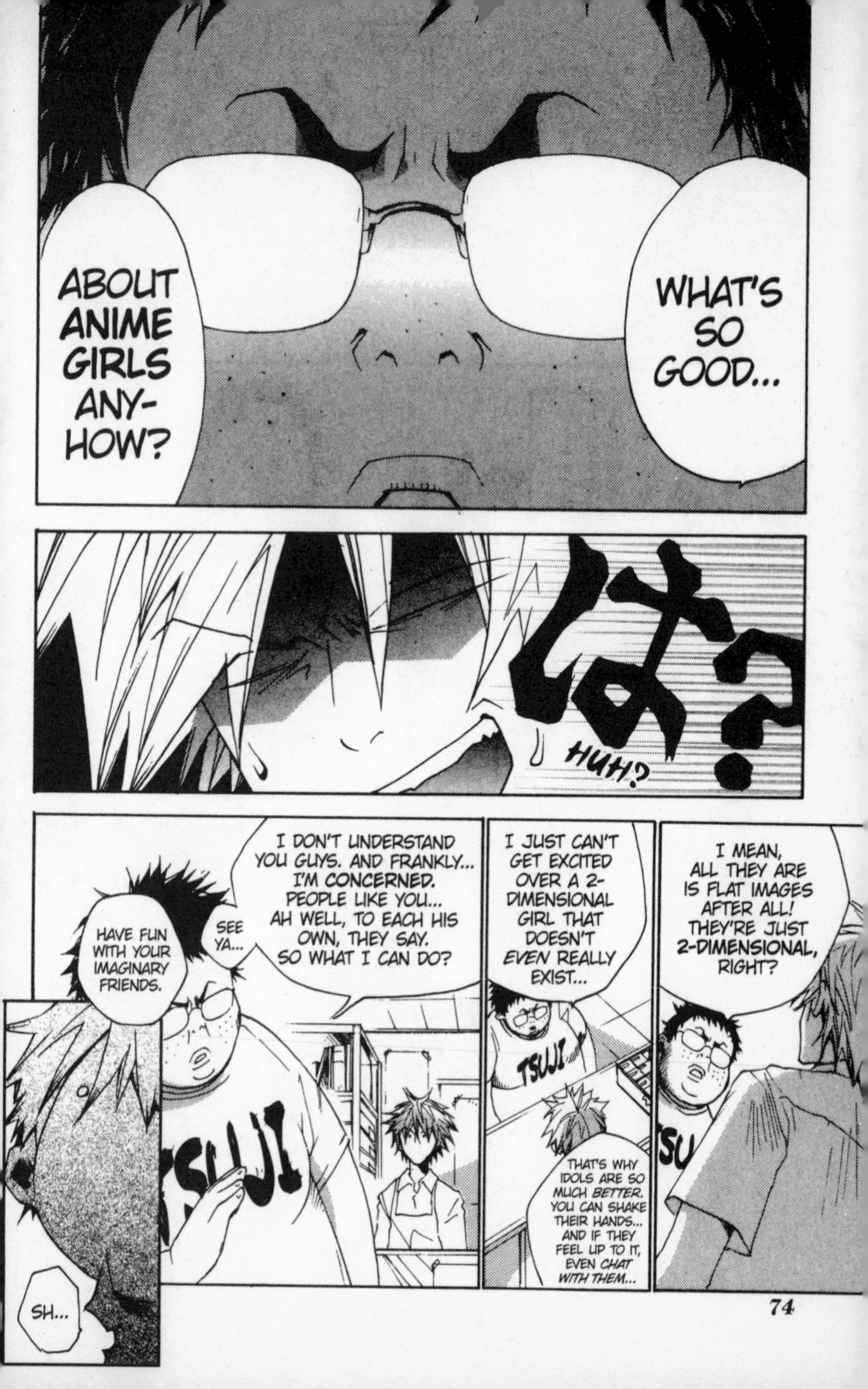
WHAT'S SO GOOD...
ABOUT ANIME GIRLS ANY-HOW?
は？
HUH?
I MEAN, ALL THEY ARE IS FLAT IMAGES AFTER ALL! THEY'RE JUST 2-DIMENSIONAL, RIGHT?
I JUST CAN'T GET EXCITED OVER A 2-DIMENSIONAL GIRL THAT DOESN'T *EVEN* REALLY EXIST...
THAT'S WHY IDOLS ARE SO MUCH *BETTER*. YOU CAN SHAKE THEIR HANDS... AND IF THEY FEEL UP TO IT, EVEN *CHAT WITH THEM*...
I DON'T UNDERSTAND YOU GUYS. AND FRANKLY... I'M CONCERNED. PEOPLE LIKE YOU... AH WELL, TO EACH HIS OWN, THEY SAY. SO WHAT I CAN DO?
SEE YA...
HAVE FUN WITH YOUR IMAGINARY FRIENDS.
TSUJI
SH...

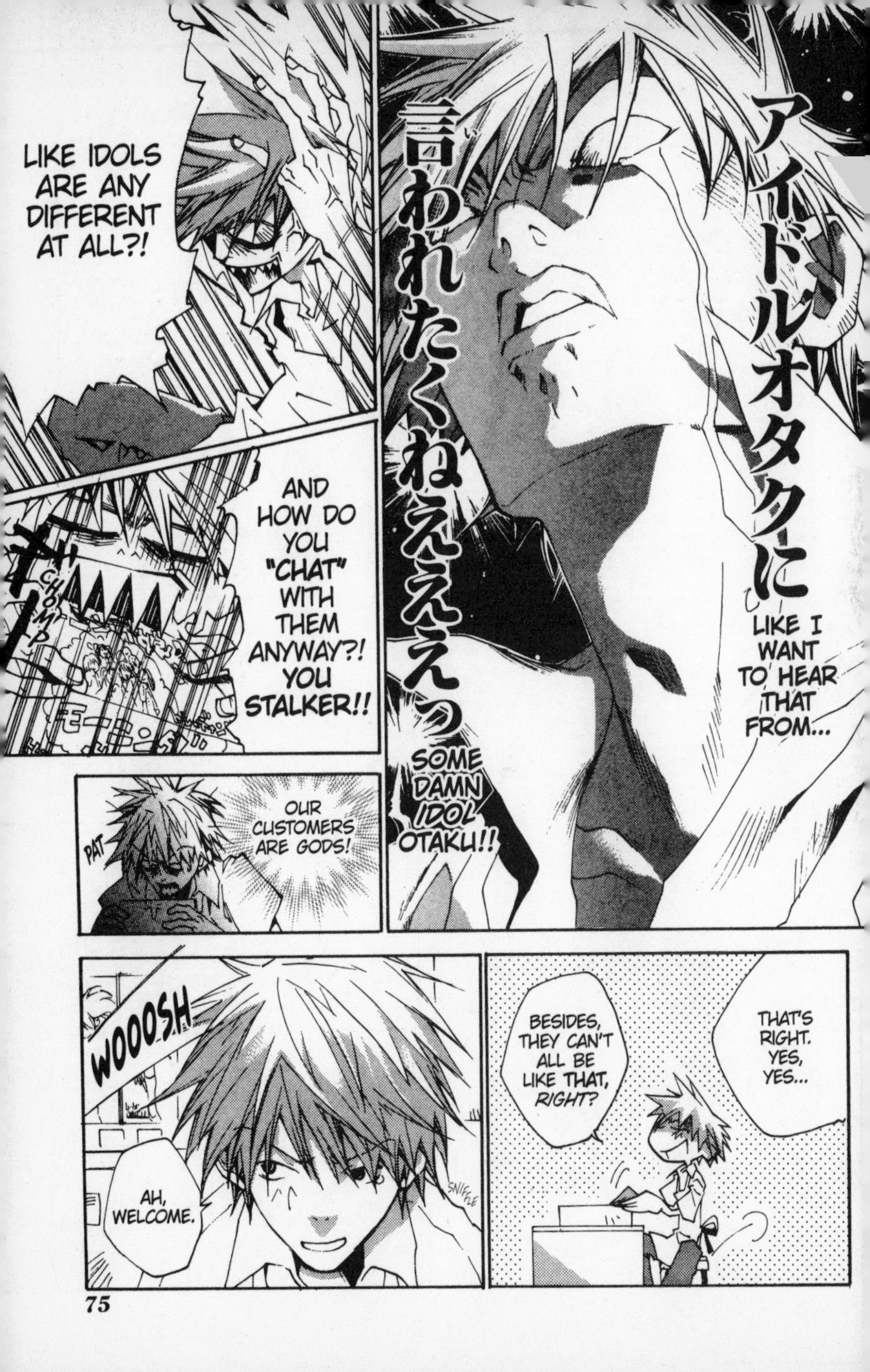
アイドルオタクに
言われたくねえええっ
LIKE I WANT TO HEAR THAT FROM...
SOME DAMN IDOL OTAKU!!
LIKE IDOLS ARE ANY DIFFERENT AT ALL?!
AND HOW DO YOU "CHAT" WITH THEM ANYWAY?! YOU STALKER!!
CHOMP
OUR CUSTOMERS ARE GODS!
PAT
THAT'S RIGHT. YES, YES...
BESIDES, THEY CAN'T ALL BE LIKE THAT, *RIGHT?*
WOOOSH
SNIFFLE
AH, WELCOME.

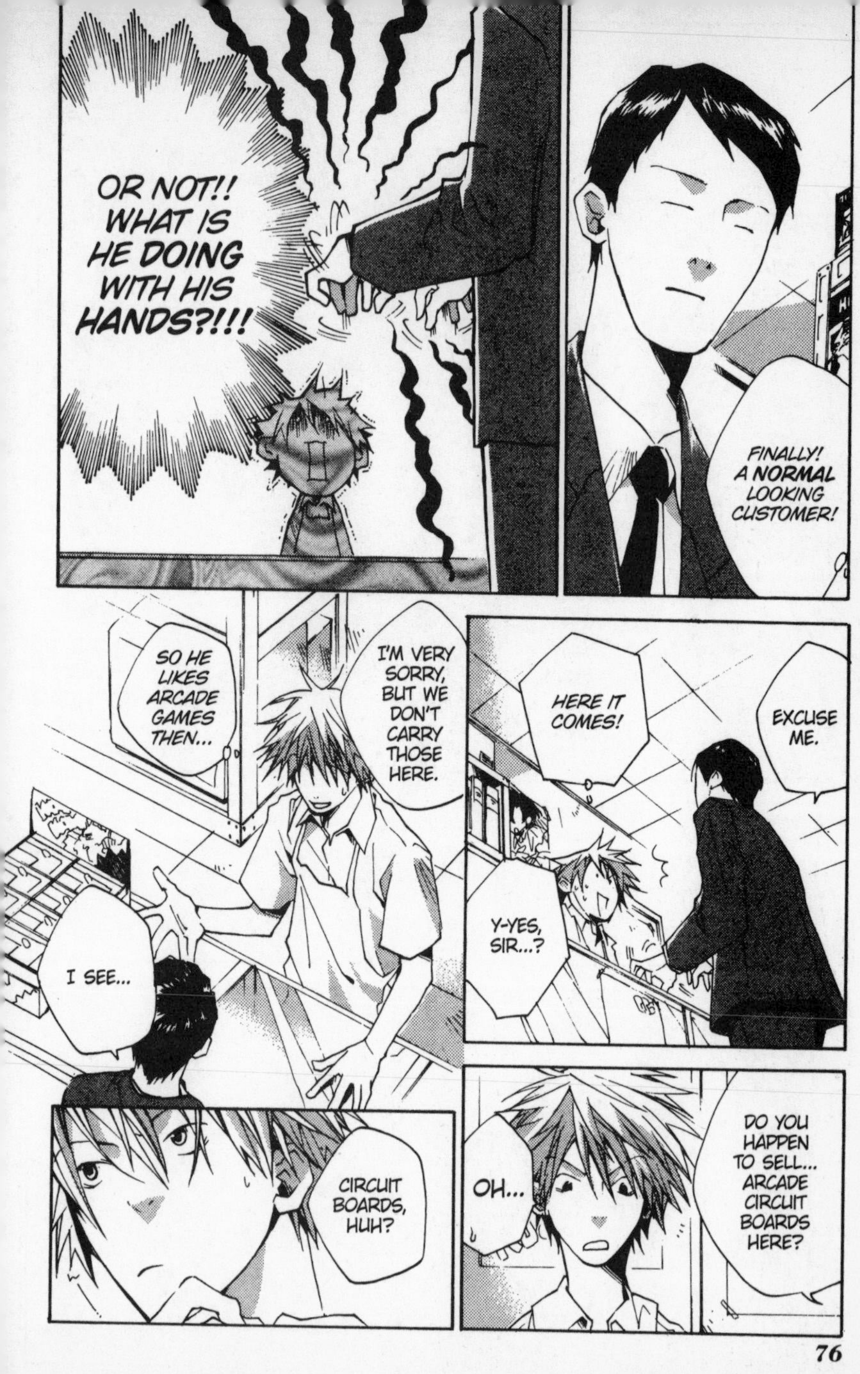
FINALLY! A NORMAL LOOKING CUSTOMER!
OR NOT!! WHAT IS HE DOING WITH HIS HANDS?!!!
EXCUSE ME.
HERE IT COMES!
Y-YES, SIR...?
DO YOU HAPPEN TO SELL... ARCADE CIRCUIT BOARDS HERE?
OH...
CIRCUIT BOARDS, HUH?
I'M VERY SORRY, BUT WE DON'T CARRY THOSE HERE.
SO HE LIKES ARCADE GAMES THEN...
I SEE...

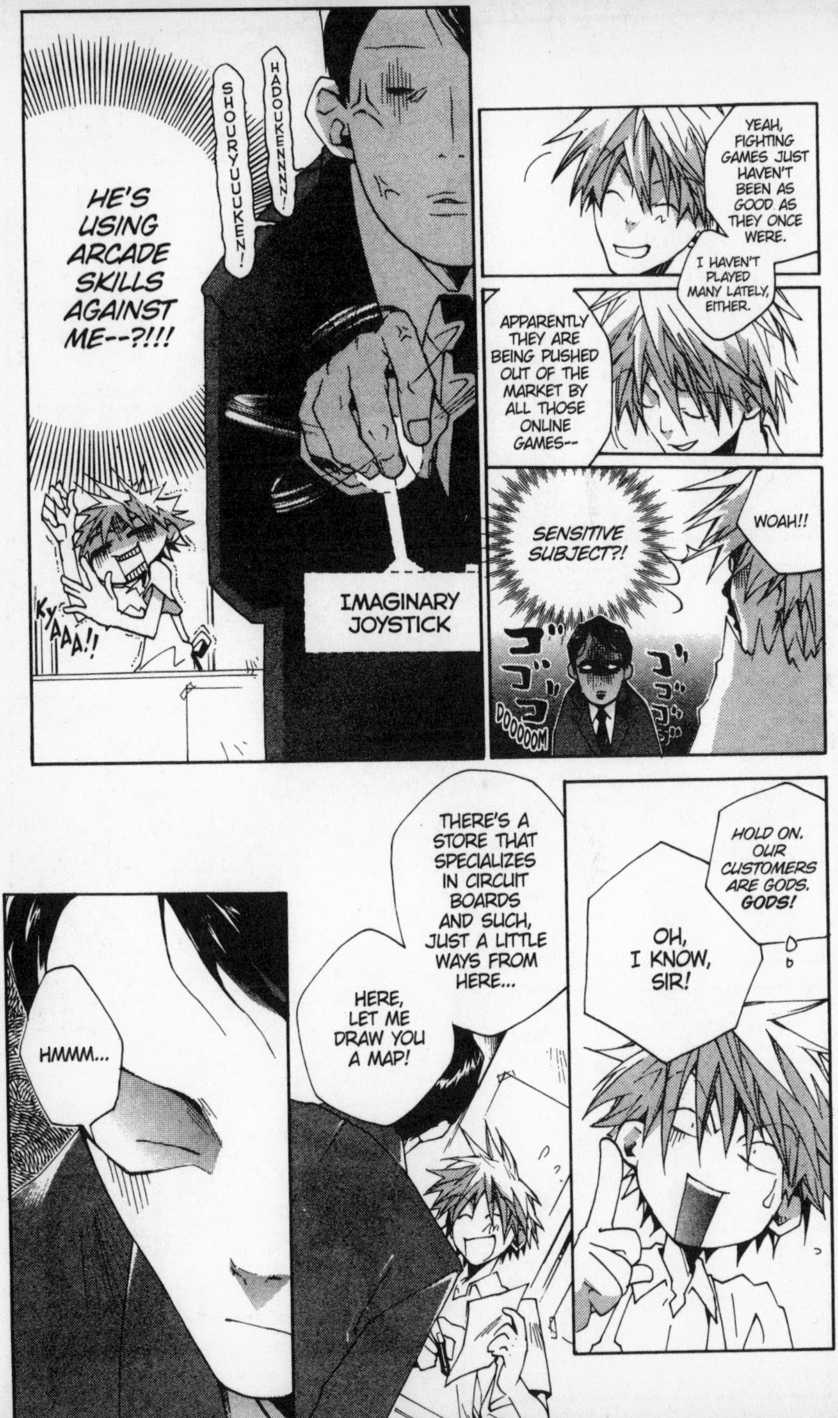
YEAH, FIGHTING GAMES JUST HAVEN'T BEEN AS GOOD AS THEY ONCE WERE.
I HAVEN'T PLAYED MANY LATELY, EITHER.
APPARENTLY THEY ARE BEING PUSHED OUT OF THE MARKET BY ALL THOSE ONLINE GAMES--
WOAH!!
SENSITIVE SUBJECT?!
DOOOOOM
HADOUKENNNN!
SHOURYUUUKEN!
HE'S USING ARCADE SKILLS AGAINST ME--?!!!
IMAGINARY JOYSTICK
KYAAA!!
HOLD ON. OUR CUSTOMERS ARE GODS. GODS!
OH, I KNOW, SIR!
THERE'S A STORE THAT SPECIALIZES IN CIRCUIT BOARDS AND SUCH, JUST A LITTLE WAYS FROM HERE...
HERE, LET ME DRAW YOU A MAP!
HMMM...

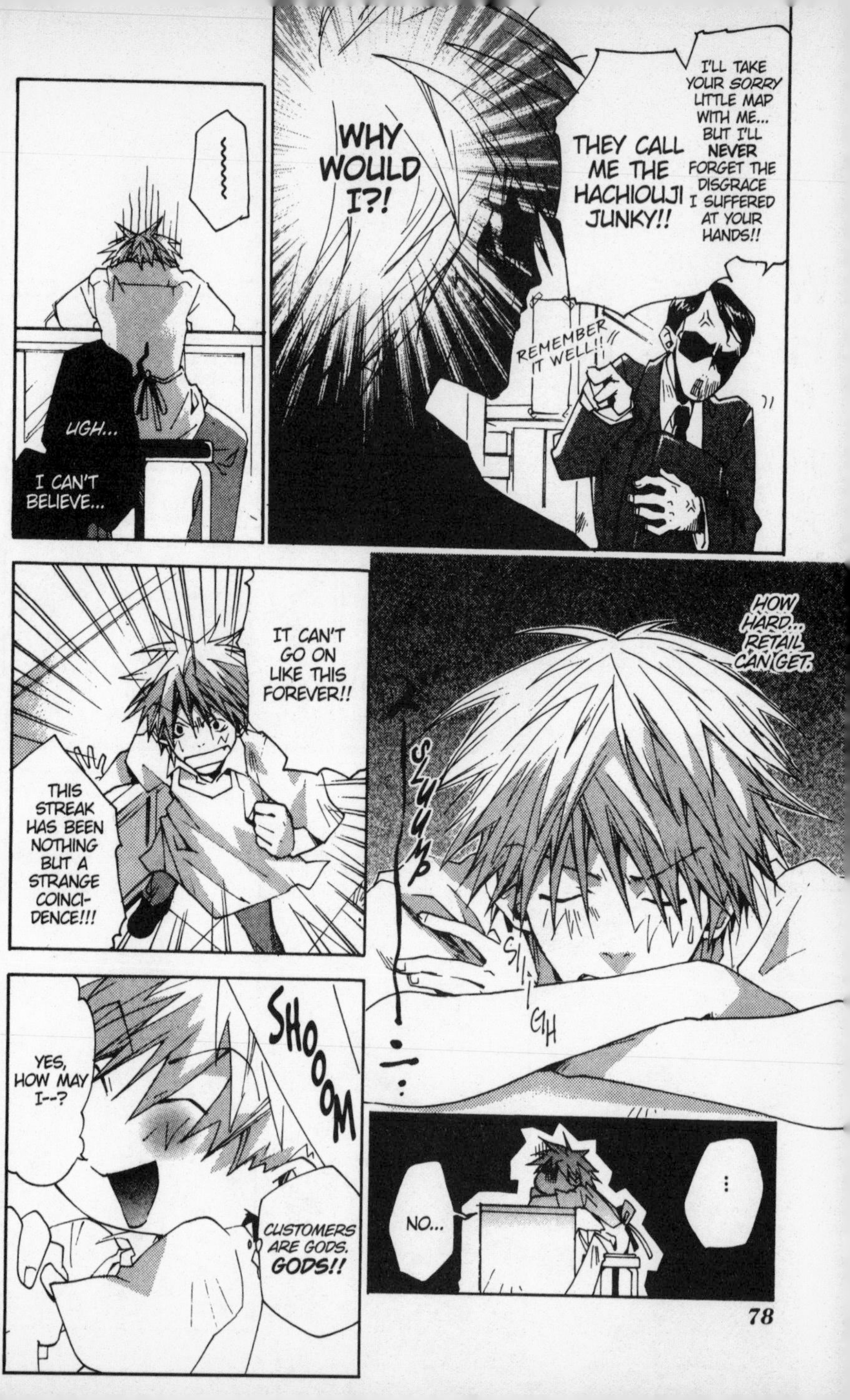

I'LL TAKE YOUR SORRY LITTLE MAP WITH ME... BUT I'LL NEVER FORGET THE DISGRACE I SUFFERED AT YOUR HANDS!!
THEY CALL ME THE HACHIOUJI JUNKY!!
REMEMBER IT WELL!!
WHY WOULD I?!
......
UGH...
I CAN'T BELIEVE...
HOW HARD... RETAIL CAN GET.
SLUUMP
SLIIIGH
...
...
NO...
IT CAN'T GO ON LIKE THIS FOREVER!!
THIS STREAK HAS BEEN NOTHING BUT A STRANGE COINCIDENCE!!!
SHOOOOM
YES, HOW MAY I--?
CUSTOMERS ARE GODS. GODS!!

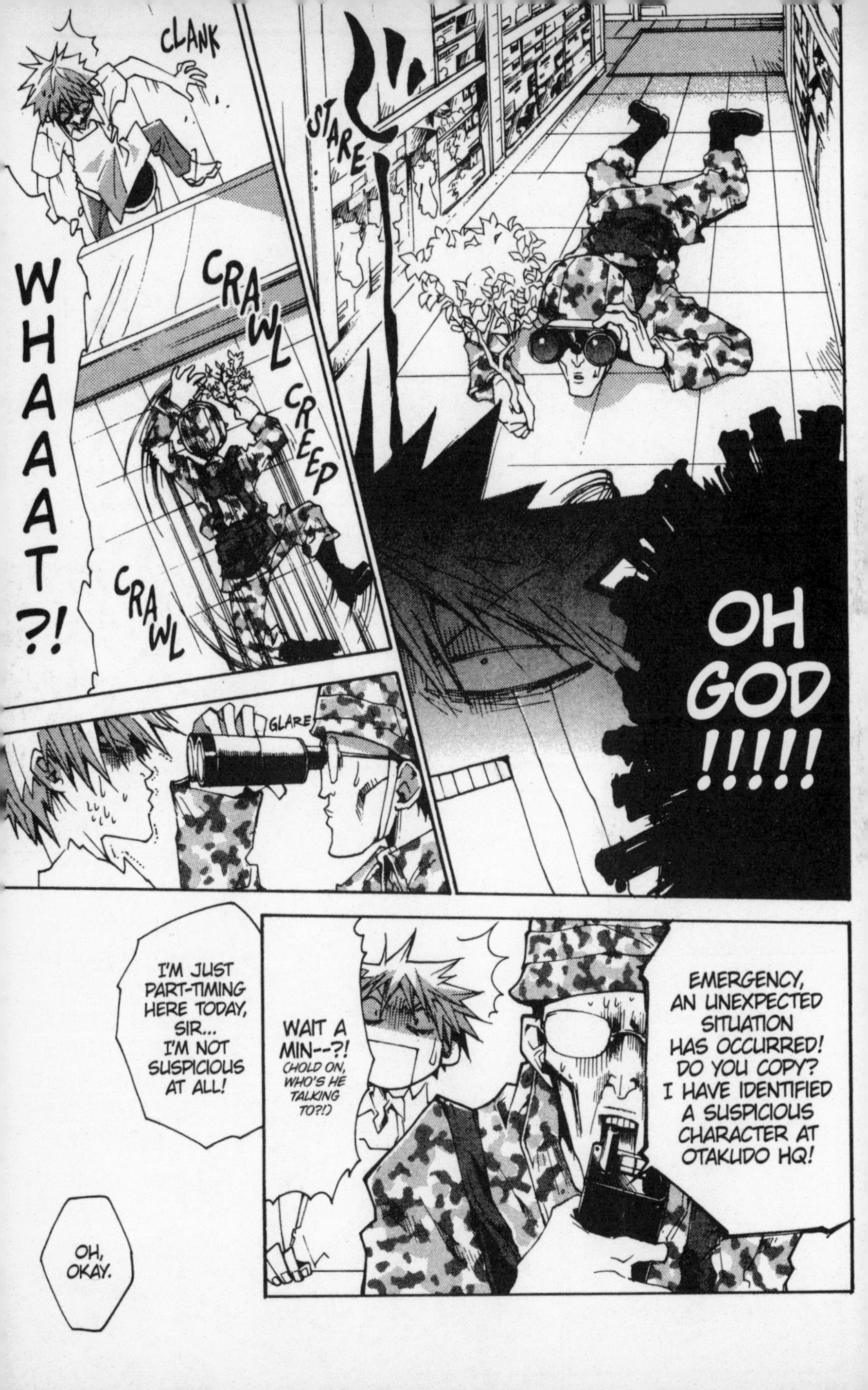
STARE
OH GOD!!!!!
CLANK
WHAAAT?!
CRAWL
CREEP
CRAWL
GLARE
EMERGENCY, AN UNEXPECTED SITUATION HAS OCCURRED! DO YOU COPY? I HAVE IDENTIFIED A SUSPICIOUS CHARACTER AT OTAKUDO HQ!
WAIT A MIN--?!
(HOLD ON, WHO'S HE TALKING TO?!)
I'M JUST PART-TIMING HERE TODAY, SIR... I'M NOT SUSPICIOUS AT ALL!
OH, OKAY.

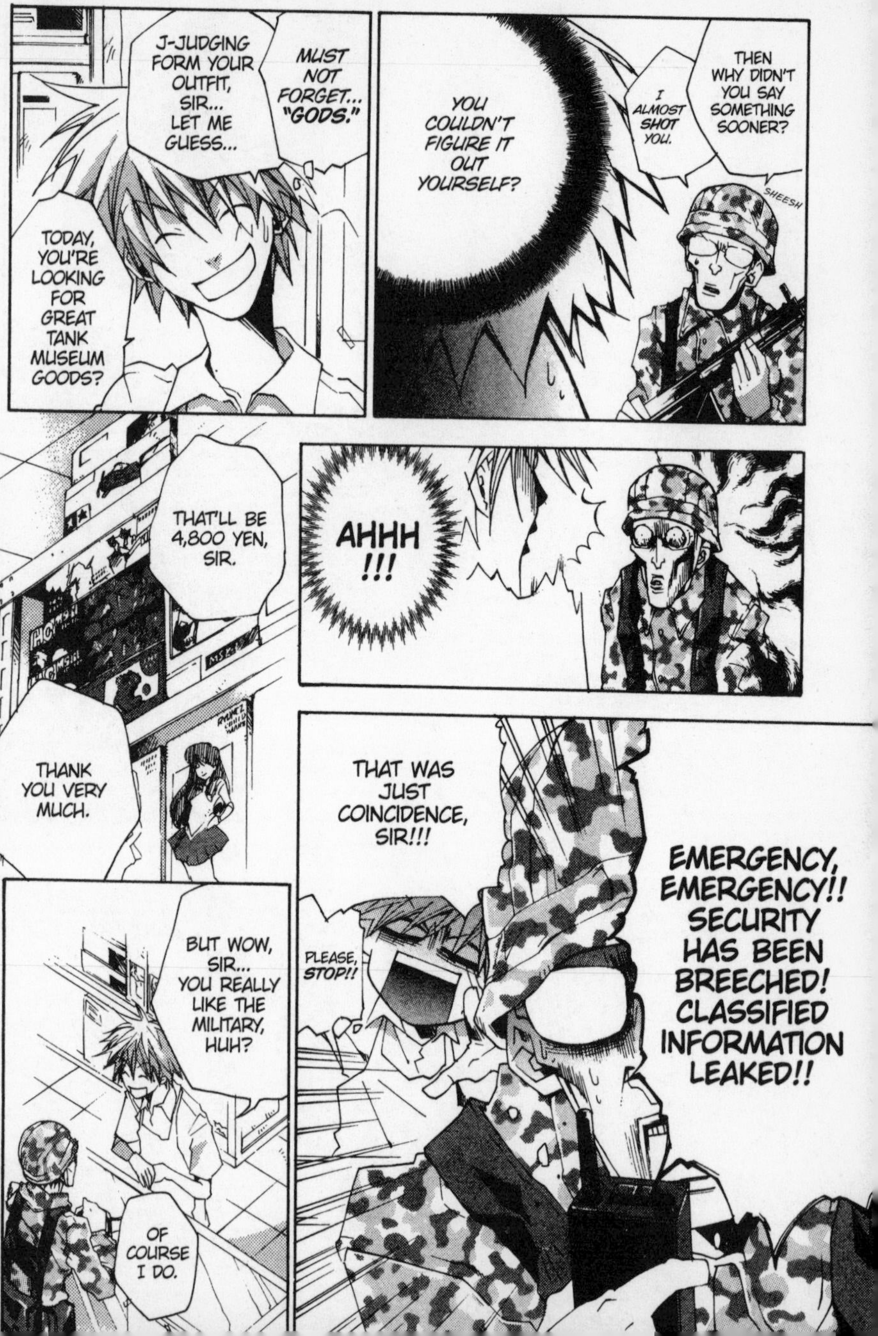
THEN WHY DIDN'T YOU SAY SOMETHING SOONER?
I ALMOST SHOT YOU.
SHEESH
YOU COULDN'T FIGURE IT OUT YOURSELF?
MUST NOT FORGET... "GODS."
J-JUDGING FORM YOUR OUTFIT, SIR... LET ME GUESS...
TODAY, YOU'RE LOOKING FOR GREAT TANK MUSEUM GOODS?
AHHH !!!
THAT WAS JUST COINCIDENCE, SIR!!!
EMERGENCY, EMERGENCY!! SECURITY HAS BEEN BREECHED! CLASSIFIED INFORMATION LEAKED!!
PLEASE, STOP!!
THAT'LL BE 4,800 YEN, SIR.
THANK YOU VERY MUCH.
BUT WOW, SIR... YOU REALLY LIKE THE MILITARY, HUH?
OF COURSE I DO.

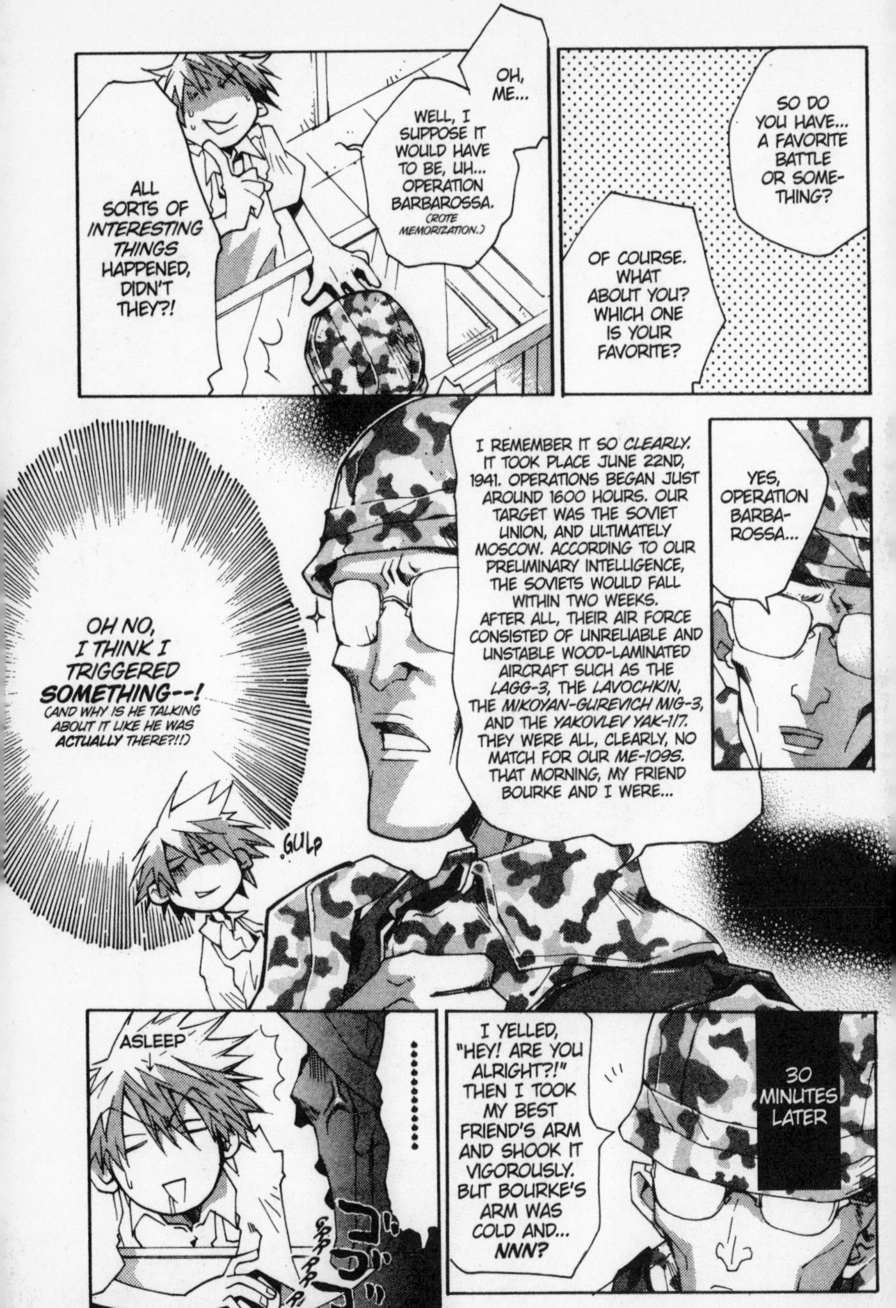
SO DO YOU HAVE... A FAVORITE BATTLE OR SOME-THING?
OF COURSE. WHAT ABOUT YOU? WHICH ONE IS YOUR FAVORITE?
OH, ME...
WELL, I SUPPOSE IT WOULD HAVE TO BE, UH... OPERATION BARBAROSSA.
(ROTE MEMORIZATION.)
ALL SORTS OF *INTERESTING* THINGS HAPPENED, DIDN'T THEY?!
YES, OPERATION BARBA-ROSSA...
I REMEMBER IT SO *CLEARLY.* IT TOOK PLACE JUNE 22ND, 1941. OPERATIONS BEGAN JUST AROUND 1600 HOURS. OUR TARGET WAS THE SOVIET UNION, AND ULTIMATELY MOSCOW. ACCORDING TO OUR PRELIMINARY INTELLIGENCE, THE SOVIETS WOULD FALL WITHIN TWO WEEKS. AFTER ALL, THEIR AIR FORCE CONSISTED OF UNRELIABLE AND UNSTABLE WOOD-LAMINATED AIRCRAFT SUCH AS THE *LAGG-3*, THE *LAVOCHKIN*, THE *MIKOYAN-GUREVICH MIG-3*, AND THE *YAKOVLEV YAK-1/7*. THEY WERE ALL, CLEARLY, NO MATCH FOR OUR *ME-109S*. THAT MORNING, MY FRIEND BOURKE AND I WERE...
OH NO, I THINK I TRIGGERED **SOMETHING--!**
(AND WHY IS HE TALKING ABOUT IT LIKE HE WAS ACTUALLY THERE?!!)
GULP
30 MINUTES LATER
I YELLED, "HEY! ARE YOU ALRIGHT?!" THEN I TOOK MY BEST FRIEND'S ARM AND SHOOK IT VIGOROUSLY. BUT BOURKE'S ARM WAS COLD AND... ***NNN?***
ASLEEP
....

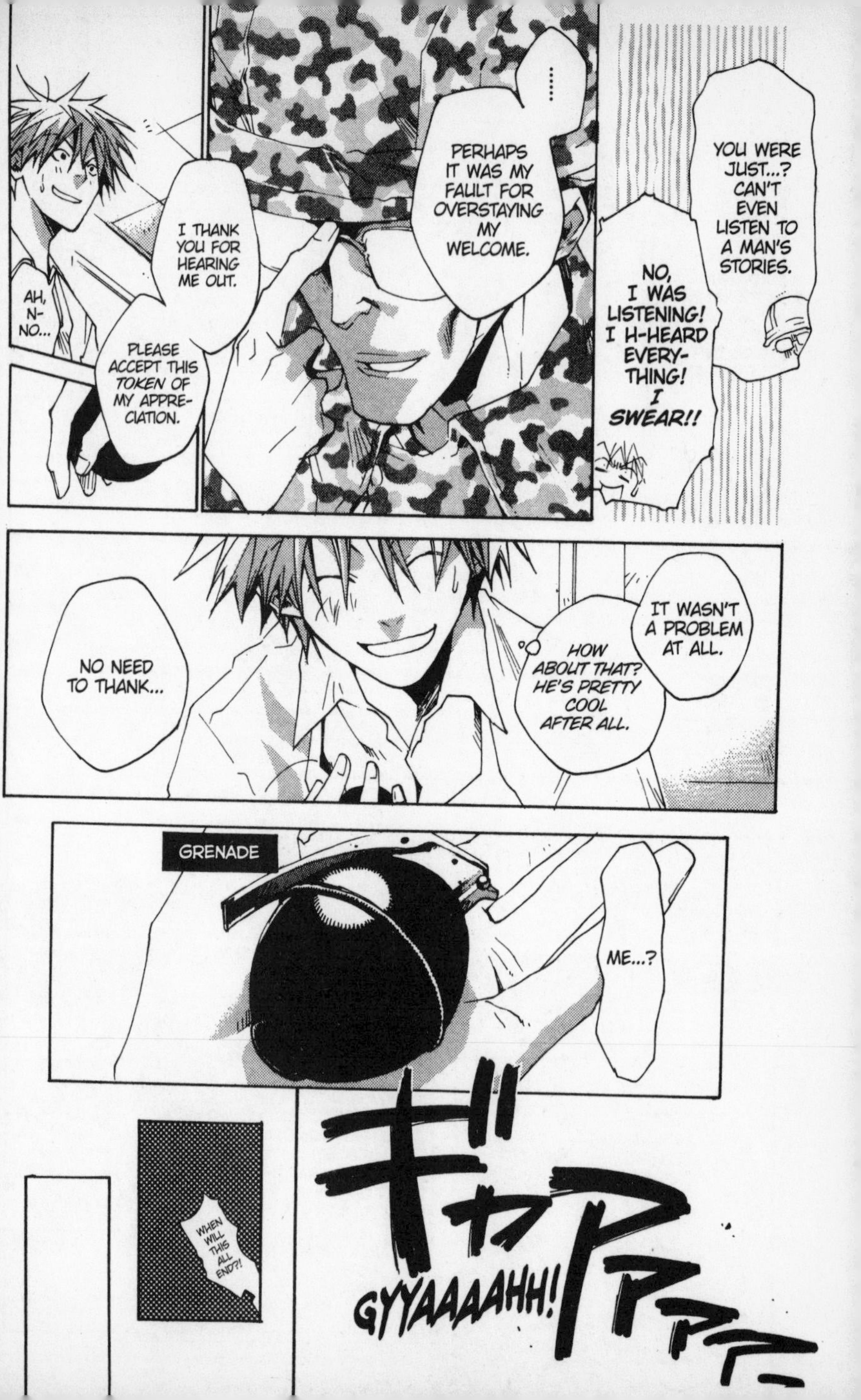
YOU WERE JUST...? CAN'T EVEN LISTEN TO A MAN'S STORIES.
NO, I WAS LISTENING! I H-HEARD EVERY-THING! I SWEAR!!
......
PERHAPS IT WAS MY FAULT FOR OVERSTAYING MY WELCOME.
I THANK YOU FOR HEARING ME OUT.
AH, N-NO...
PLEASE ACCEPT THIS TOKEN OF MY APPRE-CIATION.
IT WASN'T A PROBLEM AT ALL.
HOW ABOUT THAT? HE'S PRETTY COOL AFTER ALL.
NO NEED TO THANK...
ME...?
GRENADE
GYYAAAAHH!
WHEN WILL THIS ALL END?!

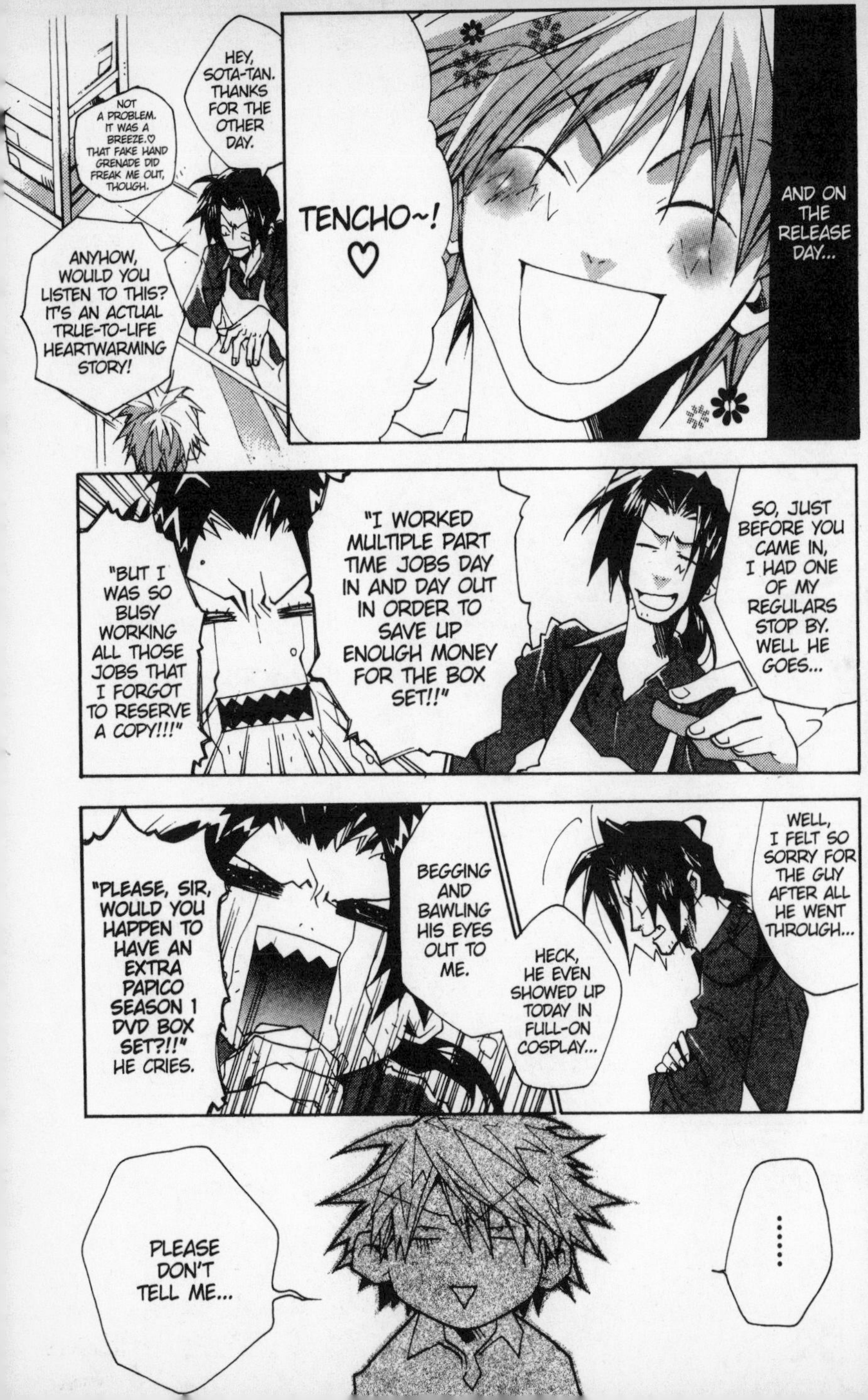
AND ON THE RELEASE DAY...
TENCHO~! ♡
HEY, SOTA-TAN. THANKS FOR THE OTHER DAY.
NOT A PROBLEM. IT WAS A BREEZE.♡ THAT FAKE HAND GRENADE DID FREAK ME OUT, THOUGH.
ANYHOW, WOULD YOU LISTEN TO THIS? IT'S AN ACTUAL TRUE-TO-LIFE HEARTWARMING STORY!
SO, JUST BEFORE YOU CAME IN, I HAD ONE OF MY REGULARS STOP BY. WELL HE GOES...
"I WORKED MULTIPLE PART TIME JOBS DAY IN AND DAY OUT IN ORDER TO SAVE UP ENOUGH MONEY FOR THE BOX SET!!"
"BUT I WAS SO BUSY WORKING ALL THOSE JOBS THAT I FORGOT TO RESERVE A COPY!!!"
WELL, I FELT SO SORRY FOR THE GUY AFTER ALL HE WENT THROUGH...
HECK, HE EVEN SHOWED UP TODAY IN FULL-ON COSPLAY...
BEGGING AND BAWLING HIS EYES OUT TO ME.
"PLEASE, SIR, WOULD YOU HAPPEN TO HAVE AN EXTRA PAPICO SEASON 1 DVD BOX SET?!!" HE CRIES.
......
PLEASE DON'T TELL ME...

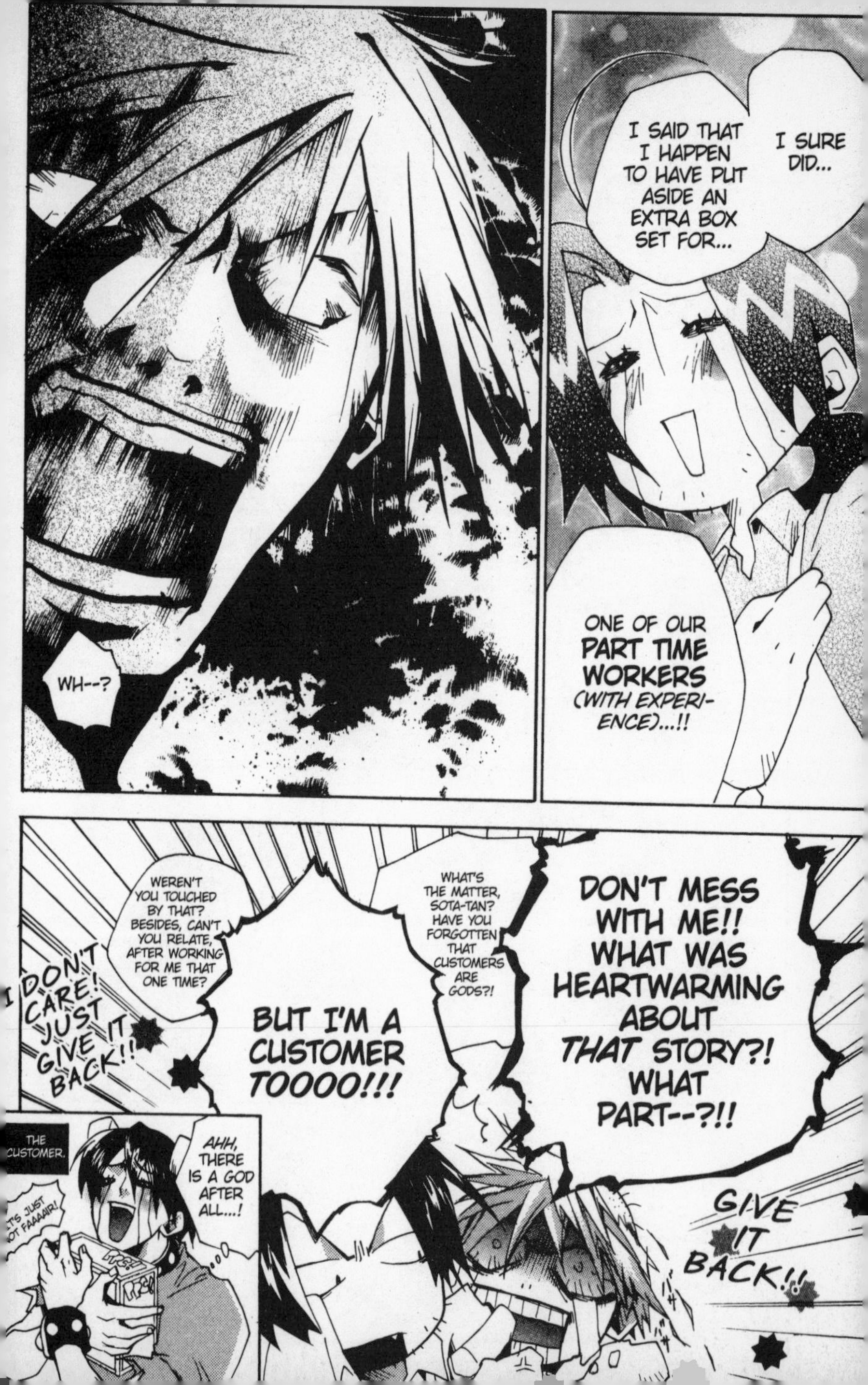
I SURE DID...
I SAID THAT I HAPPEN TO HAVE PUT ASIDE AN EXTRA BOX SET FOR...
ONE OF OUR PART TIME WORKERS (WITH EXPERIENCE)...!!
WH--?
DON'T MESS WITH ME!! WHAT WAS HEARTWARMING ABOUT THAT STORY?! WHAT PART--?!!
WHAT'S THE MATTER, SOTA-TAN? HAVE YOU FORGOTTEN THAT CUSTOMERS ARE GODS?!
BUT I'M A CUSTOMER TOOOO!!!
WEREN'T YOU TOUCHED BY THAT? BESIDES, CAN'T YOU RELATE, AFTER WORKING FOR ME THAT ONE TIME?
I DON'T CARE! JUST GIVE IT BACK!!
GIVE IT BACK!!
THE CUSTOMER.
AHH, THERE IS A GOD AFTER ALL...!
T'S JUST OT FAAAAIR!

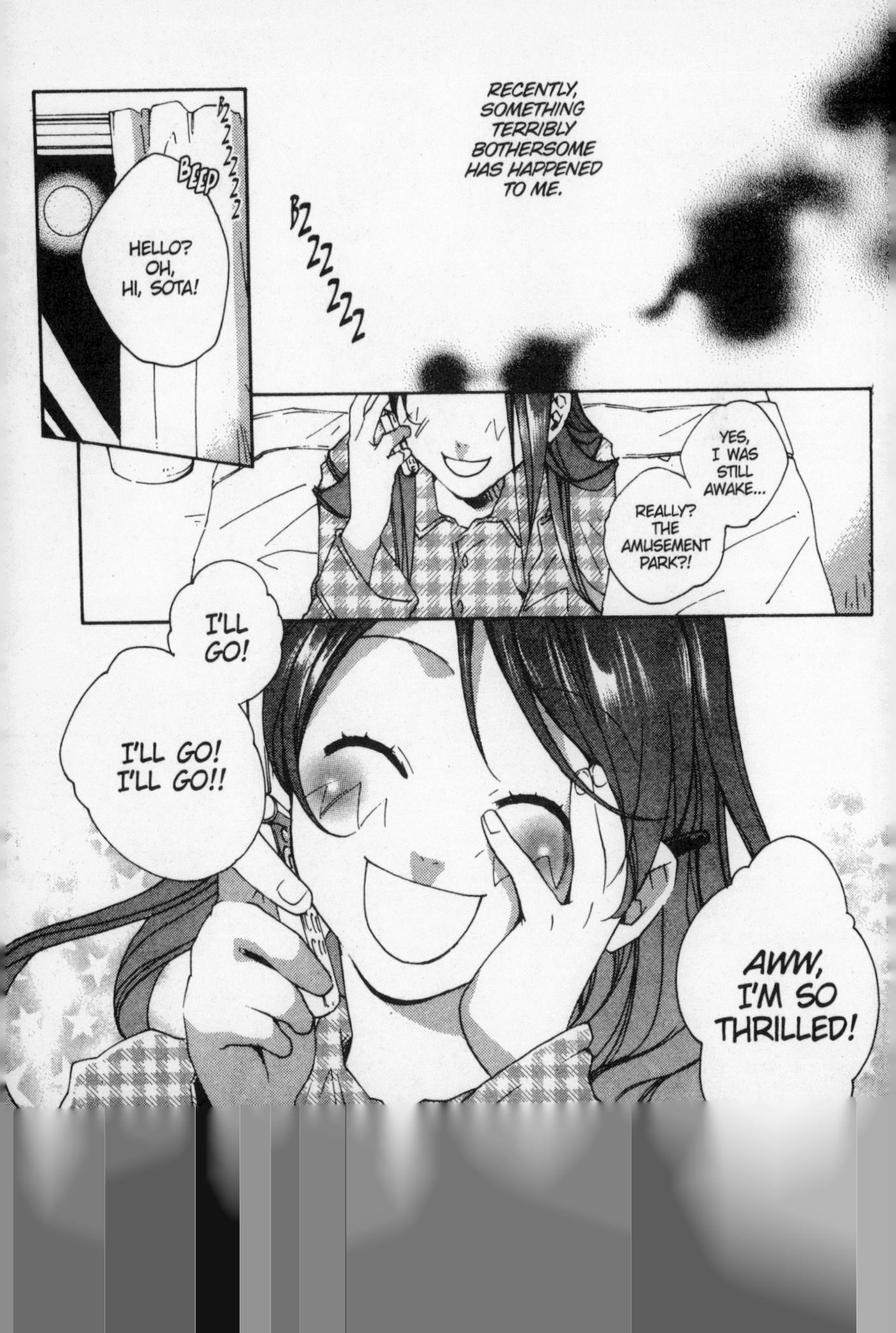
RECENTLY, SOMETHING TERRIBLY BOTHERSOME HAS HAPPENED TO ME.
BZZZZZZ
BZZZZZZ
BEEP
HELLO? OH, HI, SOTA!
YES, I WAS STILL AWAKE...
REALLY? THE AMUSEMENT PARK?!
I'LL GO!
I'LL GO! I'LL GO!!
AWW, I'M SO THRILLED!

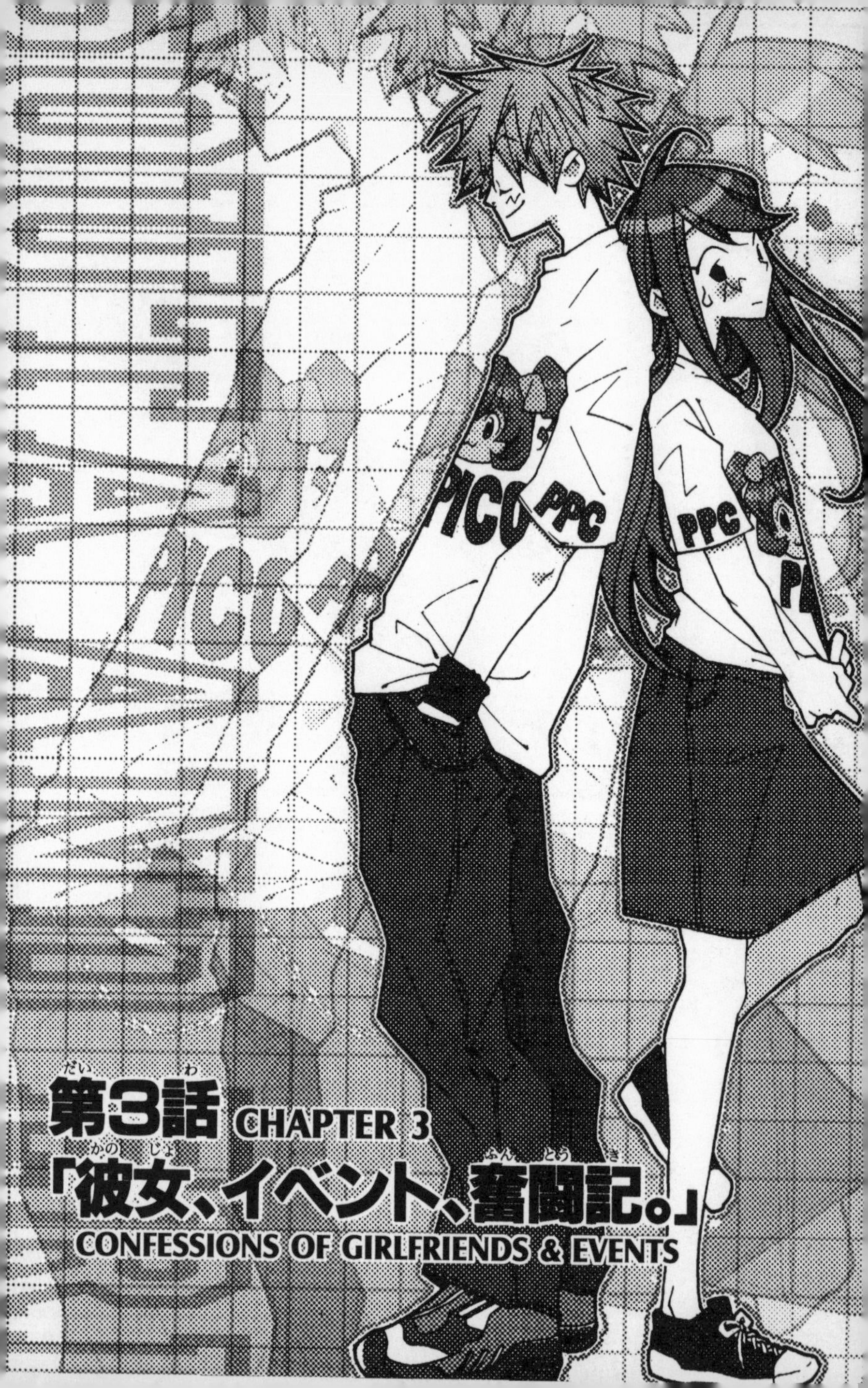
PICO
PPC
PPC
第3話 CHAPTER 3
「彼女、イベント、奮闘記。」
CONFESSIONS OF GIRLFRIENDS & EVENTS

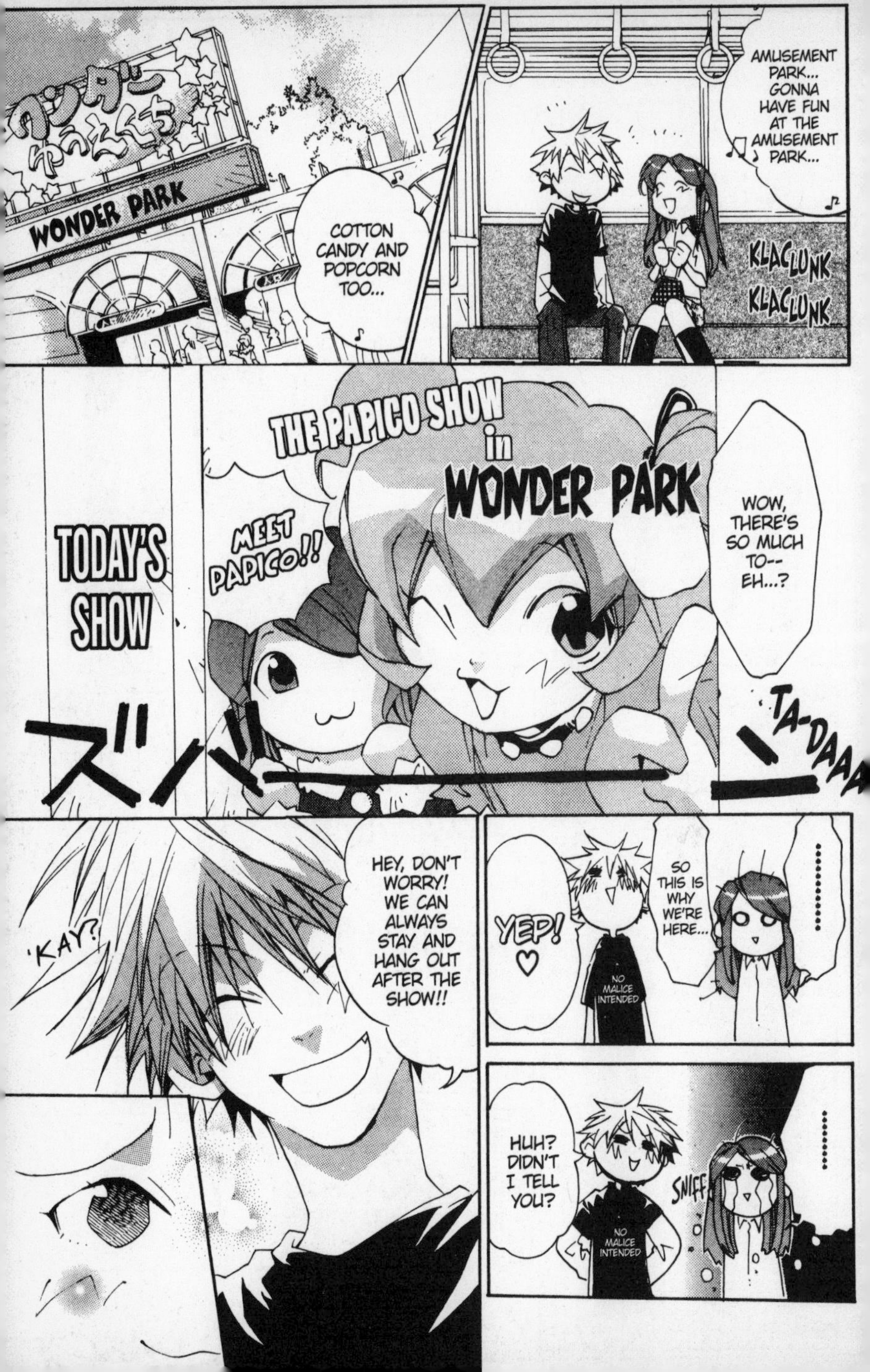
AMUSEMENT PARK... GONNA HAVE FUN AT THE AMUSEMENT PARK...
KLACLUNK KLACLUNK
COTTON CANDY AND POPCORN TOO...
WONDER PARK
WOW, THERE'S SO MUCH TO-- EH...?
THE PAPICO SHOW in WONDER PARK
MEET PAPICO!!
TODAY'S SHOW
TA-DAAA
SO THIS IS WHY WE'RE HERE...
YEP!
NO MALICE INTENDED
......
HUH? DIDN'T I TELL YOU?
NO MALICE INTENDED
SNIFF
......
HEY, DON'T WORRY! WE CAN ALWAYS STAY AND HANG OUT AFTER THE SHOW!!
'KAY?

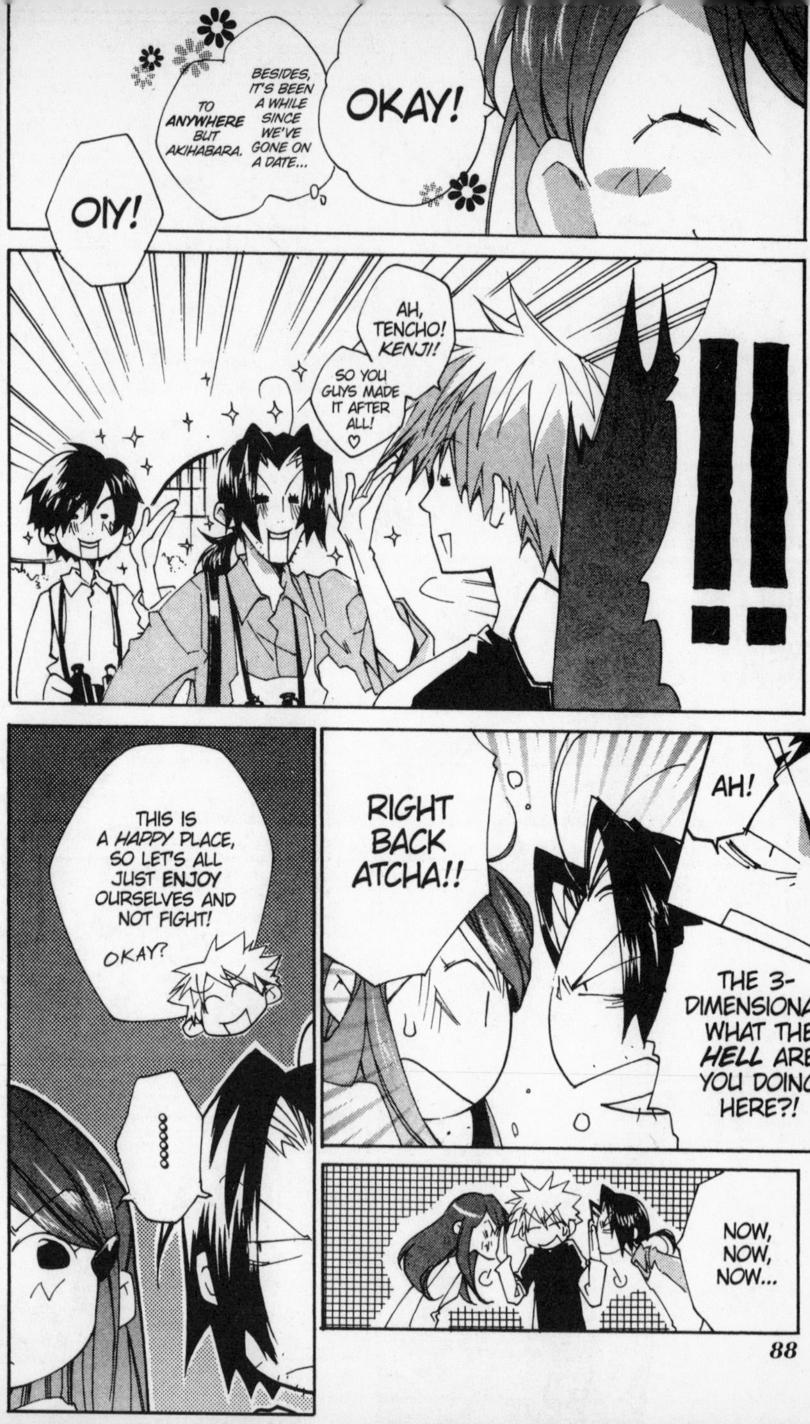
OKAY!
BESIDES, IT'S BEEN A WHILE SINCE WE'VE GONE ON A DATE...
TO ANYWHERE BUT AKIHABARA.
OIY!
!!
AH, TENCHO! KENJI!
SO YOU GUYS MADE IT AFTER ALL! ♡
AH!
THE 3-DIMENSIONAL! WHAT THE HELL ARE YOU DOING HERE?!
RIGHT BACK ATCHA!!
NOW, NOW, NOW...
THIS IS A HAPPY PLACE, SO LET'S ALL JUST ENJOY OURSELVES AND NOT FIGHT!
OKAY?
......

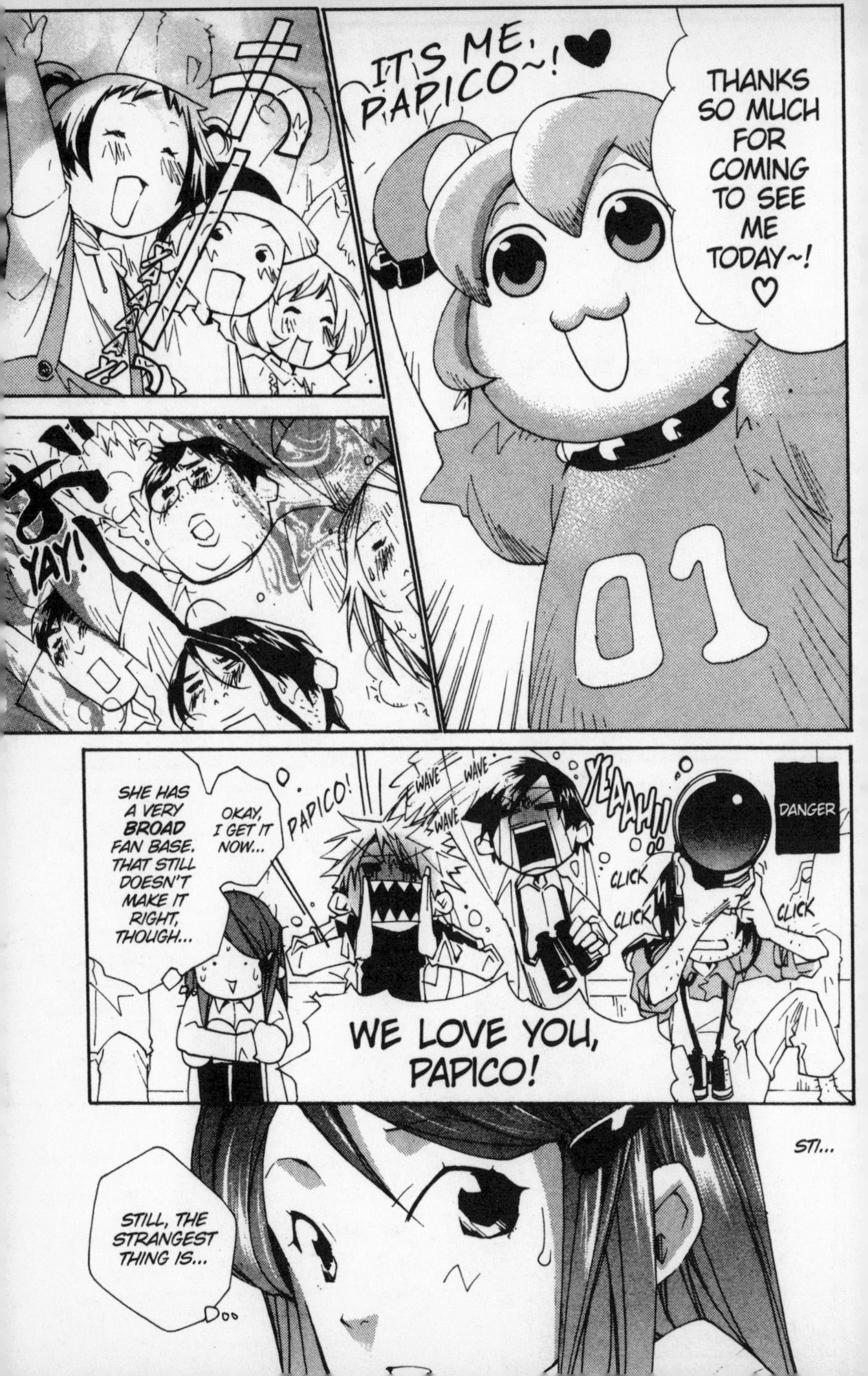
IT'S ME, PAPICO~! ♥
THANKS SO MUCH FOR COMING TO SEE ME TODAY~! ♡
YAY!
DANGER
YEAAAH!!
CLICK
CLICK
CLICK
WAVE
WAVE
WAVE
PAPICO!
OKAY, I GET IT NOW...
SHE HAS A VERY BROAD FAN BASE. THAT STILL DOESN'T MAKE IT RIGHT, THOUGH...
WE LOVE YOU, PAPICO!
STI...
STILL, THE STRANGEST THING IS...

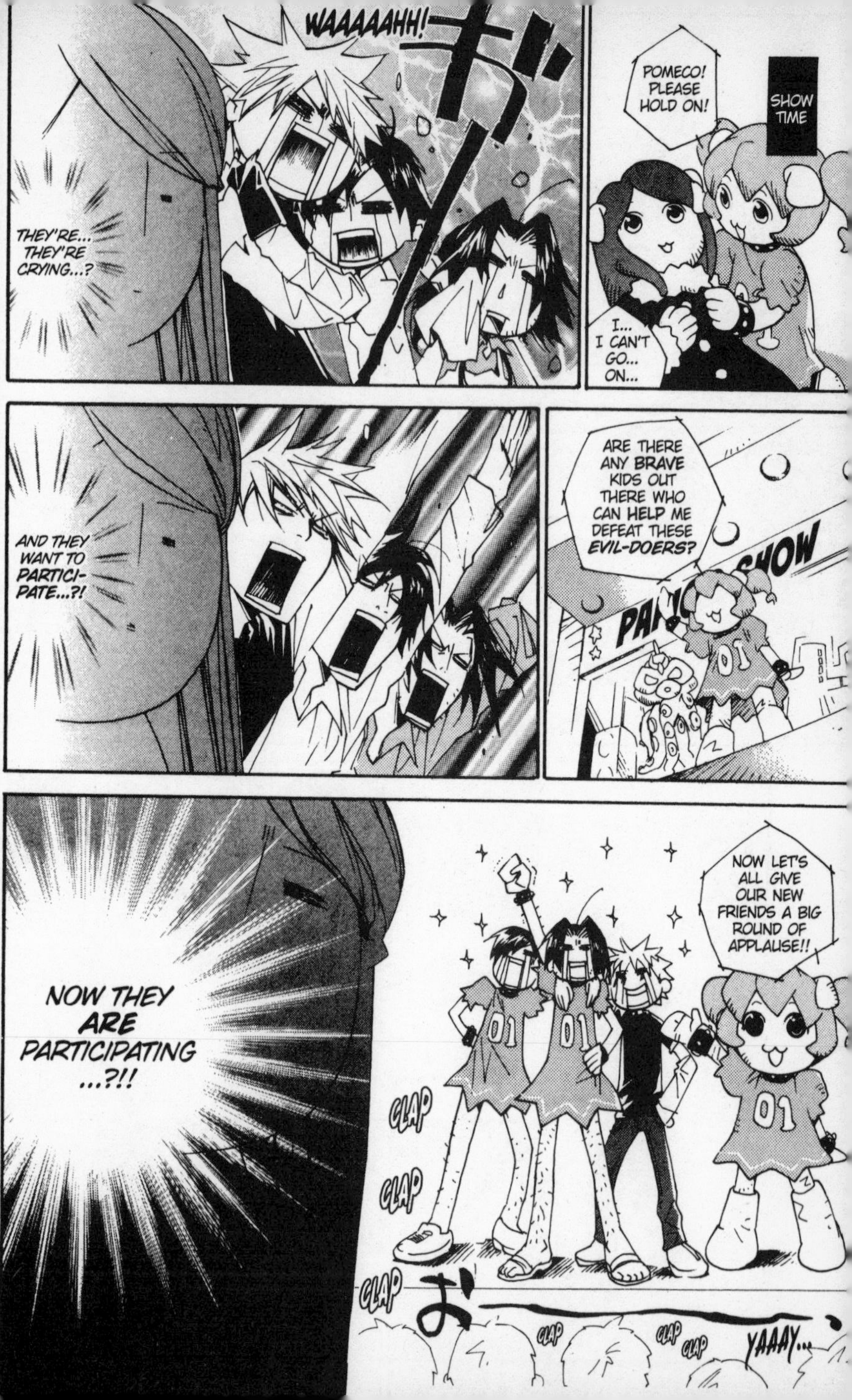
SHOW TIME
POMECO! PLEASE HOLD ON!
I... I CAN'T GO... ON...
WAAAAAHH!
THEY'RE... THEY'RE CRYING...?
ARE THERE ANY BRAVE KIDS OUT THERE WHO CAN HELP ME DEFEAT THESE EVIL-DOERS?
AND THEY WANT TO PARTICI-PATE...?!
NOW LET'S ALL GIVE OUR NEW FRIENDS A BIG ROUND OF APPLAUSE!!
CLAP
CLAP
CLAP
CLAP
CLAP
CLAP
CLAP
YAAAY...
お
NOW THEY ARE PARTICIPATING ...?!!

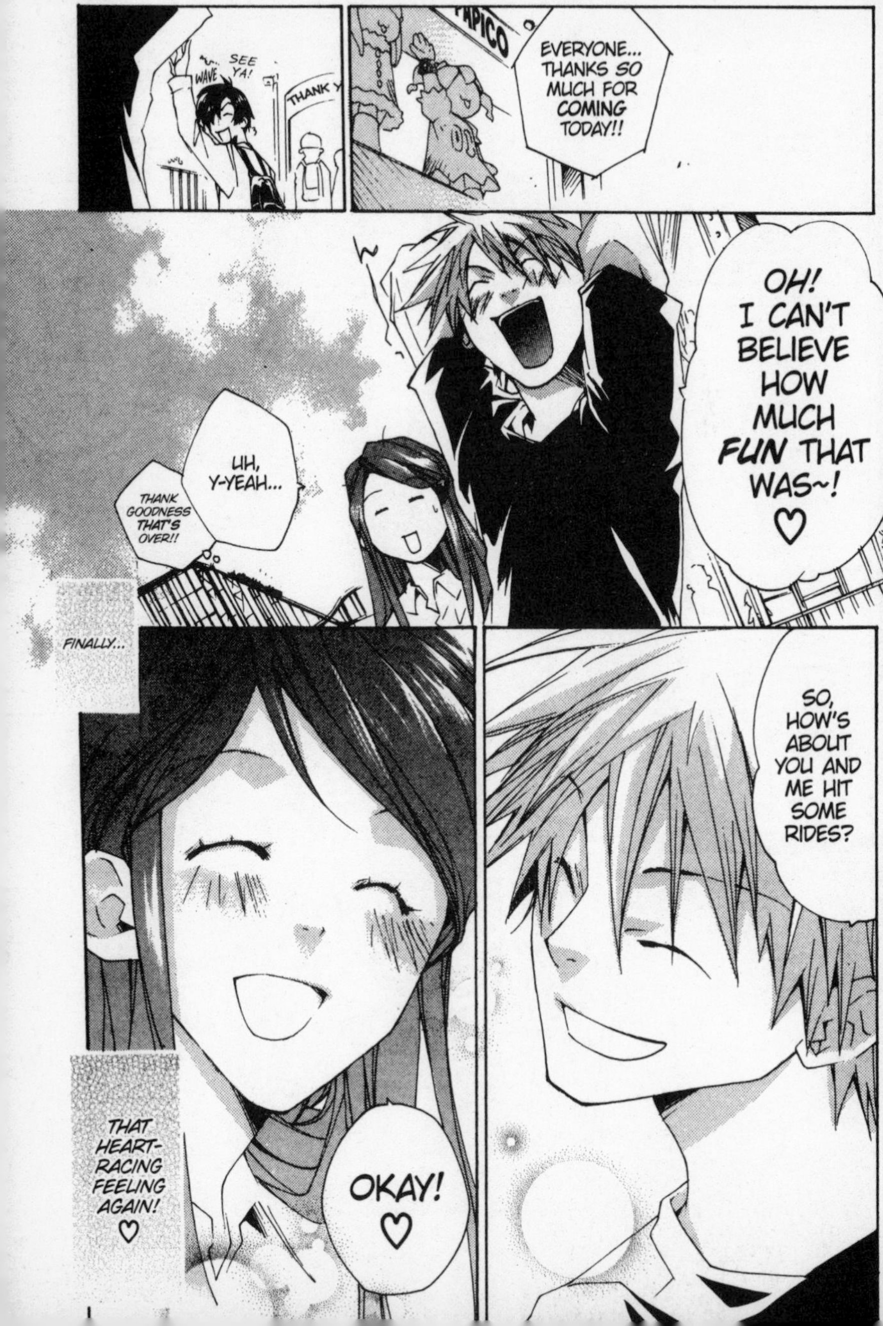
APICO
EVERYONE... THANKS SO MUCH FOR COMING TODAY!!
WAVE
SEE YA!
THANK Y
OH! I CAN'T BELIEVE HOW MUCH FUN THAT WAS~! ♡
UH, Y-YEAH...
THANK GOODNESS THAT'S OVER!!
SO, HOW'S ABOUT YOU AND ME HIT SOME RIDES?
FINALLY...
OKAY! ♡
THAT HEART-RACING FEELING AGAIN! ♡

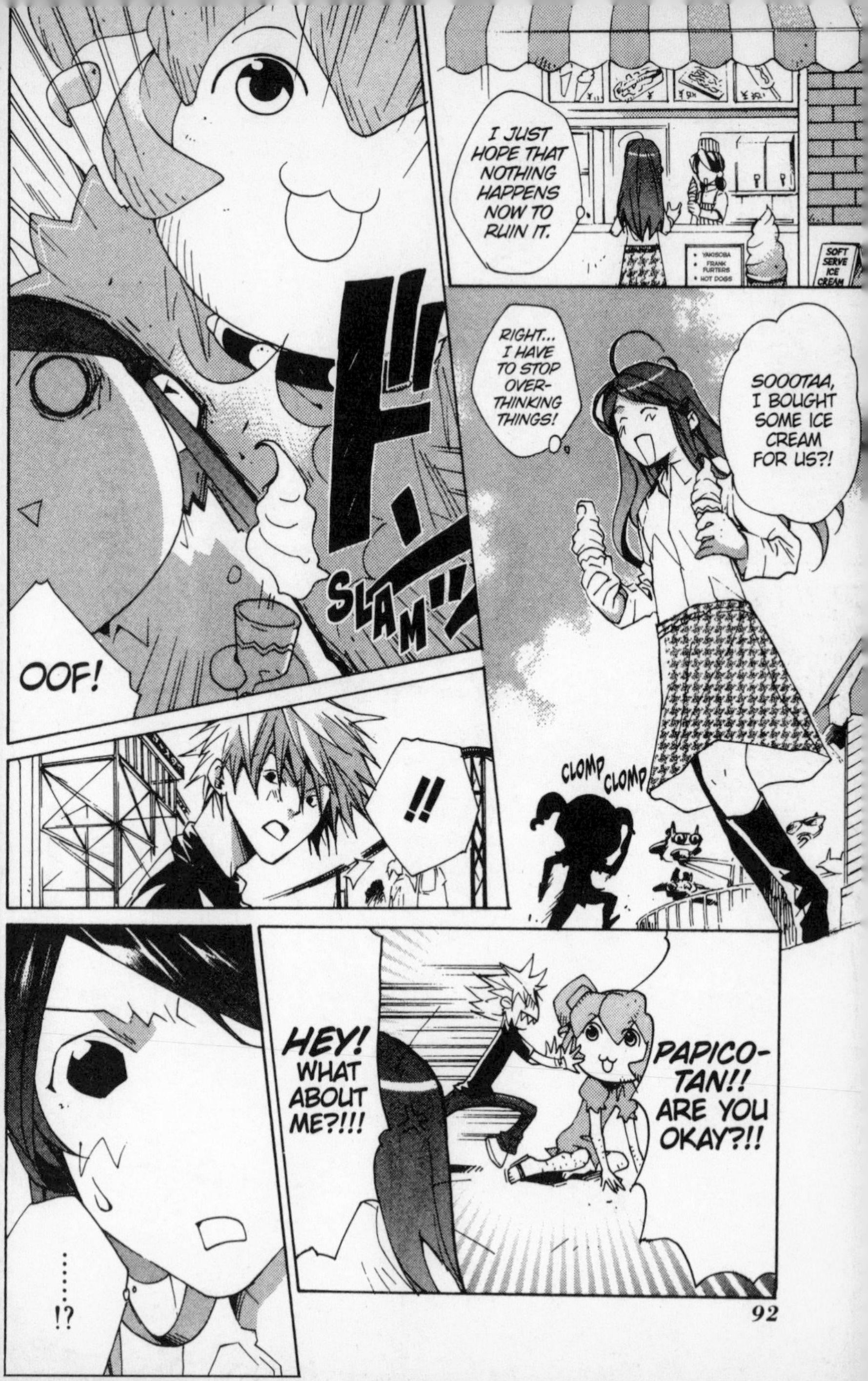
I JUST HOPE THAT NOTHING HAPPENS NOW TO RUIN IT.
YAKISOBA
FRANK FURTERS
HOT DOGS
SOFT SERVE ICE CREAM
SOOOTAA, I BOUGHT SOME ICE CREAM FOR US?!
RIGHT... I HAVE TO STOP OVER-THINKING THINGS!
CLOMP CLOMP
SLAM!!
OOF!
!!
PAPICO-TAN!! ARE YOU OKAY?!!
HEY! WHAT ABOUT ME?!!!
......!?

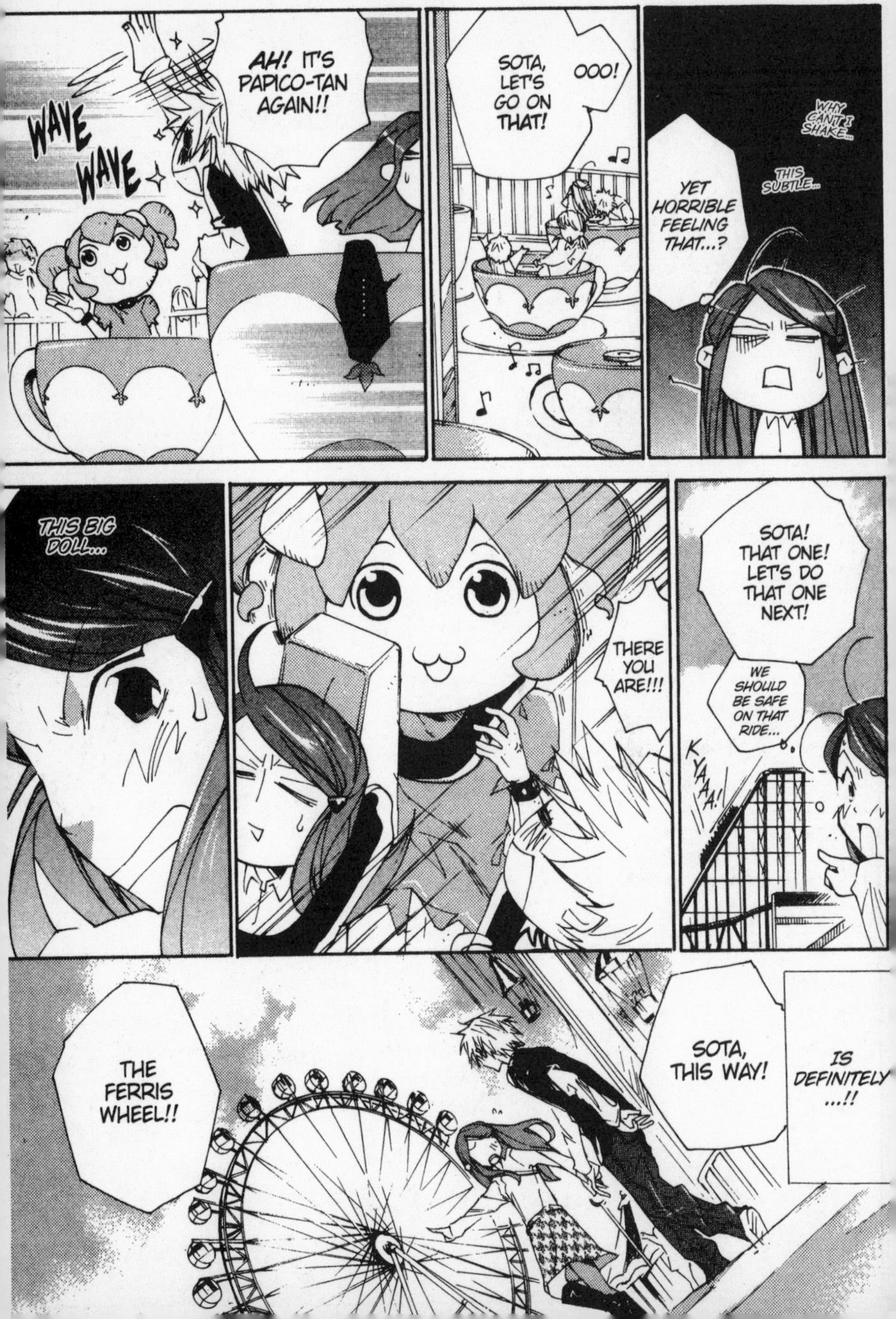
WHY CAN'T I SHAKE...
THIS SUBTLE...
YET HORRIBLE FEELING THAT...?
SOTA, LET'S GO ON THAT!
OOO!
AH! IT'S PAPICO-TAN AGAIN!!
WAVE WAVE
SOTA! THAT ONE! LET'S DO THAT ONE NEXT!
WE SHOULD BE SAFE ON THAT RIDE...
KYAAA!
THERE YOU ARE!!!
THIS BIG DOLL...
IS DEFINITELY ...!!
SOTA, THIS WAY!
THE FERRIS WHEEL!!

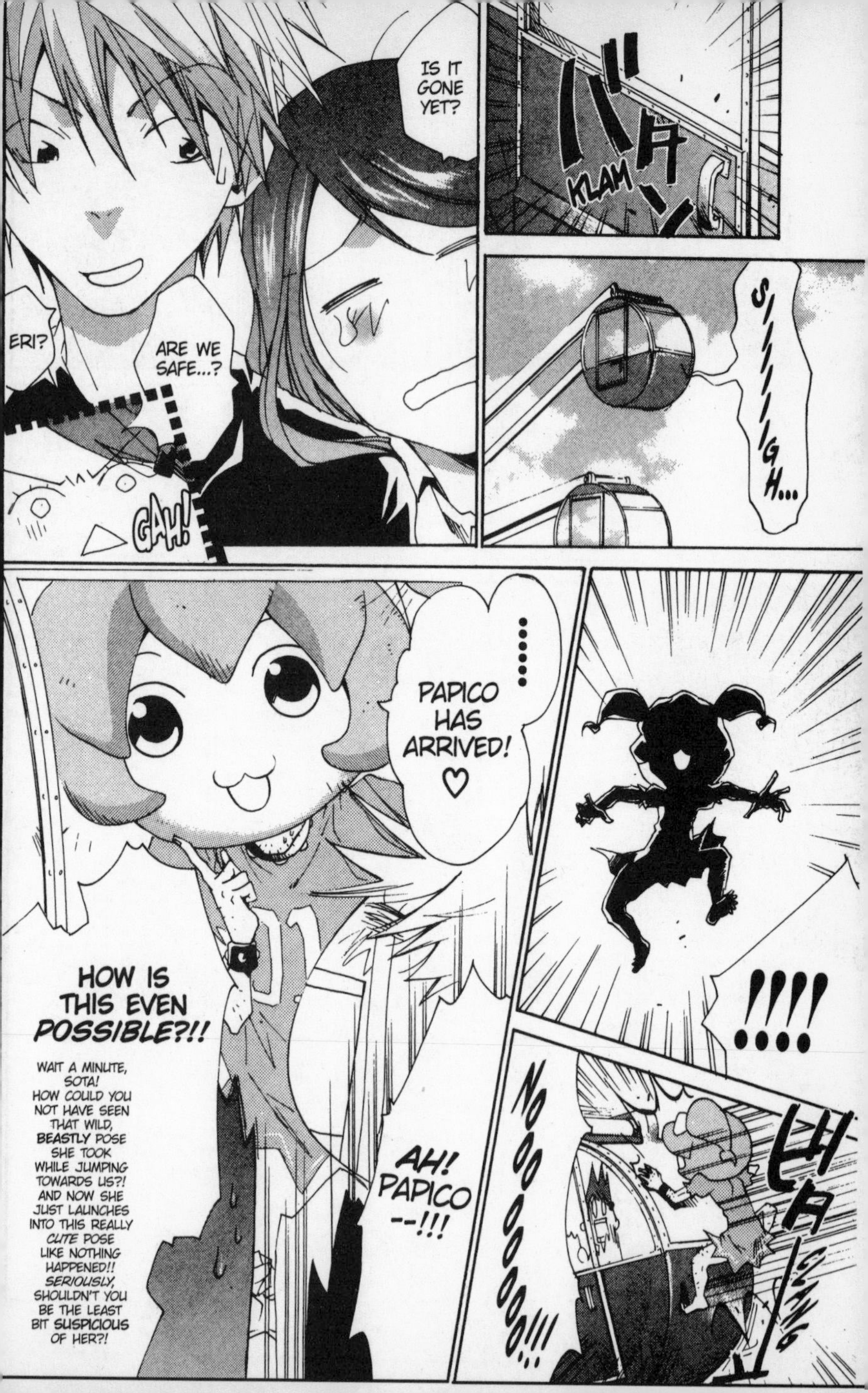
KLAM
SIIIIIIGH...
IS IT GONE YET?
ARE WE SAFE...?
ERI?
GAH!
!!!!
NOOOOOOOOOOO!!!
CLANG
......
PAPICO HAS ARRIVED! ♡
AH! PAPICO--!!!
HOW IS THIS EVEN *POSSIBLE?!!*
WAIT A MINUTE, SOTA! HOW COULD YOU NOT HAVE SEEN THAT WILD, **BEASTLY** POSE SHE TOOK WHILE JUMPING TOWARDS US?! AND NOW SHE JUST LAUNCHES INTO THIS REALLY *CUTE* POSE LIKE NOTHING HAPPENED!! *SERIOUSLY,* SHOULDN'T YOU BE THE LEAST BIT **SUSPICIOUS** OF HER?!

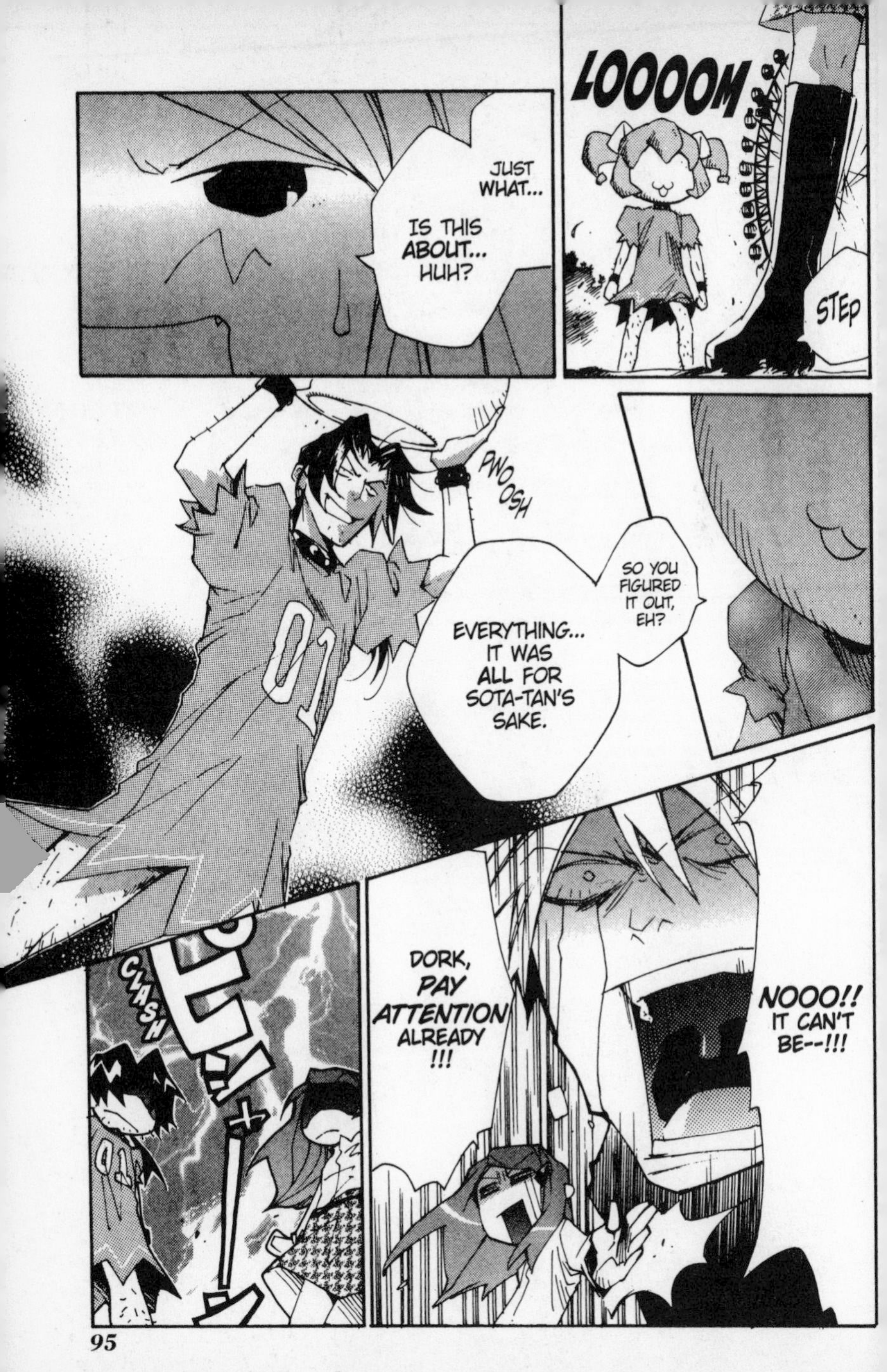
LOOOOM
STEP
JUST WHAT...
IS THIS ABOUT... HUH?
SO YOU FIGURED IT OUT, EH?
PWOOSH
EVERYTHING... IT WAS ALL FOR SOTA-TAN'S SAKE.
NOOO!! IT CAN'T BE--!!!
DORK, PAY ATTENTION ALREADY !!!
CLASH

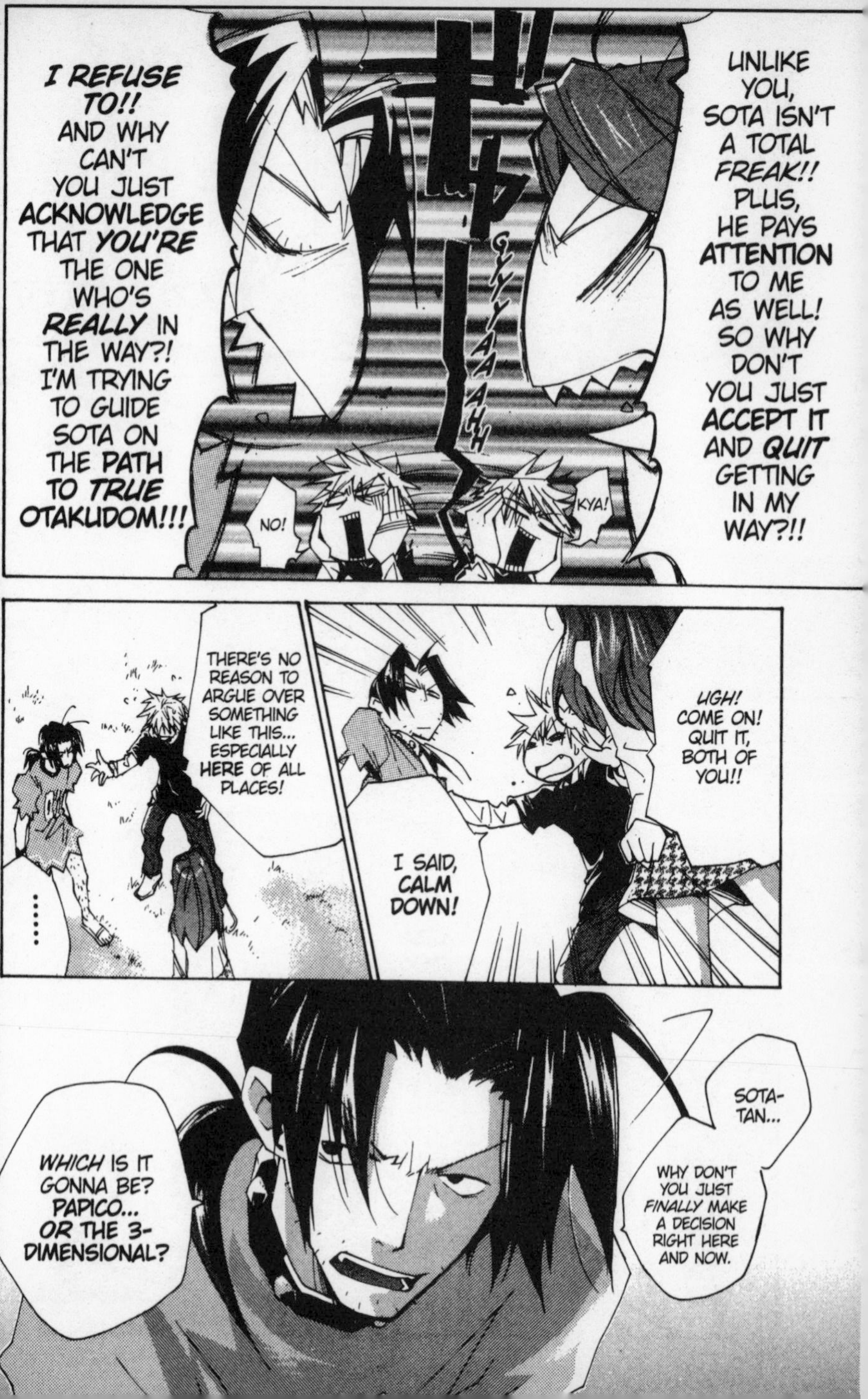
UNLIKE YOU, SOTA ISN'T A TOTAL FREAK!! PLUS, HE PAYS ATTENTION TO ME AS WELL! SO WHY DON'T YOU JUST ACCEPT IT AND QUIT GETTING IN MY WAY?!!
I REFUSE TO!! AND WHY CAN'T YOU JUST ACKNOWLEDGE THAT YOU'RE THE ONE WHO'S REALLY IN THE WAY?! I'M TRYING TO GUIDE SOTA ON THE PATH TO TRUE OTAKUDOM!!!
GYYYAAAAHH
KYA!
NO!
UGH! COME ON! QUIT IT, BOTH OF YOU!!
I SAID, CALM DOWN!
THERE'S NO REASON TO ARGUE OVER SOMETHING LIKE THIS... ESPECIALLY HERE OF ALL PLACES!
......
SOTA-TAN...
WHY DON'T YOU JUST FINALLY MAKE A DECISION RIGHT HERE AND NOW.
WHICH IS IT GONNA BE? PAPICO... OR THE 3-DIMENSIONAL?

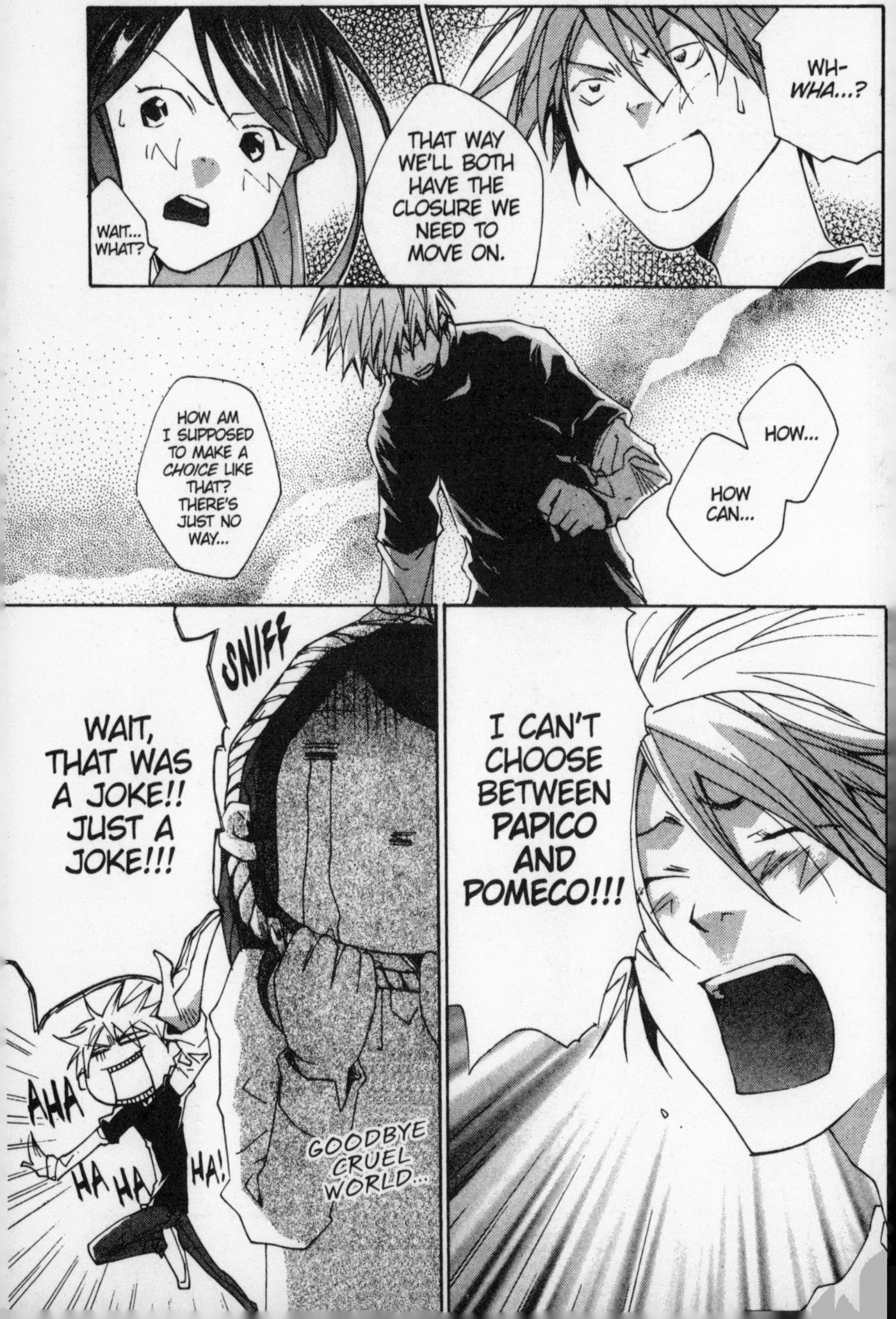
WH-
WHA...?
THAT WAY WE'LL BOTH HAVE THE CLOSURE WE NEED TO MOVE ON.
WAIT... WHAT?
HOW...
HOW CAN...
HOW AM I SUPPOSED TO MAKE A *CHOICE* LIKE THAT? THERE'S JUST NO WAY...
I CAN'T CHOOSE BETWEEN PAPICO AND POMECO!!!
SNIFF
WAIT, THAT WAS A JOKE!! JUST A JOKE!!!
GOODBYE CRUEL WORLD...
AHA
HA
HA
HA!

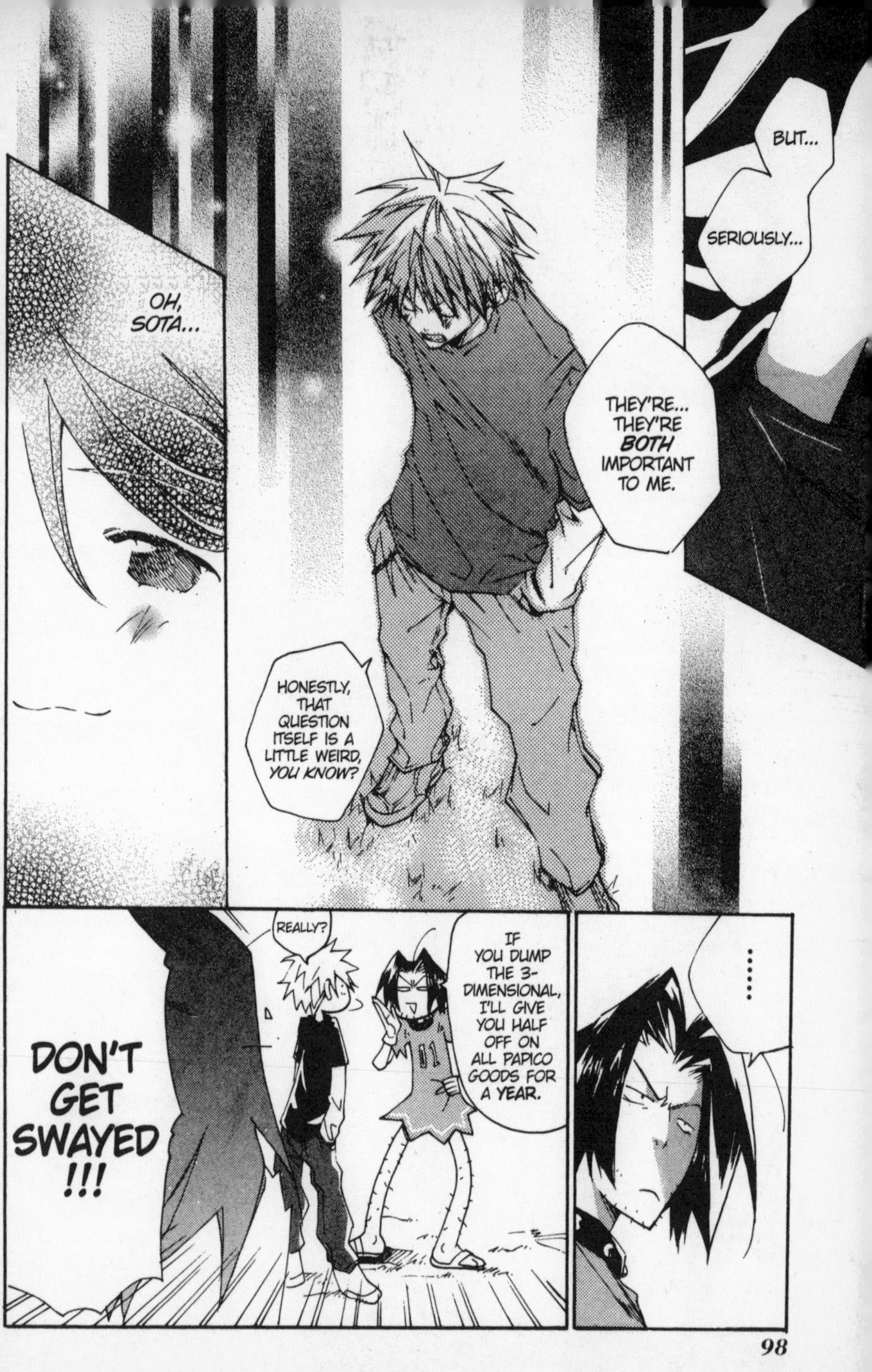
BUT...
SERIOUSLY...
THEY'RE... THEY'RE *BOTH* IMPORTANT TO ME.
HONESTLY, THAT QUESTION ITSELF IS A LITTLE WEIRD, *YOU KNOW?*
OH, SOTA...
——
......
IF YOU DUMP THE 3-DIMENSIONAL, I'LL GIVE YOU HALF OFF ON ALL PAPICO GOODS FOR A YEAR.
REALLY?
DON'T GET SWAYED!!!

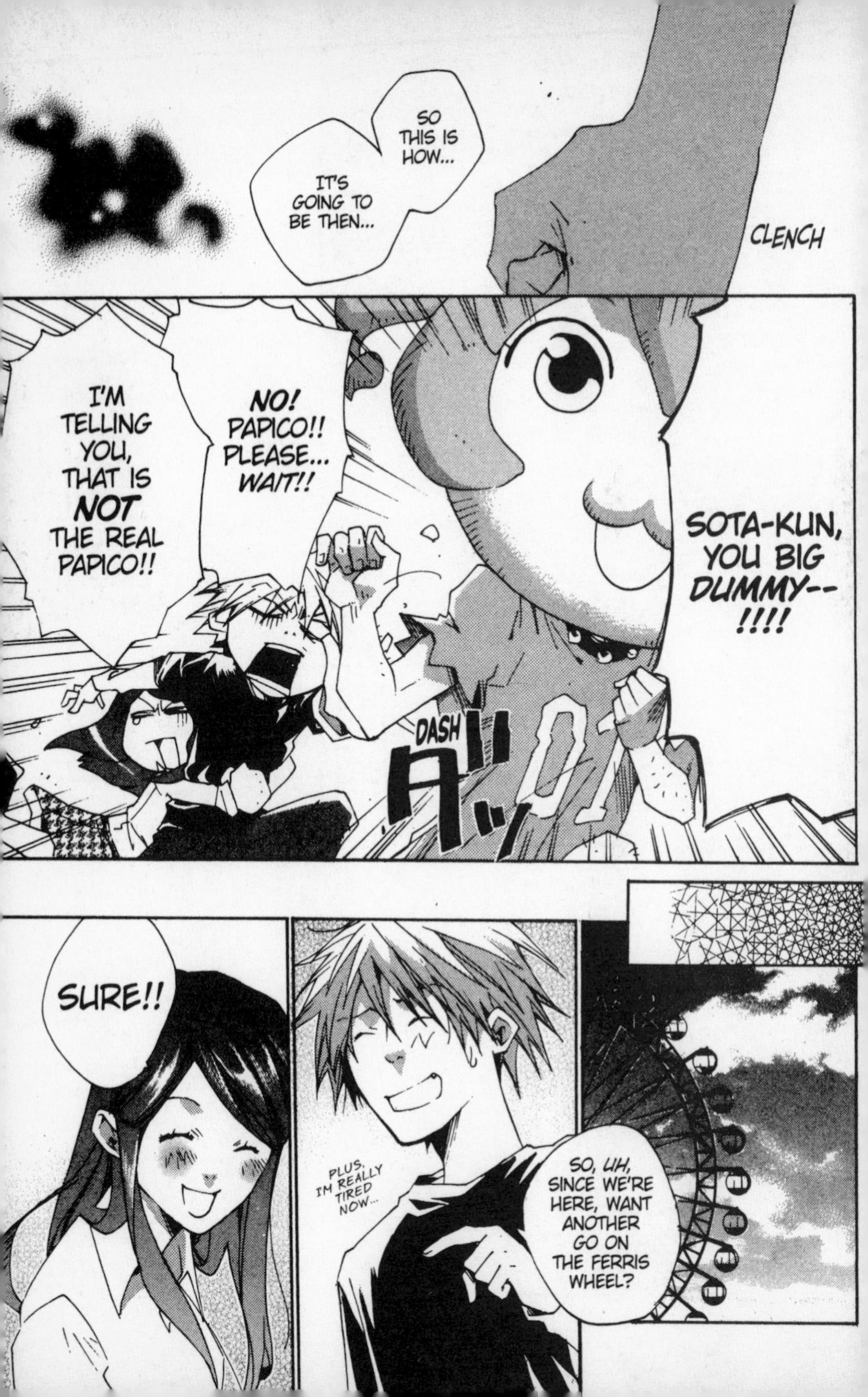
SO THIS IS HOW... IT'S GOING TO BE THEN...
CLENCH
SOTA-KUN, YOU BIG DUMMY--!!!!
DASH
NO! PAPICO!! PLEASE... WAIT!!
I'M TELLING YOU, THAT IS NOT THE REAL PAPICO!!
SO, UH, SINCE WE'RE HERE, WANT ANOTHER GO ON THE FERRIS WHEEL?
PLUS, I'M REALLY TIRED NOW...
SURE!!

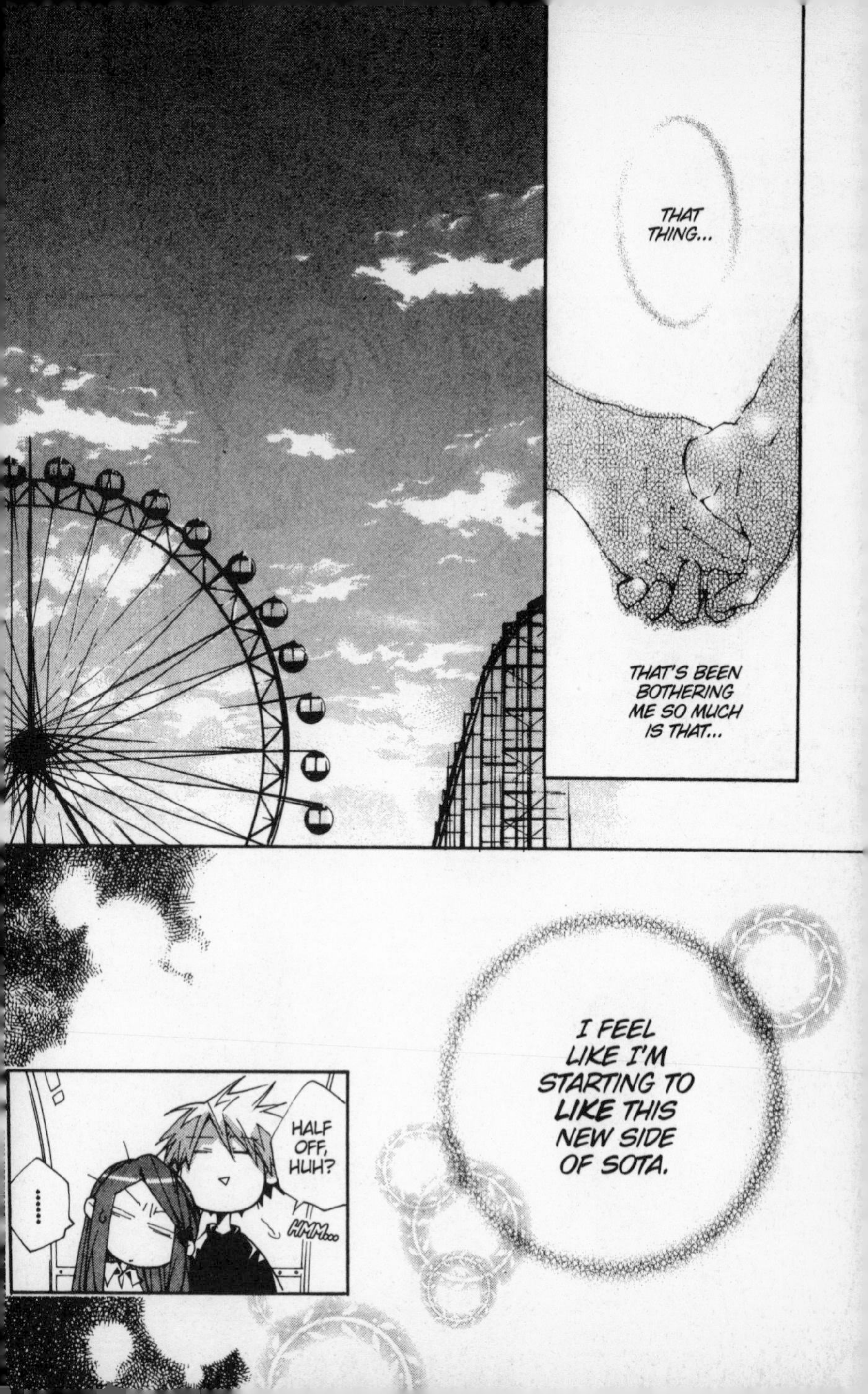
THAT THING...
THAT'S BEEN BOTHERING ME SO MUCH IS THAT...
I FEEL LIKE I'M STARTING TO **LIKE** THIS NEW SIDE OF SOTA.
HALF OFF, HUH?
HMM...
......

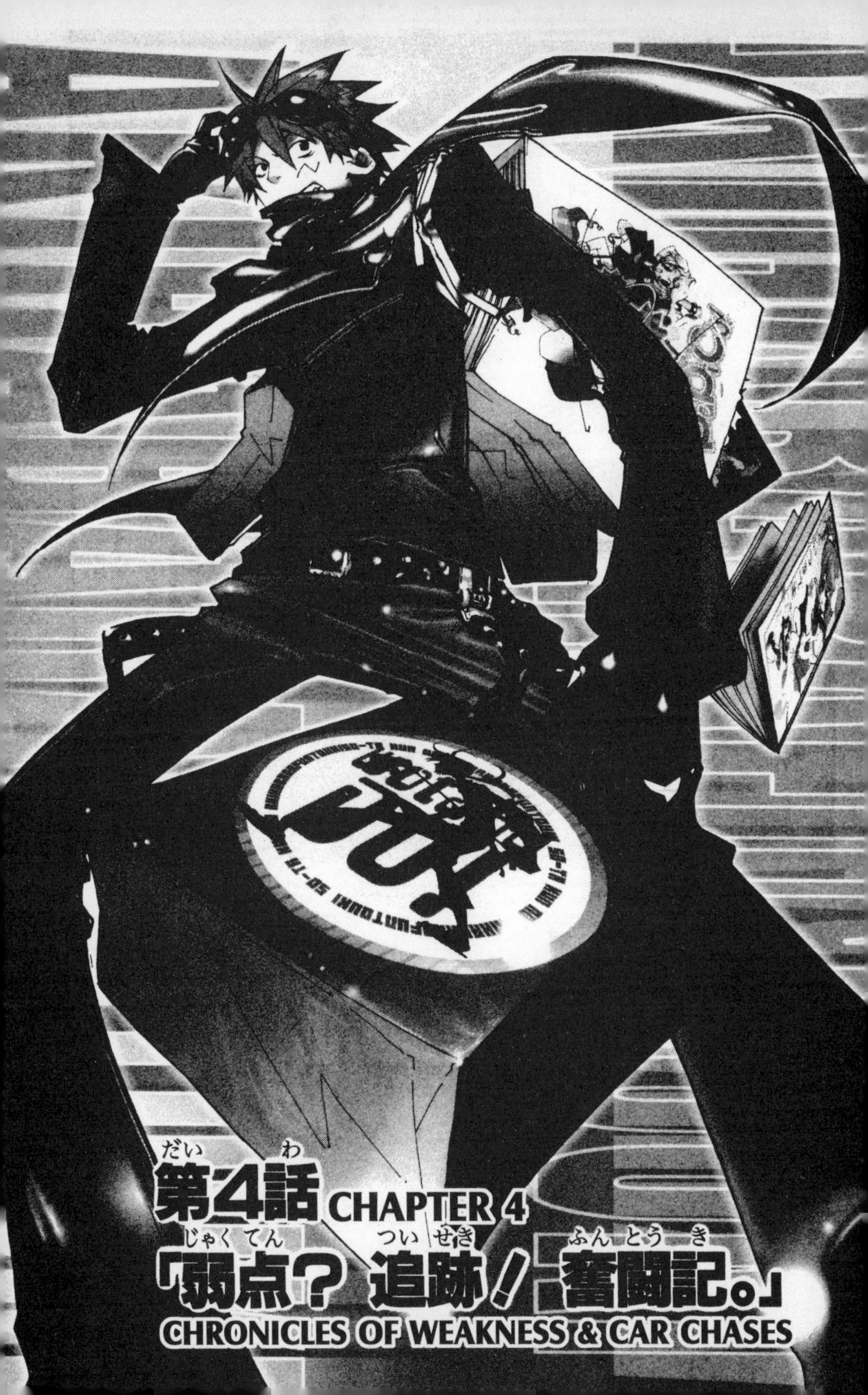

第4話 CHAPTER 4

「弱点？ 追跡！ 奮闘記。」

CHRONICLES OF WEAKNESS & CAR CHASES

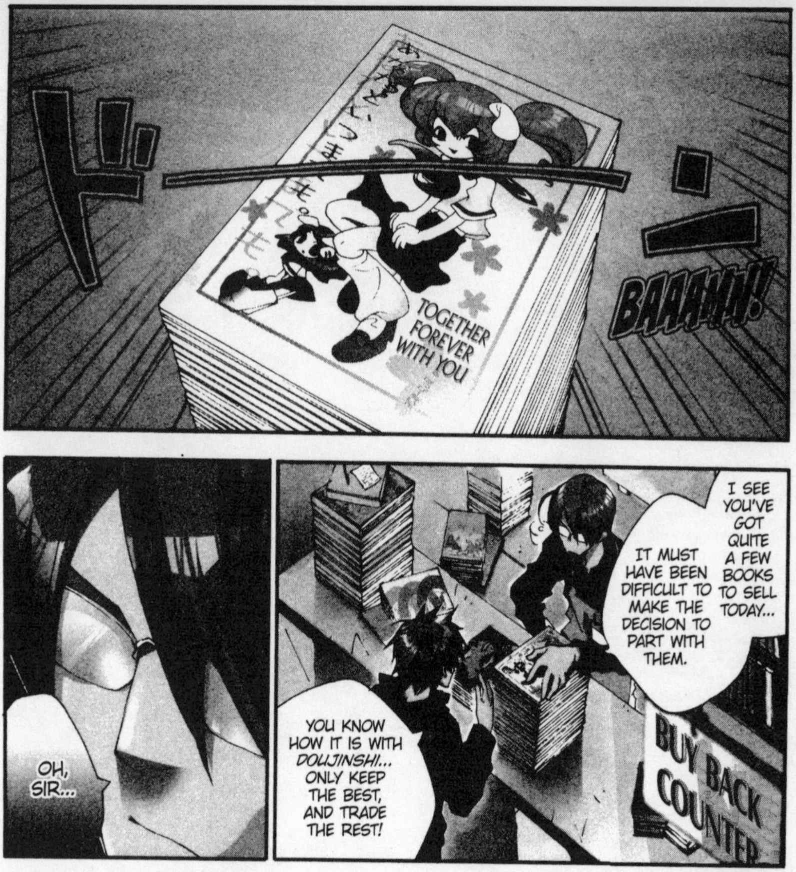
TOGETHER FOREVER WITH YOU
BAAAMN!
I SEE YOU'VE GOT QUITE A FEW BOOKS TO SELL TODAY...
IT MUST HAVE BEEN DIFFICULT TO MAKE THE DECISION TO PART WITH THEM.
BUY BACK COUNTER
YOU KNOW HOW IT IS WITH *DOUJINSHI*... ONLY KEEP THE BEST, AND TRADE THE REST!
OH, SIR...
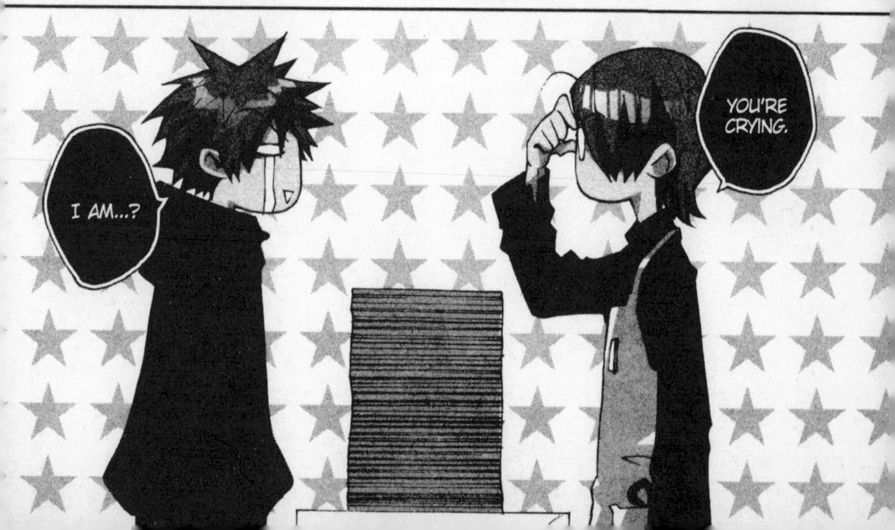
YOU'RE CRYING.
I AM...?

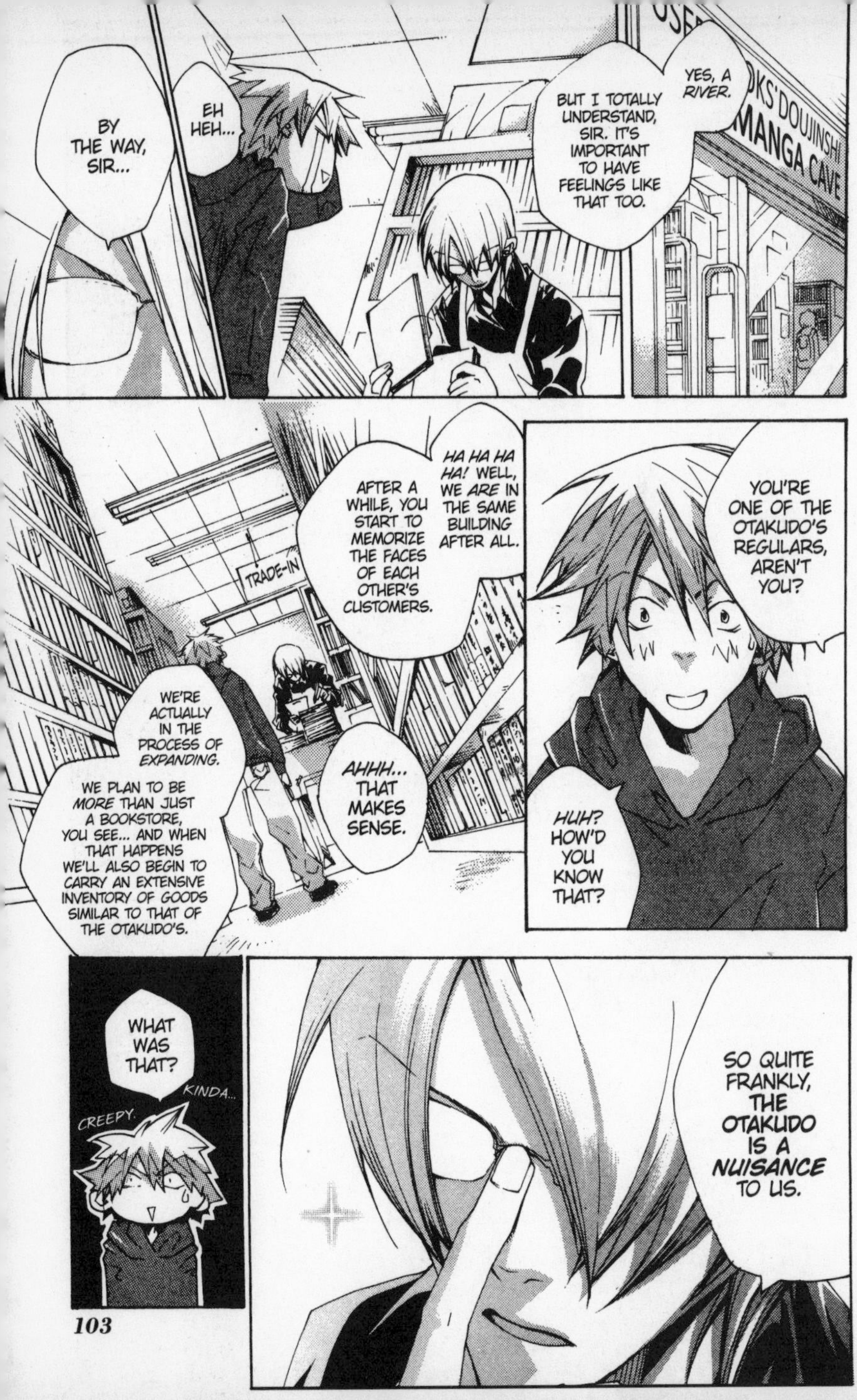
MANGA CAVE
YES, A RIVER.
BUT I TOTALLY UNDERSTAND, SIR. IT'S IMPORTANT TO HAVE FEELINGS LIKE THAT TOO.
EH HEH...
BY THE WAY, SIR...
YOU'RE ONE OF THE OTAKUDO'S REGULARS, AREN'T YOU?
HUH? HOW'D YOU KNOW THAT?
HA HA HA HA! WELL, WE ARE IN THE SAME BUILDING AFTER ALL.
AFTER A WHILE, YOU START TO MEMORIZE THE FACES OF EACH OTHER'S CUSTOMERS.
TRADE-IN
AHHH... THAT MAKES SENSE.
WE'RE ACTUALLY IN THE PROCESS OF EXPANDING.
WE PLAN TO BE MORE THAN JUST A BOOKSTORE, YOU SEE... AND WHEN THAT HAPPENS WE'LL ALSO BEGIN TO CARRY AN EXTENSIVE INVENTORY OF GOODS SIMILAR TO THAT OF THE OTAKUDO'S.
SO QUITE FRANKLY, THE OTAKUDO IS A NUISANCE TO US.
WHAT WAS THAT?
KINDA...
CREEPY.

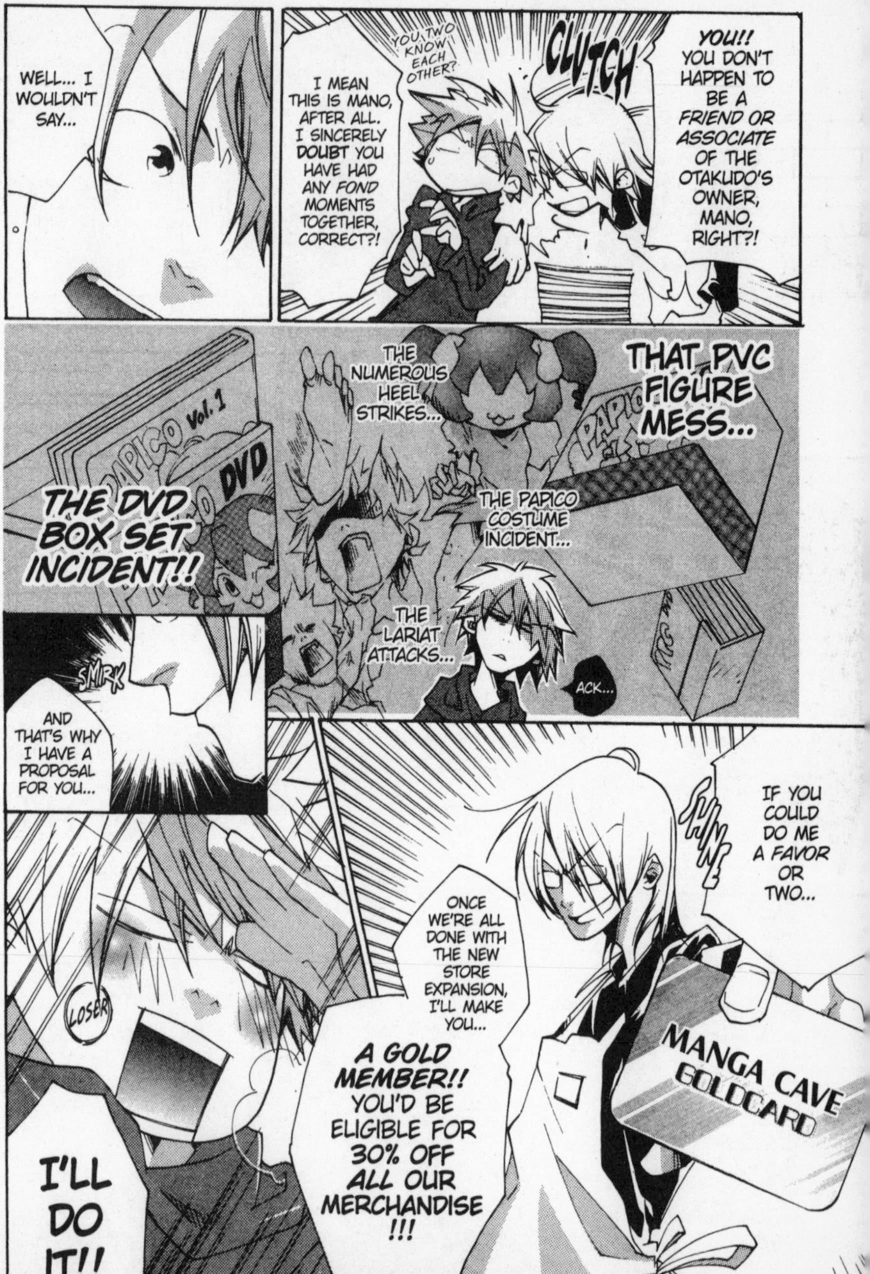

YOU!! YOU DON'T HAPPEN TO BE A FRIEND OR ASSOCIATE OF THE OTAKUDO'S OWNER, MANO, RIGHT?!
CLUTCH
I MEAN THIS IS MANO, AFTER ALL. I SINCERELY DOUBT YOU HAVE HAD ANY FOND MOMENTS TOGETHER, CORRECT?!
YOU, TWO KNOW EACH OTHER?
WELL... I WOULDN'T SAY...
THAT PVC FIGURE MESS...
THE NUMEROUS HEEL STRIKES...
PAPICO Vol. 1
DVD
THE DVD BOX SET INCIDENT!!
THE PAPICO COSTUME INCIDENT...
THE LARIAT ATTACKS...
ACK...
SMIRK
AND THAT'S WHY I HAVE A PROPOSAL FOR YOU...
SHINE
IF YOU COULD DO ME A FAVOR OR TWO...
ONCE WE'RE ALL DONE WITH THE NEW STORE EXPANSION, I'LL MAKE YOU...
A GOLD MEMBER!! YOU'D BE ELIGIBLE FOR 30% OFF ALL OUR MERCHANDISE!!!
MANGA CAVE GOLDCARD
LOSER
I'LL DO IT!!

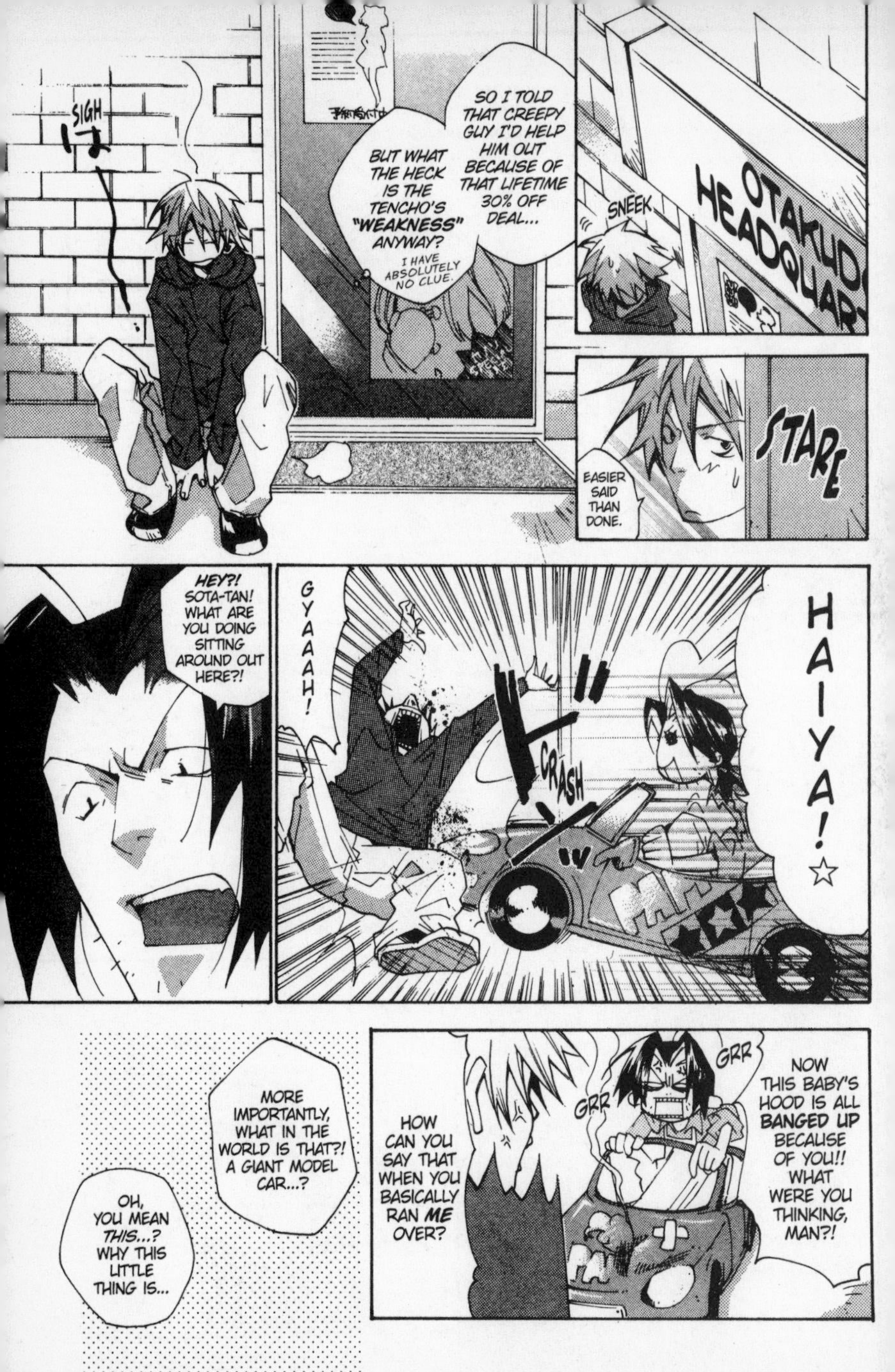
OTAKUDO HEADQUARTERS
SNEEK
STARE
EASIER SAID THAN DONE.
SIGH
は
SO I TOLD THAT CREEPY GUY I'D HELP HIM OUT BECAUSE OF THAT LIFETIME 30% OFF DEAL...
BUT WHAT THE HECK IS THE TENCHO'S "WEAKNESS" ANYWAY?
I HAVE ABSOLUTELY NO CLUE.
HAIYA!☆
CRASH
GYAAAAH!
HEY?! SOTA-TAN! WHAT ARE YOU DOING SITTING AROUND OUT HERE?!
NOW THIS BABY'S HOOD IS ALL BANGED UP BECAUSE OF YOU!! WHAT WERE YOU THINKING, MAN?!
GRR
GRR
HOW CAN YOU SAY THAT WHEN YOU BASICALLY RAN ME OVER?
MORE IMPORTANTLY, WHAT IN THE WORLD IS THAT?! A GIANT MODEL CAR...?
OH, YOU MEAN THIS...? WHY THIS LITTLE THING IS...

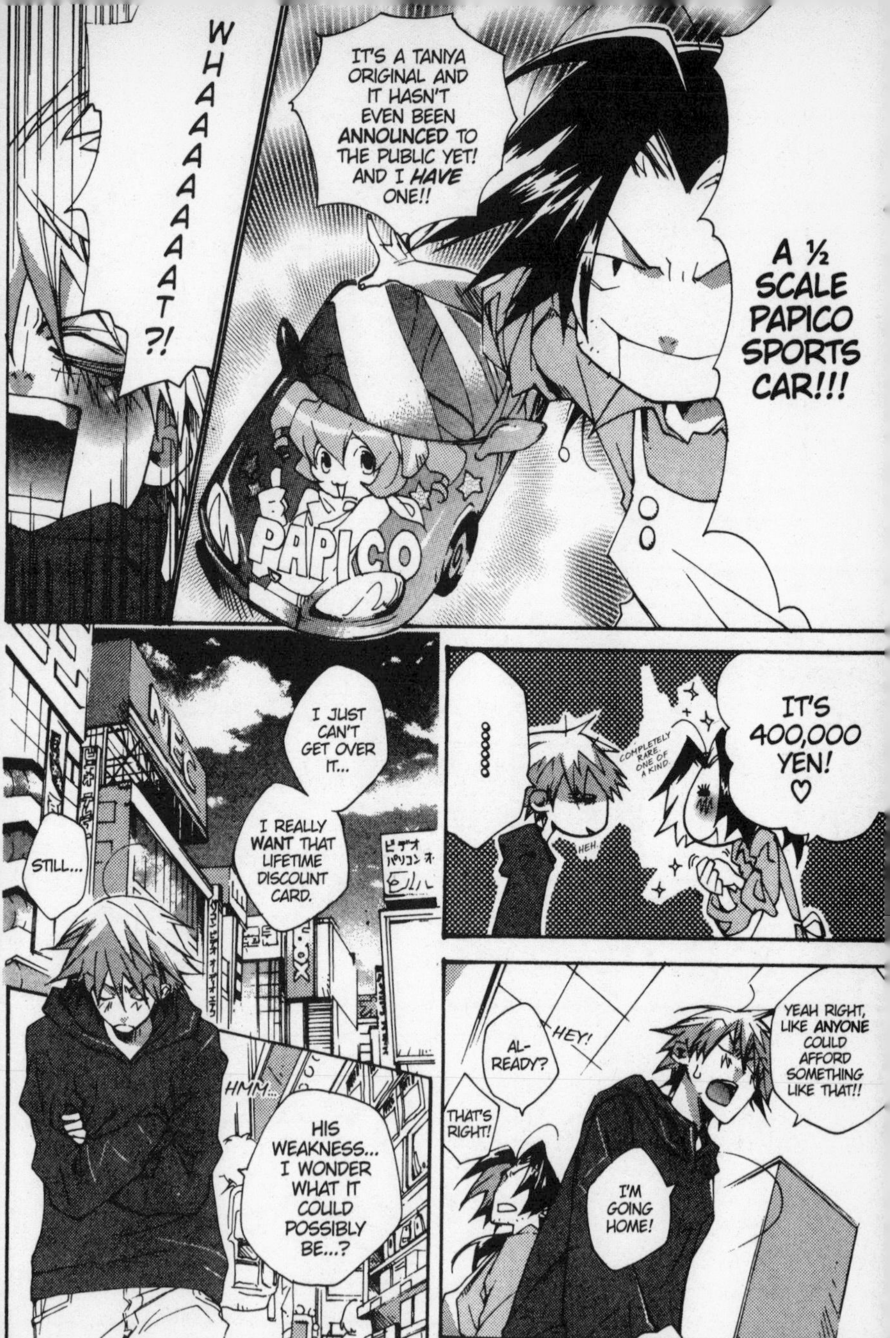
IT'S A TANIYA ORIGINAL AND IT HASN'T EVEN BEEN ANNOUNCED TO THE PUBLIC YET! AND I HAVE ONE!!
A ½ SCALE PAPICO SPORTS CAR!!!
PAPICO
WHAAAAAAAT?!
.....
IT'S 400,000 YEN! ♡
COMPLETELY RARE, ONE OF A KIND.
HEH.
YEAH RIGHT, LIKE ANYONE COULD AFFORD SOMETHING LIKE THAT!!
HEY!
AL-READY?
THAT'S RIGHT!
I'M GOING HOME!
I JUST CAN'T GET OVER IT...
I REALLY WANT THAT LIFETIME DISCOUNT CARD.
STILL...
HMM...
HIS WEAKNESS... I WONDER WHAT IT COULD POSSIBLY BE...?

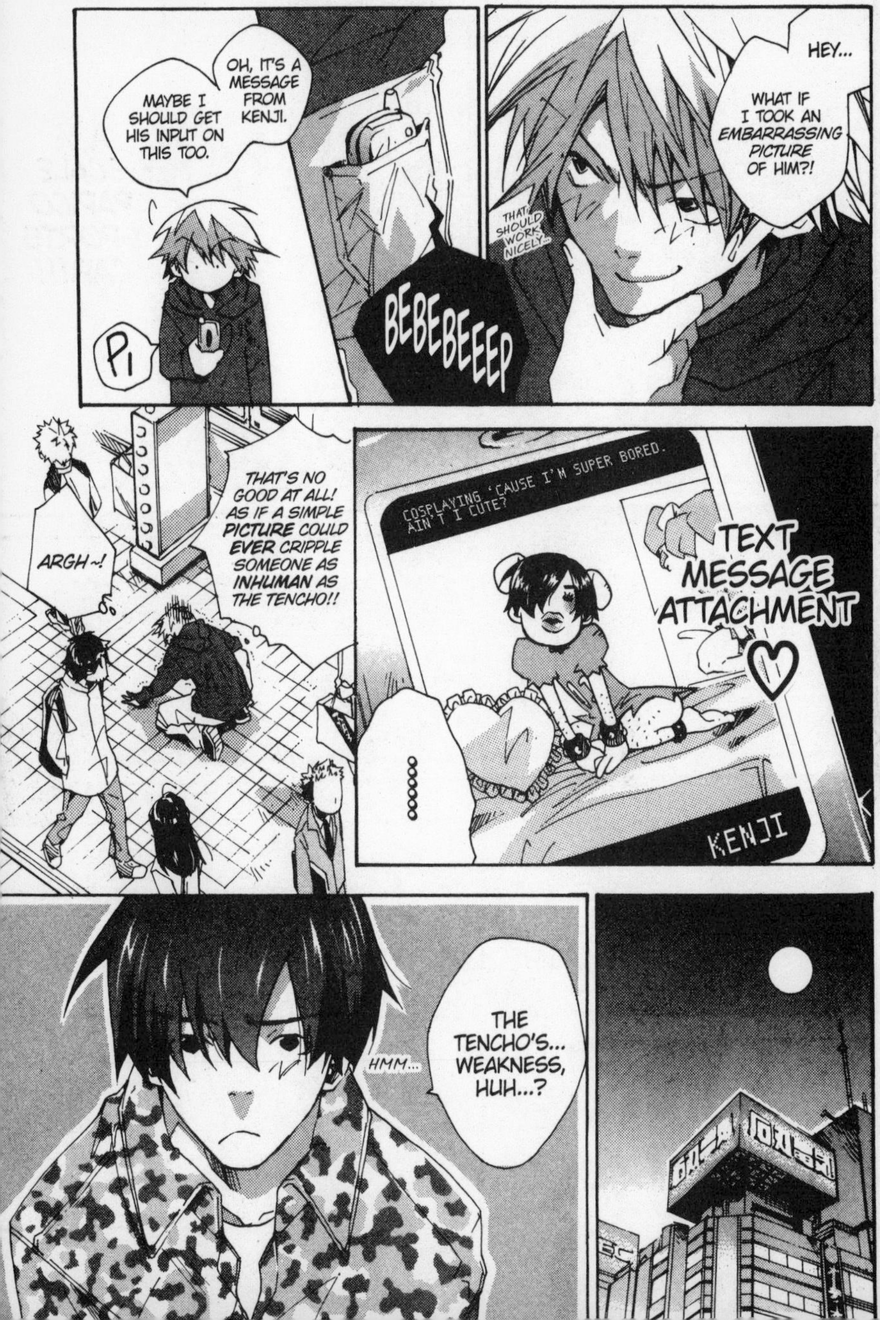
HEY...
WHAT IF I TOOK AN EMBARRASSING PICTURE OF HIM?!
THAT SHOULD WORK NICELY...
BEBEBEEEEP
OH, IT'S A MESSAGE FROM KENJI.
MAYBE I SHOULD GET HIS INPUT ON THIS TOO.
PI
COSPLAYING 'CAUSE I'M SUPER BORED. AIN'T I CUTE?
TEXT MESSAGE ATTACHMENT
KENJI
......
THAT'S NO GOOD AT ALL! AS IF A SIMPLE PICTURE COULD EVER CRIPPLE SOMEONE AS INHUMAN AS THE TENCHO!!
ARGH~!
THE TENCHO'S... WEAKNESS, HUH...?
HMM...

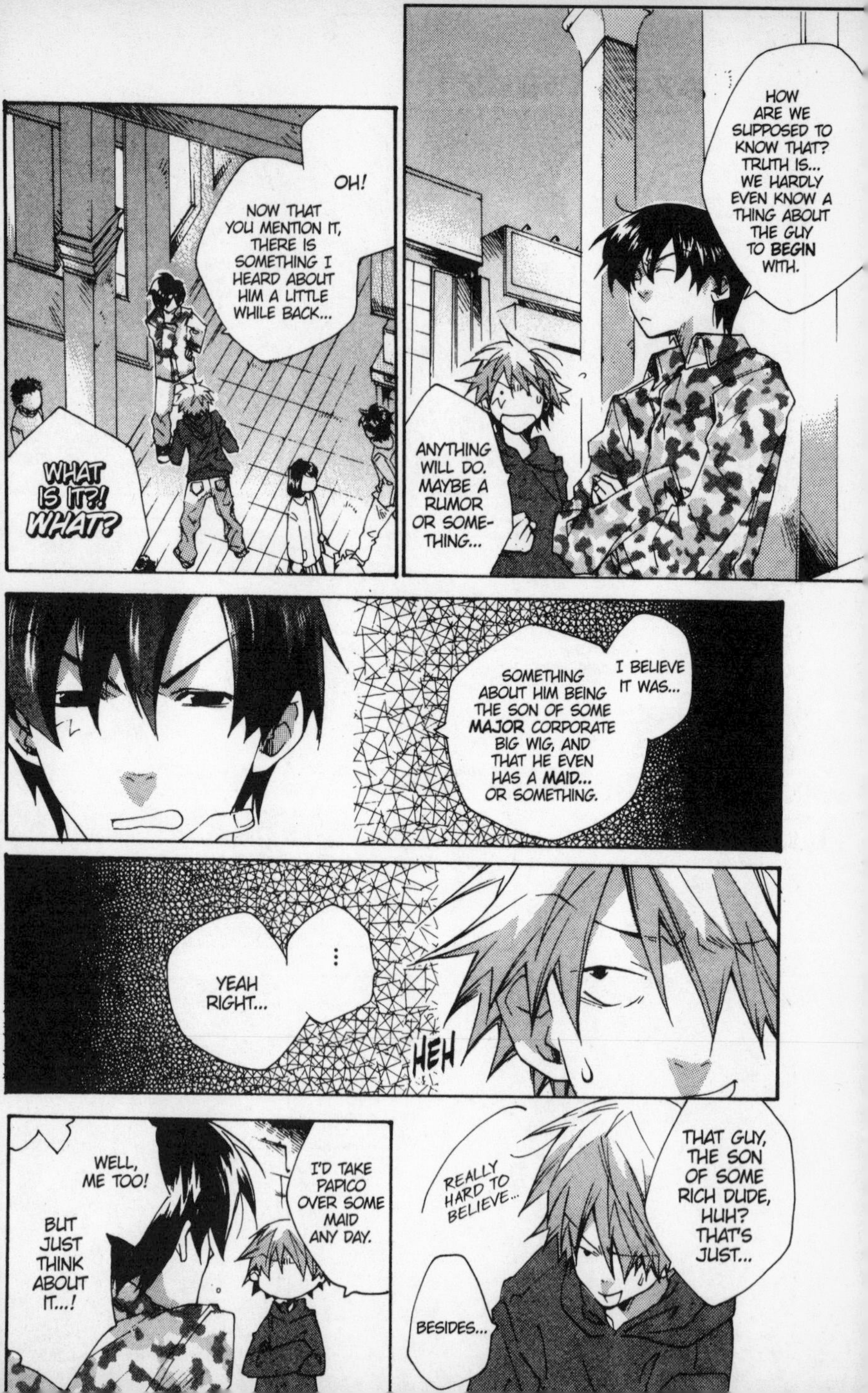
HOW ARE WE SUPPOSED TO KNOW THAT? TRUTH IS... WE HARDLY EVEN KNOW A THING ABOUT THE GUY TO BEGIN WITH.
ANYTHING WILL DO. MAYBE A RUMOR OR SOME-THING...
OH!
NOW THAT YOU MENTION IT, THERE IS SOMETHING I HEARD ABOUT HIM A LITTLE WHILE BACK...
WHAT IS IT?! WHAT?
I BELIEVE IT WAS...
SOMETHING ABOUT HIM BEING THE SON OF SOME MAJOR CORPORATE BIG WIG, AND THAT HE EVEN HAS A MAID... OR SOMETHING.
HEH
...
YEAH RIGHT...
THAT GUY, THE SON OF SOME RICH DUDE, HUH? THAT'S JUST...
REALLY HARD TO BELIEVE...
BESIDES...
I'D TAKE PAPICO OVER SOME MAID ANY DAY.
WELL, ME TOO!
BUT JUST THINK ABOUT IT...!

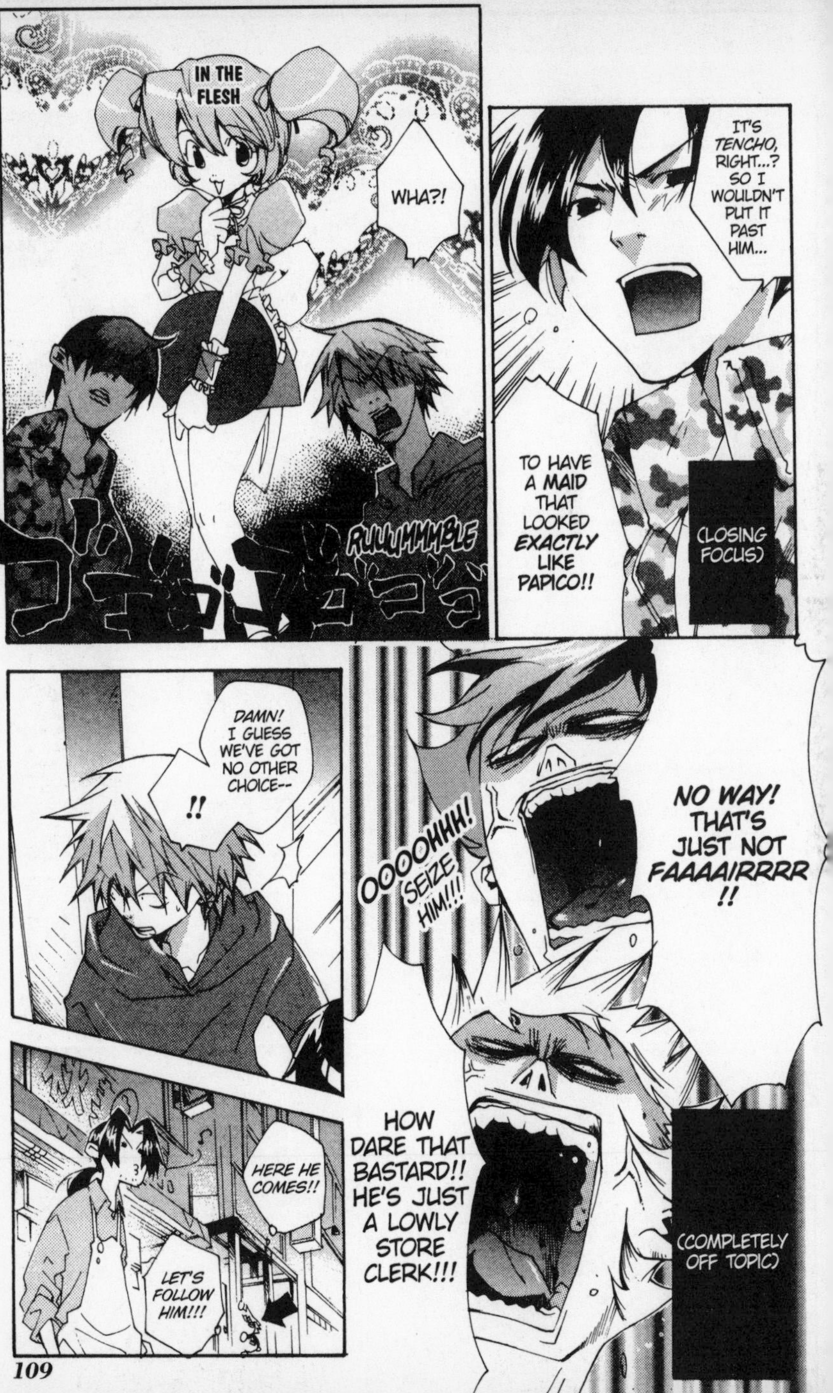
IT'S TENCHO, RIGHT...? SO I WOULDN'T PUT IT PAST HIM...
TO HAVE A MAID THAT LOOKED EXACTLY LIKE PAPICO!!
(LOSING FOCUS)
IN THE FLESH
WHA?!
RUUUMMMBLE
NO WAY! THAT'S JUST NOT FAAAAIRRRR!!
OOOOHHH! SEIZE HIM!!!
HOW DARE THAT BASTARD!! HE'S JUST A LOWLY STORE CLERK!!!
(COMPLETELY OFF TOPIC)
DAMN! I GUESS WE'VE GOT NO OTHER CHOICE--
!!
HERE HE COMES!!
LET'S FOLLOW HIM!!!

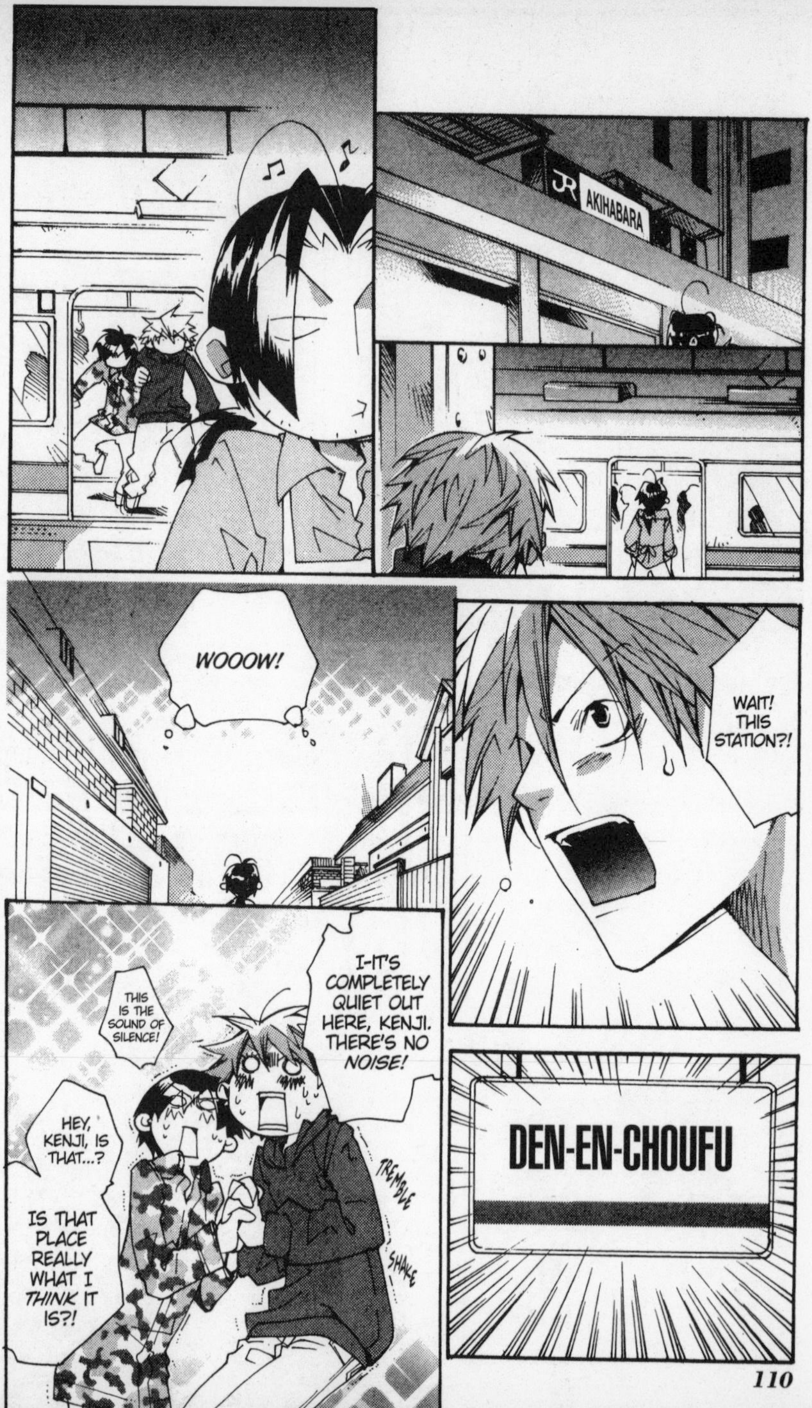
JR AKIHABARA
WAIT! THIS STATION?!
WOOOW!
DEN-EN-CHOUFU
I-IT'S COMPLETELY QUIET OUT HERE, KENJI. THERE'S NO *NOISE*!
THIS IS THE SOUND OF SILENCE!
TREMBLE
SHAKE
HEY, KENJI, IS THAT...?
IS THAT PLACE REALLY WHAT I *THINK* IT IS?!

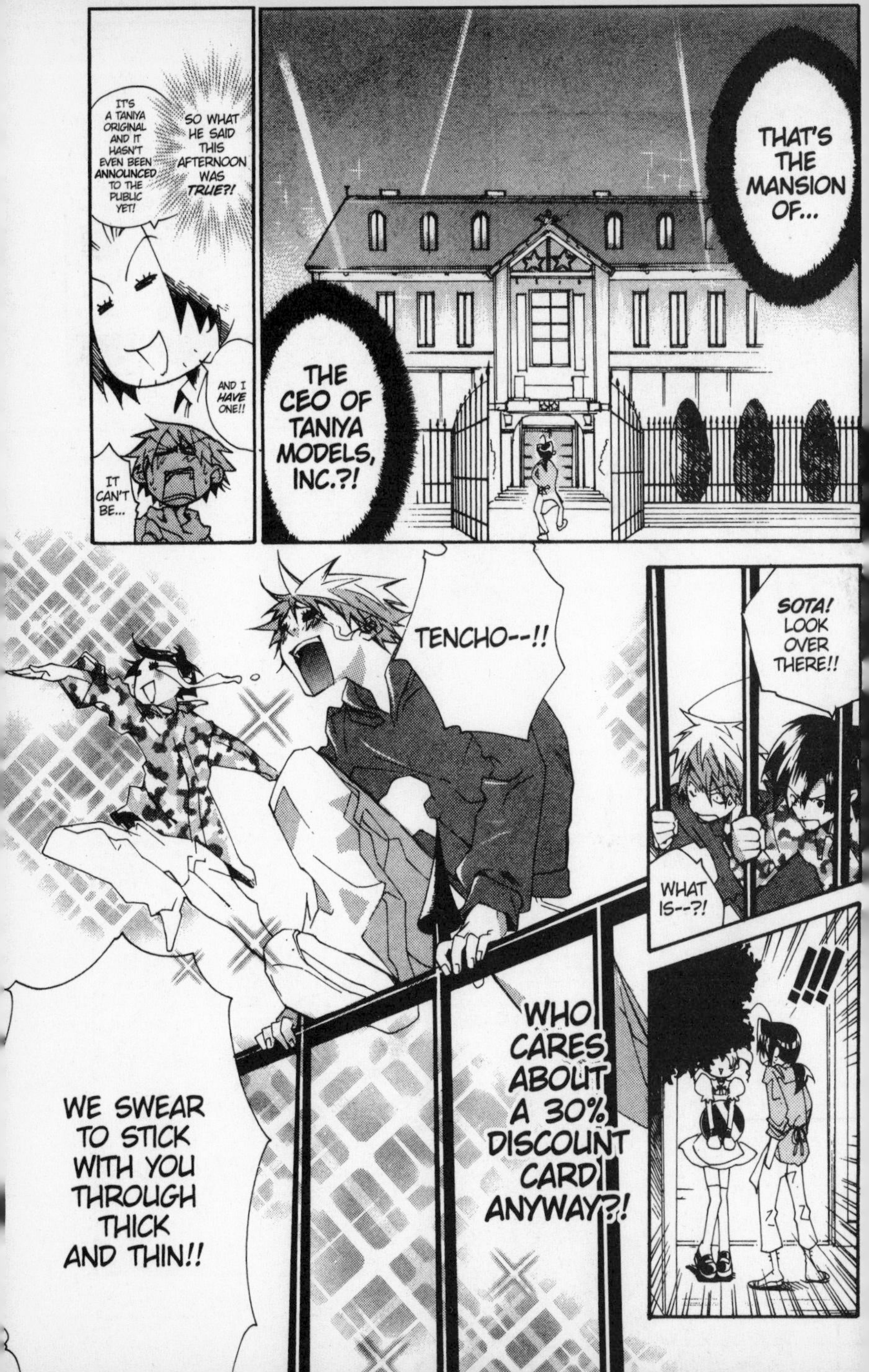
THAT'S THE MANSION OF...
THE CEO OF TANIYA MODELS, INC.?!
SO WHAT HE SAID THIS AFTERNOON WAS *TRUE?!*
IT'S A TANIYA ORIGINAL AND IT HASN'T EVEN BEEN ANNOUNCED TO THE PUBLIC YET!
AND I *HAVE* ONE!!
IT CAN'T BE...
SOTA! LOOK OVER THERE!!
WHAT IS--?!
!!!
TENCHO--!!
WHO CARES ABOUT A 30% DISCOUNT CARD ANYWAY?!
WE SWEAR TO STICK WITH YOU THROUGH THICK AND THIN!!

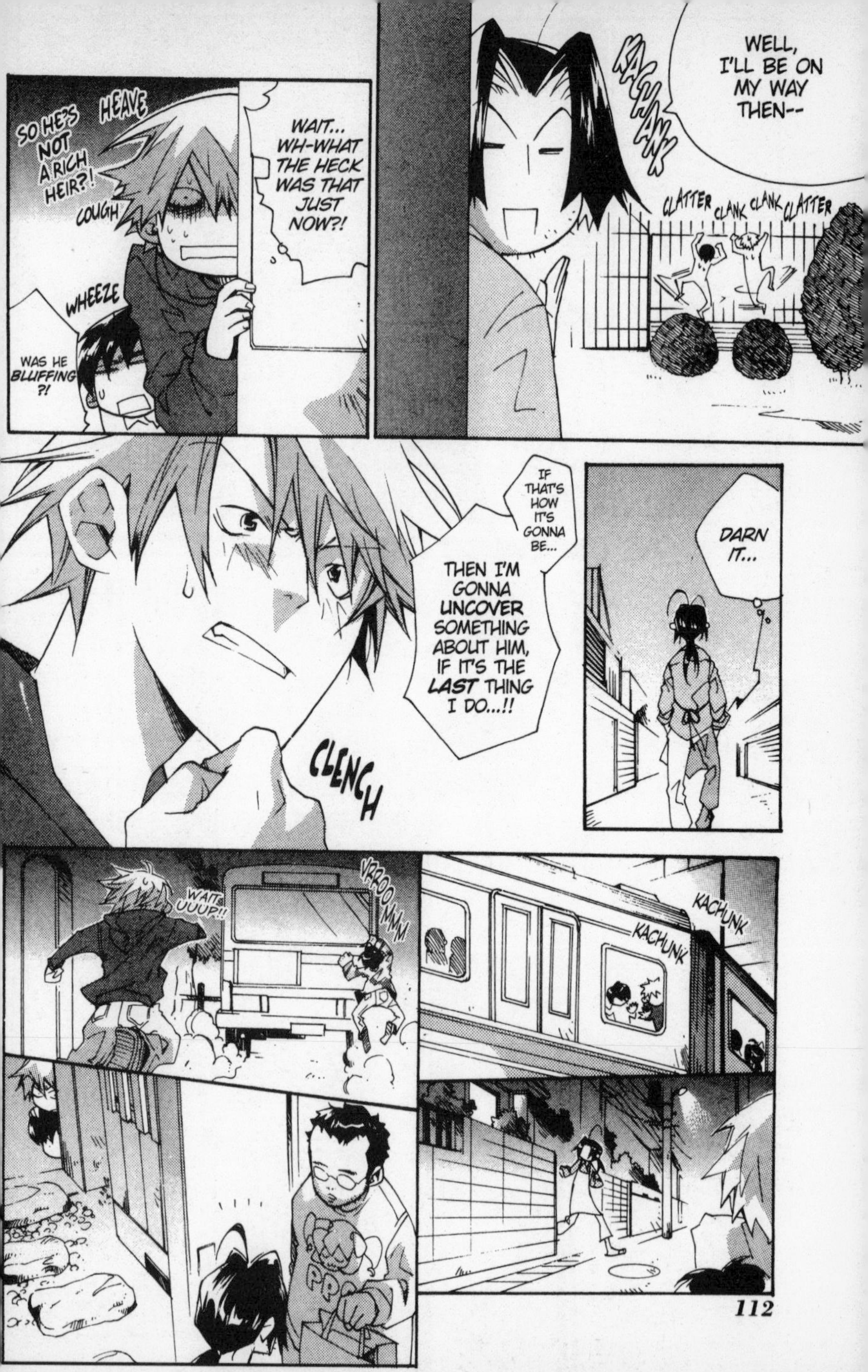
WELL, I'LL BE ON MY WAY THEN--
KACHANK
CLATTER CLANK CLANK CLATTER
WAIT... WH-WHAT THE HECK WAS THAT JUST NOW?!
HEAVE
SO HE'S NOT A RICH HEIR?!
COUGH
WHEEZE
WAS HE BLUFFING?!
DARN IT...
IF THAT'S HOW IT'S GONNA BE...
THEN I'M GONNA UNCOVER SOMETHING ABOUT HIM, IF IT'S THE LAST THING I DO...!!
CLENCH
KACHUNK
KACHUNK
VRROOMMM
WAIT UUUP!!

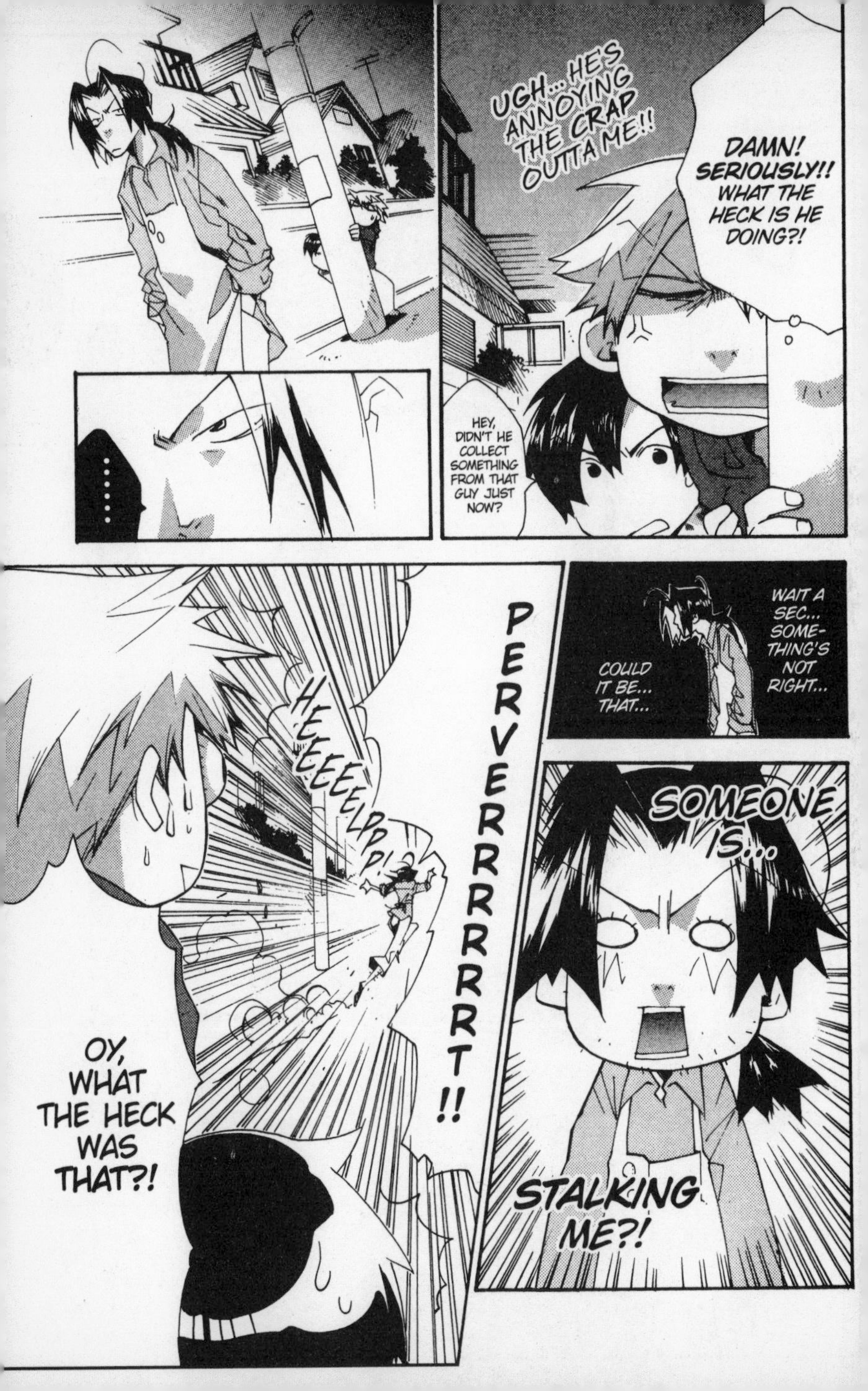
DAMN! SERIOUSLY!! WHAT THE HECK IS HE DOING?!
UGH... HE'S ANNOYING THE CRAP OUTTA ME!!
HEY, DIDN'T HE COLLECT SOMETHING FROM THAT GUY JUST NOW?
......
WAIT A SEC... SOMETHING'S NOT RIGHT...
COULD IT BE... THAT...
SOMEONE IS...
STALKING ME?!
PERVERRRRRRRT!!
HEEEEEELPP!
OY, WHAT THE HECK WAS THAT?!

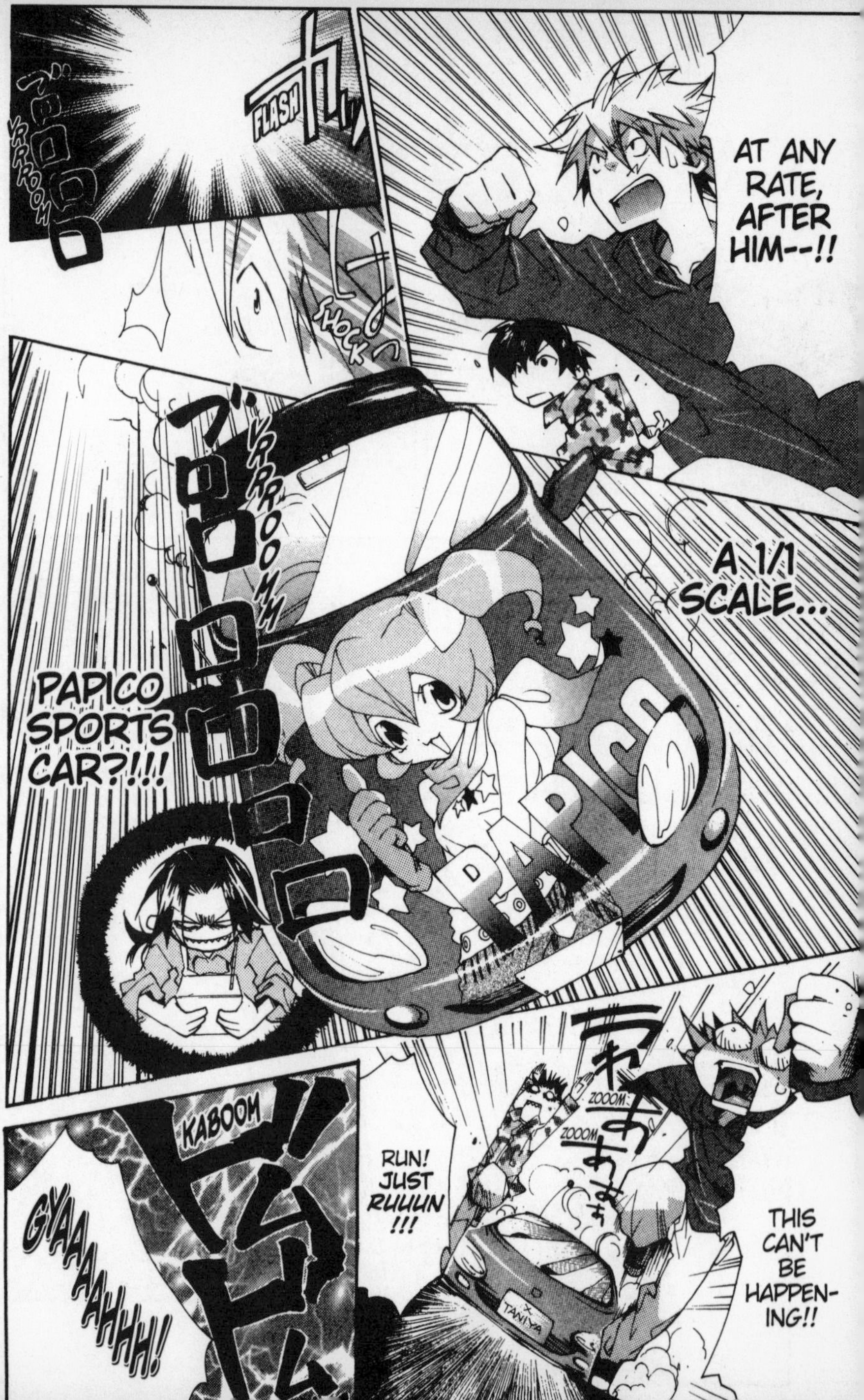
AT ANY RATE, AFTER HIM--!!
FLASH
VRRROOM
SHOCK
A 1/1 SCALE...
VRRROOOMMM
PAPICO SPORTS CAR?!!!
PAPICO
ZOOOM
ZOOOM
THIS CAN'T BE HAPPENING!!
RUN! JUST RUUUN!!!
TANIYA
KABOOM
GYAAAAAHHH!

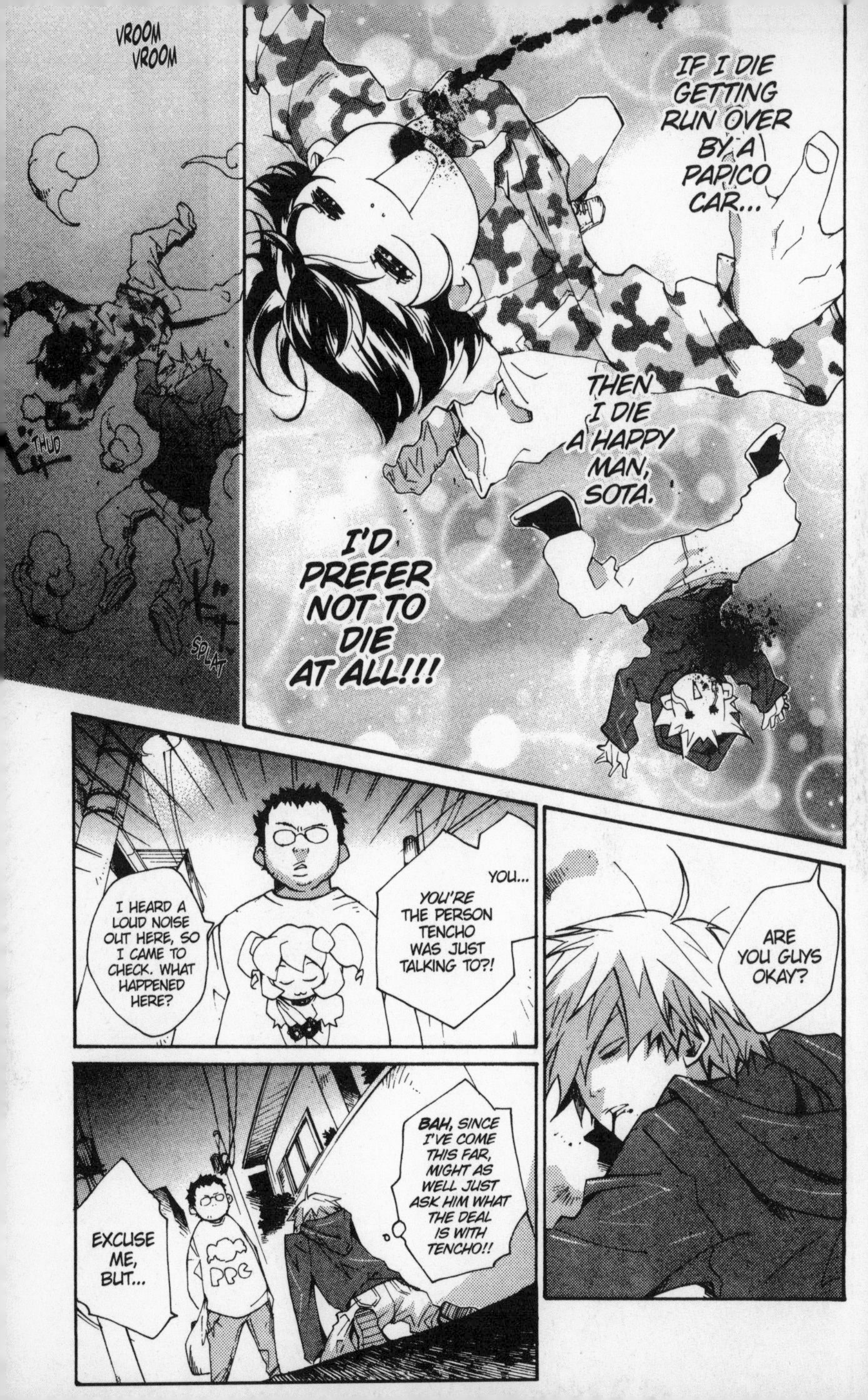
IF I DIE GETTING RUN OVER BY A PAPICO CAR...
THEN I DIE A HAPPY MAN, SOTA.
I'D PREFER NOT TO DIE AT ALL!!!
VROOM VROOM
THUD
SPLAT
ARE YOU GUYS OKAY?
YOU...
YOU'RE THE PERSON TENCHO WAS JUST TALKING TO?!
I HEARD A LOUD NOISE OUT HERE, SO I CAME TO CHECK. WHAT HAPPENED HERE?
BAH, SINCE I'VE COME THIS FAR, MIGHT AS WELL JUST ASK HIM WHAT THE DEAL IS WITH TENCHO!!
EXCUSE ME, BUT...

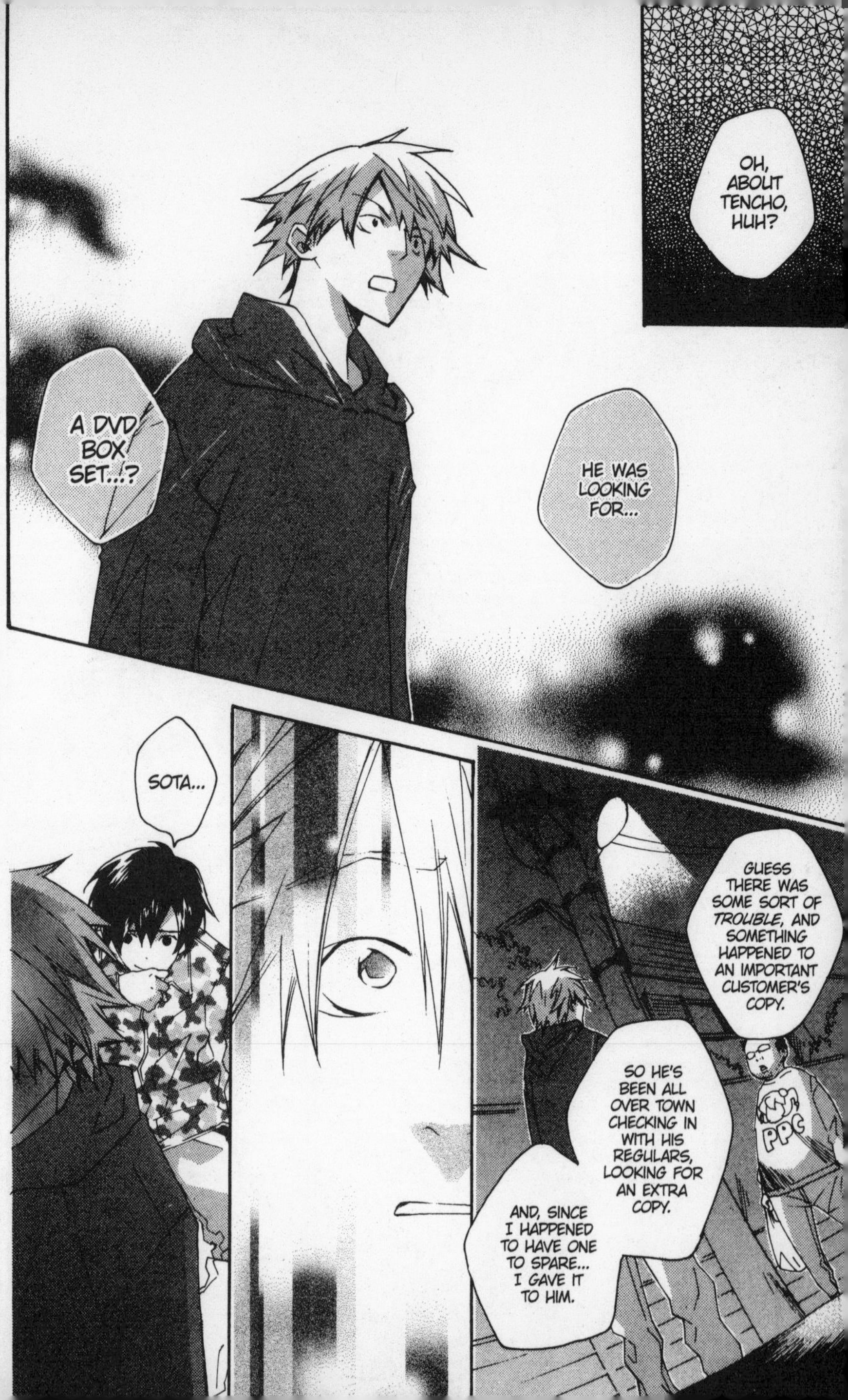
OH, ABOUT TENCHO, HUH?
HE WAS LOOKING FOR...
A DVD BOX SET...?
GUESS THERE WAS SOME SORT OF *TROUBLE*, AND SOMETHING HAPPENED TO AN IMPORTANT CUSTOMER'S COPY.
SO HE'S BEEN ALL OVER TOWN CHECKING IN WITH HIS REGULARS, LOOKING FOR AN EXTRA COPY.
AND, SINCE I HAPPENED TO HAVE ONE TO SPARE... I GAVE IT TO HIM.
PPC
SOTA...

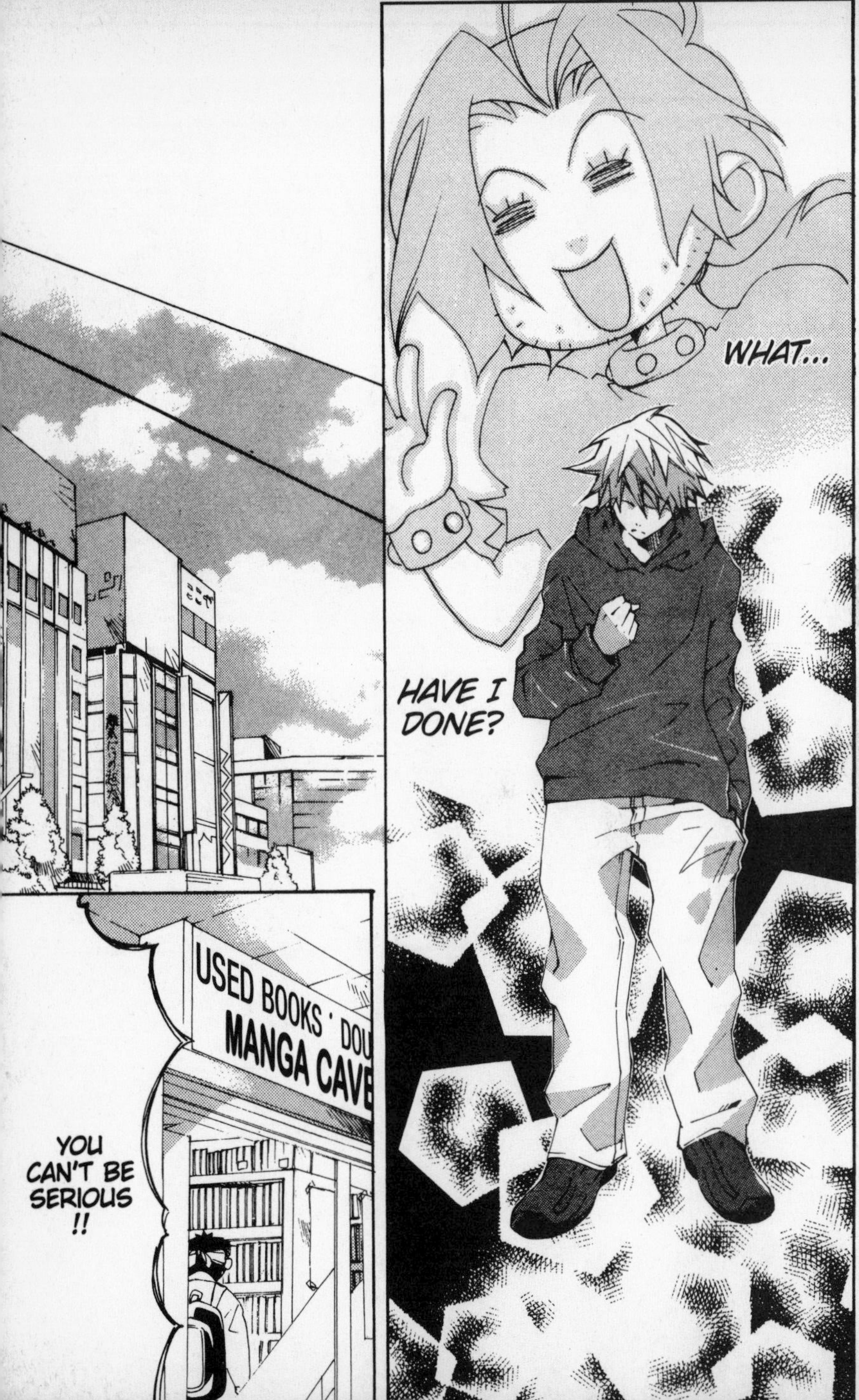
WHAT...
HAVE I DONE?
USED BOOKS ' DOU
MANGA CAVE
YOU CAN'T BE SERIOUS !!

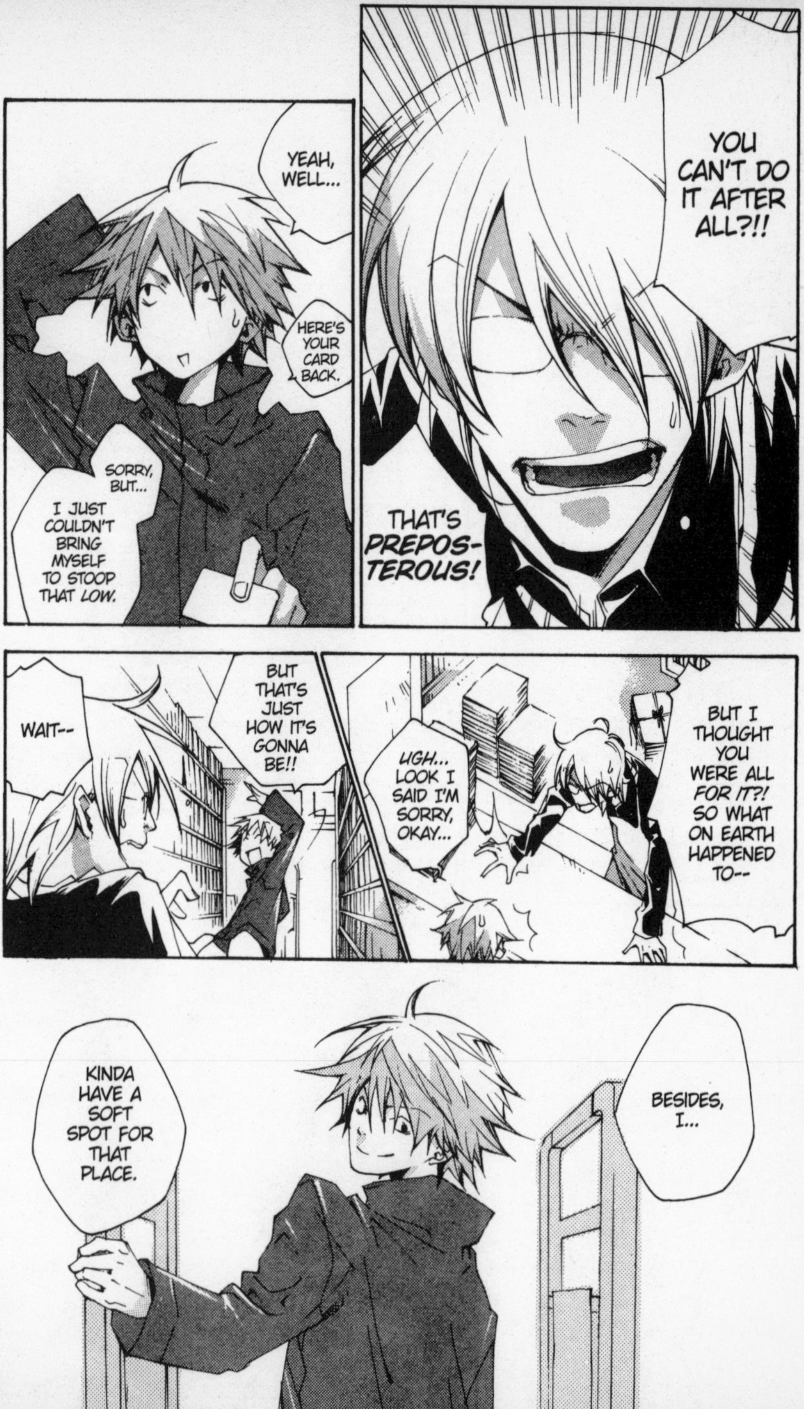

YOU CAN'T DO IT AFTER ALL?!!
THAT'S *PREPOSTEROUS!*
YEAH, WELL...
HERE'S YOUR CARD BACK.
SORRY, BUT...
I JUST COULDN'T BRING MYSELF TO STOOP THAT *LOW.*
BUT I THOUGHT YOU WERE ALL *FOR IT?!* SO WHAT ON EARTH HAPPENED TO--
UGH... LOOK I SAID I'M SORRY, OKAY...
BUT THAT'S JUST HOW IT'S GONNA BE!!
WAIT--
BESIDES, I...
KINDA HAVE A SOFT SPOT FOR THAT PLACE.

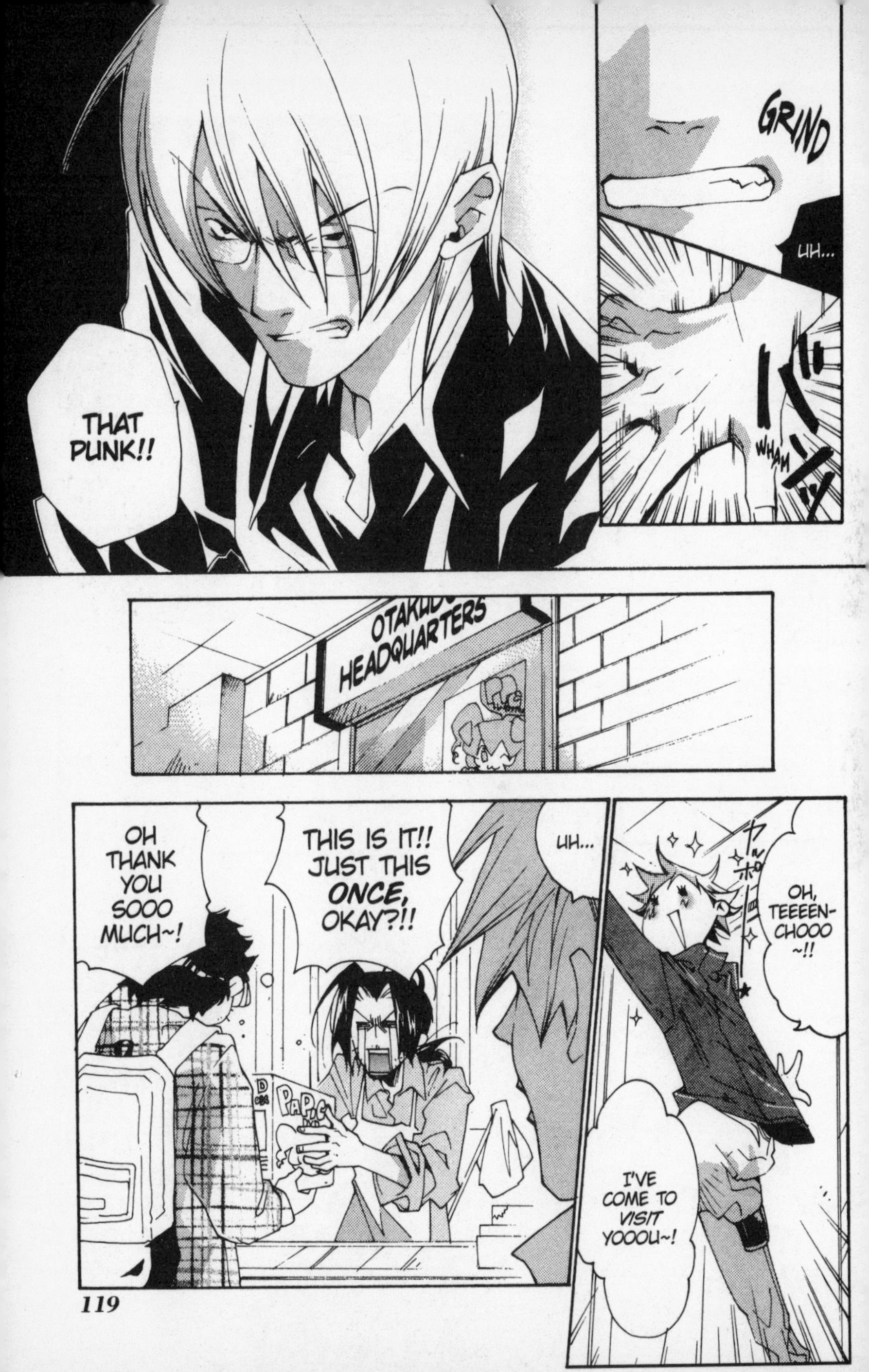
GRIND
UH...
WHAM
THAT PUNK!!
HEADQUARTERS
OH, TEEEEN-CHOOO~!!
I'VE COME TO VISIT YOOOU~!
UH...
THIS IS IT!! JUST THIS ONCE, OKAY?!!
OH THANK YOU SOOO MUCH~!

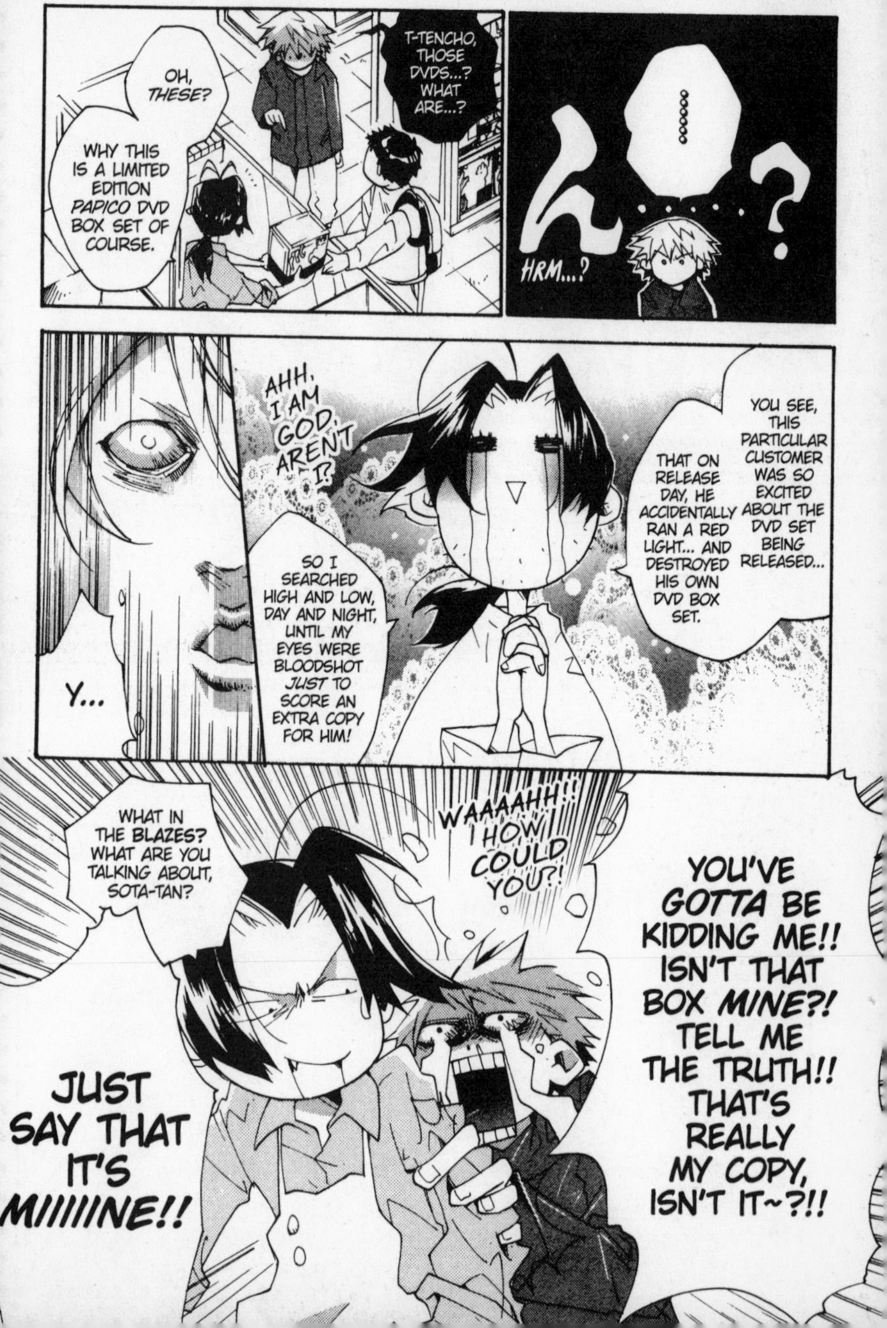

......
HRM...?
T-TENCHO, THOSE DVDS...? WHAT ARE...?
OH, *THESE?*
WHY THIS IS A LIMITED EDITION *PAPICO* DVD BOX SET OF COURSE.
YOU SEE, THIS PARTICULAR CUSTOMER WAS SO EXCITED ABOUT THE DVD SET BEING RELEASED...
THAT ON RELEASE DAY, HE ACCIDENTALLY RAN A RED LIGHT... AND DESTROYED HIS OWN DVD BOX SET.
AHH, I AM GOD, AREN'T I?
SO I SEARCHED HIGH AND LOW, DAY AND NIGHT, UNTIL MY EYES WERE BLOODSHOT *JUST* TO SCORE AN EXTRA COPY FOR HIM!
Y...
YOU'VE *GOTTA* BE KIDDING ME!! ISN'T THAT BOX *MINE?!* TELL ME THE TRUTH!! THAT'S REALLY MY COPY, ISN'T IT~?!!
WAAAAHH!! HOW COULD YOU?!
WHAT IN THE BLAZES? WHAT ARE YOU TALKING ABOUT, SOTA-TAN?
JUST SAY THAT IT'S *MIIIIINE!!*

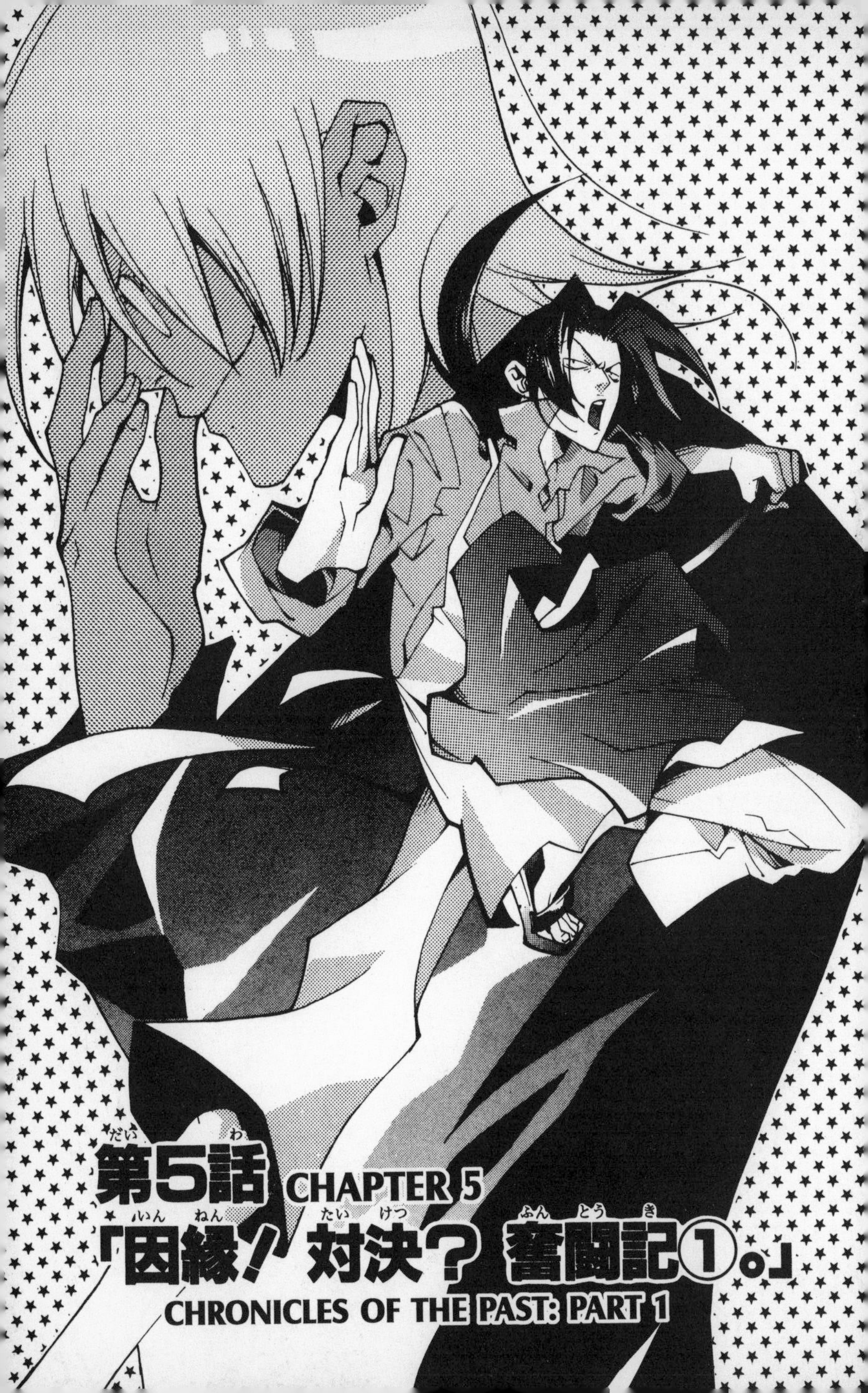

第5話 CHAPTER 5
「因縁！ 対決？ 奮闘記①。」
CHRONICLES OF THE PAST: PART 1

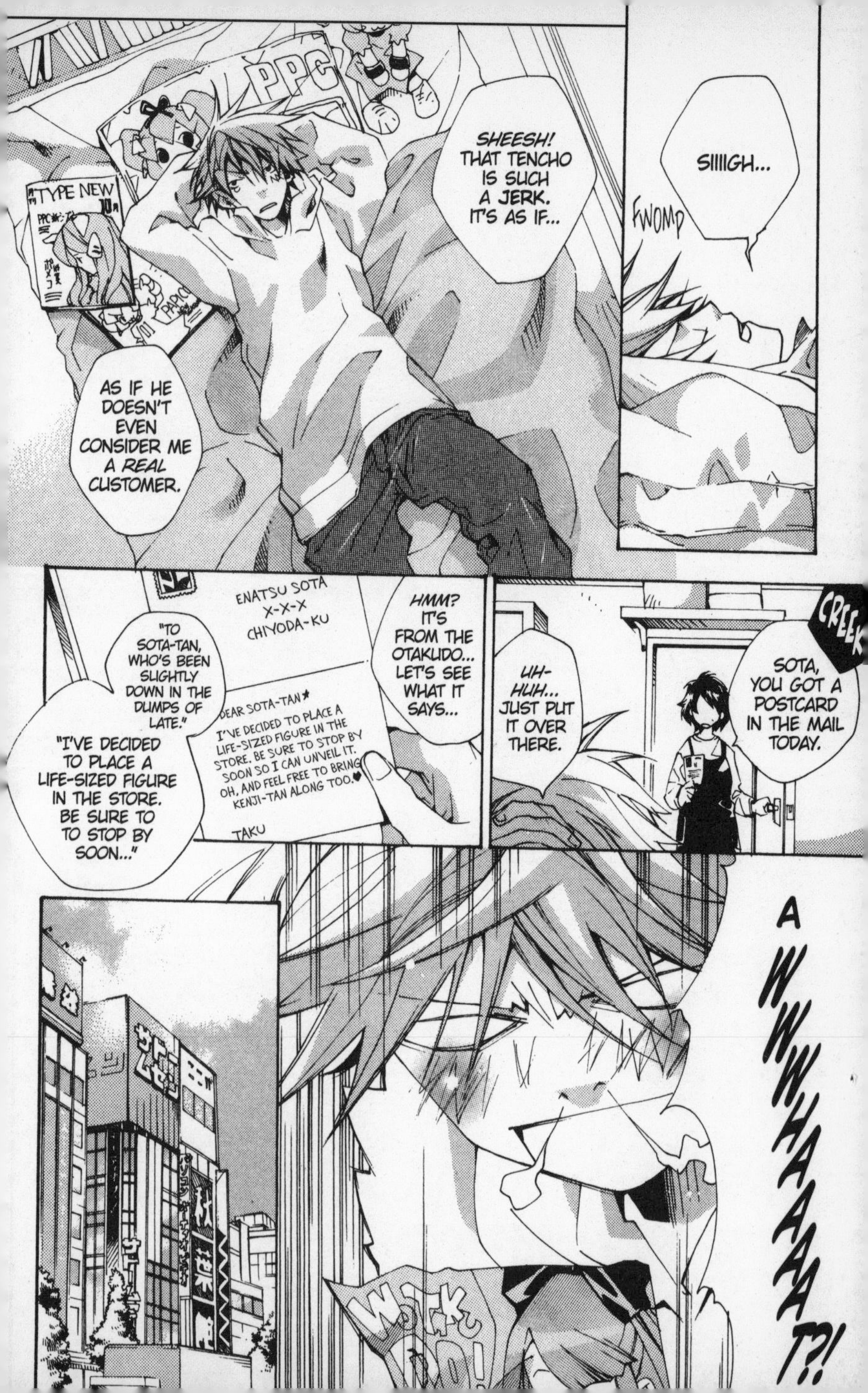
FWOMP
SIIIGH...
PPC
TYPE NEW
SHEESH! THAT TENCHO IS SUCH A JERK. IT'S AS IF...
AS IF HE DOESN'T EVEN CONSIDER ME A *REAL* CUSTOMER.
CREEK
SOTA, YOU GOT A POSTCARD IN THE MAIL TODAY.
UH-HUH... JUST PUT IT OVER THERE.
HMM? IT'S FROM THE OTAKUDO... LET'S SEE WHAT IT SAYS...
ENATSU SOTA X-X-X CHIYODA-KU
DEAR SOTA-TAN★ I'VE DECIDED TO PLACE A LIFE-SIZED FIGURE IN THE STORE. BE SURE TO STOP BY SOON SO I CAN UNVEIL IT. OH, AND FEEL FREE TO BRING KENJI-TAN ALONG TOO.♥
TAKU
"TO SOTA-TAN, WHO'S BEEN SLIGHTLY DOWN IN THE DUMPS OF LATE."
"I'VE DECIDED TO PLACE A LIFE-SIZED FIGURE IN THE STORE. BE SURE TO TO STOP BY SOON..."
AWWWHAAAAAT?!

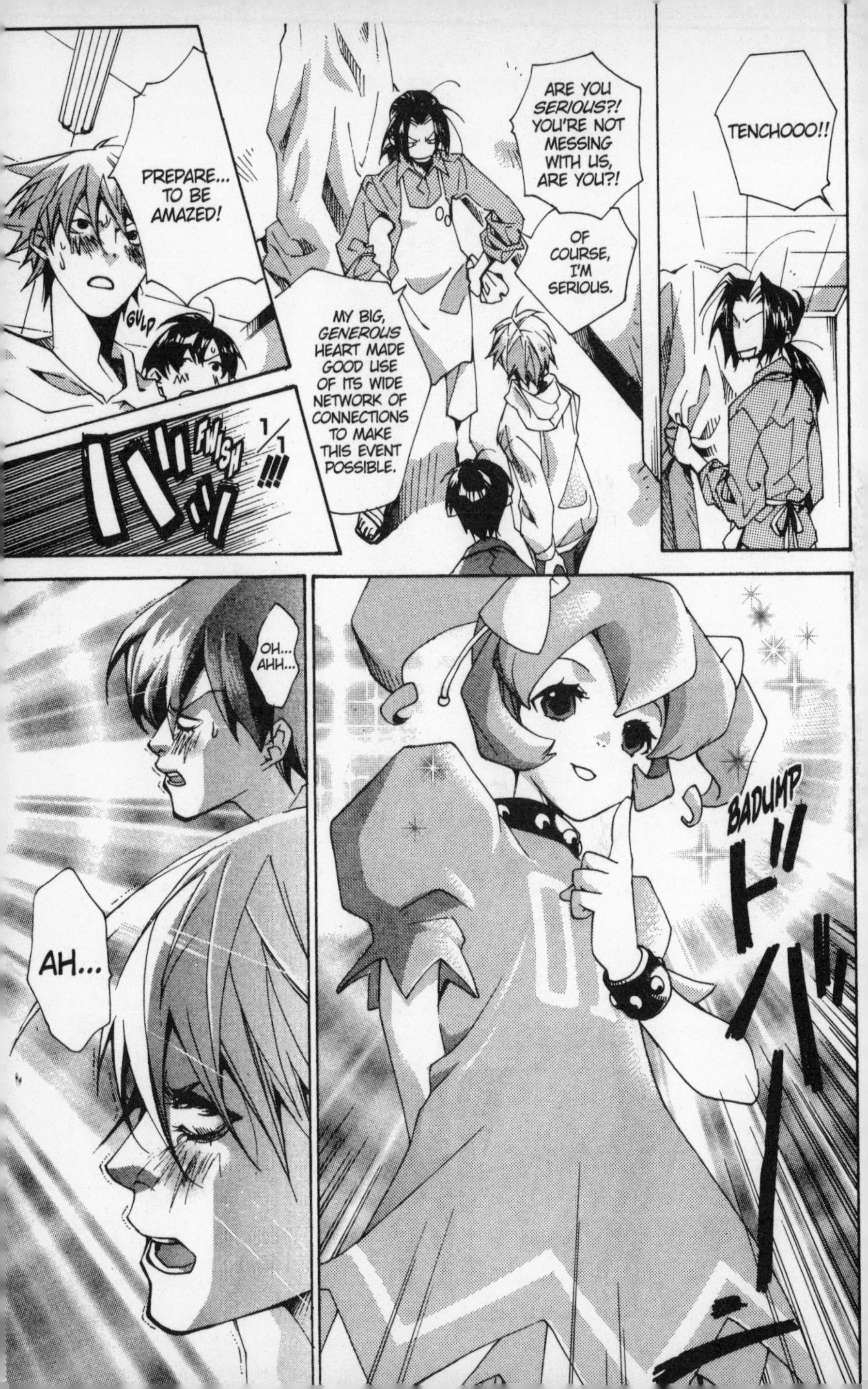
TENCHOOO!!
ARE YOU SERIOUS?! YOU'RE NOT MESSING WITH US, ARE YOU?!
OF COURSE, I'M SERIOUS.
MY BIG, GENEROUS HEART MADE GOOD USE OF ITS WIDE NETWORK OF CONNECTIONS TO MAKE THIS EVENT POSSIBLE.
PREPARE... TO BE AMAZED!
GULP
FWISH
BADUMP
OH... AHH...
AH...

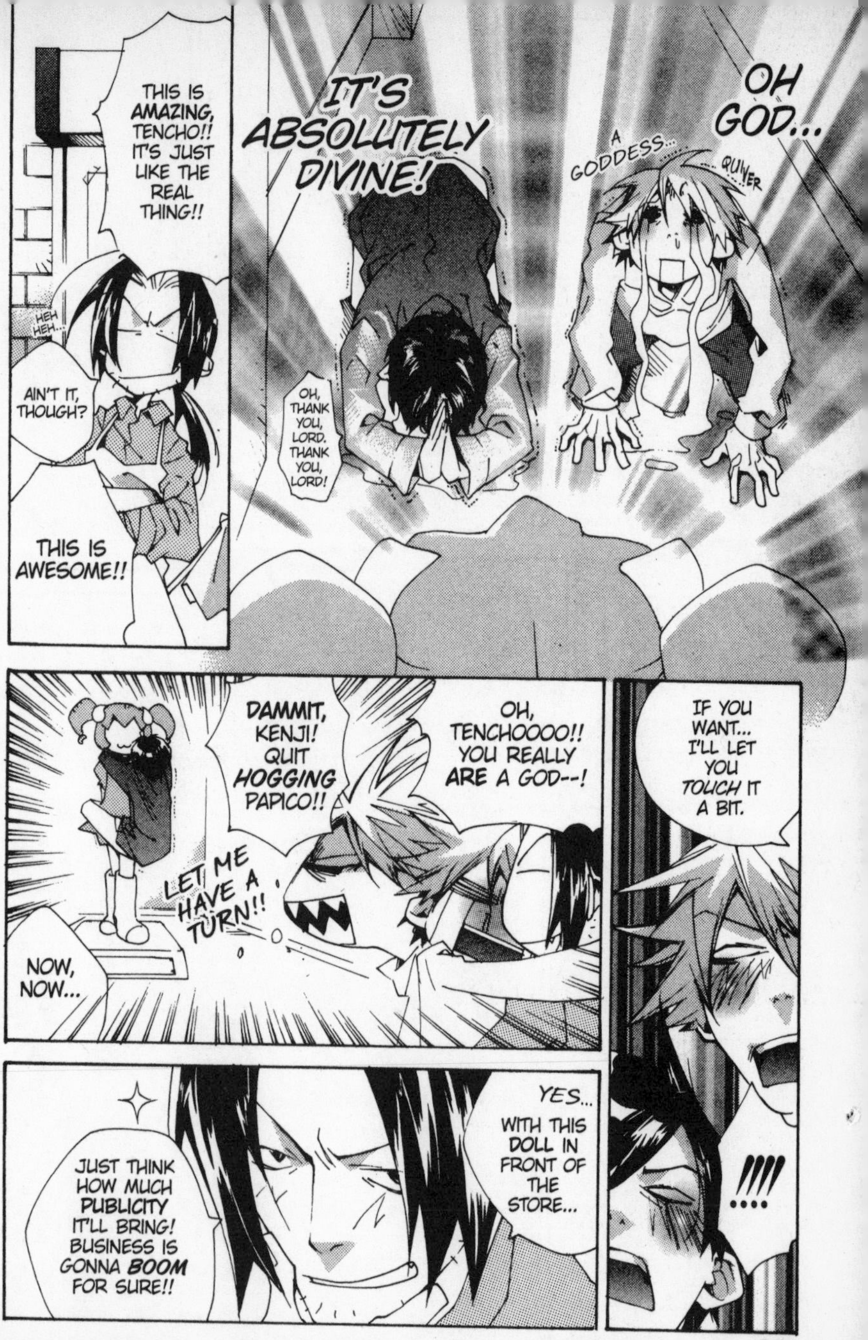
OH GOD...
A GODDESS...
QUIVER
IT'S ABSOLUTELY DIVINE!
OH, THANK YOU, LORD. THANK YOU, LORD!
THIS IS AMAZING, TENCHO!! IT'S JUST LIKE THE REAL THING!!
HEH HEH...
AIN'T IT, THOUGH?
THIS IS AWESOME!!
IF YOU WANT... I'LL LET YOU TOUCH IT A BIT.
!!!!....
OH, TENCHOOOO!! YOU REALLY ARE A GOD--!
DAMMIT, KENJI! QUIT HOGGING PAPICO!!
LET ME HAVE A TURN!!
NOW, NOW...
YES... WITH THIS DOLL IN FRONT OF THE STORE...
JUST THINK HOW MUCH PUBLICITY IT'LL BRING! BUSINESS IS GONNA BOOM FOR SURE!!

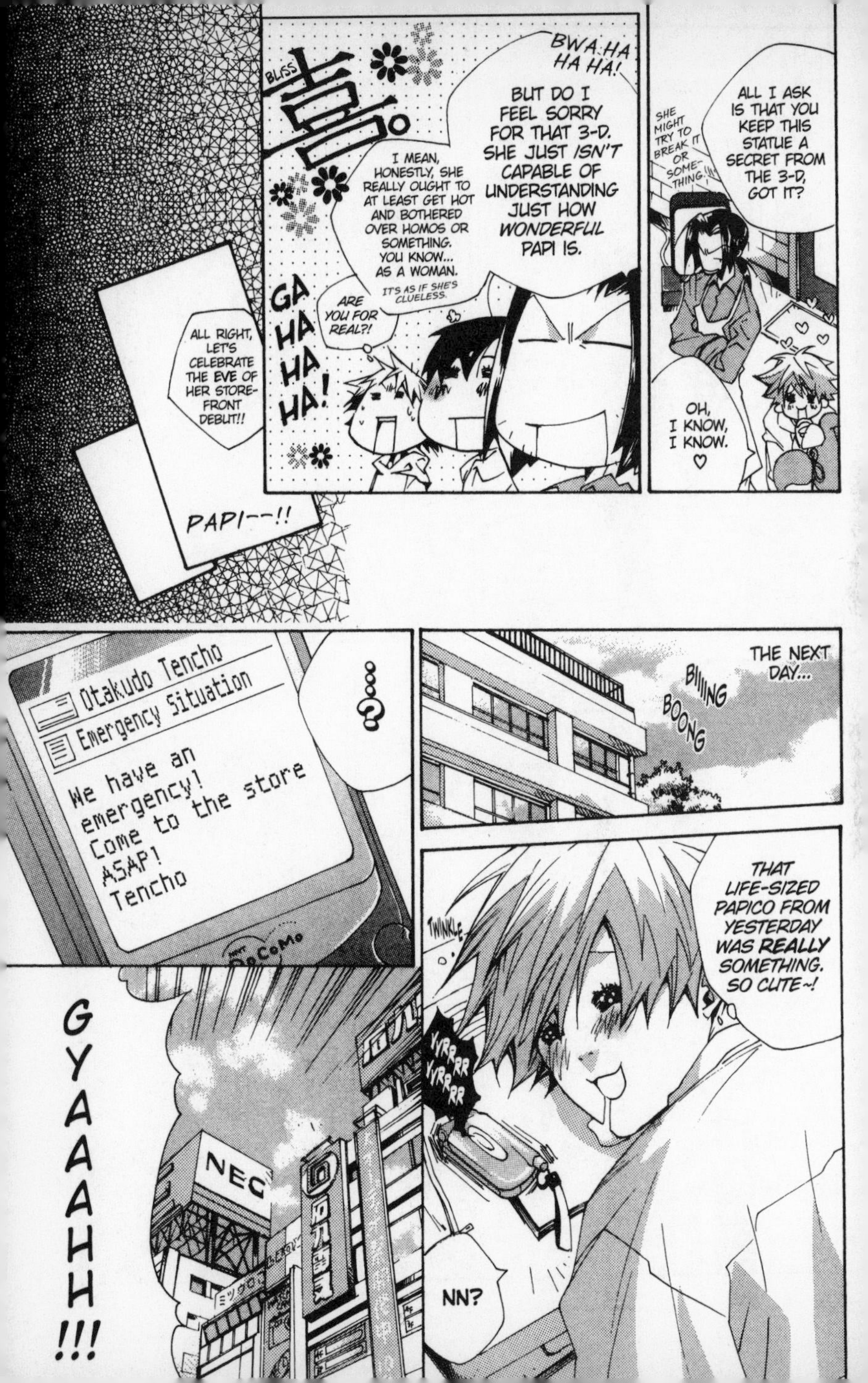
ALL I ASK IS THAT YOU KEEP THIS STATUE A SECRET FROM THE 3-D, GOT IT?
SHE MIGHT TRY TO BREAK IT OR SOMETHING!!
OH, I KNOW, I KNOW. ♡
BWA HA HA HA!
BUT DO I FEEL SORRY FOR THAT 3-D. SHE JUST *ISN'T* CAPABLE OF UNDERSTANDING JUST HOW *WONDERFUL* PAPI IS.
BLISS
I MEAN, HONESTLY, SHE REALLY OUGHT TO AT LEAST GET HOT AND BOTHERED OVER HOMOS OR SOMETHING. YOU KNOW... AS A WOMAN.
IT'S AS IF SHE'S CLUELESS.
GA HA HA HA!
ARE YOU FOR REAL?!
ALL RIGHT, LET'S CELEBRATE THE EVE OF HER STORE-FRONT DEBUT!!
PAPI--!!
THE NEXT DAY...
BIIIING BOONG
TWINKLE
THAT LIFE-SIZED PAPICO FROM YESTERDAY WAS REALLY SOMETHING. SO CUTE~!
VVRRRR VVRRRR
NN?
Otakudo Tencho
Emergency Situation
We have an emergency! Come to the store ASAP! Tencho
...?
DoCoMo
NEC
GYAAAAHH!!!

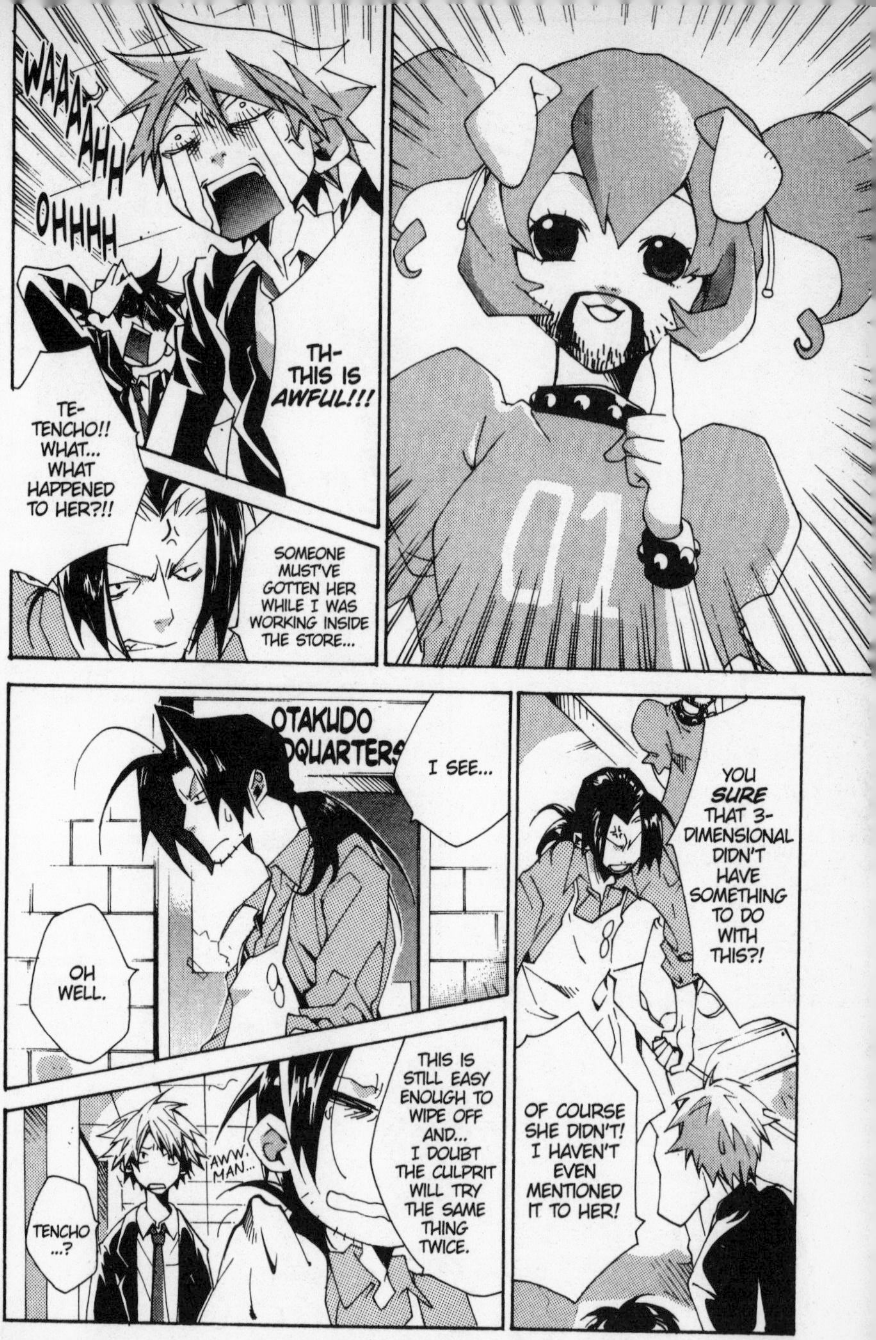
WAAAAAHHH OHHHH
TH- THIS IS AWFUL!!!
TE- TENCHO!! WHAT... WHAT HAPPENED TO HER?!!
SOMEONE MUST'VE GOTTEN HER WHILE I WAS WORKING INSIDE THE STORE...
YOU SURE THAT 3-DIMENSIONAL DIDN'T HAVE SOMETHING TO DO WITH THIS?!
OF COURSE SHE DIDN'T! I HAVEN'T EVEN MENTIONED IT TO HER!
OTAKUDO
DQUARTERS
I SEE...
OH WELL.
THIS IS STILL EASY ENOUGH TO WIPE OFF AND... I DOUBT THE CULPRIT WILL TRY THE SAME THING TWICE.
AWW. MAN...
TENCHO ...?

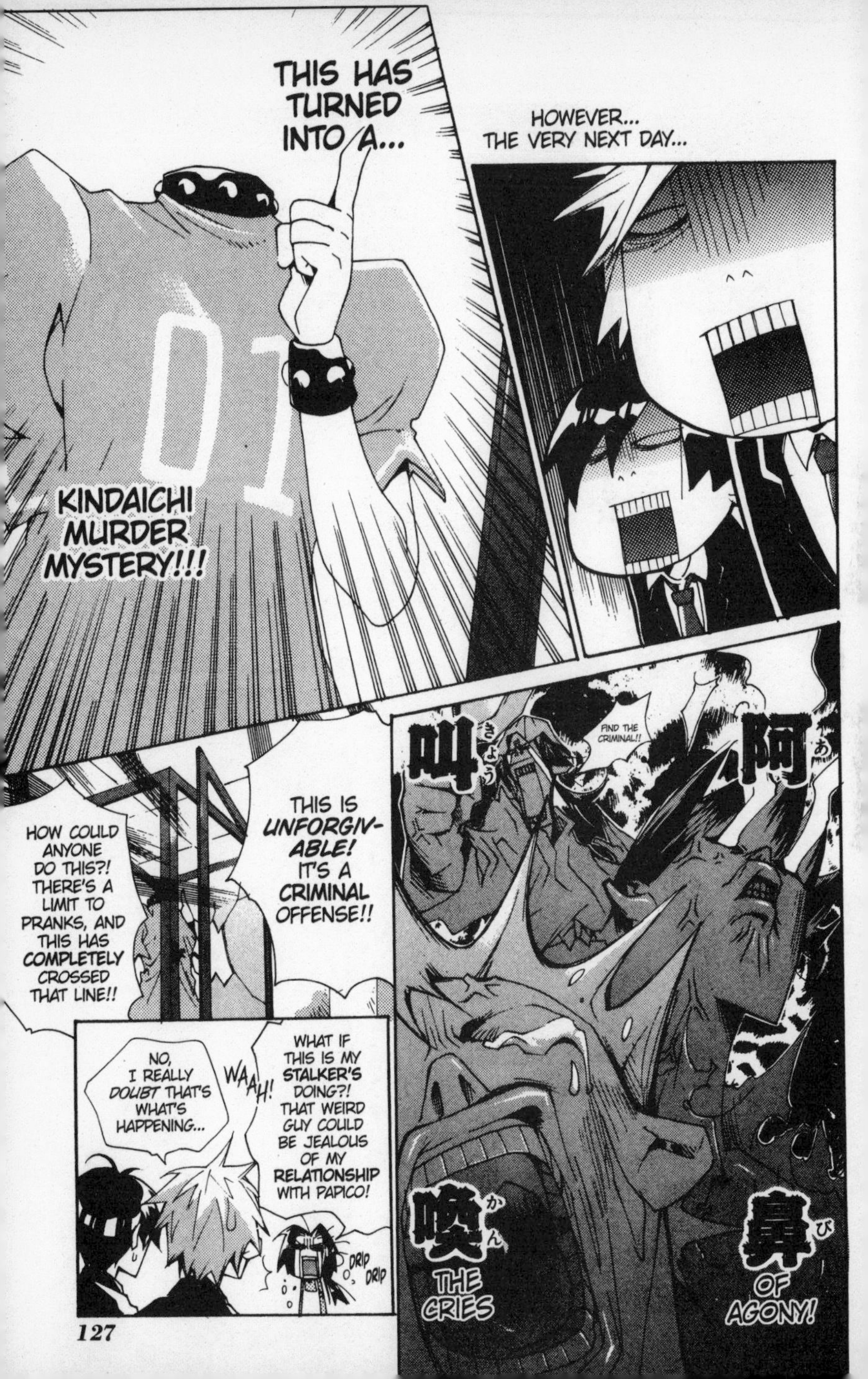
HOWEVER... THE VERY NEXT DAY...
THIS HAS TURNED INTO A...
KINDAICHI MURDER MYSTERY!!!
FIND THE CRIMINAL!!
阿(あ)鼻(び)叫(きょう)喚(かん)
THE CRIES OF AGONY!
THIS IS *UNFORGIVABLE!* IT'S A CRIMINAL OFFENSE!!
HOW COULD ANYONE DO THIS?! THERE'S A LIMIT TO PRANKS, AND THIS HAS COMPLETELY CROSSED THAT LINE!!
WHAT IF THIS IS MY STALKER'S DOING?! THAT WEIRD GUY COULD BE JEALOUS OF MY RELATIONSHIP WITH PAPICO!
WAAH!
DRIP DRIP
NO, I REALLY *DOUBT* THAT'S WHAT'S HAPPENING...

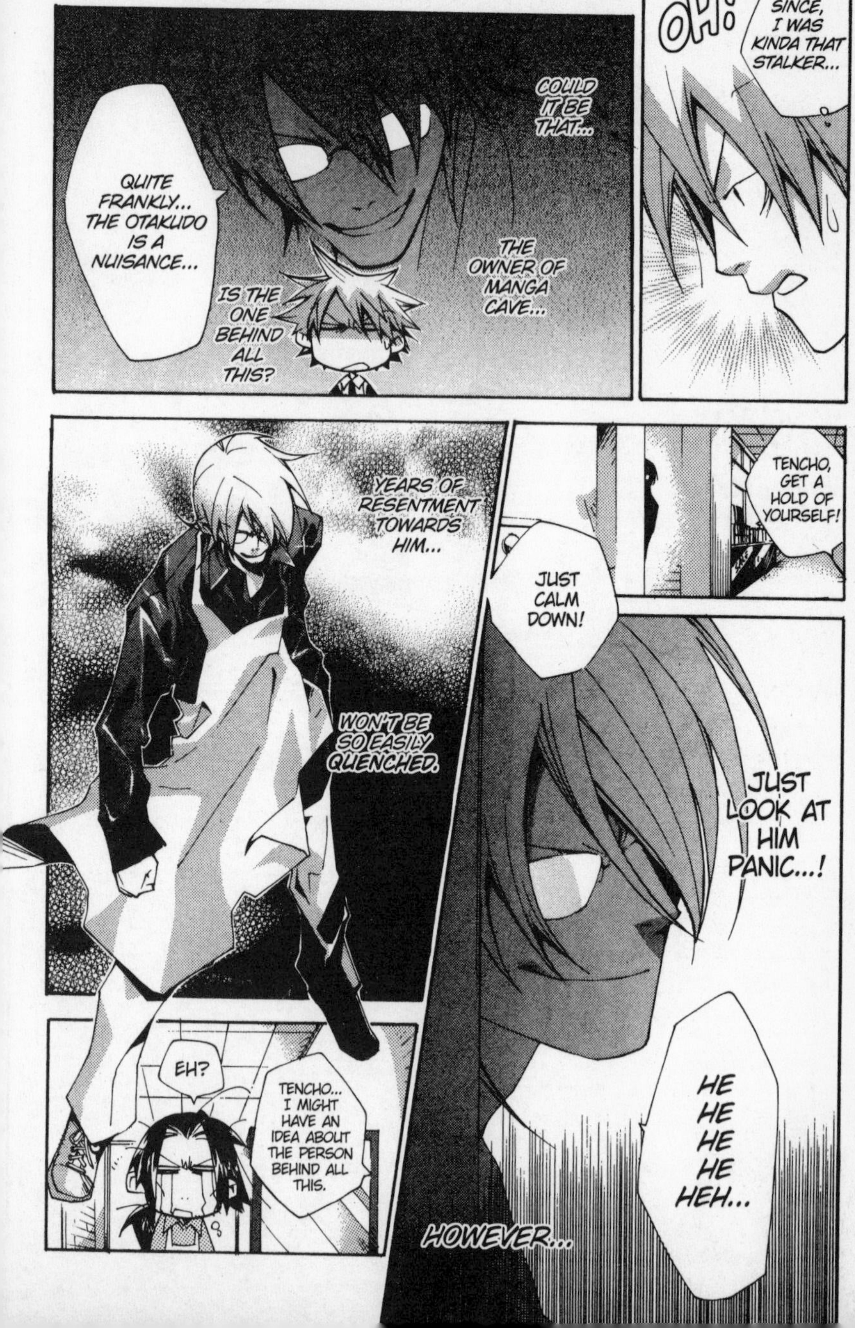
OH!
SINCE, I WAS KINDA THAT STALKER...
COULD IT BE THAT...
THE OWNER OF MANGA CAVE...
IS THE ONE BEHIND ALL THIS?
QUITE FRANKLY... THE OTAKUDO IS A NUISANCE...
TENCHO, GET A HOLD OF YOURSELF!
JUST CALM DOWN!
JUST LOOK AT HIM PANIC...!
HE HE HE HE HEH...
HOWEVER...
YEARS OF RESENTMENT TOWARDS HIM...
WON'T BE SO EASILY QUENCHED.
TENCHO... I MIGHT HAVE AN IDEA ABOUT THE PERSON BEHIND ALL THIS.
EH?

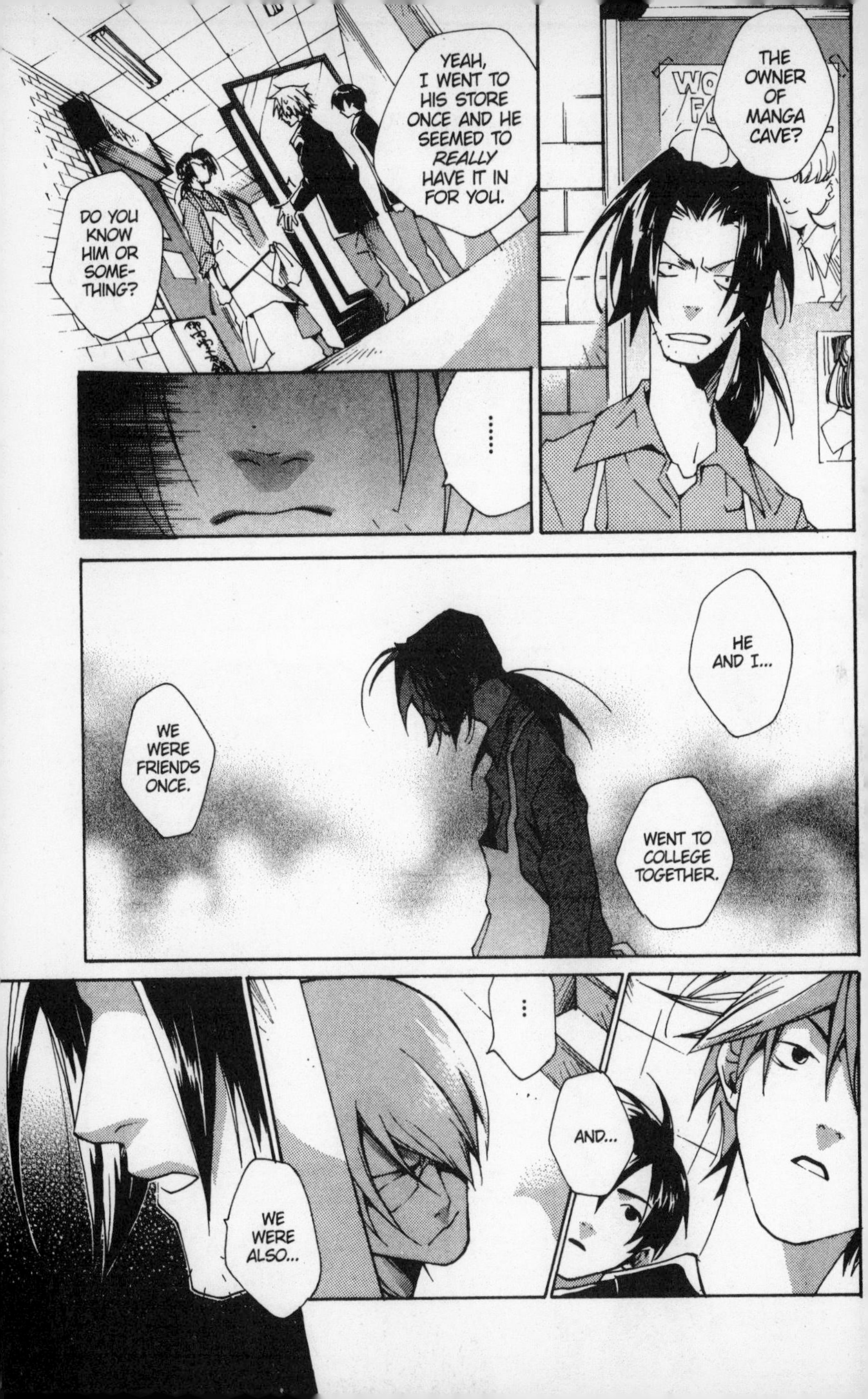
THE OWNER OF MANGA CAVE?
YEAH, I WENT TO HIS STORE ONCE AND HE SEEMED TO *REALLY* HAVE IT IN FOR YOU.
DO YOU KNOW HIM OR SOME-THING?
......
HE AND I...
WENT TO COLLEGE TOGETHER.
WE WERE FRIENDS ONCE.
AND...
...
WE WERE ALSO...

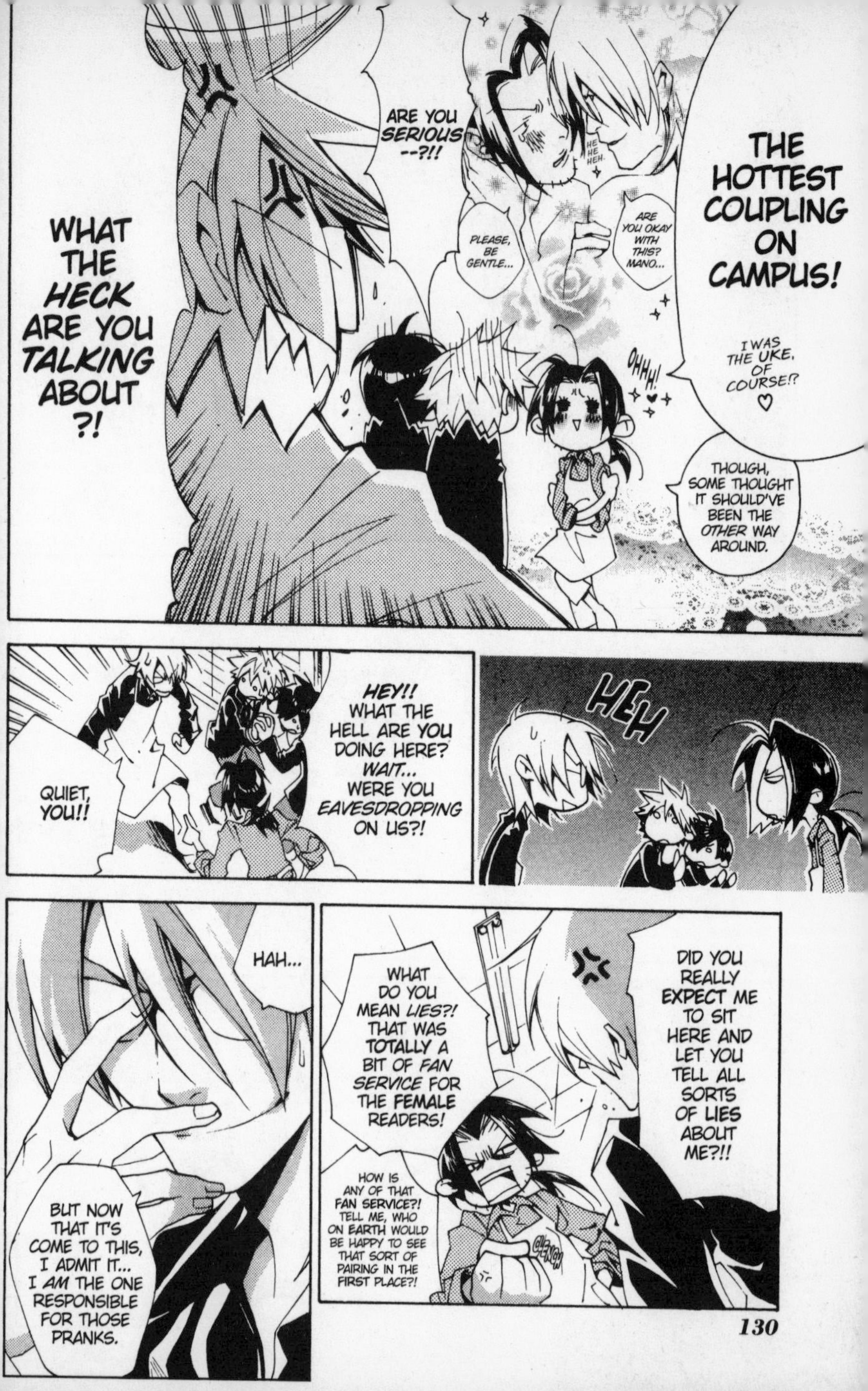
THE HOTTEST COUPLING ON CAMPUS!
ARE YOU OKAY WITH THIS? MANO...
HE HE HEH.
PLEASE, BE GENTLE...
ARE YOU SERIOUS--?!!
I WAS THE UKE, OF COURSE!?
OHHH!
THOUGH, SOME THOUGHT IT SHOULD'VE BEEN THE OTHER WAY AROUND.
WHAT THE HECK ARE YOU TALKING ABOUT ?!
HEH
HEY!! WHAT THE HELL ARE YOU DOING HERE? WAIT... WERE YOU EAVESDROPPING ON US?!
QUIET, YOU!!
DID YOU REALLY EXPECT ME TO SIT HERE AND LET YOU TELL ALL SORTS OF LIES ABOUT ME?!!
WHAT DO YOU MEAN LIES?! THAT WAS TOTALLY A BIT OF FAN SERVICE FOR THE FEMALE READERS!
HOW IS ANY OF THAT FAN SERVICE?! TELL ME, WHO ON EARTH WOULD BE HAPPY TO SEE THAT SORT OF PAIRING IN THE FIRST PLACE?!
CLENCH
HAH...
BUT NOW THAT IT'S COME TO THIS, I ADMIT IT... I AM THE ONE RESPONSIBLE FOR THOSE PRANKS.

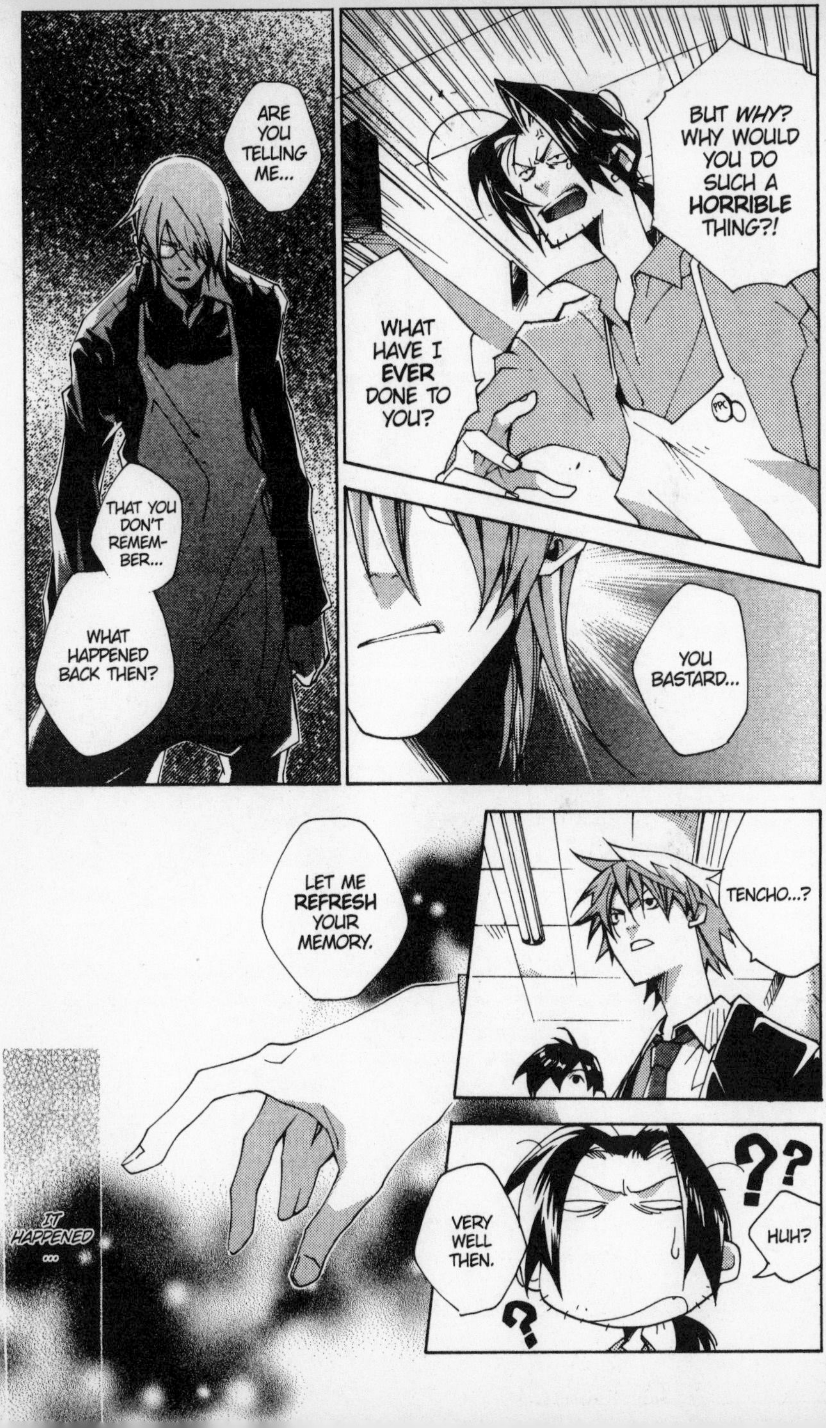
BUT WHY? WHY WOULD YOU DO SUCH A HORRIBLE THING?!
WHAT HAVE I EVER DONE TO YOU?
YOU BASTARD...
ARE YOU TELLING ME...
THAT YOU DON'T REMEMBER...
WHAT HAPPENED BACK THEN?
TENCHO...?
HUH?
VERY WELL THEN.
LET ME REFRESH YOUR MEMORY.
IT HAPPENED...

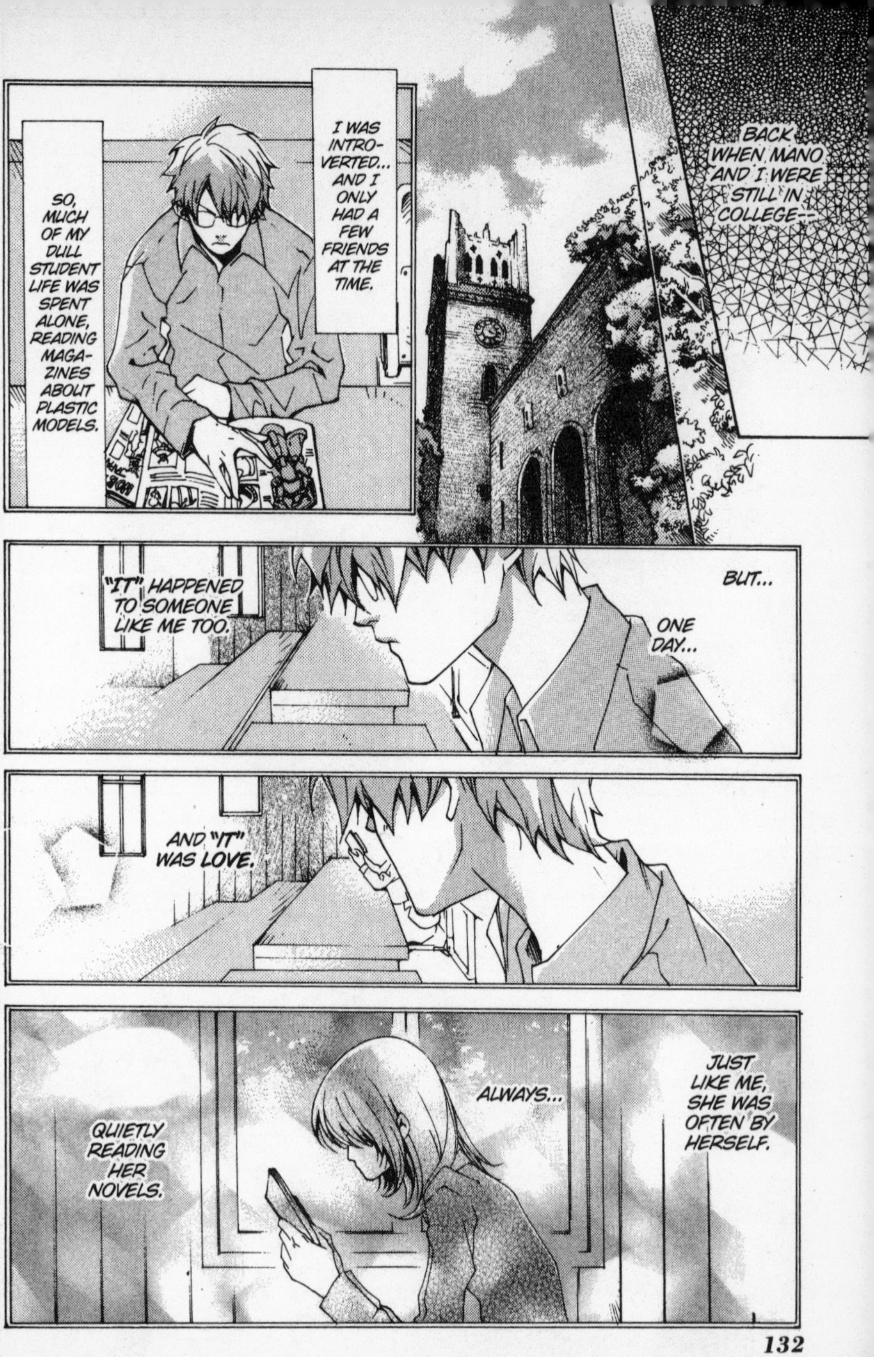
BACK WHEN MANO AND I WERE STILL IN COLLEGE--
I WAS INTROVERTED... AND I ONLY HAD A FEW FRIENDS AT THE TIME.
SO, MUCH OF MY DULL STUDENT LIFE WAS SPENT ALONE, READING MAGAZINES ABOUT PLASTIC MODELS.
BUT...
ONE DAY...
"IT" HAPPENED TO SOMEONE LIKE ME TOO.
AND "IT" WAS LOVE.
JUST LIKE ME, SHE WAS OFTEN BY HERSELF.
ALWAYS...
QUIETLY READING HER NOVELS.

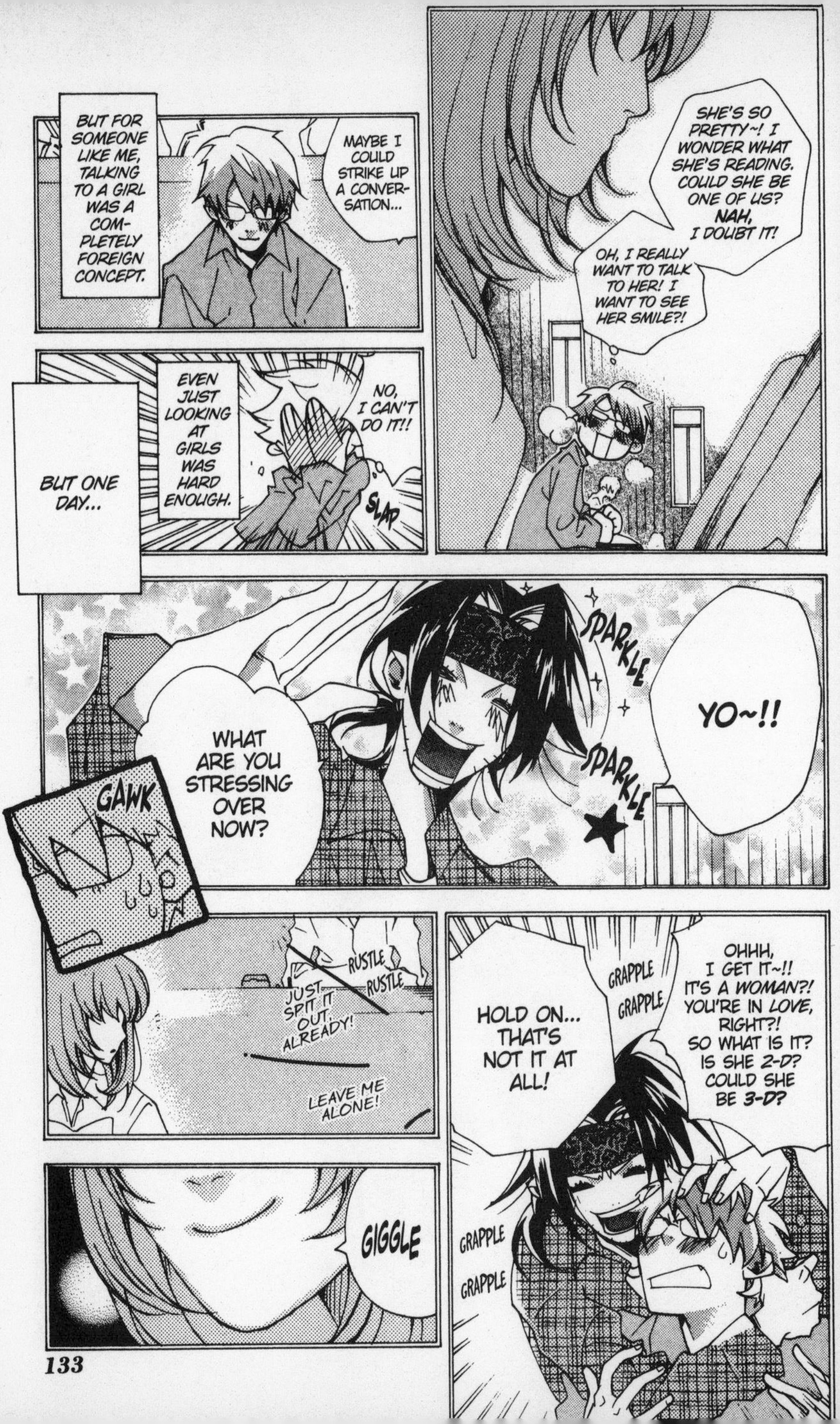
SHE'S SO PRETTY~! I WONDER WHAT SHE'S READING. COULD SHE BE ONE OF US? NAH, I DOUBT IT!
OH, I REALLY WANT TO TALK TO HER! I WANT TO SEE HER SMILE?!
MAYBE I COULD STRIKE UP A CONVERSATION...
BUT FOR SOMEONE LIKE ME, TALKING TO A GIRL WAS A COMPLETELY FOREIGN CONCEPT.
NO, I CAN'T DO IT!!
SLAP
EVEN JUST LOOKING AT GIRLS WAS HARD ENOUGH.
BUT ONE DAY...
YO~!!
SPARKLE
SPARKLE
WHAT ARE YOU STRESSING OVER NOW?
GAWK
OHHH, I GET IT~!! IT'S A WOMAN?! YOU'RE IN LOVE, RIGHT?! SO WHAT IS IT? IS SHE 2-D? COULD SHE BE 3-D?
GRAPPLE GRAPPLE
HOLD ON... THAT'S NOT IT AT ALL!
GRAPPLE GRAPPLE
RUSTLE RUSTLE
JUST SPIT IT OUT ALREADY!
LEAVE ME ALONE!
GIGGLE

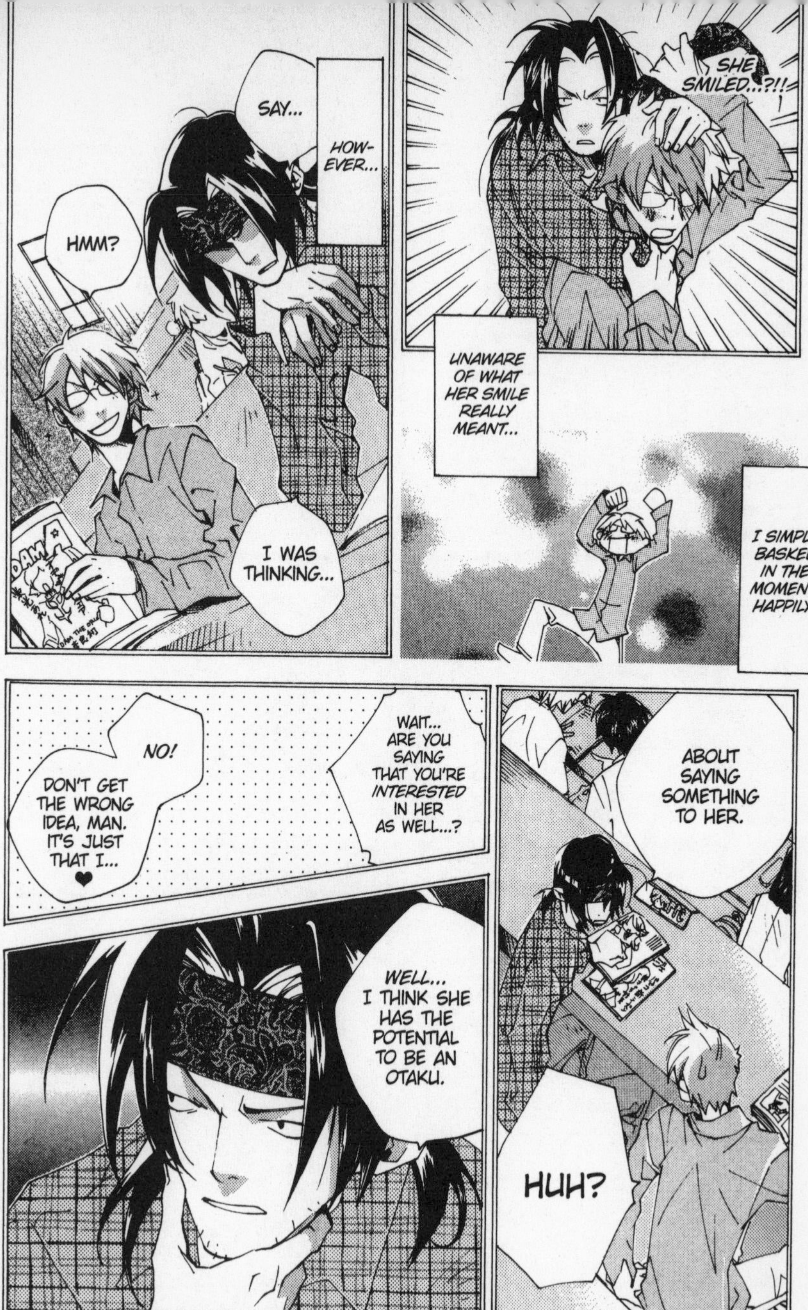
SHE SMILED...?!!
UNAWARE OF WHAT HER SMILE REALLY MEANT...
I SIMPLY BASKED IN THE MOMENT, HAPPILY.
HOW-EVER...
SAY...
HMM?
I WAS THINKING...
ABOUT SAYING SOMETHING TO HER.
HUH?
WAIT... ARE YOU SAYING THAT YOU'RE INTERESTED IN HER AS WELL...?
NO!
DON'T GET THE WRONG IDEA, MAN. IT'S JUST THAT I... ❤
WELL... I THINK SHE HAS THE POTENTIAL TO BE AN OTAKU.

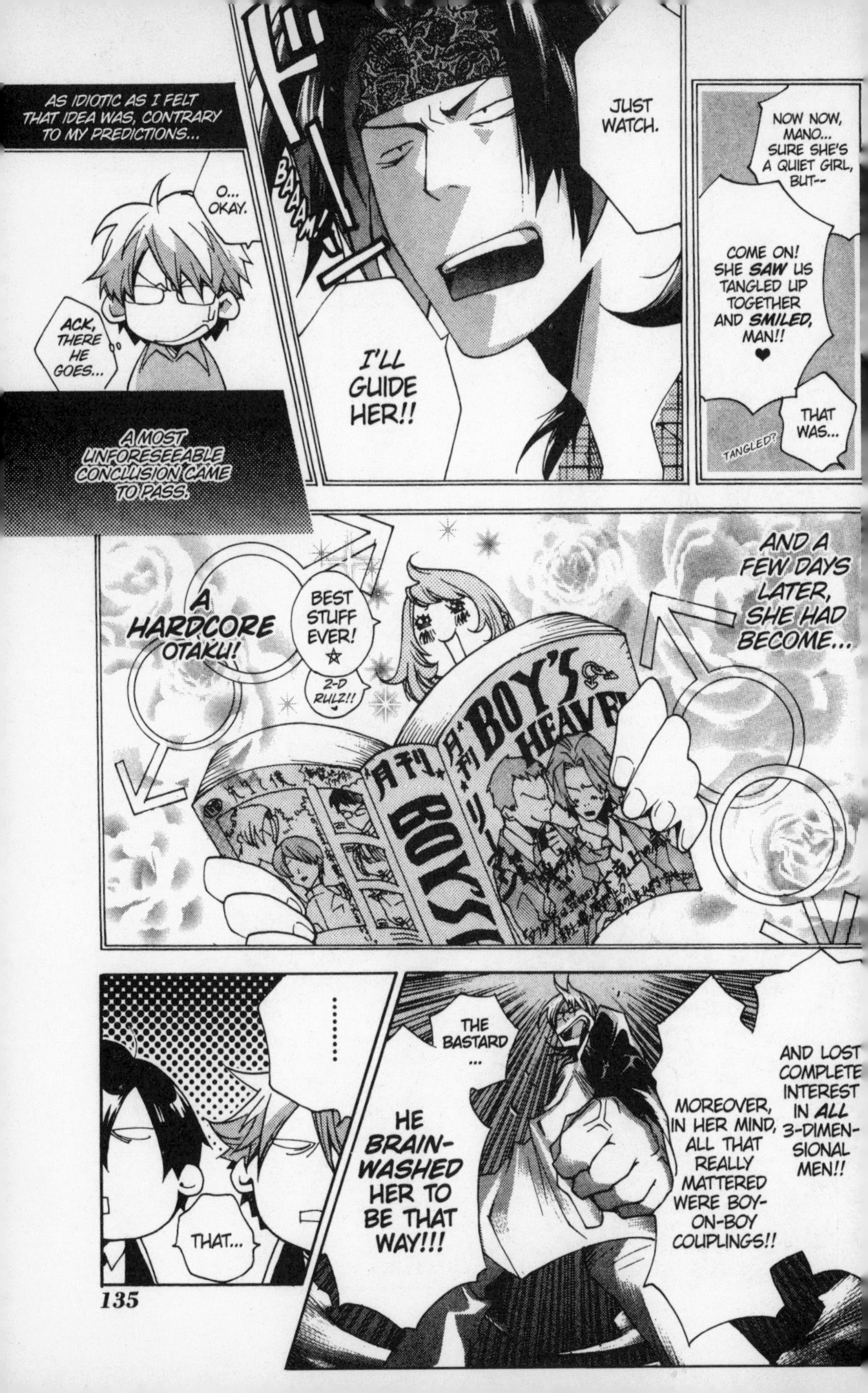
NOW NOW, MANO... SURE SHE'S A QUIET GIRL, BUT--
COME ON! SHE SAW US TANGLED UP TOGETHER AND SMILED, MAN!! ❤
THAT WAS...
TANGLED?
JUST WATCH.
BAAAM!
I'LL GUIDE HER!!
AS IDIOTIC AS I FELT THAT IDEA WAS, CONTRARY TO MY PREDICTIONS...
O... OKAY.
ACK, THERE HE GOES...
A MOST UNFORESEEABLE CONCLUSION CAME TO PASS.
AND A FEW DAYS LATER, SHE HAD BECOME...
A HARDCORE OTAKU!
BEST STUFF EVER! ☆
2-D RULZ!!
BOY'S HEAVEN
BOY'S
AND LOST COMPLETE INTEREST IN ALL 3-DIMEN-SIONAL MEN!!
MOREOVER, IN HER MIND, ALL THAT REALLY MATTERED WERE BOY-ON-BOY COUPLINGS!!
THE BASTARD ...
HE BRAIN-WASHED HER TO BE THAT WAY!!!
......
THAT...

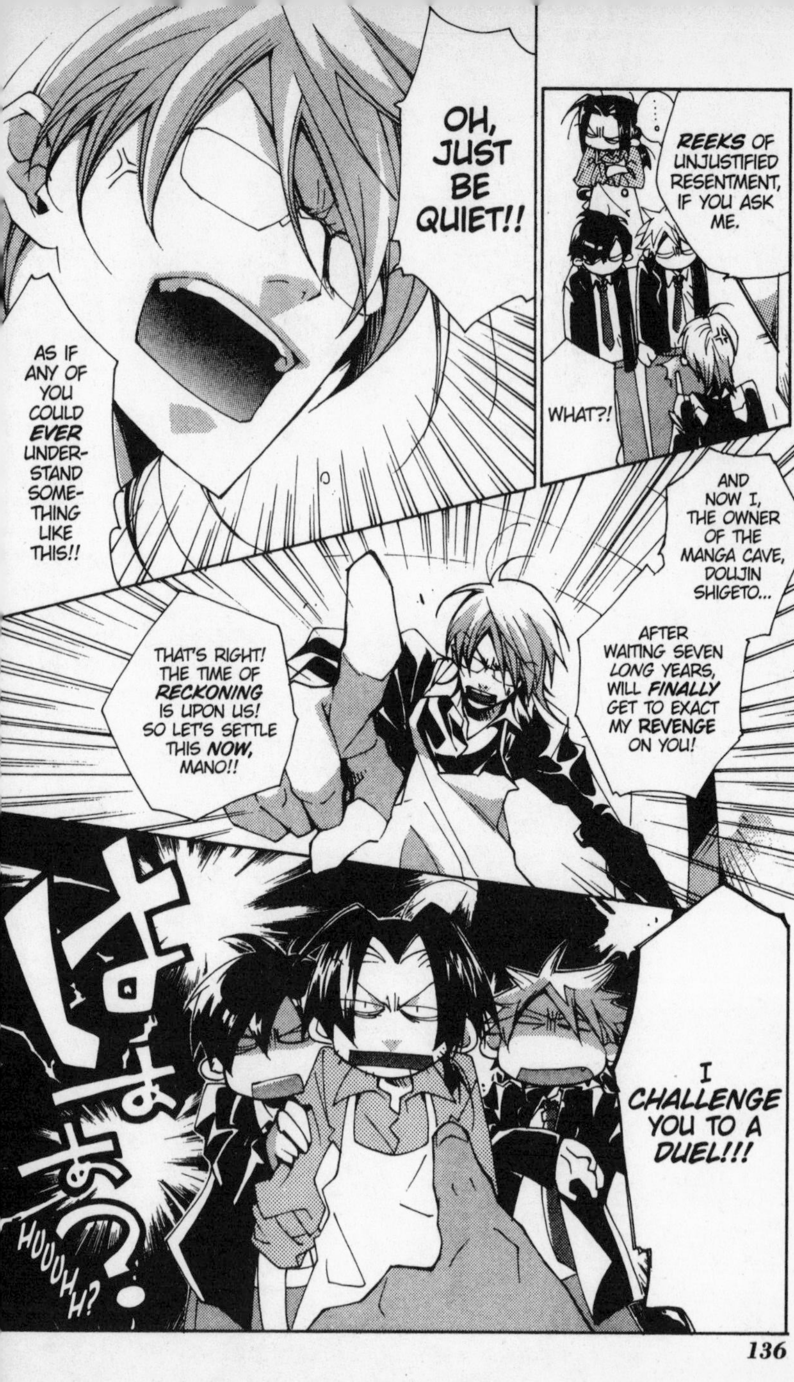
...
REEKS OF UNJUSTIFIED RESENTMENT, IF YOU ASK ME.
WHAT?!
OH, JUST BE QUIET!!
AS IF ANY OF YOU COULD EVER UNDERSTAND SOMETHING LIKE THIS!!
AND NOW I, THE OWNER OF THE MANGA CAVE, DOUJIN SHIGETO...
AFTER WAITING SEVEN LONG YEARS, WILL FINALLY GET TO EXACT MY REVENGE ON YOU!
THAT'S RIGHT! THE TIME OF RECKONING IS UPON US! SO LET'S SETTLE THIS NOW, MANO!!
I CHALLENGE YOU TO A DUEL!!!
HUUUHH?

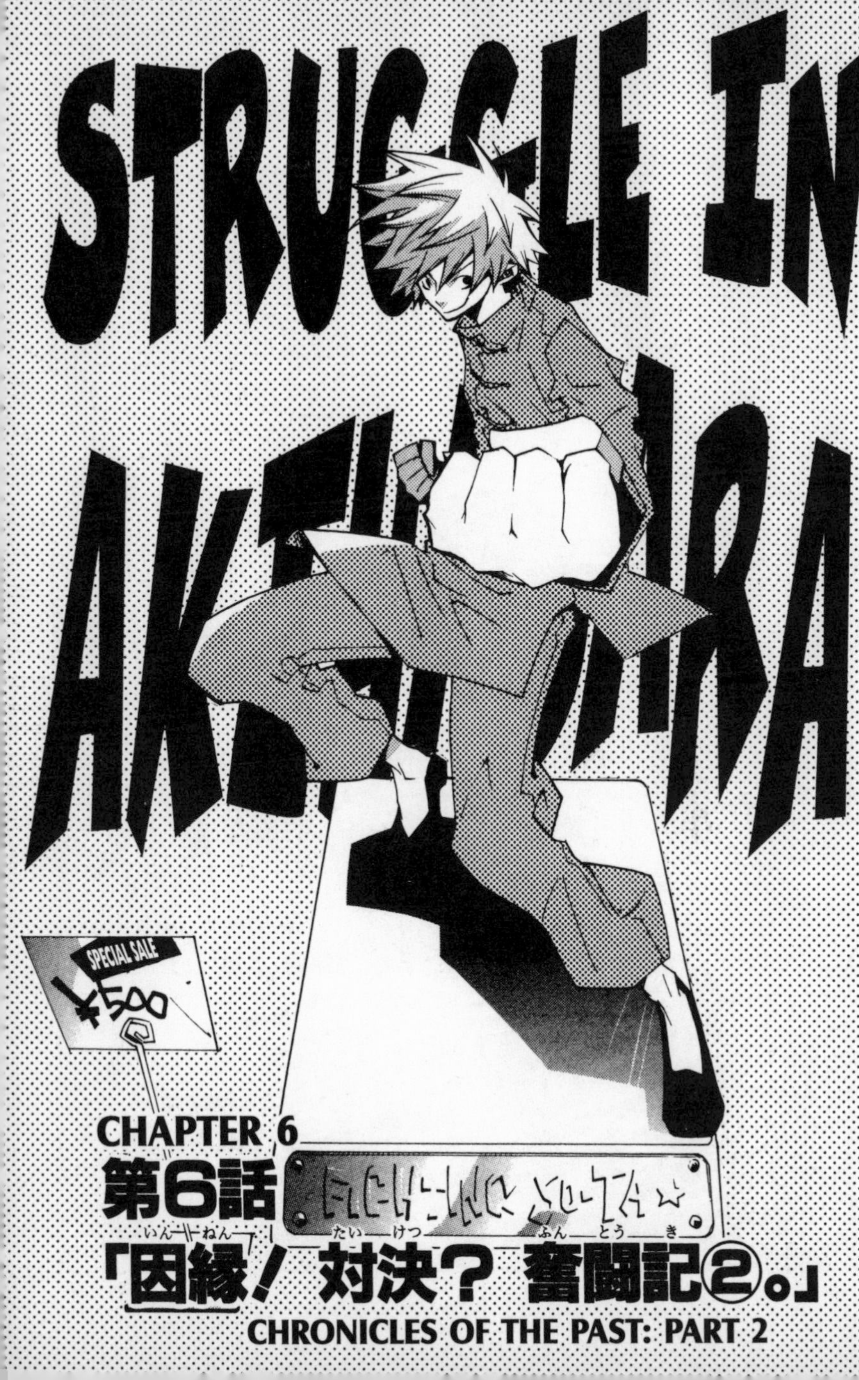
STRUGGLE IN
SPECIAL SALE
¥500

CHAPTER 6

第6話「因縁！対決？奮闘記②。」

CHRONICLES OF THE PAST: PART 2

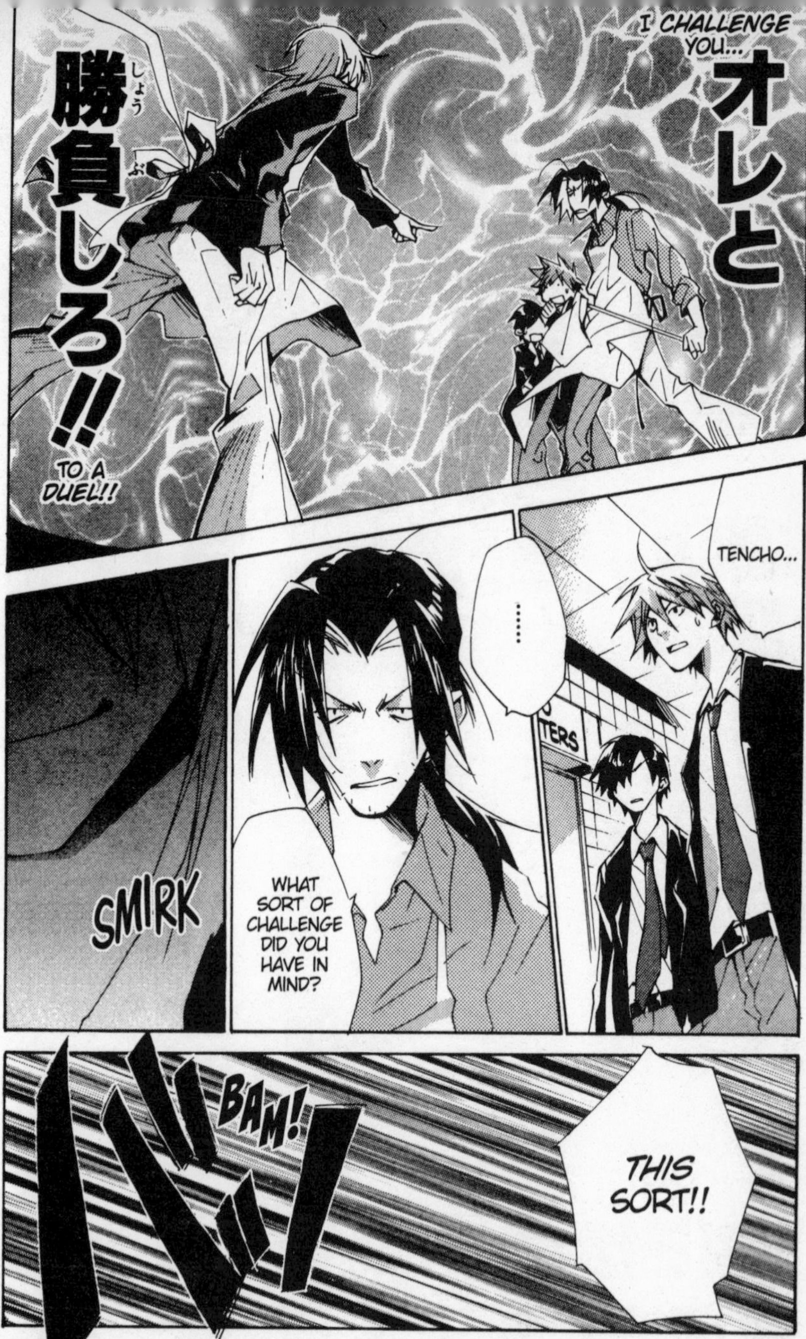
I CHALLENGE YOU...
オレと
勝負しろっ!!
TO A DUEL!!
TENCHO...
......
WHAT SORT OF CHALLENGE DID YOU HAVE IN MIND?
SMIRK
THIS SORT!!
BAM!

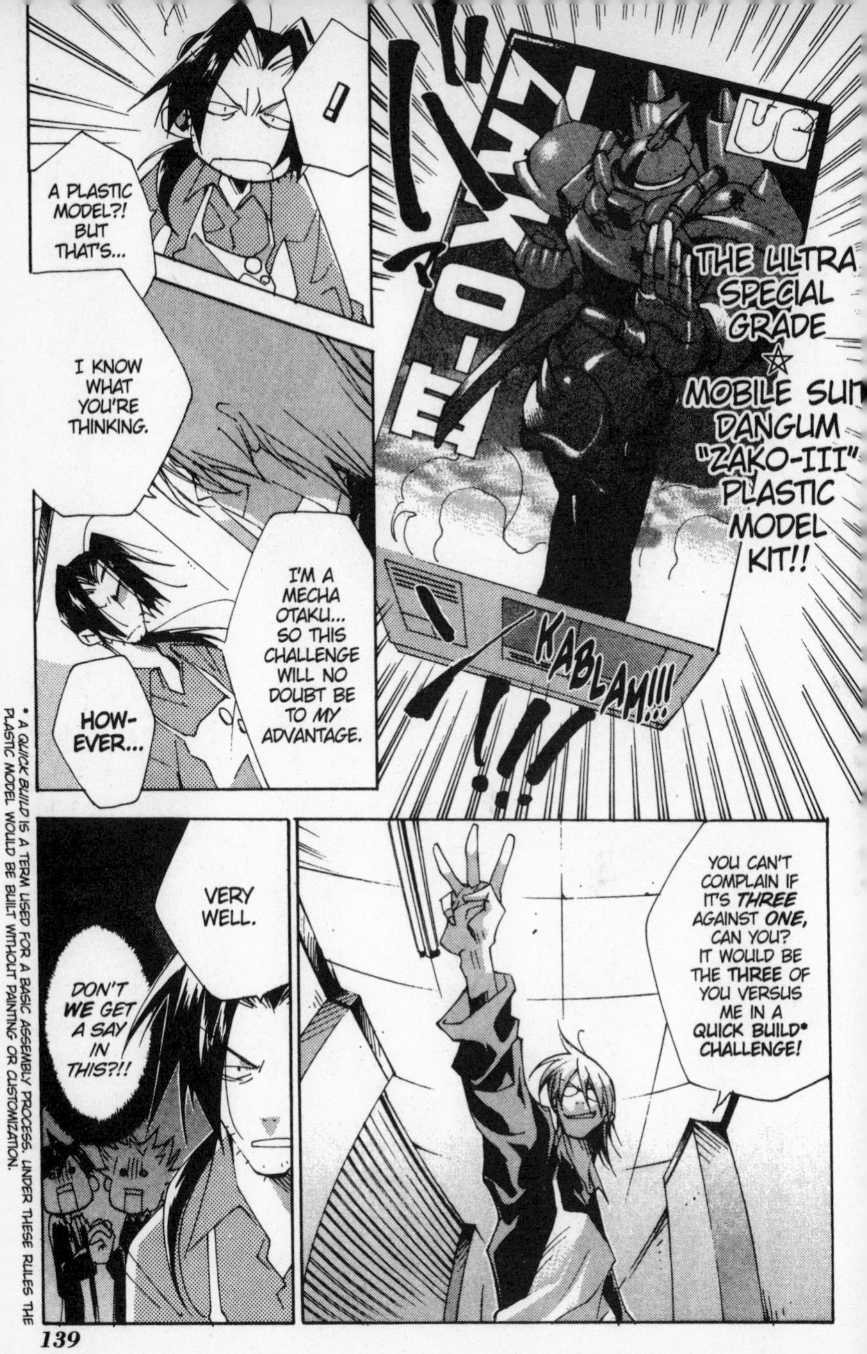
THE ULTRA SPECIAL GRADE ☆ MOBILE SUIT DANGUM "ZAKO-III" PLASTIC MODEL KIT!!
KABLAM!!!
!
A PLASTIC MODEL?! BUT THAT'S...
I KNOW WHAT YOU'RE THINKING.
I'M A MECHA OTAKU... SO THIS CHALLENGE WILL NO DOUBT BE TO *MY* ADVANTAGE.
HOW-EVER...
YOU CAN'T COMPLAIN IF IT'S ***THREE*** AGAINST ***ONE***, CAN YOU? IT WOULD BE THE **THREE** OF YOU VERSUS ME IN A QUICK BUILD* CHALLENGE!
VERY WELL.
DON'T ***WE*** *GET A SAY IN THIS?!!*

* A *QUICK BUILD* IS A TERM USED FOR A BASIC ASSEMBLY PROCESS. UNDER THESE RULES THE PLASTIC MODEL WOULD BE BUILT WITHOUT PAINTING OR CUSTOMIZATION.

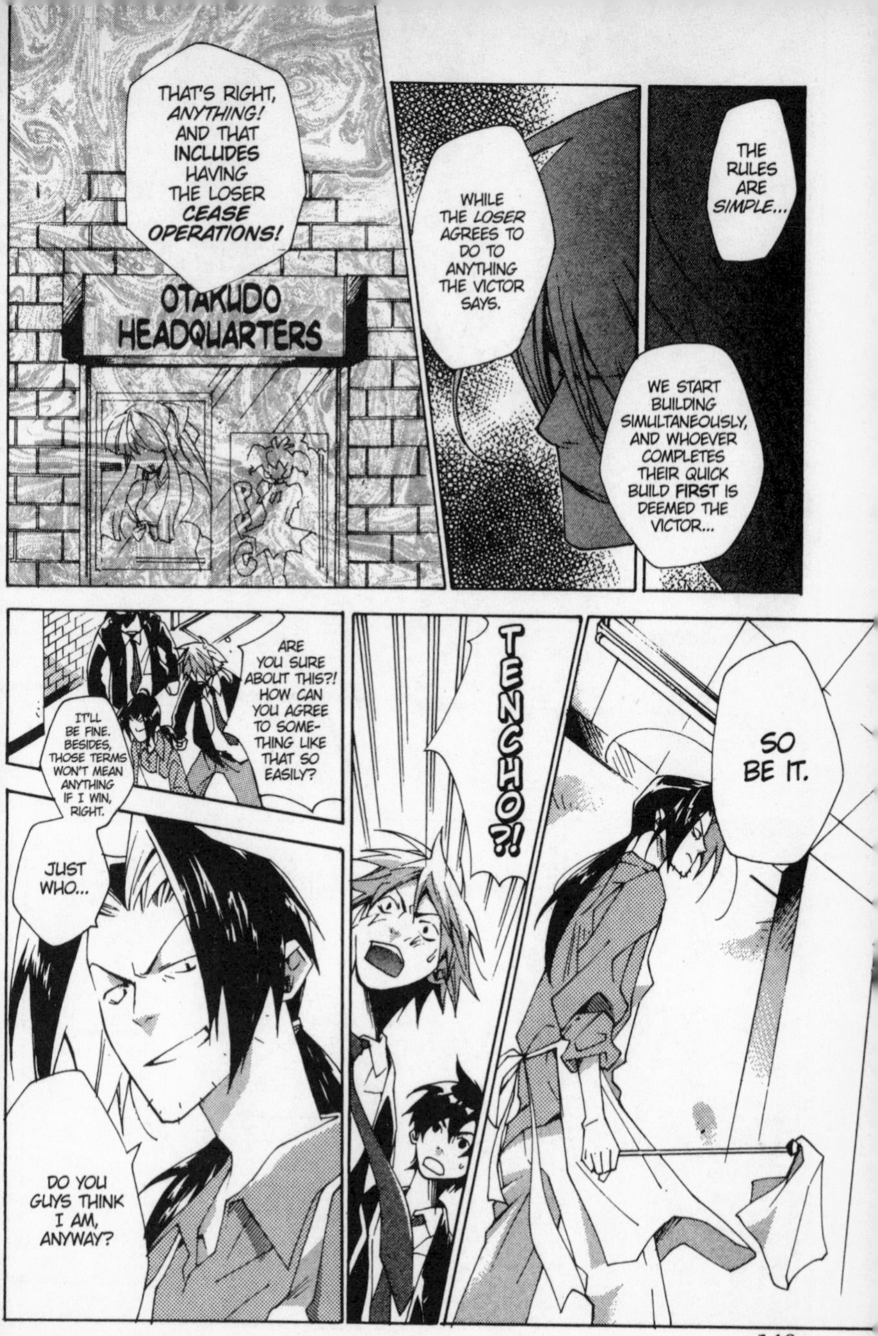
THE RULES ARE SIMPLE...
WE START BUILDING SIMULTANEOUSLY, AND WHOEVER COMPLETES THEIR QUICK BUILD FIRST IS DEEMED THE VICTOR...
WHILE THE LOSER AGREES TO DO TO ANYTHING THE VICTOR SAYS.
THAT'S RIGHT, ANYTHING! AND THAT INCLUDES HAVING THE LOSER CEASE OPERATIONS!
OTAKUDO HEADQUARTERS
SO BE IT.
TENCHO?!
ARE YOU SURE ABOUT THIS?! HOW CAN YOU AGREE TO SOME-THING LIKE THAT SO EASILY?
IT'LL BE FINE. BESIDES, THOSE TERMS WON'T MEAN ANYTHING IF I WIN, RIGHT.
JUST WHO...
DO YOU GUYS THINK I AM, ANYWAY?

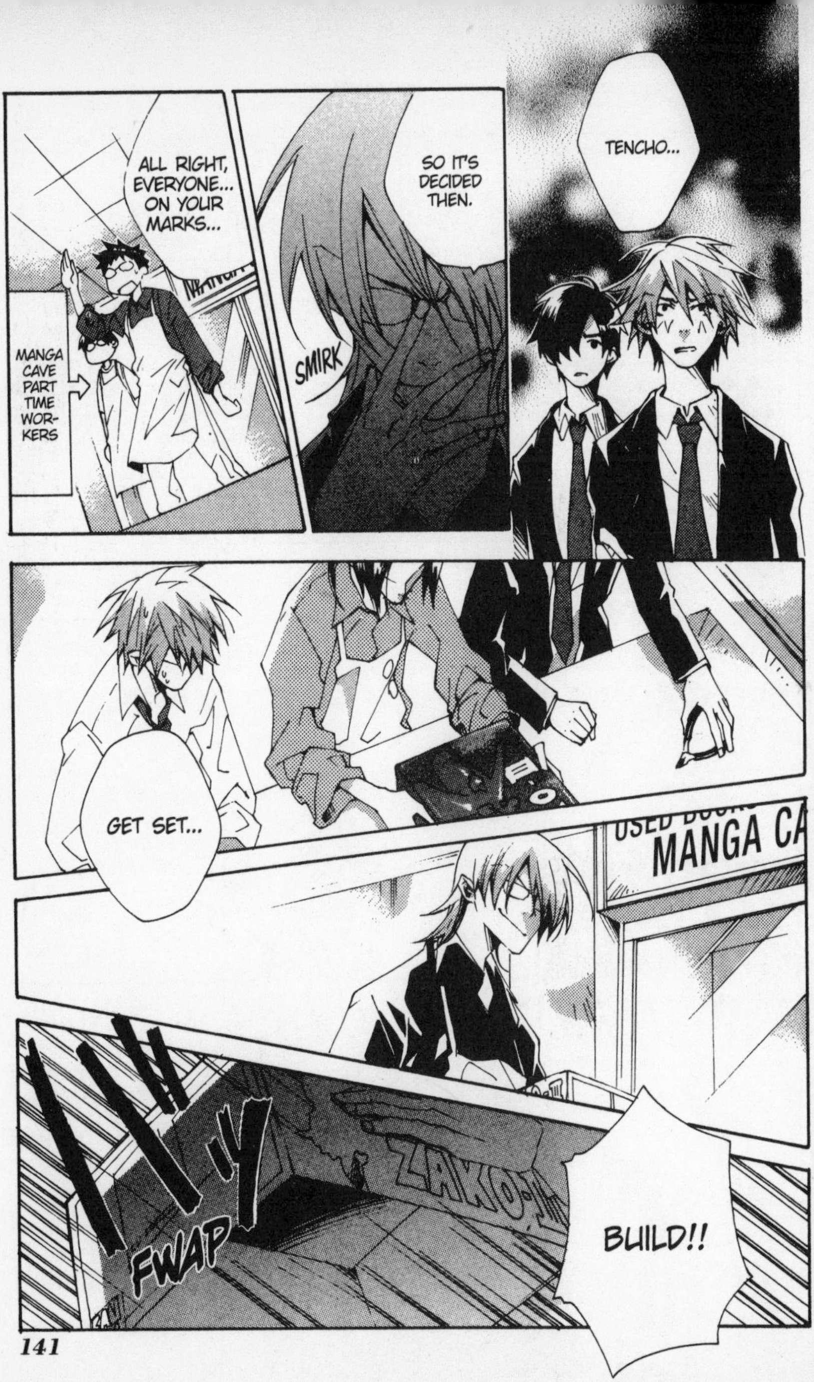
TENCHO...
SO IT'S DECIDED THEN.
SMIRK
ALL RIGHT, EVERYONE... ON YOUR MARKS...
MANGA CAVE PART TIME WORKERS
GET SET...
MANGA CA
BUILD!!
FWAP

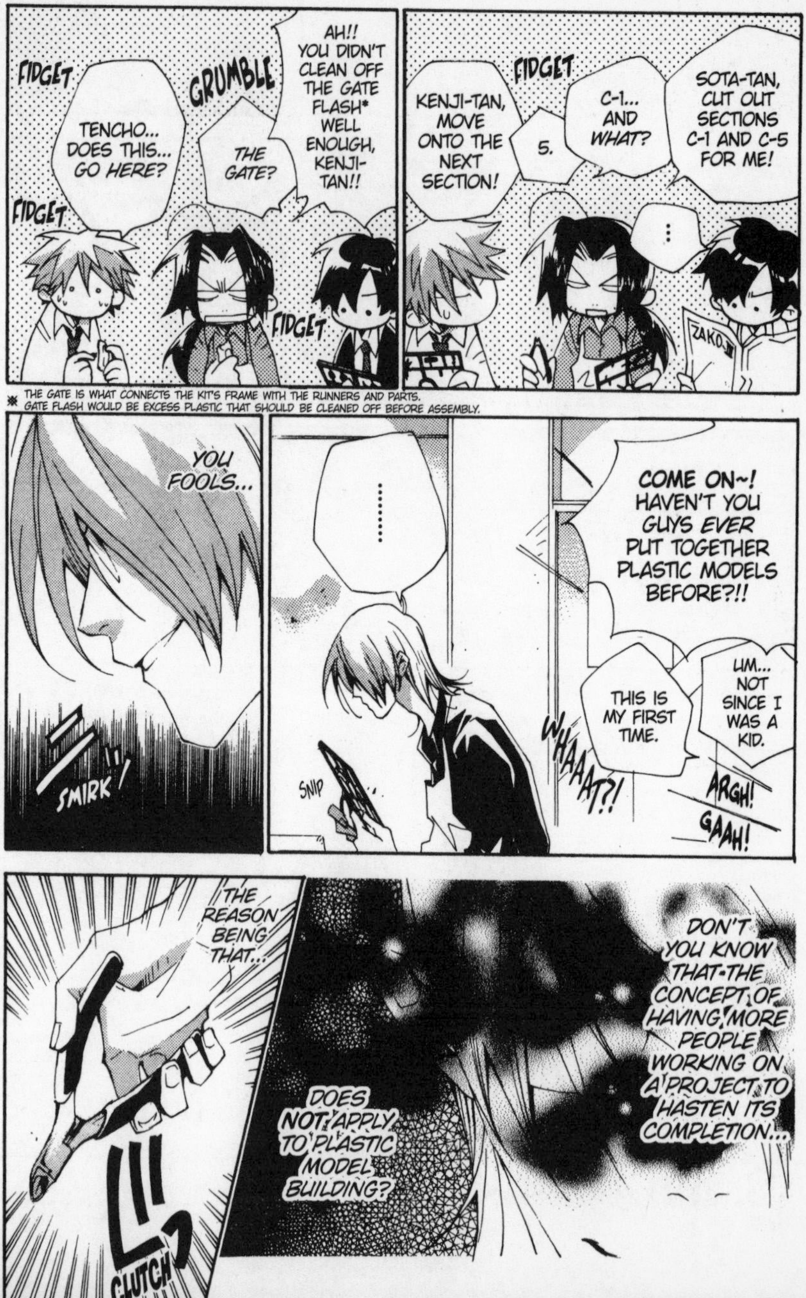
SOTA-TAN, CUT OUT SECTIONS C-1 AND C-5 FOR ME!
C-1... AND WHAT?
5.
KENJI-TAN, MOVE ONTO THE NEXT SECTION!
FIDGET
...
ZAKO
AH!! YOU DIDN'T CLEAN OFF THE GATE FLASH* WELL ENOUGH, KENJI-TAN!!
THE GATE?
GRUMBLE
FIDGET
TENCHO... DOES THIS... GO HERE?
FIDGET
FIDGET
COME ON~! HAVEN'T YOU GUYS EVER PUT TOGETHER PLASTIC MODELS BEFORE?!!
UM... NOT SINCE I WAS A KID.
THIS IS MY FIRST TIME.
WHAAAAT?!
ARGH!
GAAH!
......
SNIP
YOU FOOLS...
SMIRK
DON'T YOU KNOW THAT THE CONCEPT OF HAVING MORE PEOPLE WORKING ON A PROJECT TO HASTEN ITS COMPLETION...
DOES NOT APPLY TO PLASTIC MODEL BUILDING?
THE REASON BEING THAT...
CLUTCH

※ THE GATE IS WHAT CONNECTS THE KIT'S FRAME WITH THE RUNNERS AND PARTS. GATE FLASH WOULD BE EXCESS PLASTIC THAT SHOULD BE CLEANED OFF BEFORE ASSEMBLY.

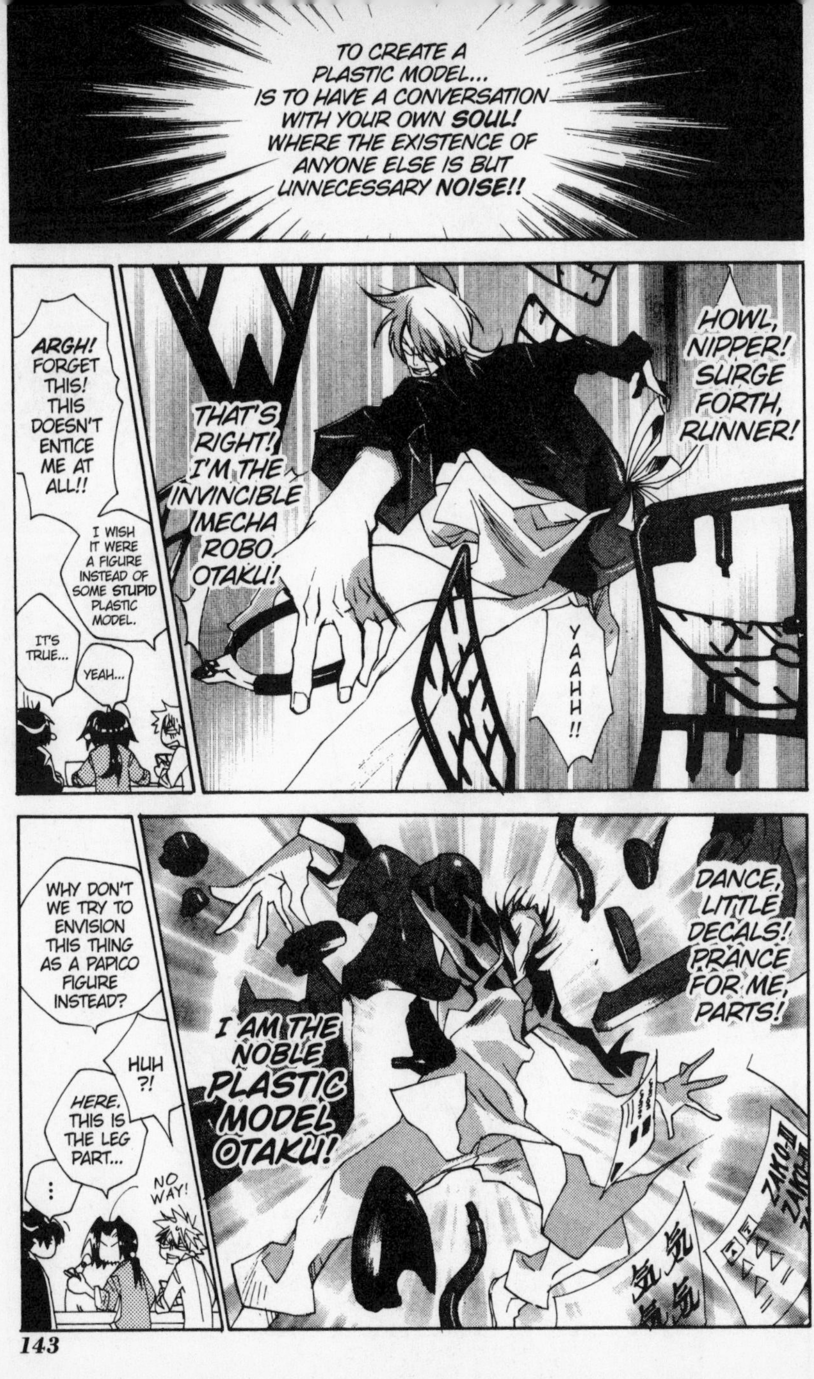
TO CREATE A PLASTIC MODEL... IS TO HAVE A CONVERSATION WITH YOUR OWN SOUL! WHERE THE EXISTENCE OF ANYONE ELSE IS BUT UNNECESSARY NOISE!!
HOWL, NIPPER! SURGE FORTH, RUNNER!
THAT'S RIGHT! I'M THE INVINCIBLE MECHA ROBO OTAKU!
YAAHH!!
ARGH! FORGET THIS! THIS DOESN'T ENTICE ME AT ALL!!
I WISH IT WERE A FIGURE INSTEAD OF SOME STUPID PLASTIC MODEL.
IT'S TRUE...
YEAH...
DANCE, LITTLE DECALS! PRANCE FOR ME, PARTS!
I AM THE NOBLE PLASTIC MODEL OTAKU!
WHY DON'T WE TRY TO ENVISION THIS THING AS A PAPICO FIGURE INSTEAD?
HUH?!
HERE. THIS IS THE LEG PART...
NO WAY!
...

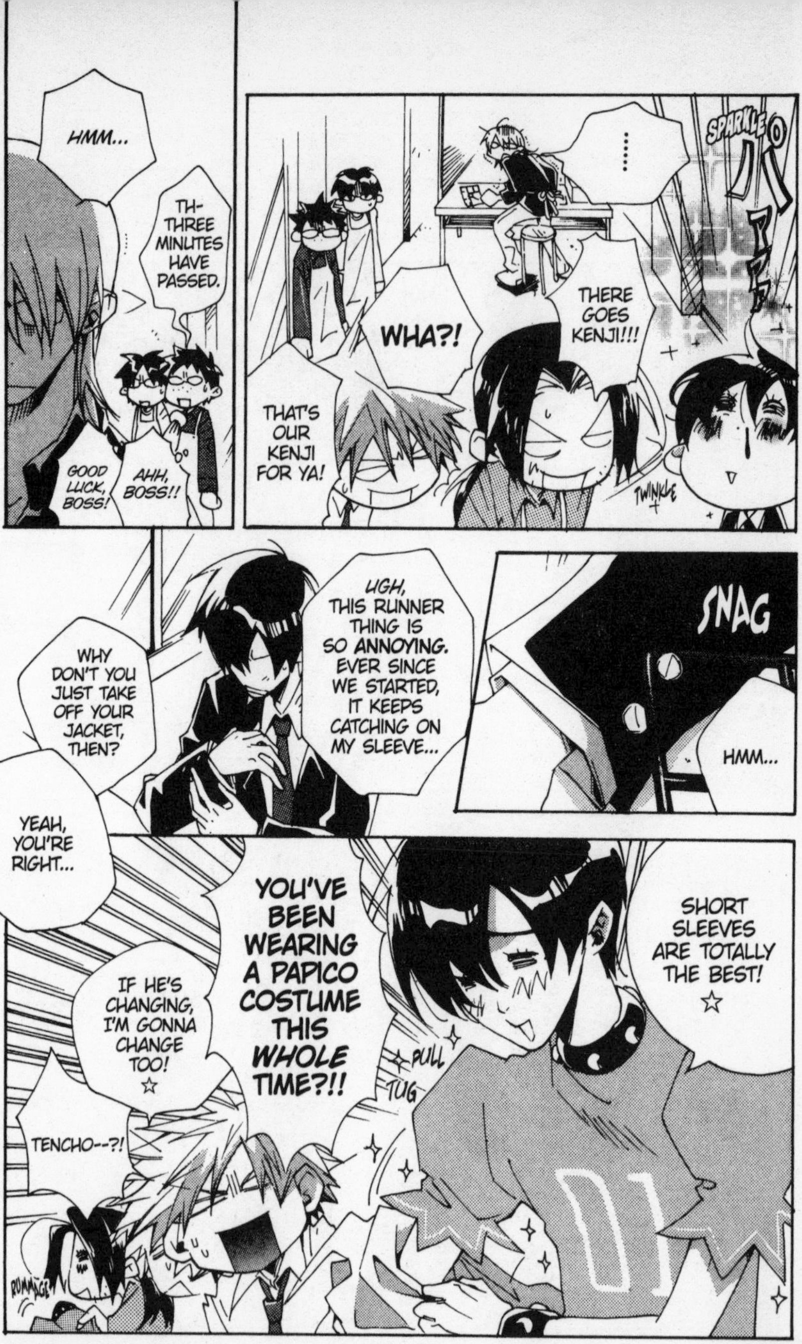
SPARKLE
......
THERE GOES KENJI!!!
TWINKLE
WHA?!
THAT'S OUR KENJI FOR YA!
HMM...
TH- THREE MINUTES HAVE PASSED.
AHH, BOSS!!
GOOD LUCK, BOSS!
SNAG
HMM...
UGH, THIS RUNNER THING IS SO ANNOYING. EVER SINCE WE STARTED, IT KEEPS CATCHING ON MY SLEEVE...
WHY DON'T YOU JUST TAKE OFF YOUR JACKET, THEN?
YEAH, YOU'RE RIGHT...
SHORT SLEEVES ARE TOTALLY THE BEST! ☆
PULL
TUG
YOU'VE BEEN WEARING A PAPICO COSTUME THIS WHOLE TIME?!!
IF HE'S CHANGING, I'M GONNA CHANGE TOO! ☆
TENCHO--?!
RUMMAGE

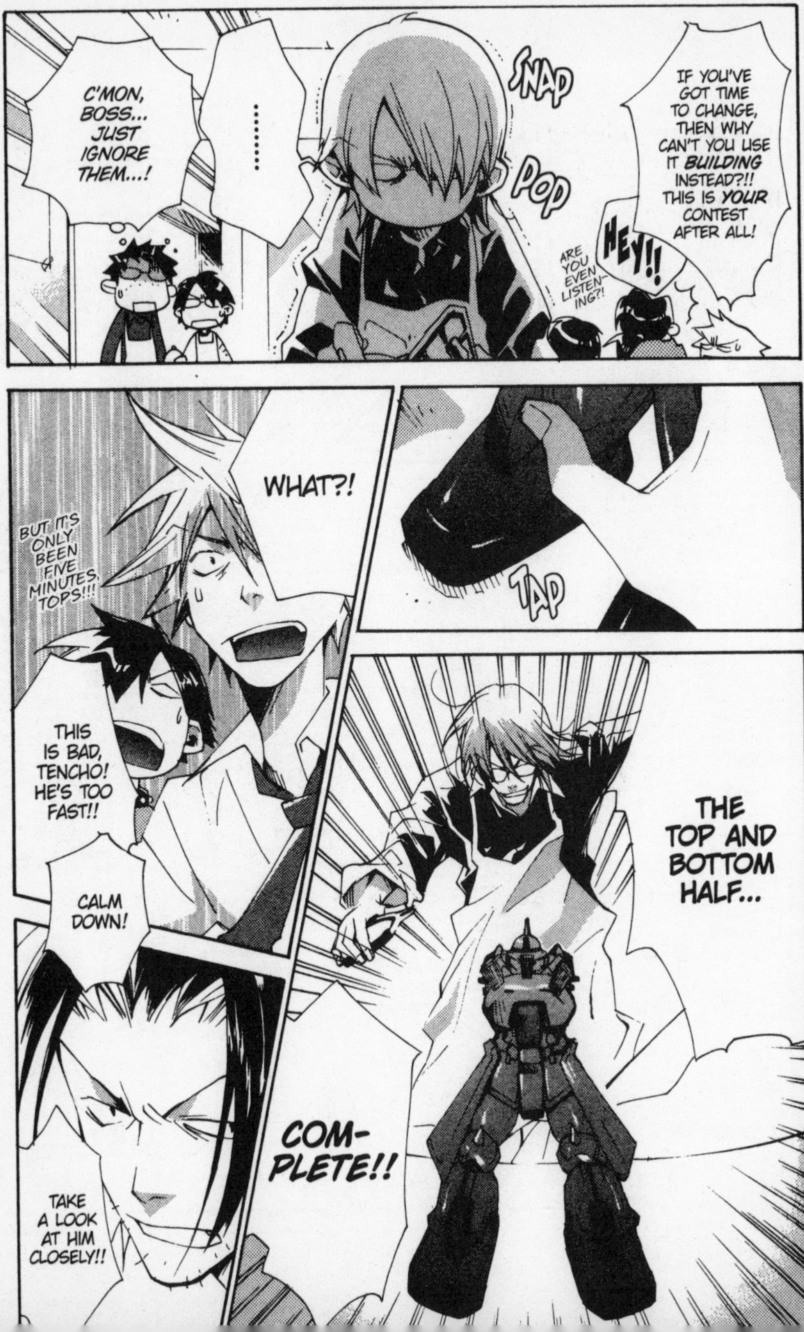
IF YOU'VE GOT TIME TO CHANGE, THEN WHY CAN'T YOU USE IT *BUILDING* INSTEAD?!! THIS IS *YOUR* CONTEST AFTER ALL!
HEY!!
ARE YOU EVEN LISTEN-ING?!
POP
SNAP
......
C'MON, BOSS... JUST IGNORE THEM...!
TAP
WHAT?!
BUT IT'S ONLY BEEN FIVE MINUTES, TOPS!!!
THIS IS BAD, TENCHO! HE'S TOO FAST!!
THE TOP AND BOTTOM HALF...
COM-PLETE!!
CALM DOWN!
TAKE A LOOK AT HIM CLOSELY!!

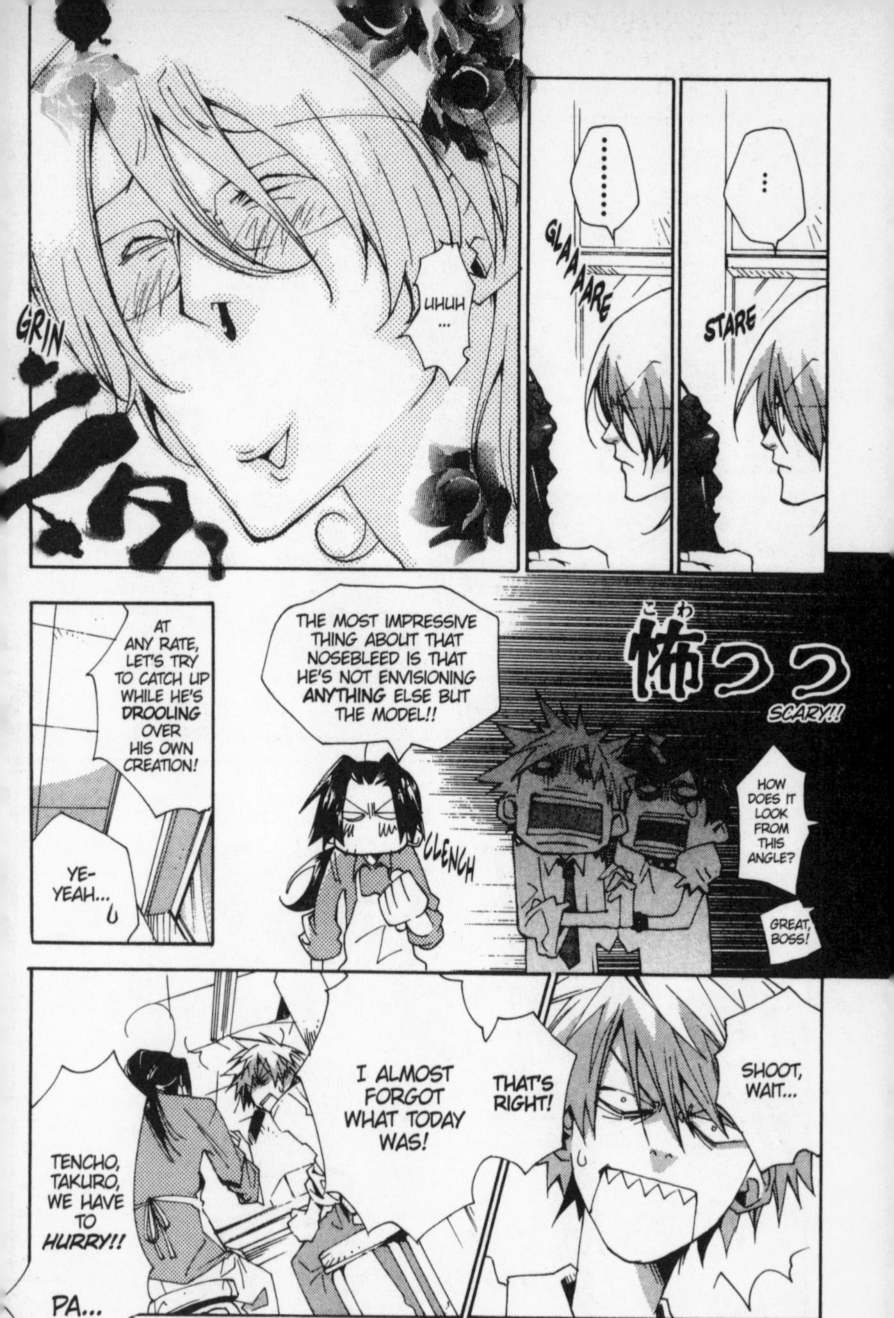

...
STARE
......
GLAAAARE
UHUH ...
GRIN
怖っっ
SCARY!!
HOW DOES IT LOOK FROM THIS ANGLE?
GREAT, BOSS!
THE MOST IMPRESSIVE THING ABOUT THAT NOSEBLEED IS THAT HE'S NOT ENVISIONING ANYTHING ELSE BUT THE MODEL!!
CLENCH
AT ANY RATE, LET'S TRY TO CATCH UP WHILE HE'S DROOLING OVER HIS OWN CREATION!
YE-YEAH...
SHOOT, WAIT...
THAT'S RIGHT!
I ALMOST FORGOT WHAT TODAY WAS!
TENCHO, TAKURO, WE HAVE TO HURRY!!
PA...

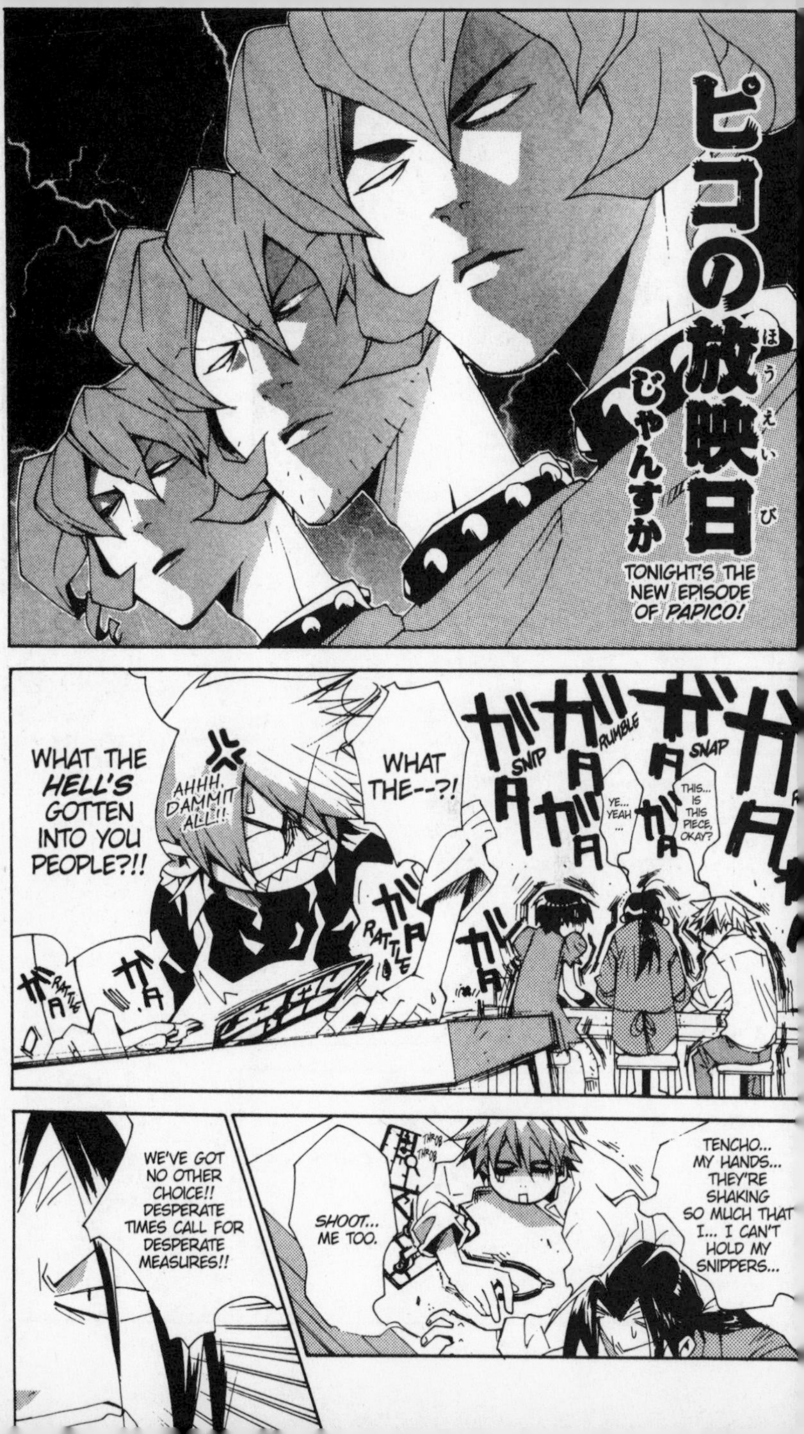

ピコの放映日じゃんすか
TONIGHT'S THE NEW EPISODE OF PAPICO!
SNAP
RUMBLE
THIS... IS THIS PIECE, OKAY?
YE... YEAH...
SNIP
WHAT THE--?!
AHHH, DAMMIT ALL!!
WHAT THE HELL'S GOTTEN INTO YOU PEOPLE?!!
RATTLE
RATTLE
TENCHO... MY HANDS... THEY'RE SHAKING SO MUCH THAT I... I CAN'T HOLD MY SNIPPERS...
THROB THROB
SHOOT... ME TOO.
WE'VE GOT NO OTHER CHOICE!! DESPERATE TIMES CALL FOR DESPERATE MEASURES!!

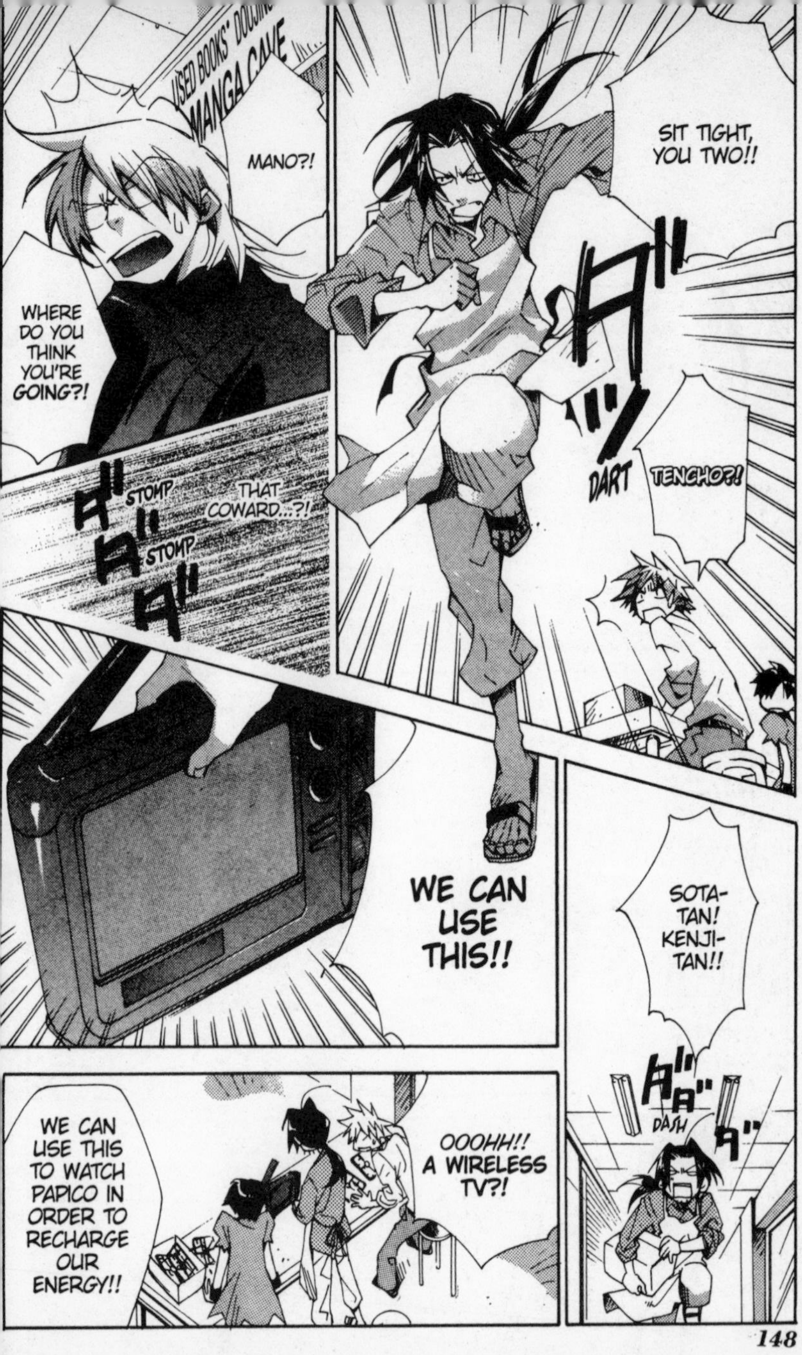
SIT TIGHT, YOU TWO!!
DART
TENCHO?!
USED BOOKS' DOUJIN
MANGA CAVE
MANO?!
WHERE DO YOU THINK YOU'RE GOING?!
STOMP
STOMP
THAT COWARD...?!
SOTA-TAN! KENJI-TAN!!
DASH
WE CAN USE THIS!!
OOOHH!! A WIRELESS TV?!
WE CAN USE THIS TO WATCH PAPICO IN ORDER TO RECHARGE OUR ENERGY!!

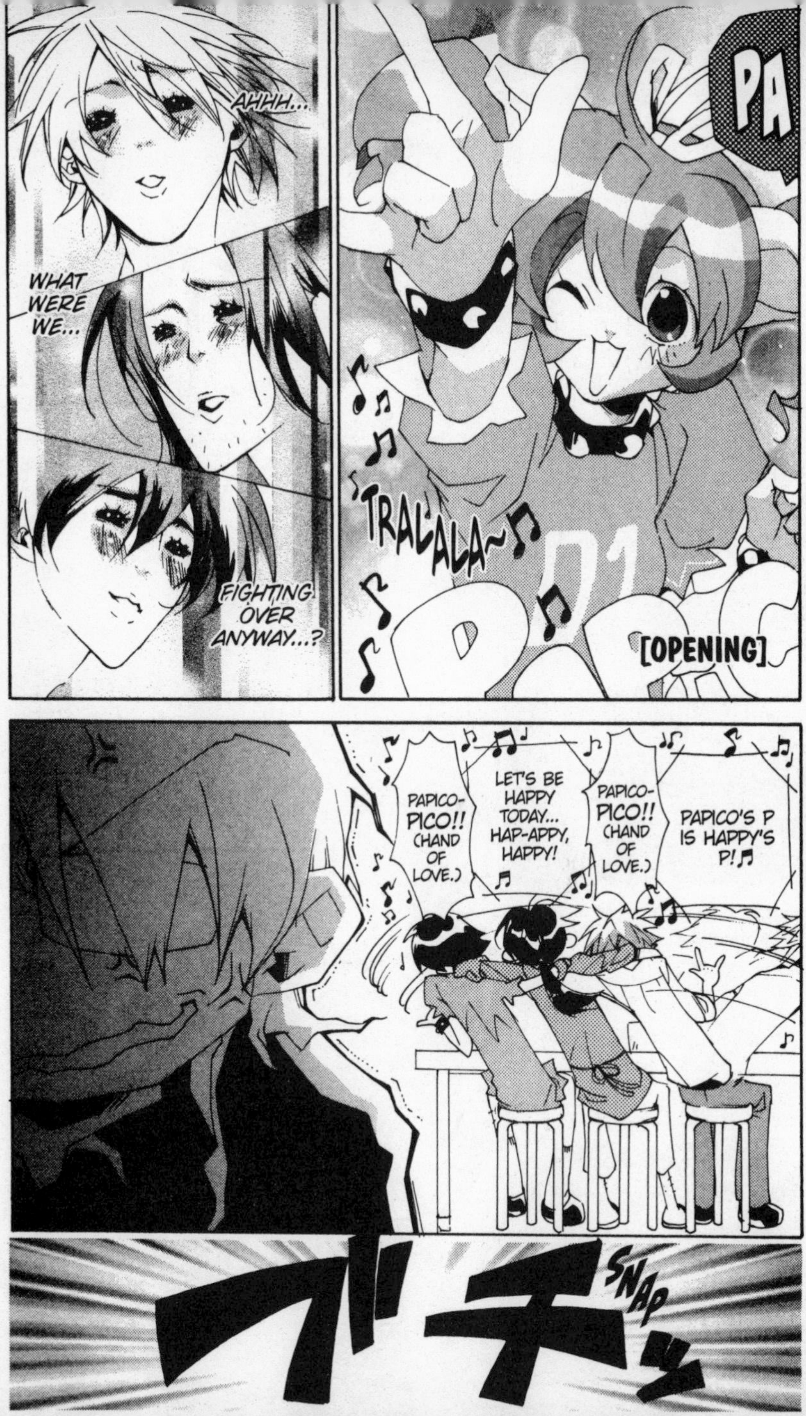
PA
TRALALA~
[OPENING]
AHHH...
WHAT WERE WE...
FIGHTING OVER ANYWAY...?
PAPICO'S P IS HAPPY'S P!♫
PAPICO-PICO!! (HAND OF LOVE.)
LET'S BE HAPPY TODAY... HAP-APPY, HAPPY! ♫
PAPICO-PICO!! (HAND OF LOVE.)
ブチッ
SNAP

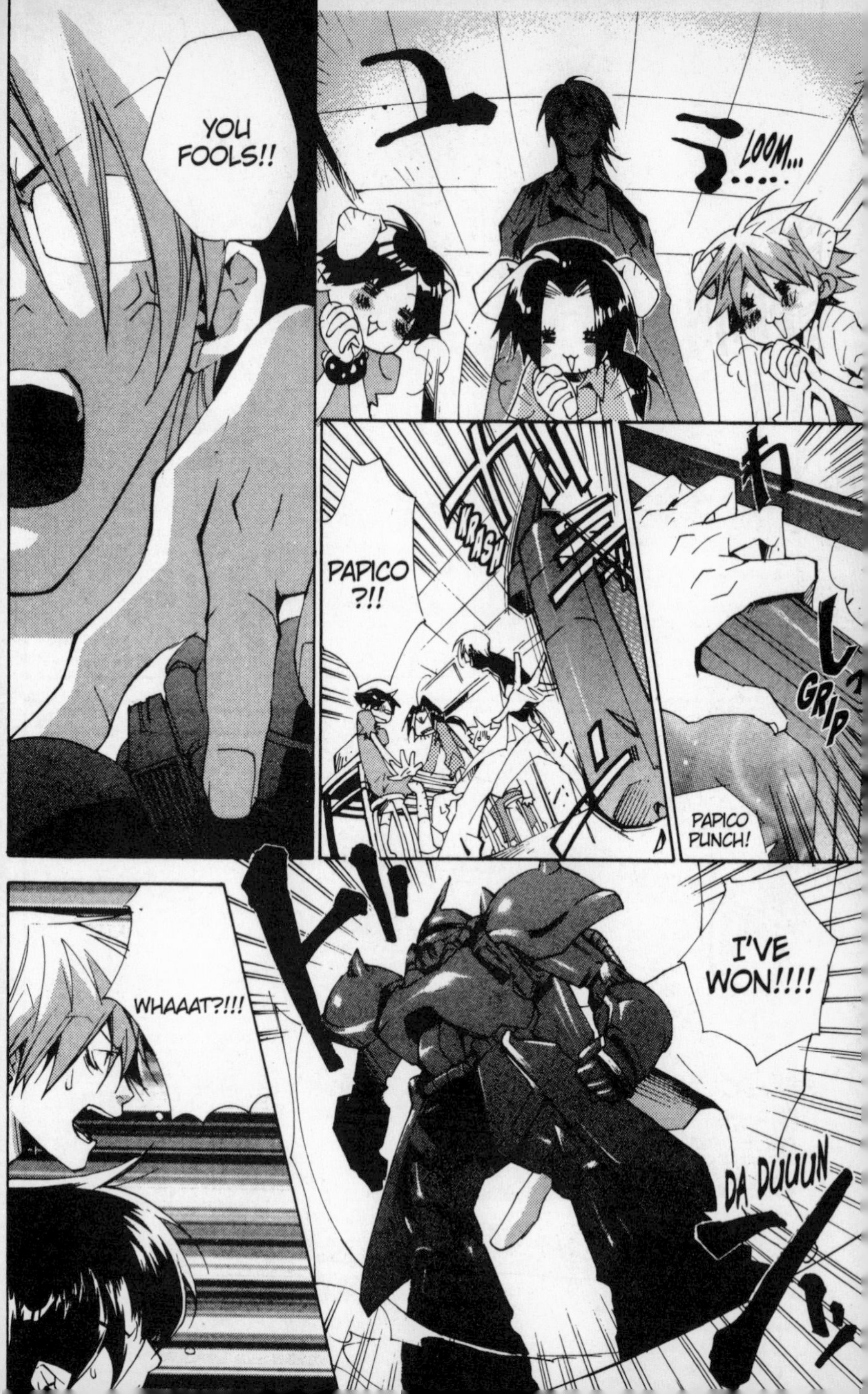
LOOM......
GRIP
PAPICO PUNCH!
KRASH
PAPICO ?!!
YOU FOOLS!!
I'VE WON!!!!
DA DUUUN
WHAAAT?!!!

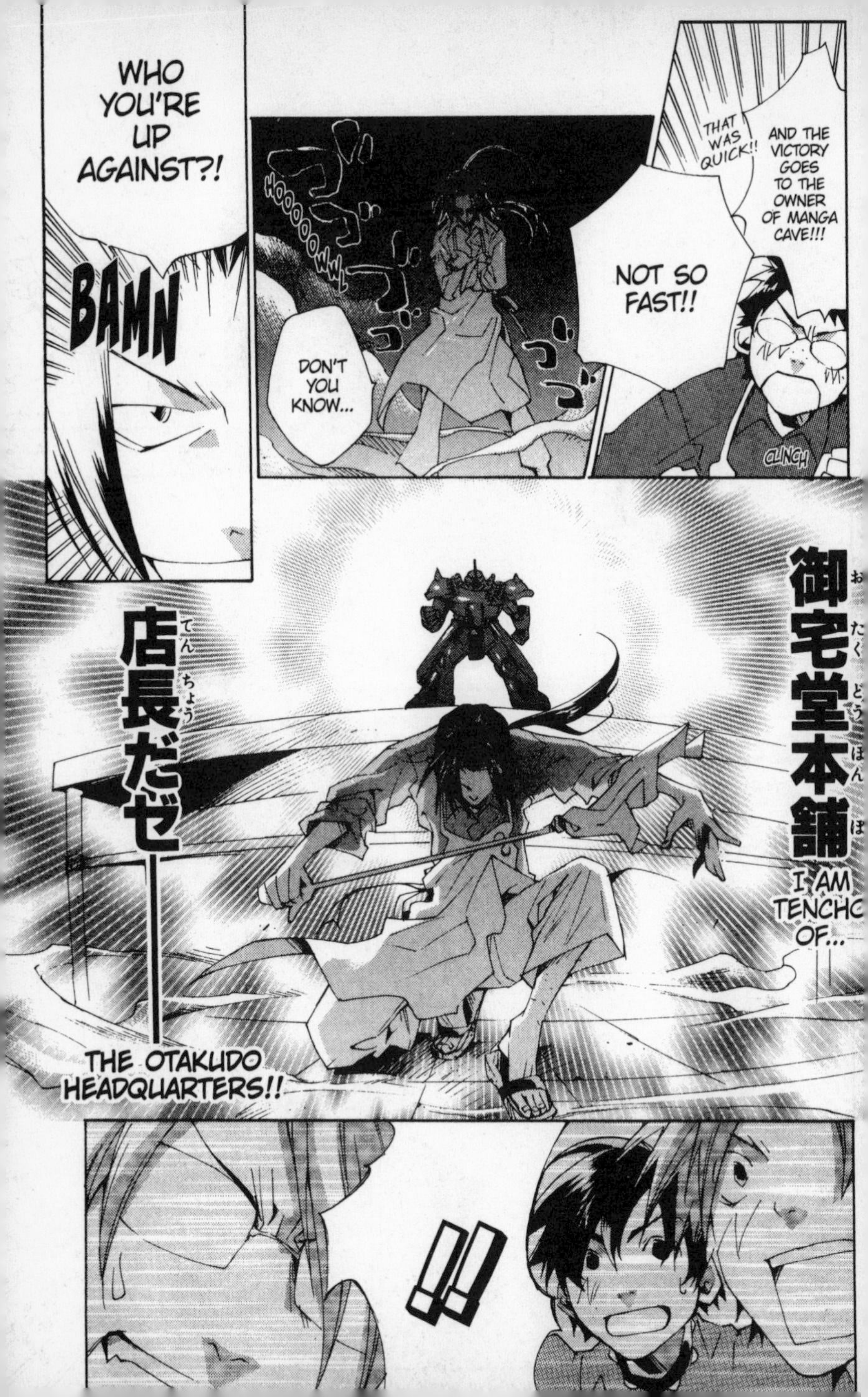
AND THE VICTORY GOES TO THE OWNER OF MANGA CAVE!!!
THAT WAS QUICK!!
NOT SO FAST!!
CLINCH
HOOOOOOWWL
DON'T YOU KNOW...
WHO YOU'RE UP AGAINST?!
BAMN
御宅堂本舗
I AM TENCHO OF...
店長だぜ
THE OTAKUDO HEADQUARTERS!!
!!

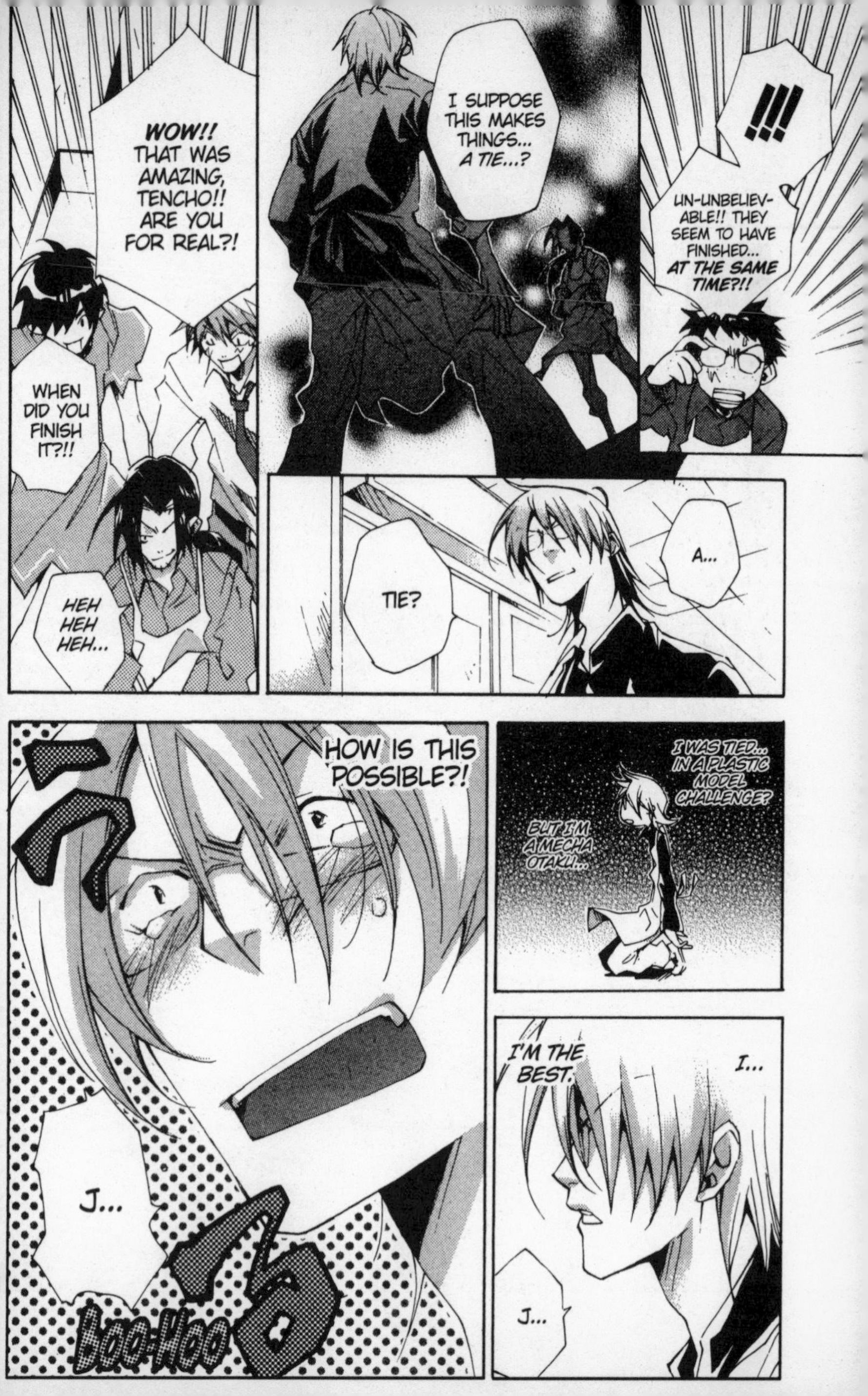
!!!
UN-UNBELIEVABLE!! THEY SEEM TO HAVE FINISHED... AT THE SAME TIME?!!
I SUPPOSE THIS MAKES THINGS... A TIE...?
A...
TIE?
WOW!! THAT WAS AMAZING, TENCHO!! ARE YOU FOR REAL?!
WHEN DID YOU FINISH IT?!!
HEH HEH HEH...
I WAS TIED... IN A PLASTIC MODEL CHALLENGE?
BUT I'M A MECHA OTAKU...
I...
I'M THE BEST.
J...
HOW IS THIS POSSIBLE?!
J...
BOO-HOO

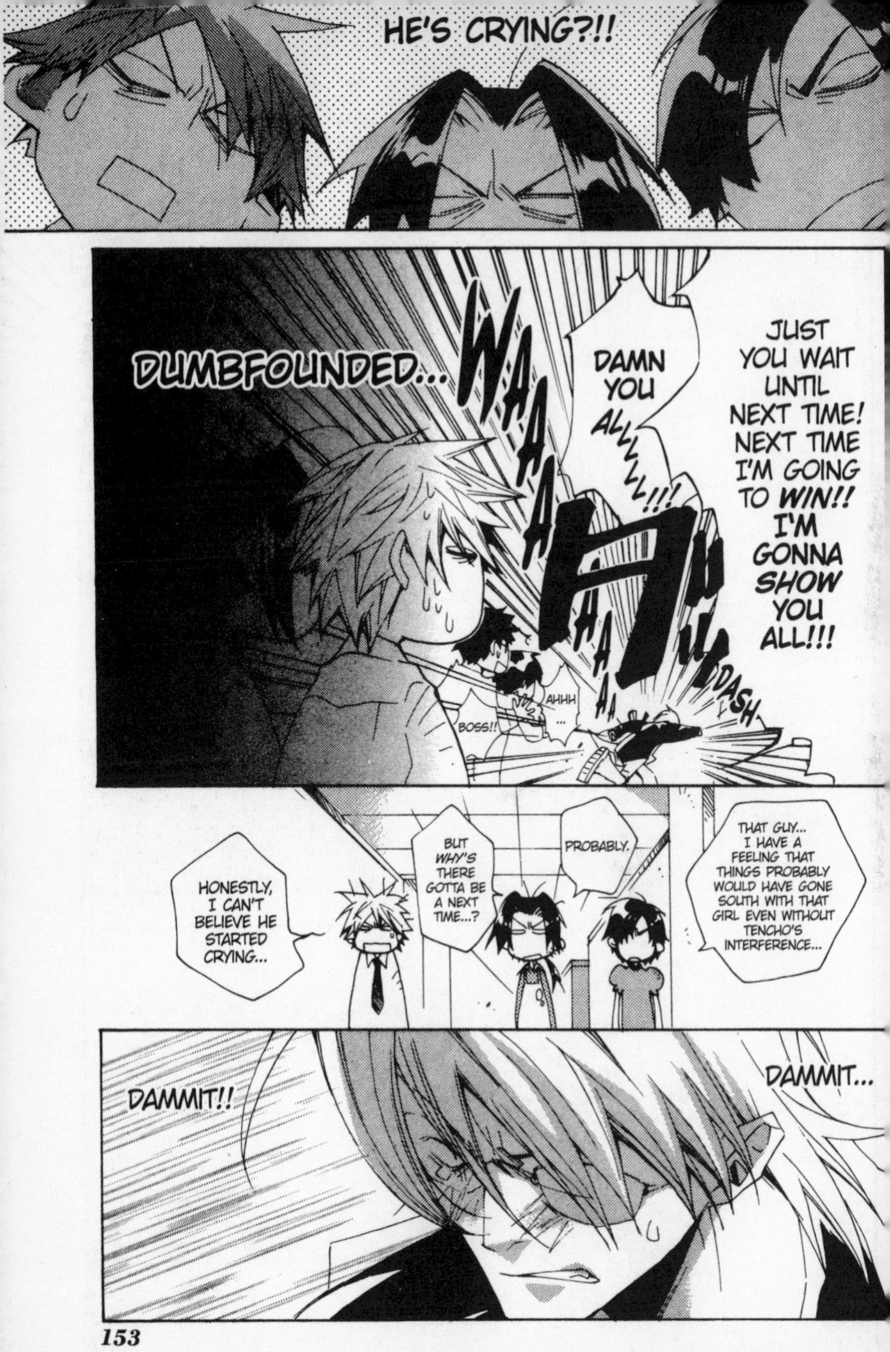
HE'S CRYING?!!
JUST YOU WAIT UNTIL NEXT TIME! NEXT TIME I'M GOING TO *WIN*!! I'M GONNA *SHOW* YOU ALL!!!
DAMN YOU ALLLLL!!!
DASH
AHHH ...
BOSS!!
DUMBFOUNDED...
THAT GUY... I HAVE A FEELING THAT THINGS PROBABLY WOULD HAVE GONE SOUTH WITH THAT GIRL EVEN WITHOUT TENCHO'S INTERFERENCE...
PROBABLY.
BUT *WHY'S* THERE GOTTA BE A NEXT TIME...?
HONESTLY, I CAN'T BELIEVE HE STARTED CRYING...
DAMMIT...
DAMMIT!!

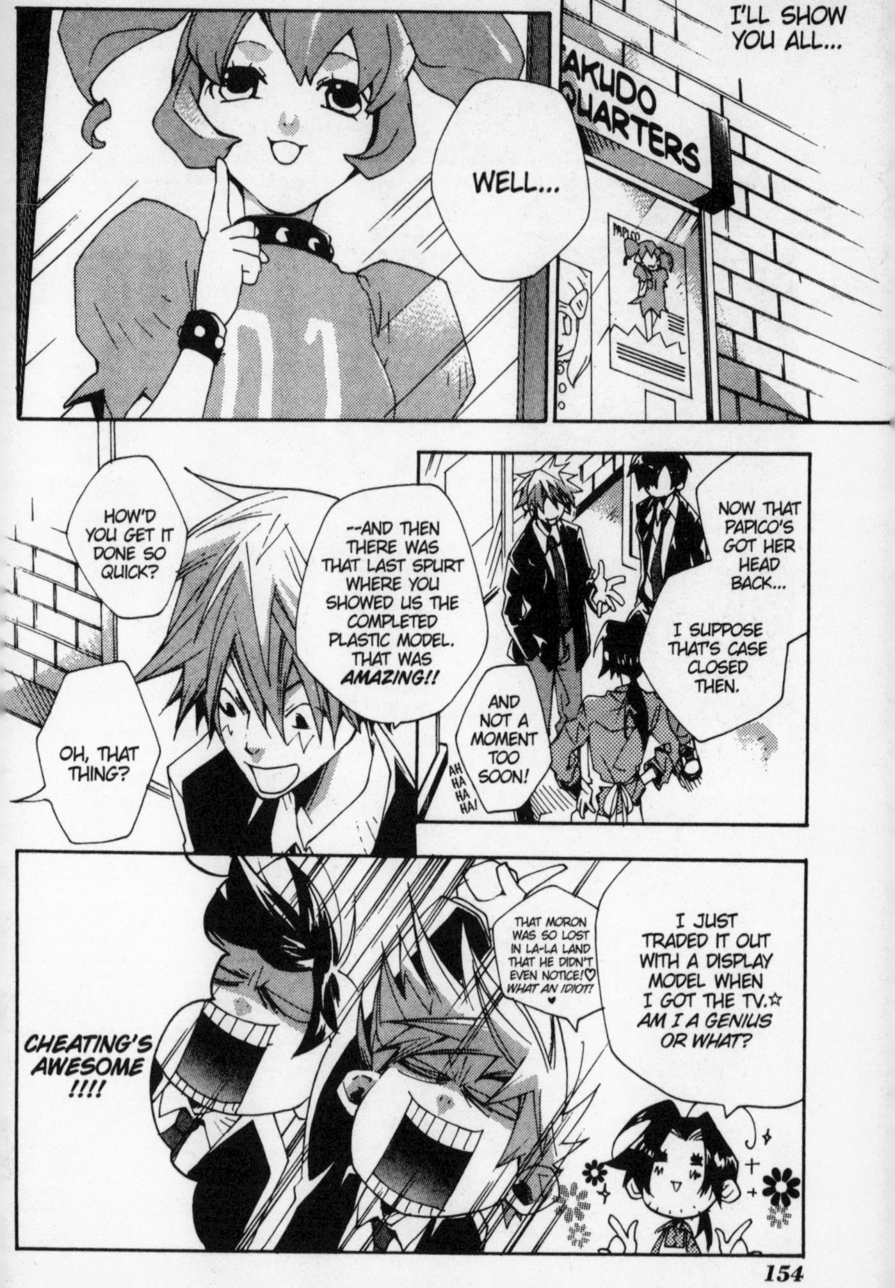

I'LL SHOW YOU ALL...
AKUDO QUARTERS
PAPICO
WELL...
NOW THAT PAPICO'S GOT HER HEAD BACK...
I SUPPOSE THAT'S CASE CLOSED THEN.
AND NOT A MOMENT TOO SOON!
AH HA HA HA!
--AND THEN THERE WAS THAT LAST SPURT WHERE YOU SHOWED US THE COMPLETED PLASTIC MODEL. THAT WAS *AMAZING!!*
HOW'D YOU GET IT DONE SO QUICK?
OH, THAT THING?
I JUST TRADED IT OUT WITH A DISPLAY MODEL WHEN I GOT THE TV.☆ *AM I A GENIUS OR WHAT?*
THAT MORON WAS SO LOST IN LA-LA LAND THAT HE DIDN'T EVEN NOTICE!♡ *WHAT AN IDIOT!*♥
CHEATING'S AWESOME!!!!

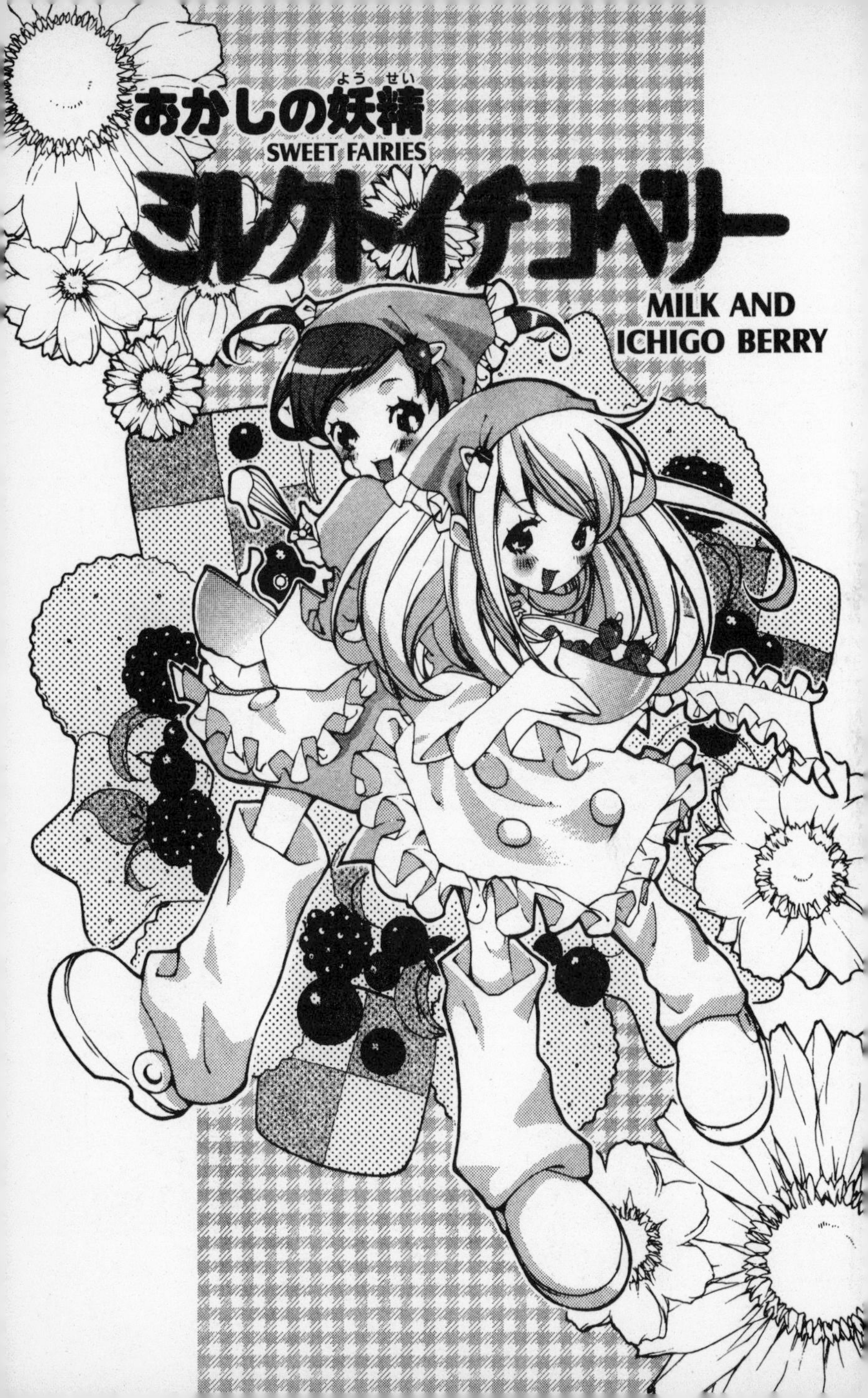

おかしの妖精
SWEET FAIRIES
ミルクトイチゴベリー
MILK AND
ICHIGO BERRY

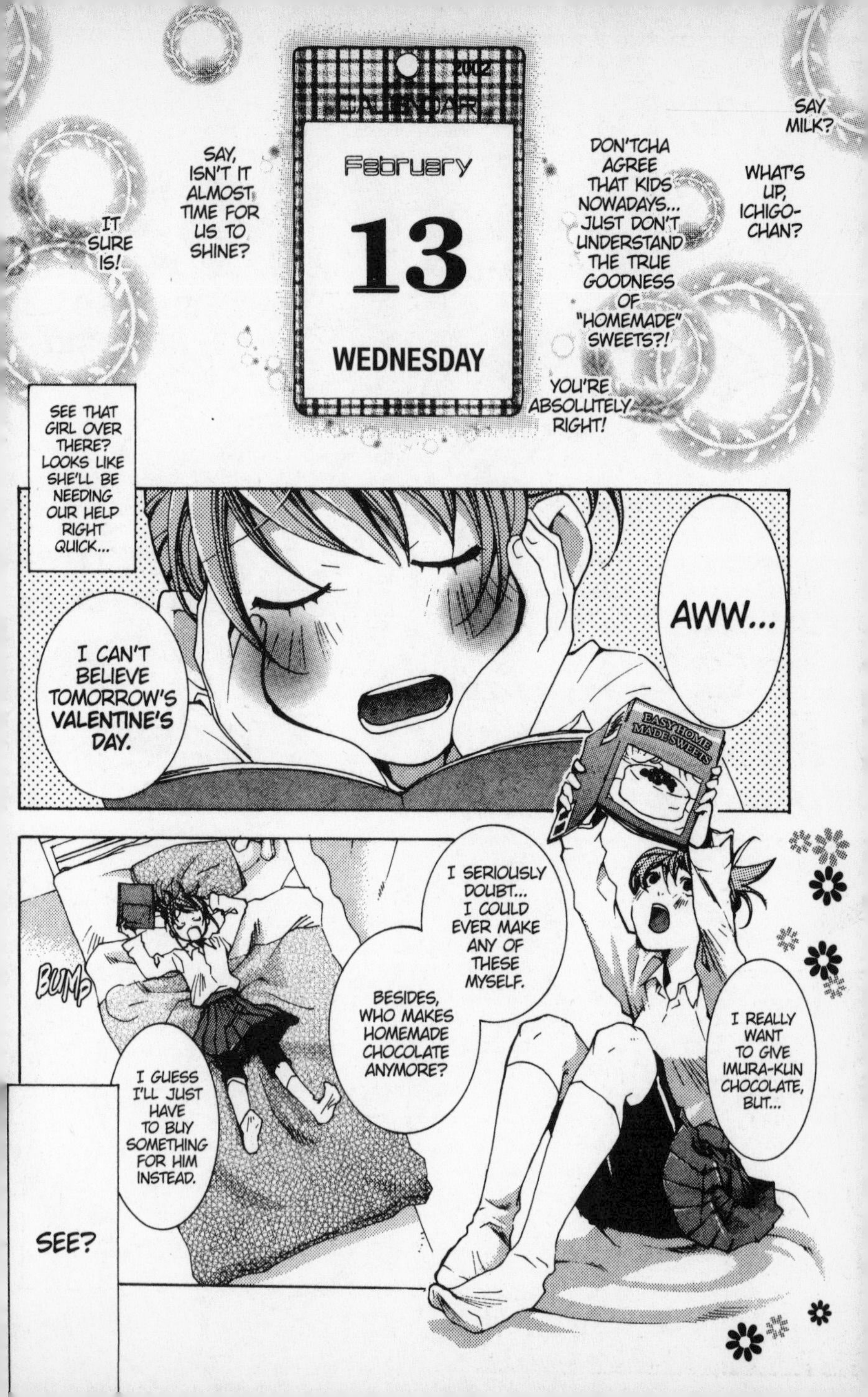
SAY MILK?
WHAT'S UP, ICHIGO-CHAN?
2002
CALENDAR
February
13
WEDNESDAY
DON'TCHA AGREE THAT KIDS NOWADAYS... JUST DON'T UNDERSTAND THE TRUE GOODNESS OF "HOMEMADE" SWEETS?!
YOU'RE ABSOLUTELY RIGHT!
SAY, ISN'T IT ALMOST TIME FOR US TO SHINE?
IT SURE IS!
SEE THAT GIRL OVER THERE? LOOKS LIKE SHE'LL BE NEEDING OUR HELP RIGHT QUICK...
AWW...
I CAN'T BELIEVE TOMORROW'S VALENTINE'S DAY.
EASY HOME MADE SWEETS
I REALLY WANT TO GIVE IMURA-KUN CHOCOLATE, BUT...
I SERIOUSLY DOUBT... I COULD EVER MAKE ANY OF THESE MYSELF.
BESIDES, WHO MAKES HOMEMADE CHOCOLATE ANYMORE?
BUMP
I GUESS I'LL JUST HAVE TO BUY SOMETHING FOR HIM INSTEAD.
SEE?

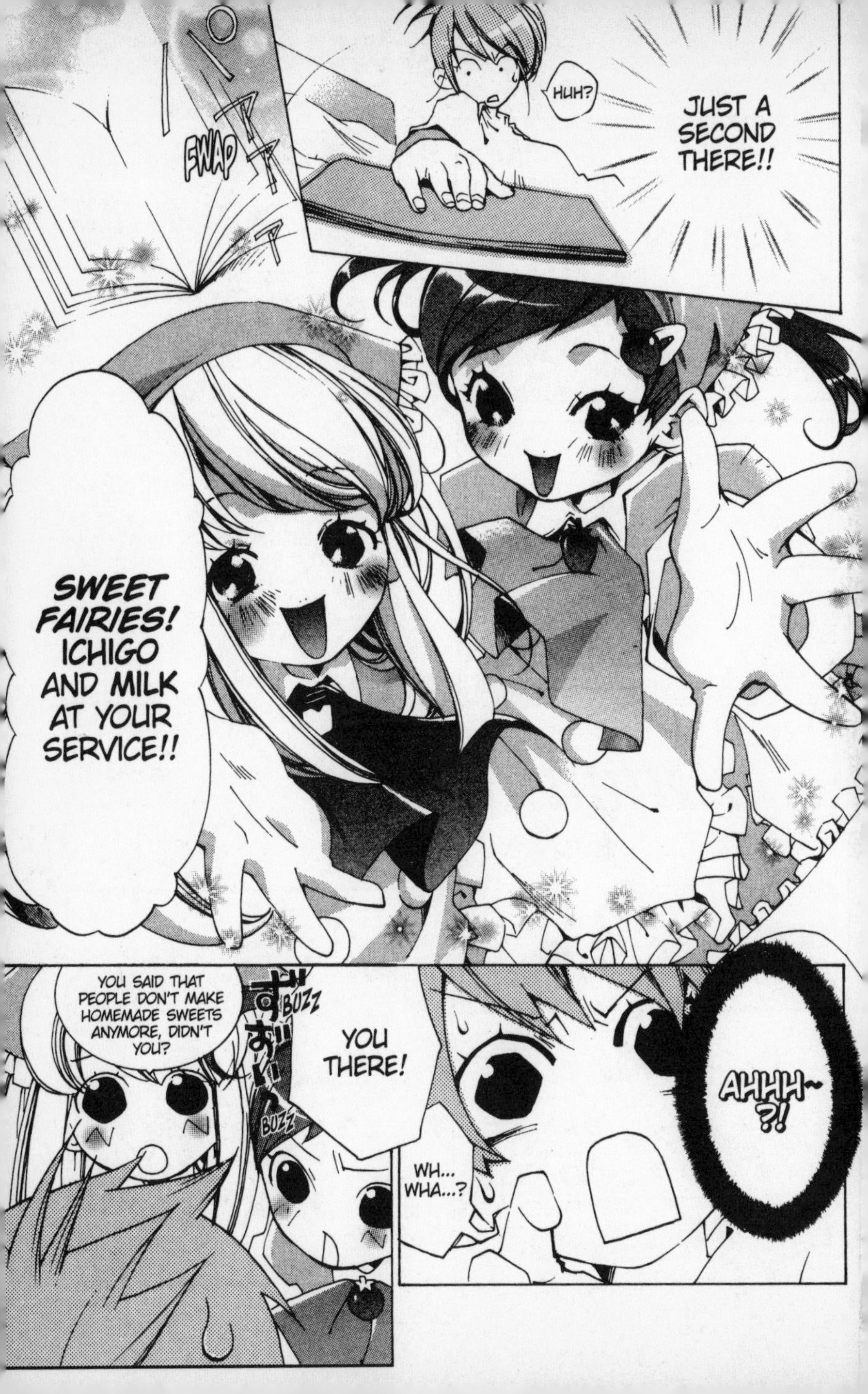
JUST A SECOND THERE!!
HUH?
FWAP
SWEET FAIRIES! ICHIGO AND MILK AT YOUR SERVICE!!
AHHH~ ?!
WH... WHA...?
YOU THERE!
BUZZ
BUZZ
YOU SAID THAT PEOPLE DON'T MAKE HOMEMADE SWEETS ANYMORE, DIDN'T YOU?

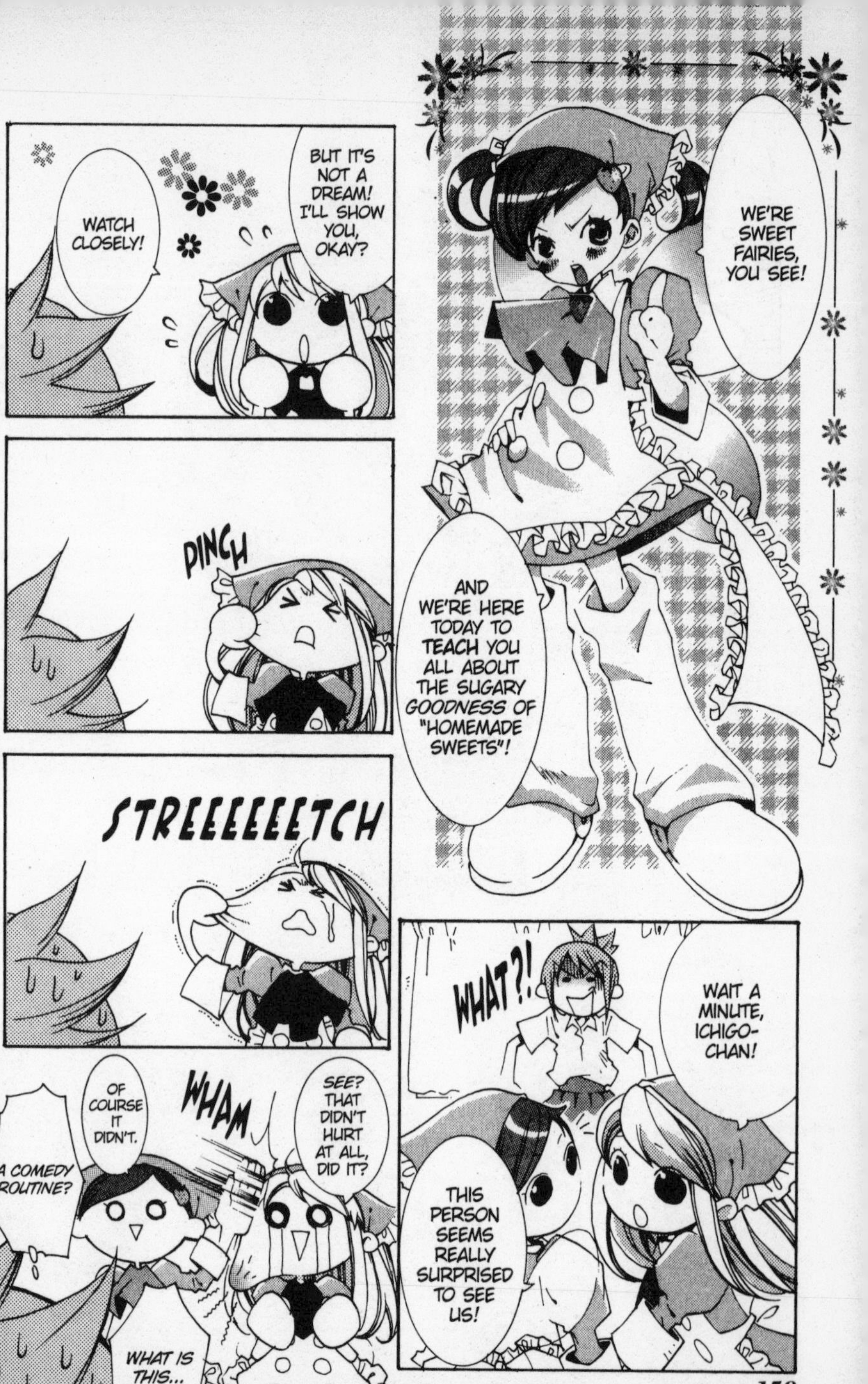
WE'RE SWEET FAIRIES, YOU SEE!
AND WE'RE HERE TODAY TO TEACH YOU ALL ABOUT THE SUGARY GOODNESS OF "HOMEMADE SWEETS"!
WAIT A MINUTE, ICHIGO-CHAN!
WHAT?!
THIS PERSON SEEMS REALLY SURPRISED TO SEE US!
BUT IT'S NOT A DREAM! I'LL SHOW YOU, OKAY?
WATCH CLOSELY!
PINCH
STREEEEEETCH
SEE? THAT DIDN'T HURT AT ALL, DID IT?
WHAM
OF COURSE IT DIDN'T.
A COMEDY ROUTINE?
WHAT IS THIS...

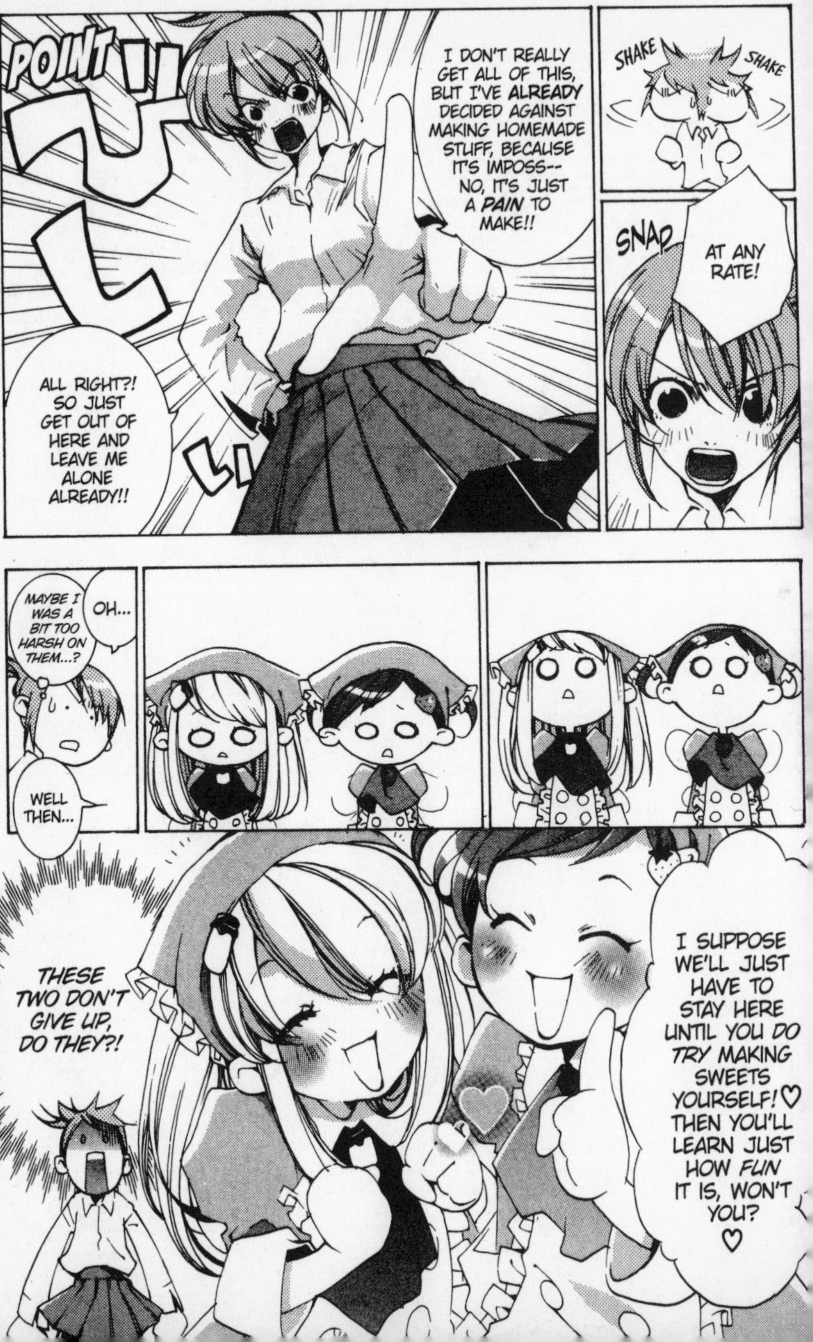

SHAKE
SHAKE
SNAP
AT ANY RATE!
POINT!!
I DON'T REALLY GET ALL OF THIS, BUT I'VE **ALREADY** DECIDED AGAINST MAKING HOMEMADE STUFF, BECAUSE IT'S IMPOSS-- NO, IT'S JUST A *PAIN* TO MAKE!!
ALL RIGHT?! SO JUST GET OUT OF HERE AND LEAVE ME ALONE ALREADY!!
OH...
MAYBE I WAS A BIT TOO HARSH ON THEM...?
WELL THEN...
I SUPPOSE WE'LL JUST HAVE TO STAY HERE UNTIL YOU *DO TRY* MAKING SWEETS YOURSELF! ♡ THEN YOU'LL LEARN JUST HOW *FUN* IT IS, WON'T YOU? ♡
THESE TWO DON'T GIVE UP, DO THEY?!

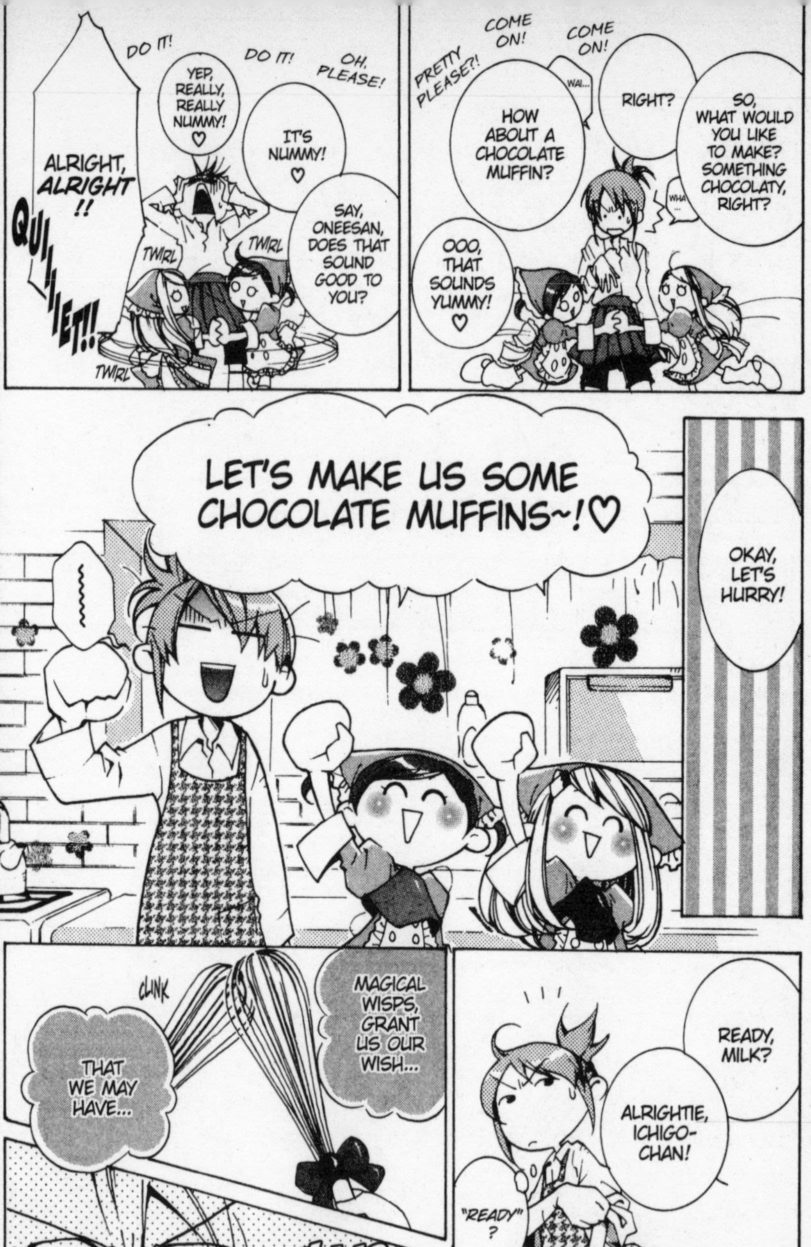
COME ON!
COME ON!
PRETTY PLEASE?!
SO, WHAT WOULD YOU LIKE TO MAKE? SOMETHING CHOCOLATY, RIGHT?
RIGHT?
WAI...
HOW ABOUT A CHOCOLATE MUFFIN?
WHA...
OOO, THAT SOUNDS YUMMY! ♡
OH, PLEASE!
DO IT!
IT'S NUMMY! ♡
YEP, REALLY, REALLY NUMMY! ♡
DO IT!
SAY, ONEESAN, DOES THAT SOUND GOOD TO YOU?
ALRIGHT, ALRIGHT!!
TWIRL
TWIRL
QUIIIIET!!
TWIRL
OKAY, LET'S HURRY!
LET'S MAKE US SOME CHOCOLATE MUFFINS~!♡
READY, MILK?
ALRIGHTIE, ICHIGO-CHAN!
"READY"?
MAGICAL WISPS, GRANT US OUR WISH...
CLINK
THAT WE MAY HAVE...
HUH?

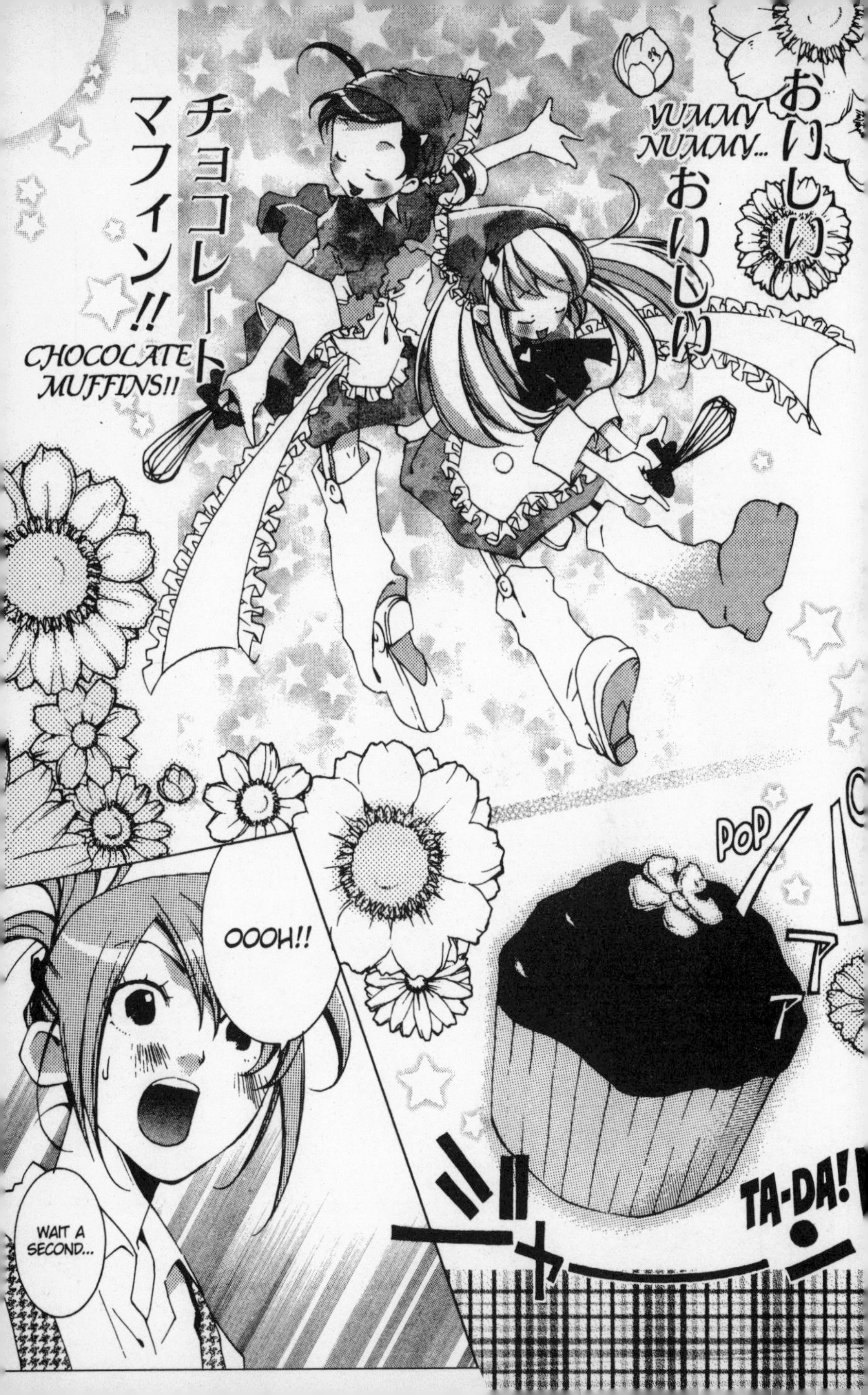

おいしい おいしい
YUMMY NUMMY...
チョコレートマフィン!!
CHOCOLATE MUFFINS!!
POP
TA-DA!
OOOH!!
WAIT A SECOND...

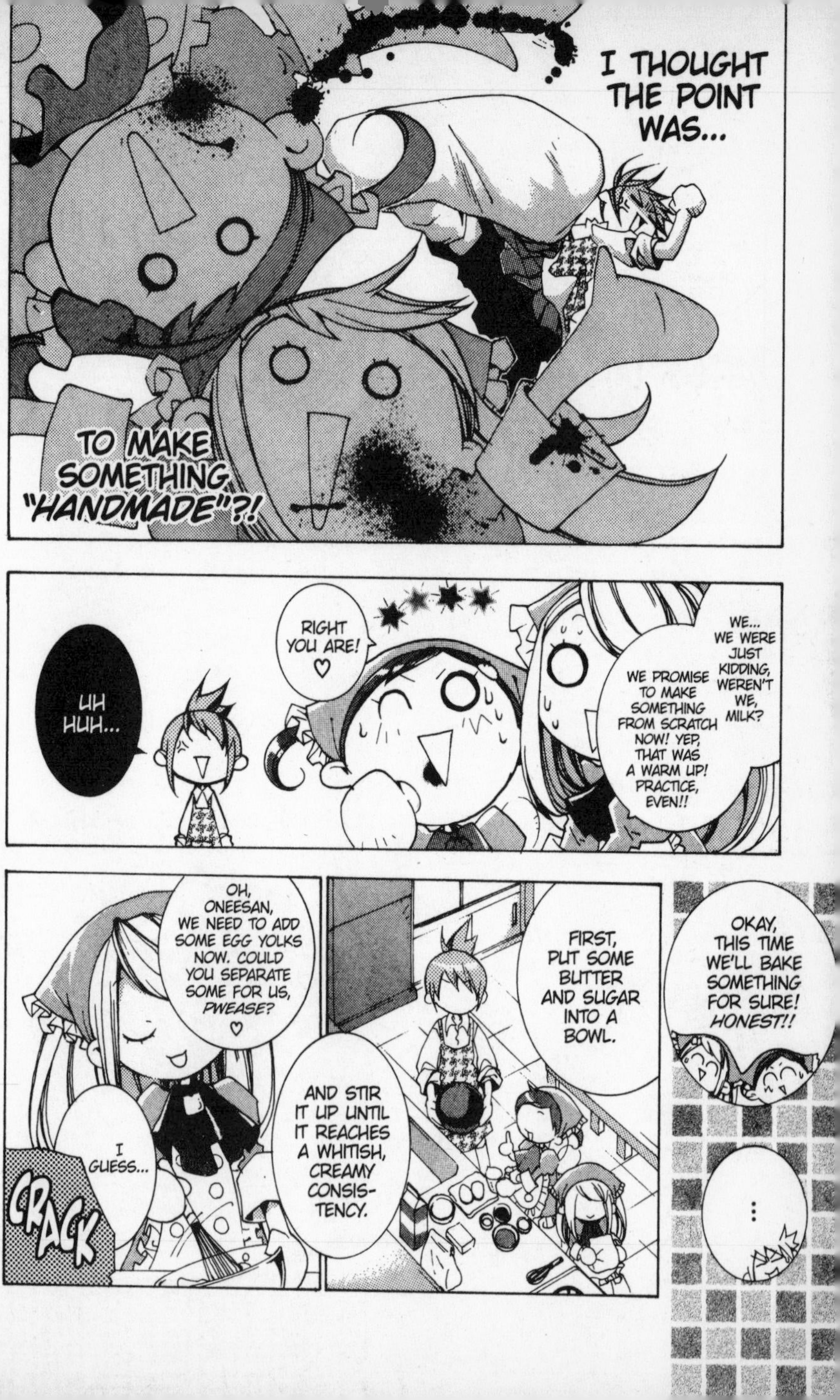
I THOUGHT THE POINT WAS...
TO MAKE SOMETHING "*HANDMADE*"?!
WE... WE WERE JUST KIDDING, WEREN'T WE, MILK?
WE PROMISE TO MAKE SOMETHING FROM SCRATCH NOW! YEP, THAT WAS A WARM UP! PRACTICE, EVEN!!
RIGHT YOU ARE! ♡
UH HUH...
OKAY, THIS TIME WE'LL BAKE SOMETHING FOR SURE! *HONEST!!*
...
FIRST, PUT SOME BUTTER AND SUGAR INTO A BOWL.
AND STIR IT UP UNTIL IT REACHES A WHITISH, CREAMY CONSISTENCY.
OH, ONEESAN, WE NEED TO ADD SOME EGG YOLKS NOW. COULD YOU SEPARATE SOME FOR US, *PWEASE?* ♡
I GUESS...
CRACK

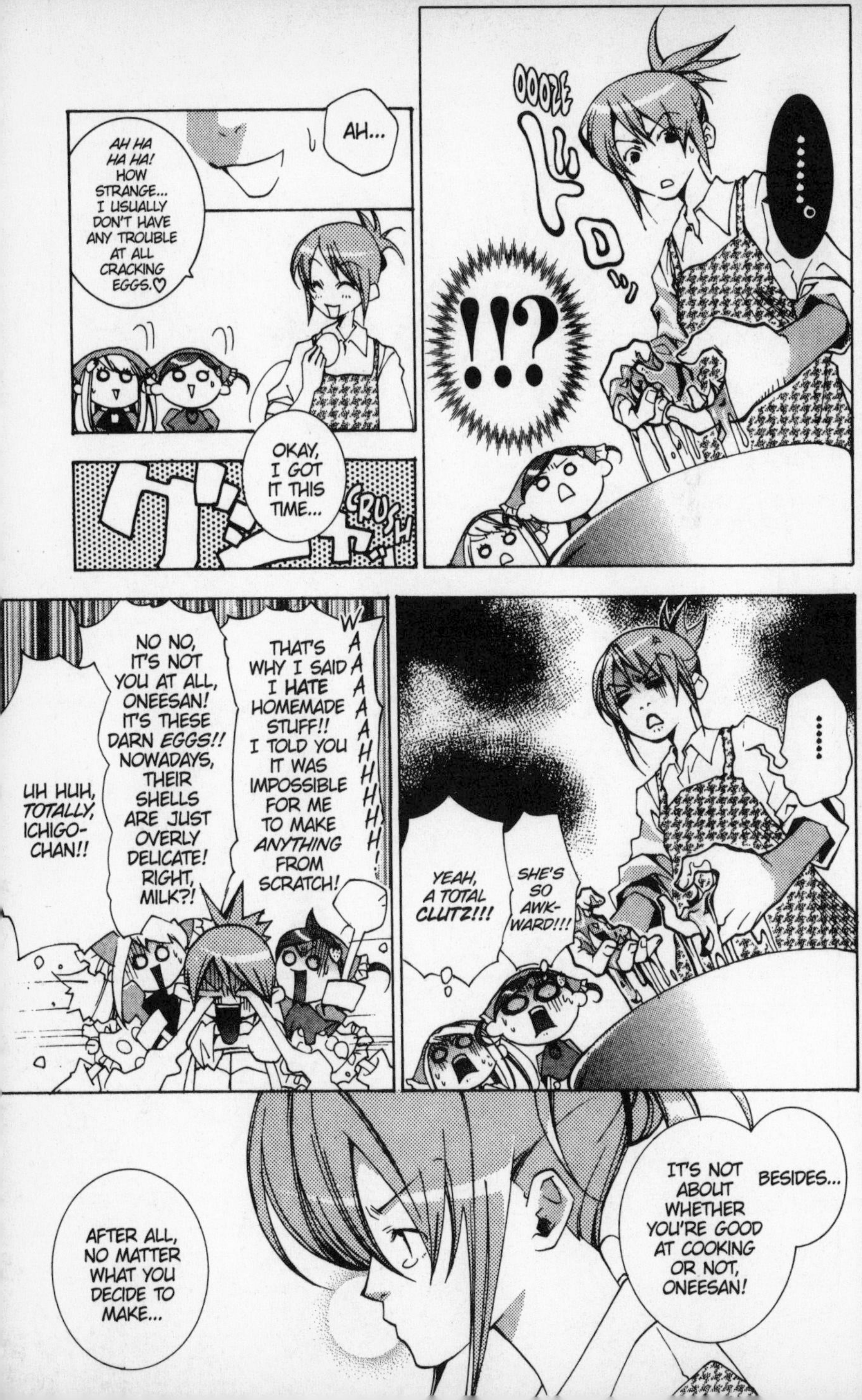
......
OOOZE
!!?
AH...
AH HA HA HA! HOW STRANGE... I USUALLY DON'T HAVE ANY TROUBLE AT ALL CRACKING EGGS.♡
OKAY, I GOT IT THIS TIME...
CRUSH
......
SHE'S SO AWKWARD!!!
YEAH, A TOTAL CLUTZ!!!
WAAAAAAHHHHH!
THAT'S WHY I SAID I HATE HOMEMADE STUFF!! I TOLD YOU IT WAS IMPOSSIBLE FOR ME TO MAKE ANYTHING FROM SCRATCH!
NO NO, IT'S NOT YOU AT ALL, ONEESAN! IT'S THESE DARN EGGS!! NOWADAYS, THEIR SHELLS ARE JUST OVERLY DELICATE! RIGHT, MILK?!
UH HUH, TOTALLY, ICHIGO-CHAN!!
BESIDES...
IT'S NOT ABOUT WHETHER YOU'RE GOOD AT COOKING OR NOT, ONEESAN!
AFTER ALL, NO MATTER WHAT YOU DECIDE TO MAKE...

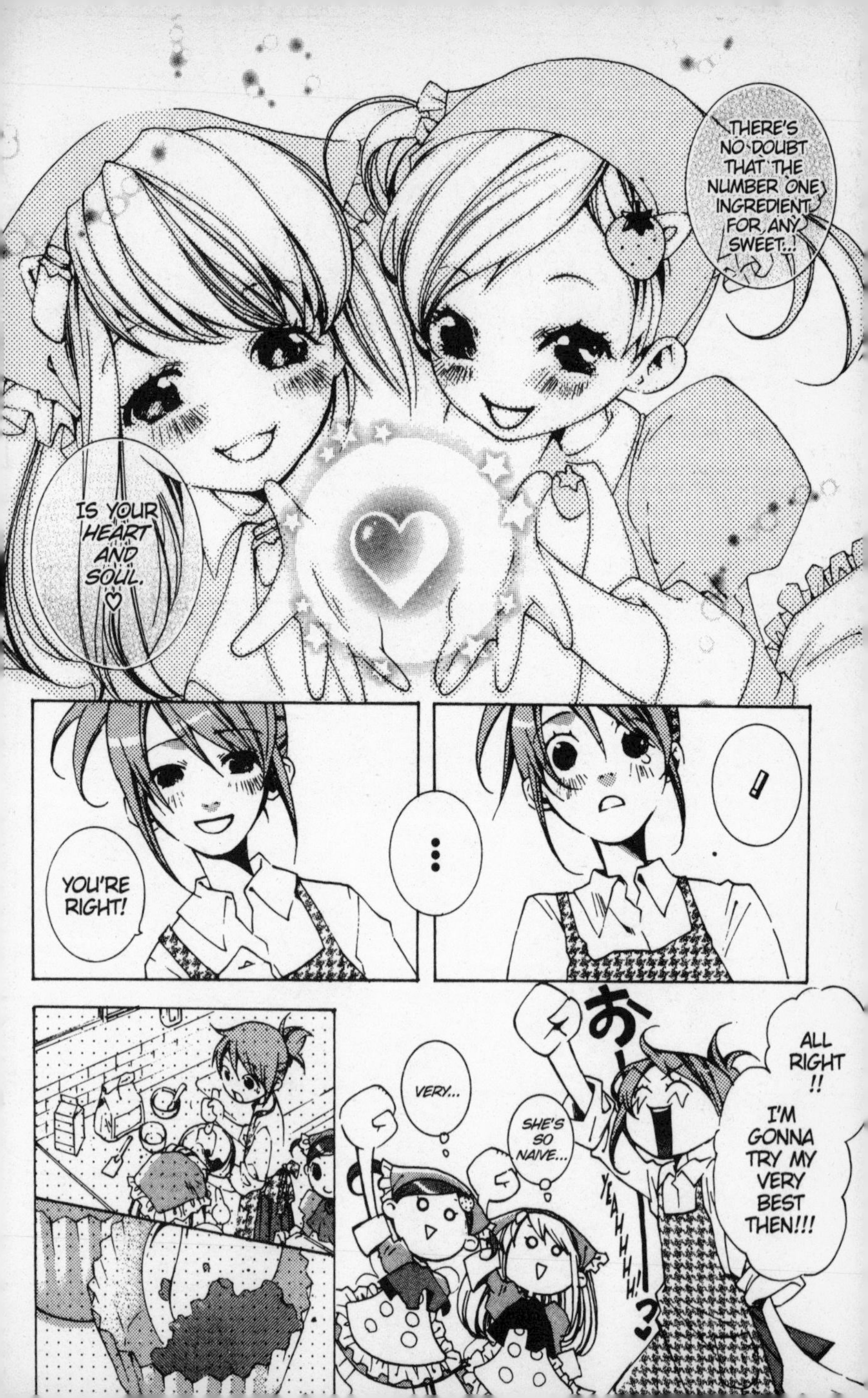
THERE'S NO DOUBT THAT THE NUMBER ONE INGREDIENT FOR ANY SWEET...!
IS YOUR HEART AND SOUL. ♡
!
•••
YOU'RE RIGHT!
ALL RIGHT!!
I'M GONNA TRY MY VERY BEST THEN!!!
おー
YEAHHHH!?
SHE'S SO NAIVE...
VERY...

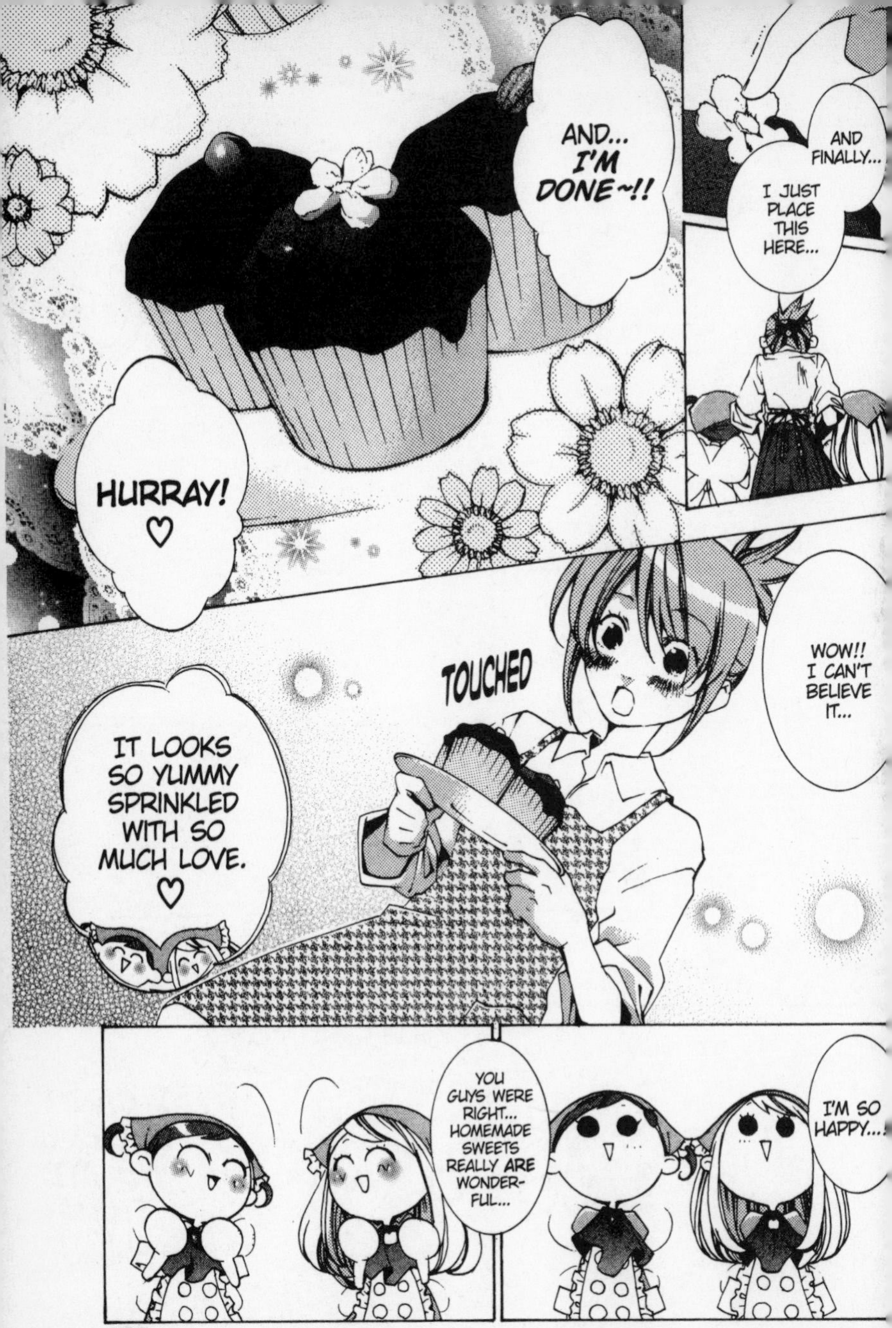
AND FINALLY...
I JUST PLACE THIS HERE...
AND... I'M DONE~!!
HURRAY! ♡
WOW!! I CAN'T BELIEVE IT...
TOUCHED
IT LOOKS SO YUMMY SPRINKLED WITH SO MUCH LOVE. ♡
I'M SO HAPPY...
YOU GUYS WERE RIGHT... HOMEMADE SWEETS REALLY ARE WONDERFUL...

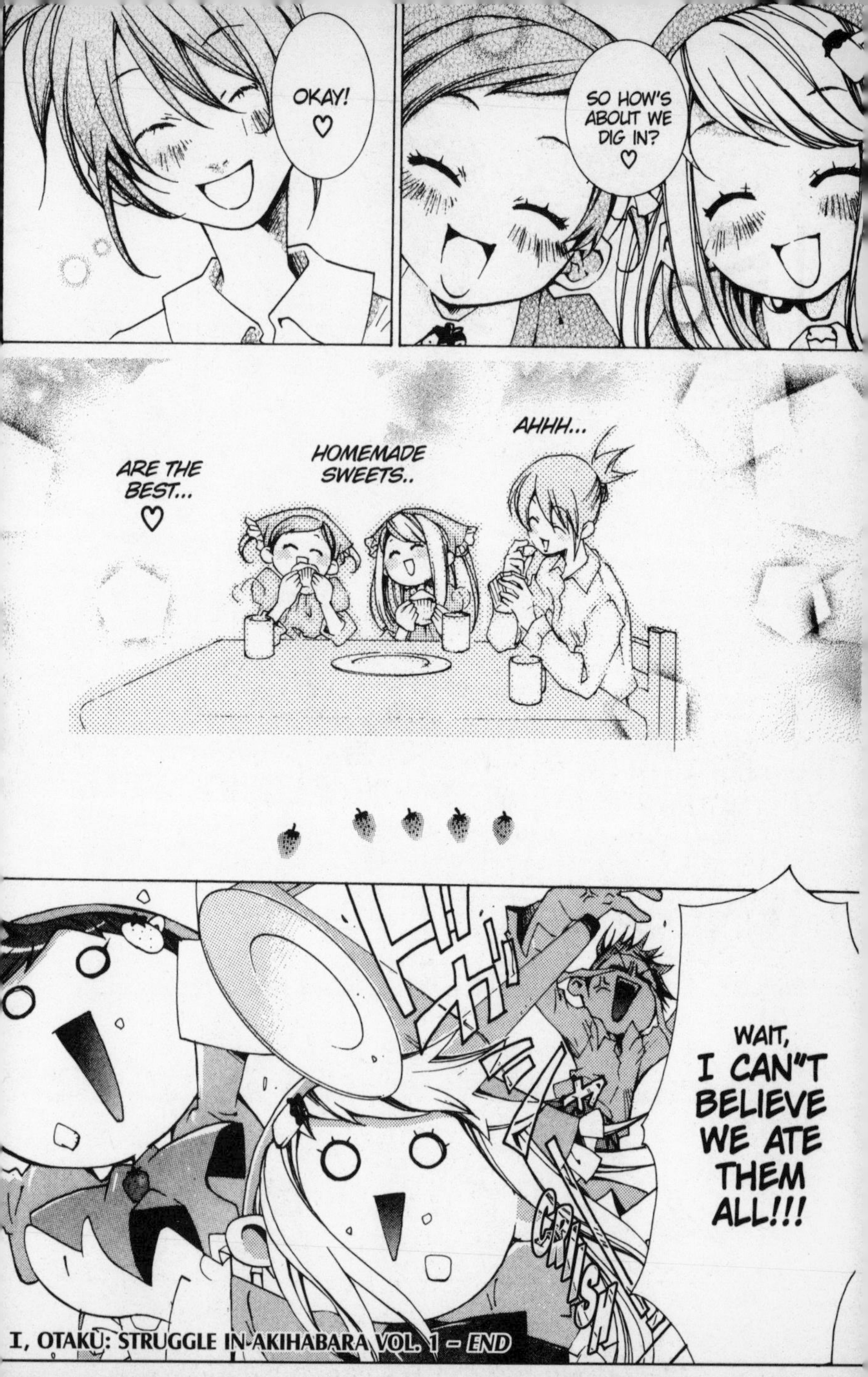
SO HOW'S ABOUT WE DIG IN? ♡
OKAY! ♡
AHHH...
HOMEMADE SWEETS..
ARE THE BEST... ♡
WAIT, I CAN"T BELIEVE WE ATE THEM ALL!!!
I, OTAKU: STRUGGLE IN AKIHABARA VOL. 1 - *END*

Illustration Gallery

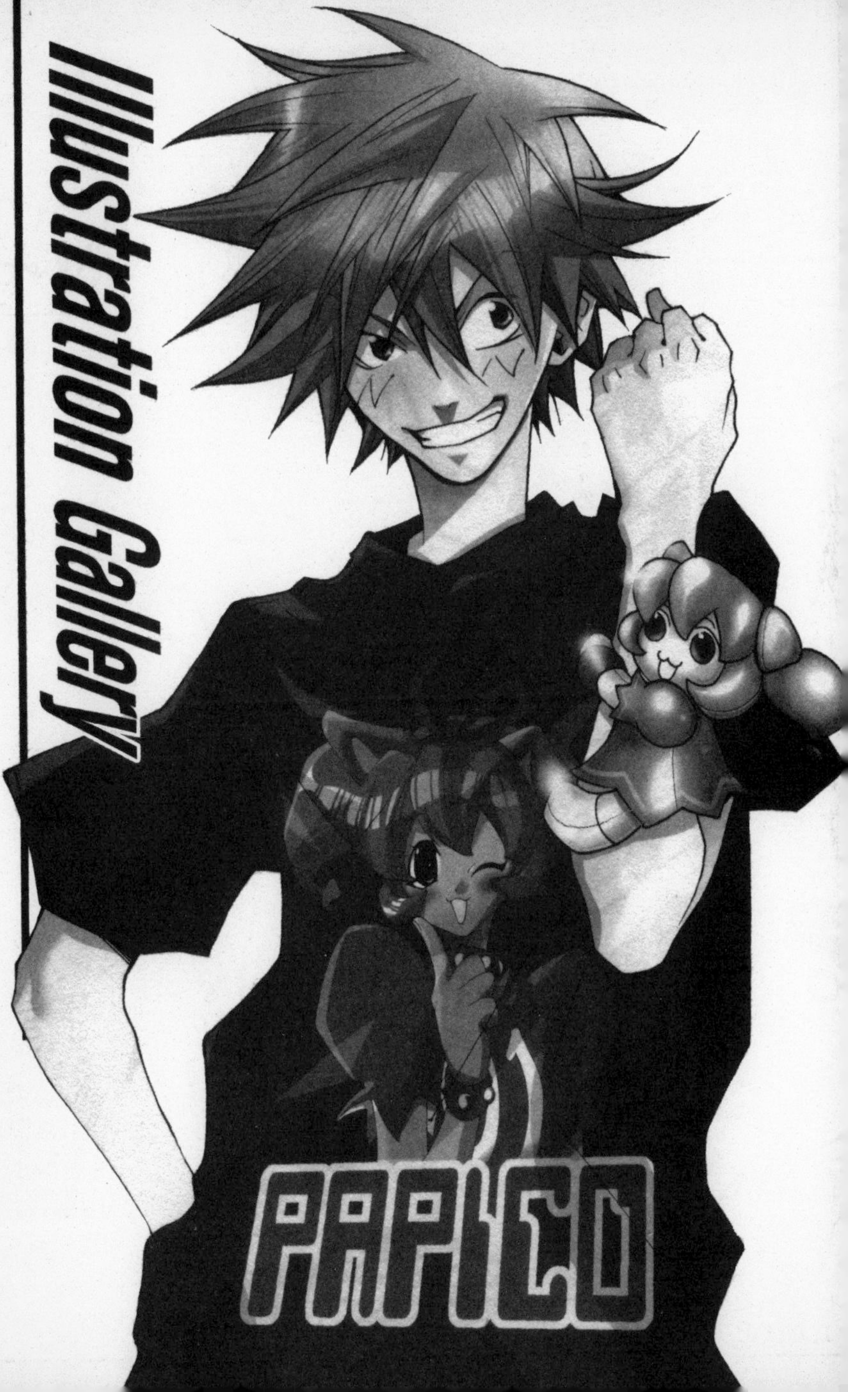
PAPICO

ENATSU SOTA

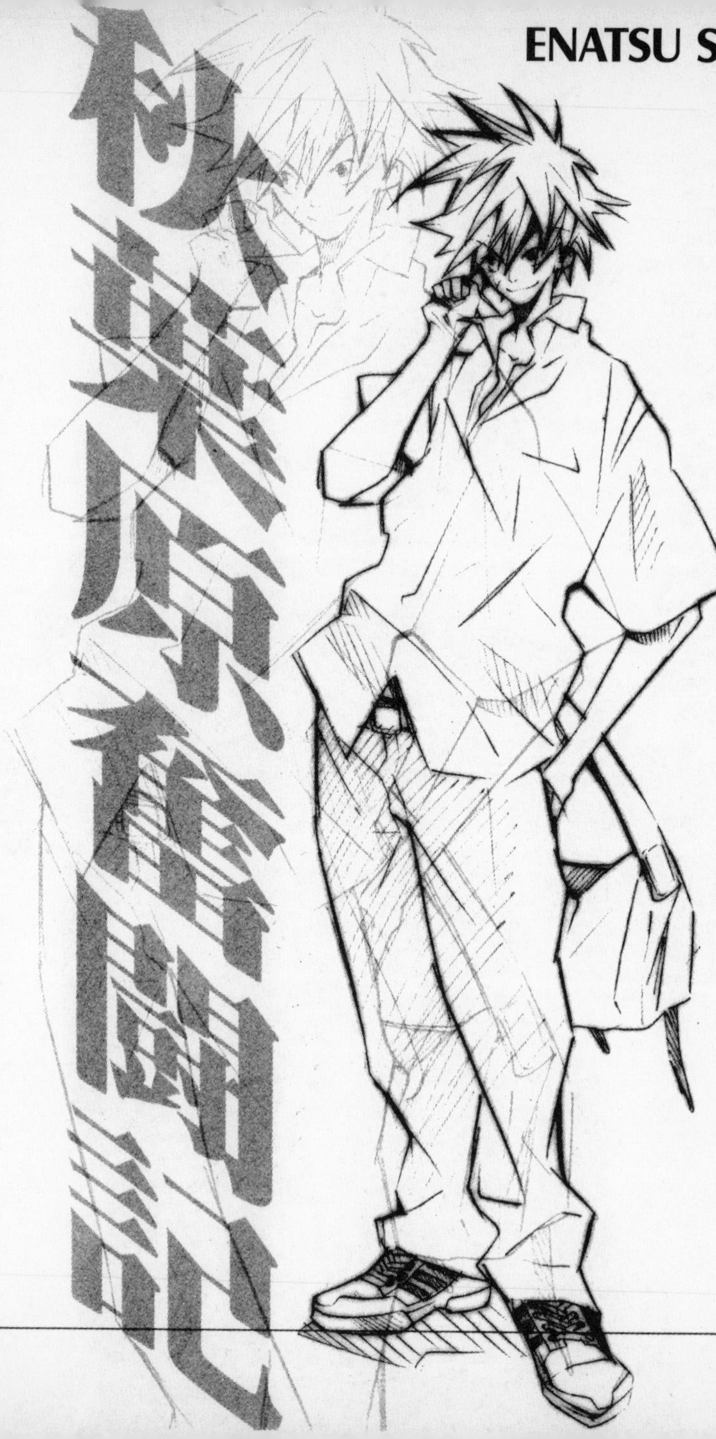

height-171/weight-58/bloodtype-a/birth-07/20

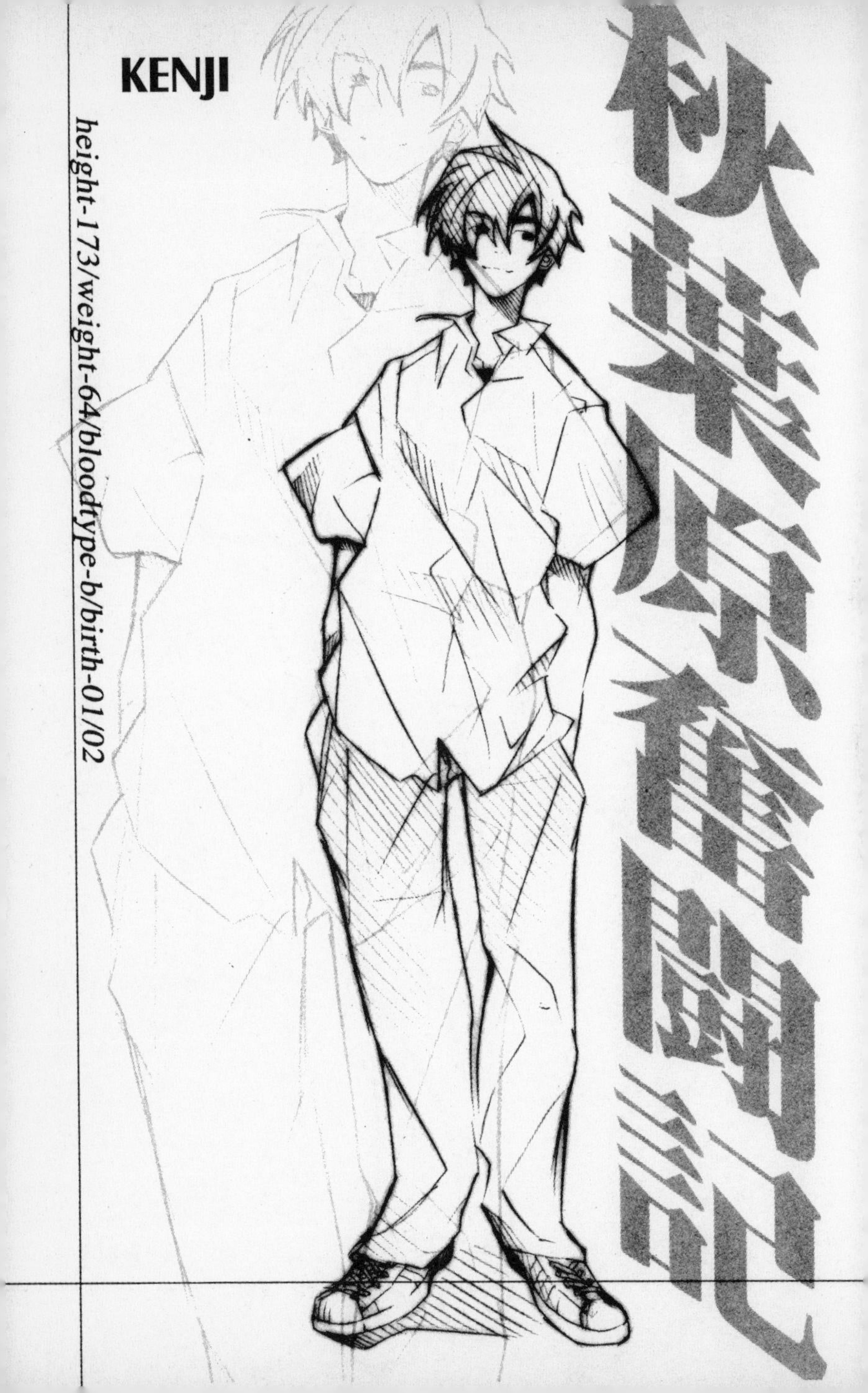
秋葉原奮闘記
KENJI
height-173/weight-64/bloodtype-b/birth-01/02

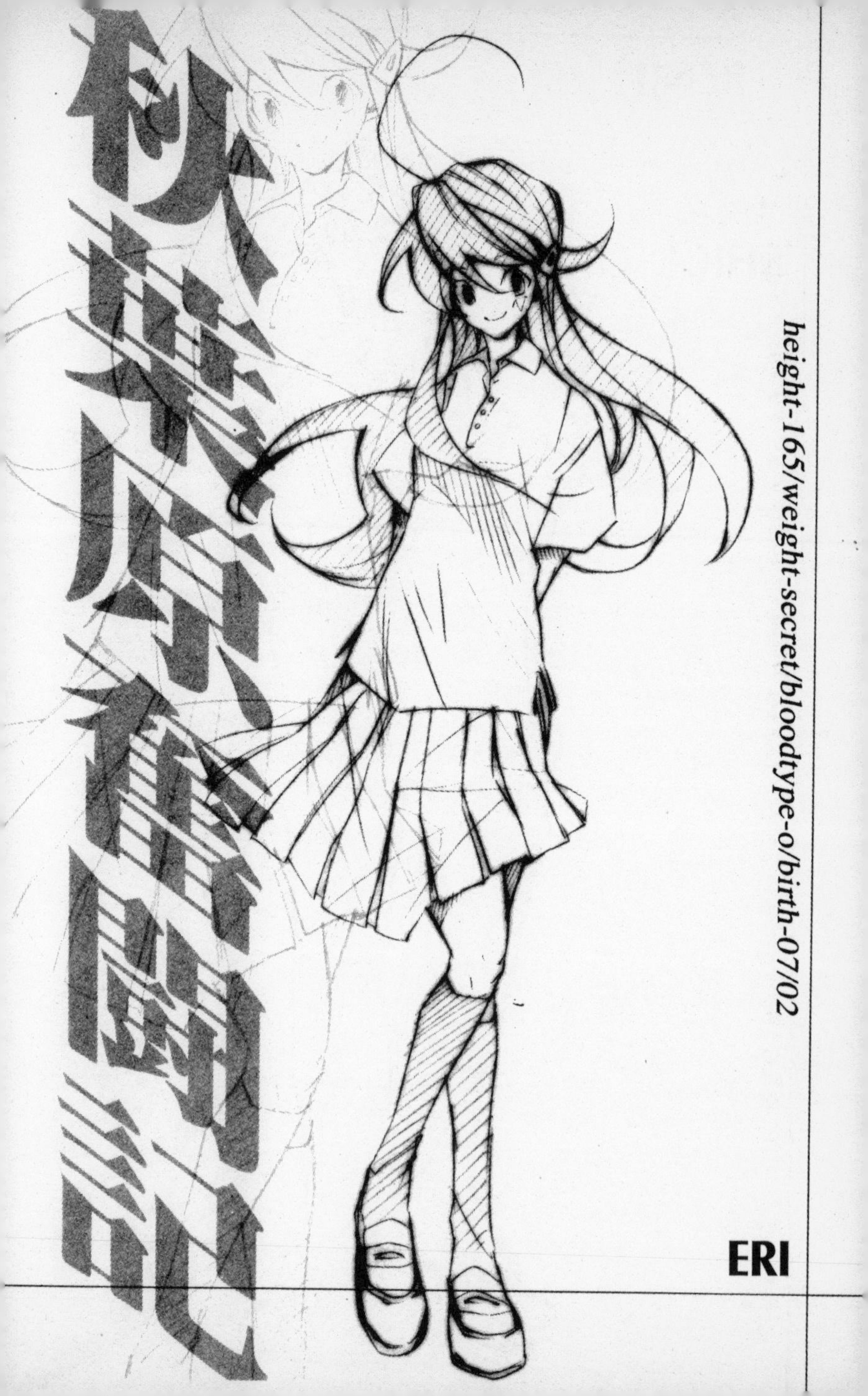
height-165/weight-secret/bloodtype-o/birth-07/02
ERI

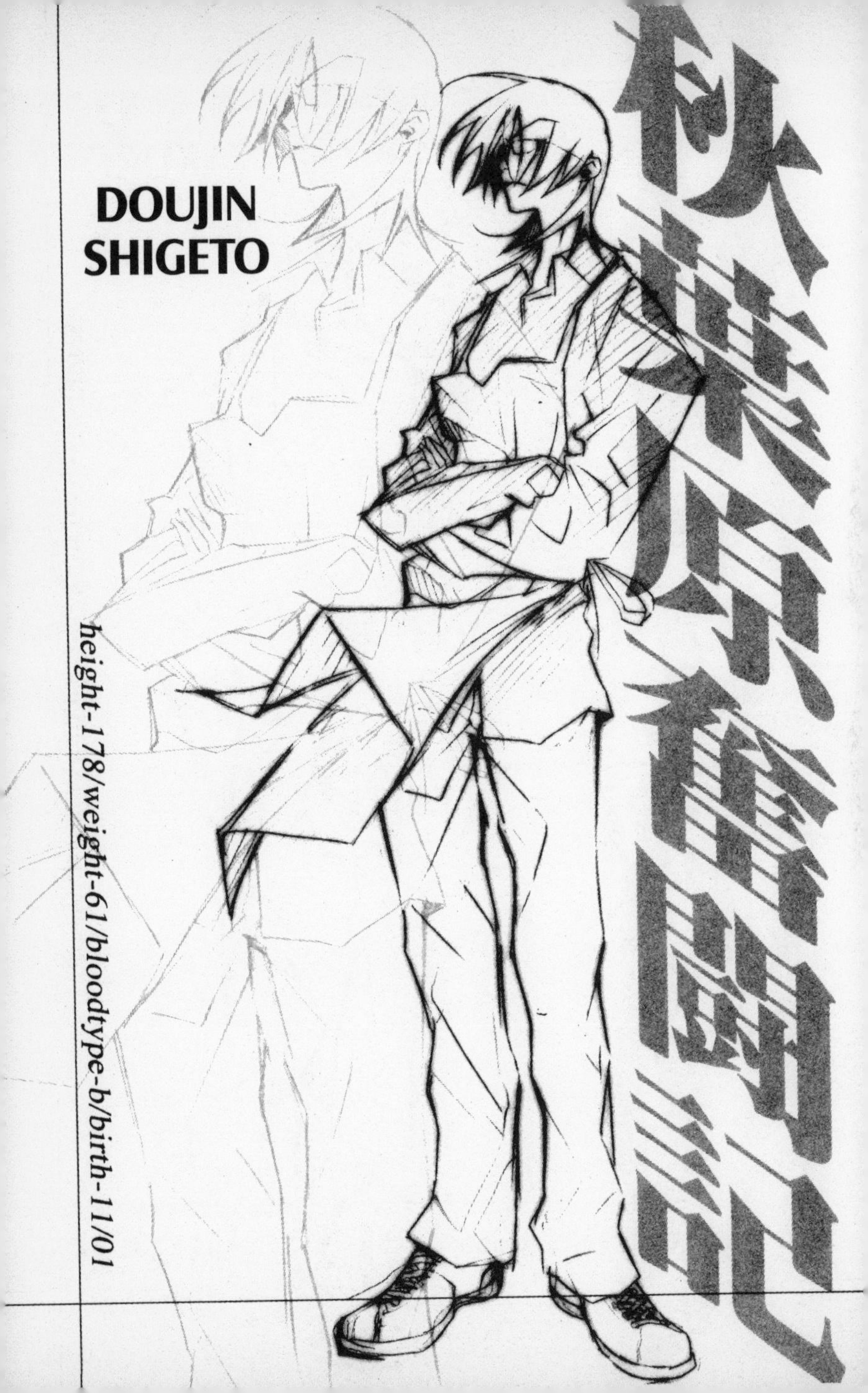
秋葉原奮闘記
DOUJIN
SHIGETO
height-178/weight-61/bloodtype-b/birth-11/01

MANO TAKURO

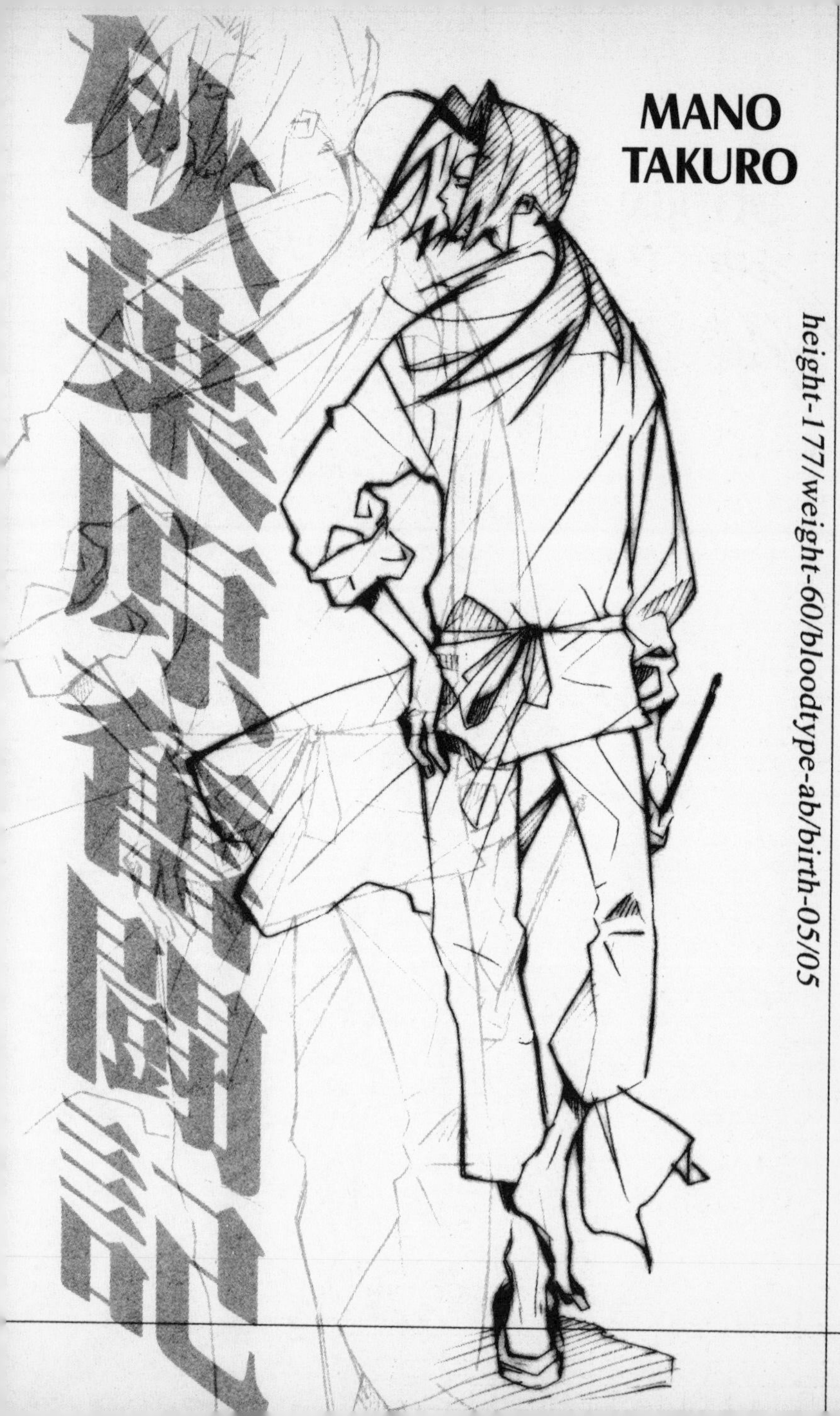

height-177/weight-60/bloodtype-ab/birth-05/05

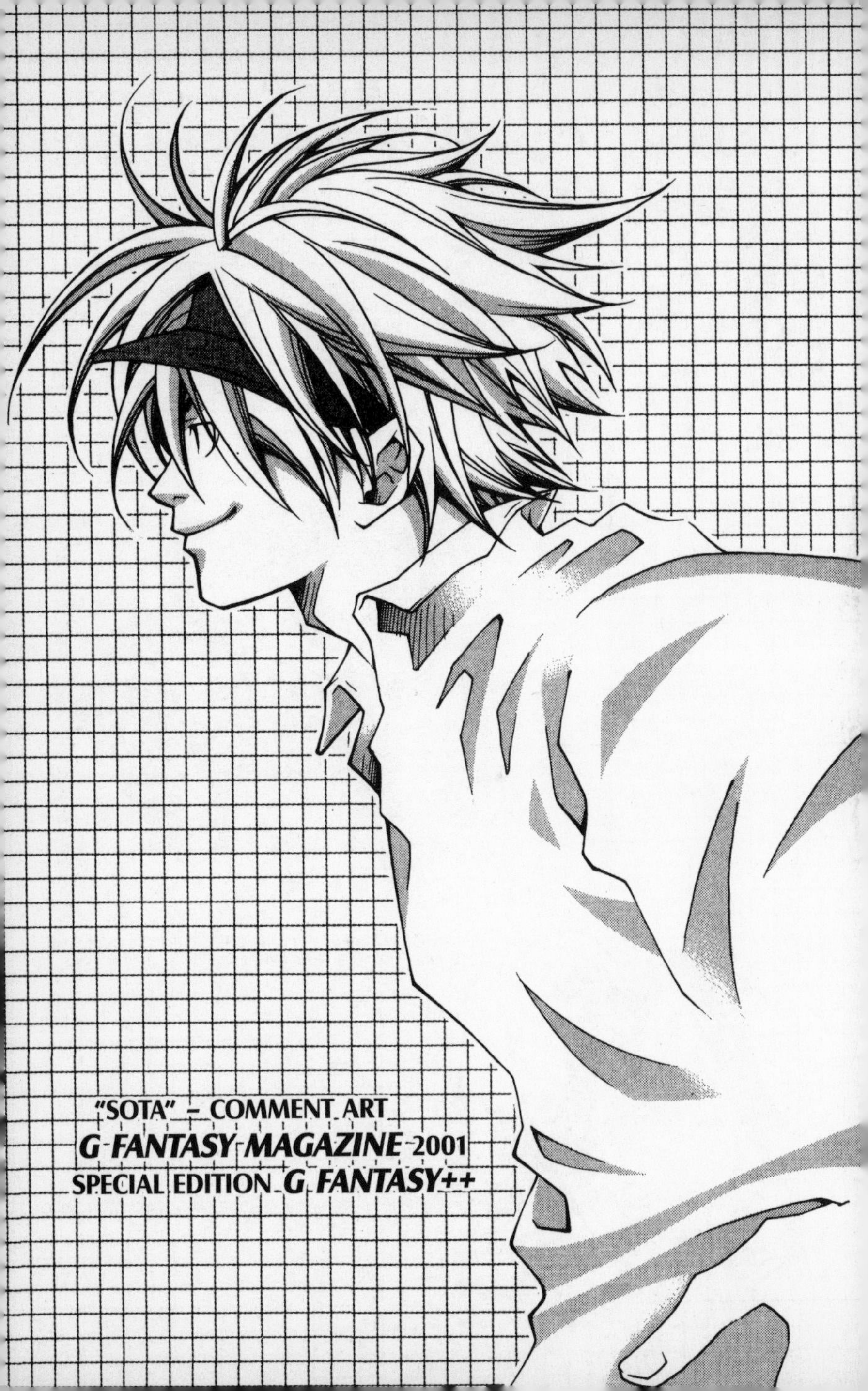
"SOTA" – COMMENT ART
G FANTASY MAGAZINE 2001
SPECIAL EDITION *G FANTASY++*

SOTA-KUN NO AKIHABARA FUNTOHKI

壮太君の アキハバラ 奮闘記

ソウタクンノアキハバラフントウキ

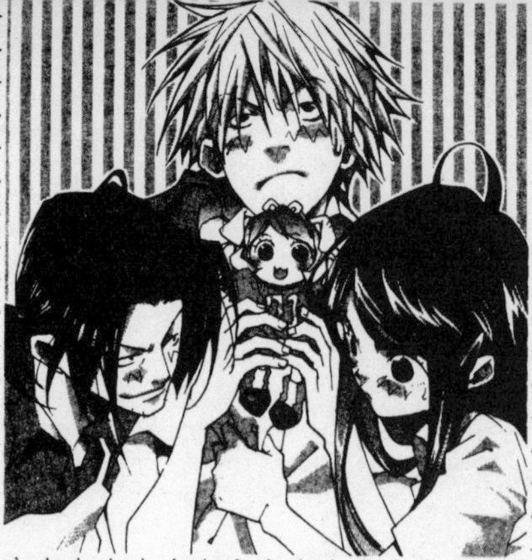

"SOTA-KUN & ERI-CHAN'S AKIHABARA STRUGGLES 2" – PREVIEW ART
G FANTASY MAGAZINE FEBRUARY, 2002

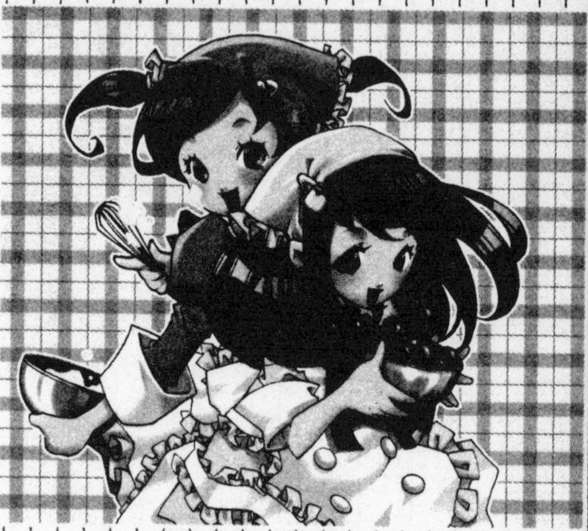

"SWEETS FAIRIES MILK AND ICHIGOBERRY" – COVER ART
G FANTASY MAGAZINE MAY, 2002

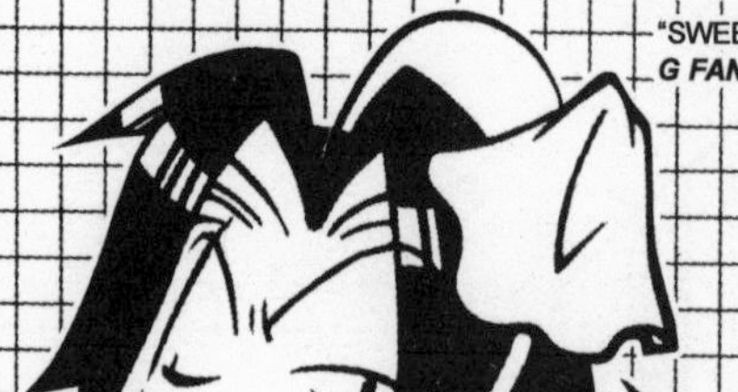
はつばいび
RELEASE DATE

"TENCHO STAMP" – READER MAIL-IN CONTEST GIFT
G FANTASY MAGAZINE DECEMBER, 2002

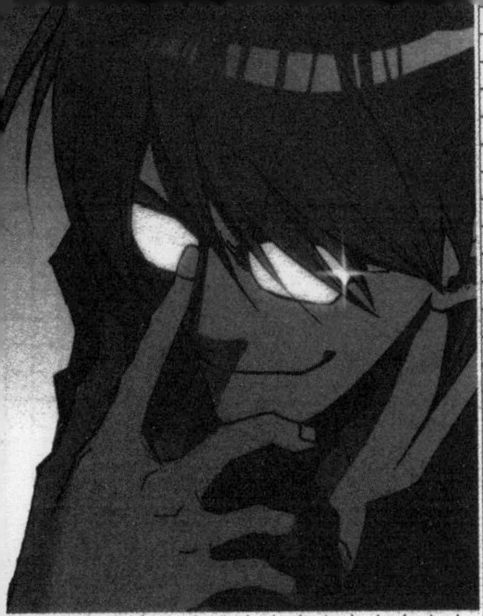

"THE MANGA CAVE TENCHO" – PREVIEW ART
G FANTASY MAGAZINE MARCH, 2003

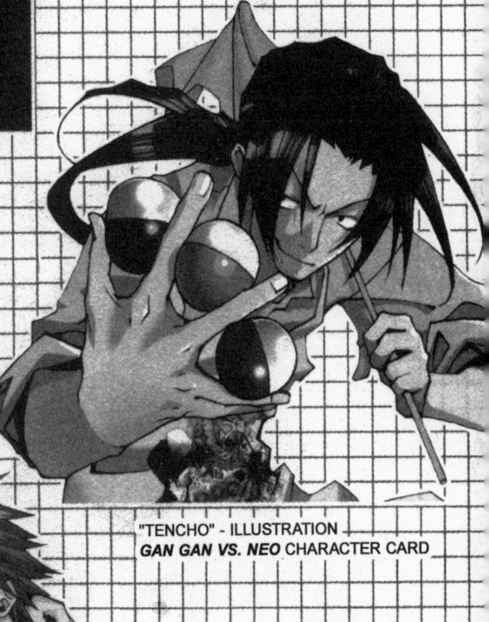

"TENCHO" - ILLUSTRATION
GAN GAN VS. NEO CHARACTER CARD

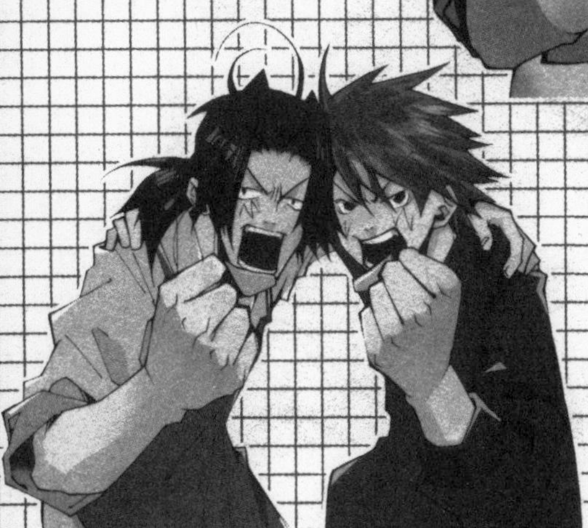

"SOTA AND THE TENCHO" – COVER ART
G FANTASY MAGAZINE APRIL, 2003

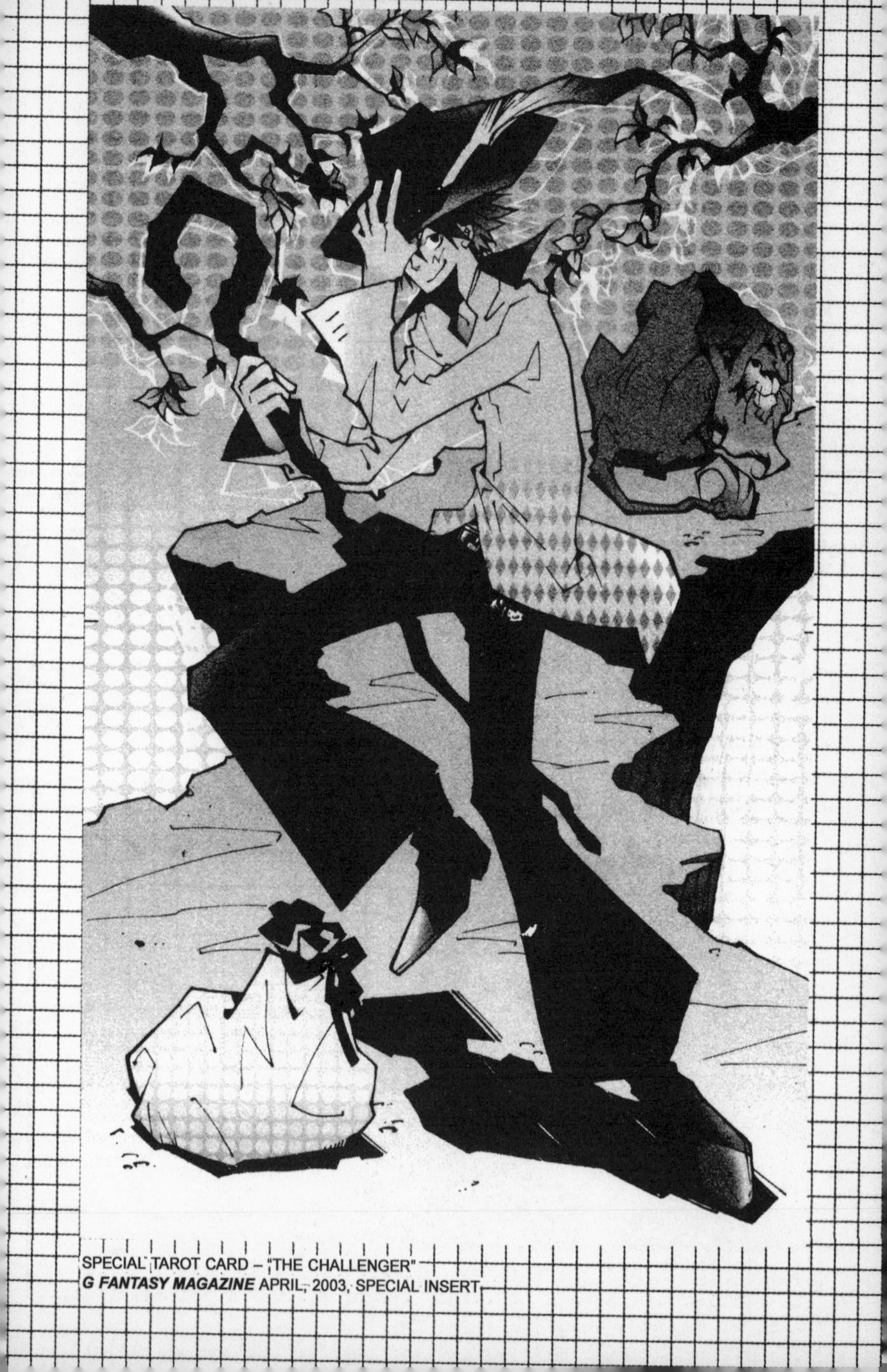

SPECIAL TAROT CARD – "THE CHALLENGER"
G FANTASY MAGAZINE APRIL, 2003, SPECIAL INSERT

SOTA-KUN'S STUGGLE IN AKIHABARA 4-KOMA THEATRE

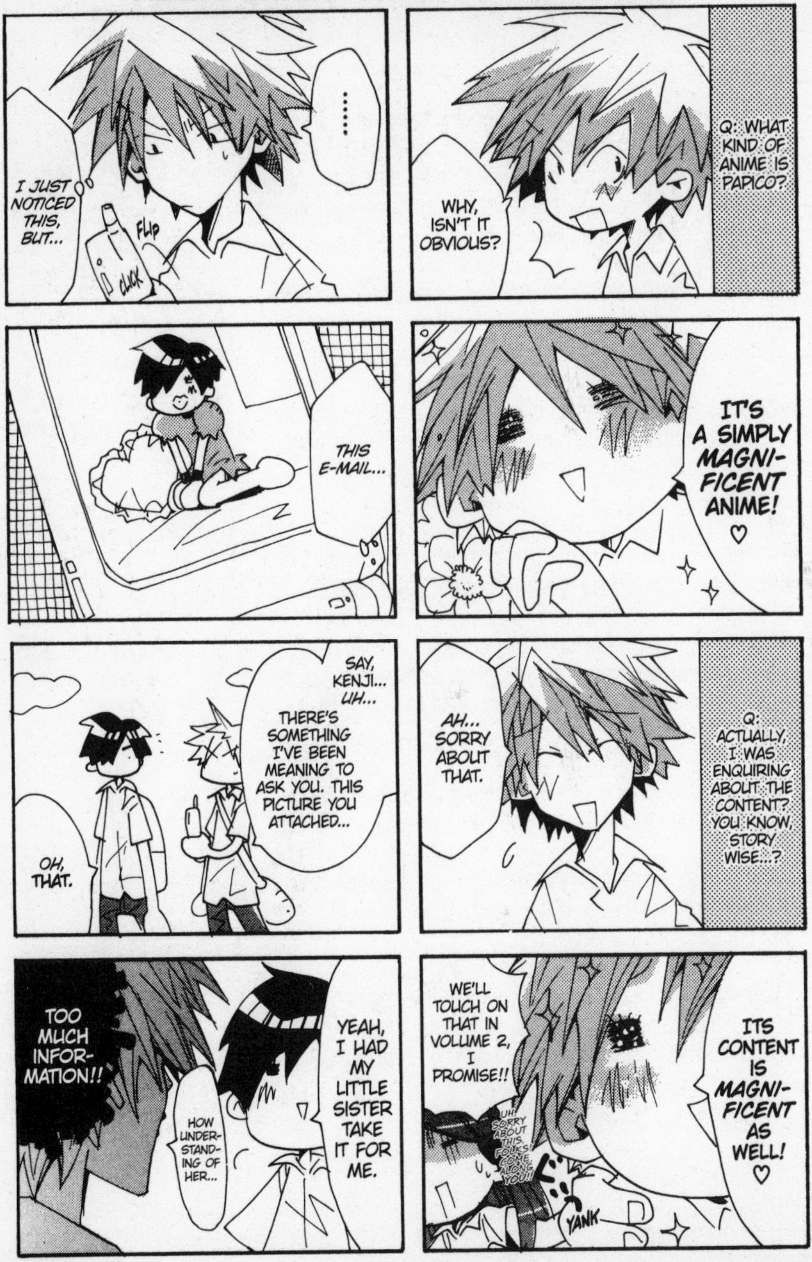

Q: WHAT KIND OF ANIME IS PAPICO?
WHY, ISN'T IT OBVIOUS?
IT'S A SIMPLY MAGNIFICENT ANIME! ♡
Q: ACTUALLY, I WAS ENQUIRING ABOUT THE CONTENT? YOU KNOW, STORY WISE...?
AH... SORRY ABOUT THAT.
ITS CONTENT IS MAGNIFICENT AS WELL! ♡
WE'LL TOUCH ON THAT IN VOLUME 2, I PROMISE!!
UH! SORRY ABOUT THIS, FOLKS! COME ALONG, YOU!!
YANK
......
I JUST NOTICED THIS, BUT...
FLIP
CLICK
THIS E-MAIL...
SAY, KENJI... UH... THERE'S SOMETHING I'VE BEEN MEANING TO ASK YOU. THIS PICTURE YOU ATTACHED...
OH, THAT.
YEAH, I HAD MY LITTLE SISTER TAKE IT FOR ME.
HOW UNDER-STAND-ING OF HER...
TOO MUCH INFOR-MATION!!

JAPANESE HONORIFICS GUIDE

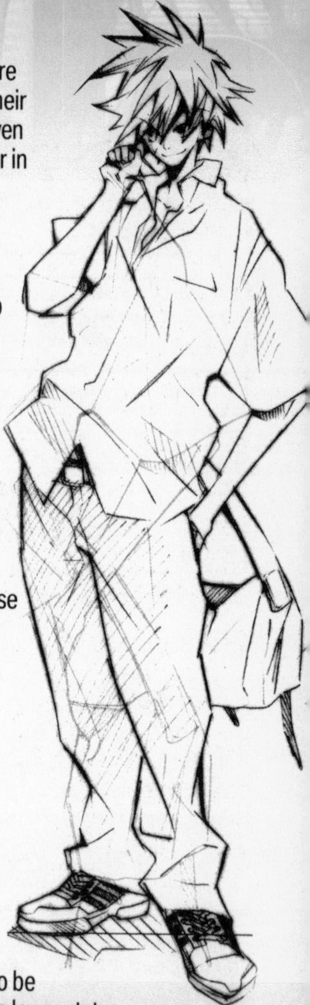

To ensure that all character relationships appear as they were originally intended, all character names have been kept in their original Japanese name order with family name first and given name second. For copyright reasons, creator names appear in standard English name order.

In addition to preserving the original Japanese name order, Seven Seas is committed to ensuring that honorifics—polite speech that indicates a person's status or relationship towards another individual—are retained within this book. Politeness is an integral facet of Japanese culture and we believe that maintaining honorifics in our translations helps bring out the same character nuances as seen in the original work.

The following are some of the more common honorifics you may come across while reading this and other books:

-san – The most common of all honorifics, it is an all-purpose suffix that can be used in any situation where politeness is expected. Generally seen as the equivalent to Mr., Miss, Ms., Mrs., etc.

-sama – This suffix is one level higher than "-san" and is used to confer great respect upon an individual.

-dono – Stemming from the word "tono," meaning "lord," "-dono" signifies an even higher level than "-sama," and confers the utmost respect.

-kun – This suffix is commonly used at the end of boys' names to express either familiarity or endearment. It can also be used when addressing someone younger than oneself or of a lower status.

-chan **–** Another common honorific. This suffix is mainly used to express endearment towards girls, but can also be used when referring to little boys or even pets. Couples are also known to use the term amongst each other to convey a sense of cuteness and intimacy.

Sempai **–** This title is used towards one's senior or "superior"in a particular group or organization. "Sempai" is most often used in a school setting, where underclassmen refer to upperclassmen as "sempai," though it is also commonly said by employees when addressing fellow employees who hold seniority in the workplace.

Sensei **–** Literally meaning "one who has come before," this title is used for teachers, doctors, or masters of any profession or art.

Oniisan **–** This title literally means "big brother." First and foremost, it is used by younger siblings towards older male siblings. It can be used by itself or attached to a person's name as a suffix (niisan). It is often used by a younger person toward an older person unrelated by blood, but as a sign of respect. Other forms include the informal "oniichan" and the more respectful "oniisama."

Oneesan **–** This title is the opposite of "oniisan" and means "big sister." Other forms include the informal "oneechan" and the more respectful "oneesama."

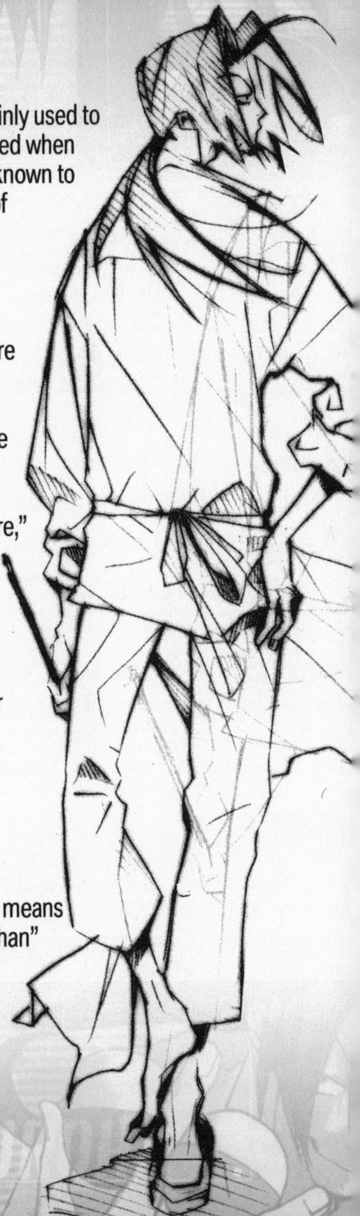

TRANSLATION NOTES

PAGE 3.1

In the original, the "Otakudo Headquarters" is actually called *Otakudo Honpo,* which literally translates to "Otaku Shrine Main Shop." The "Do" in Otakudo can mean shrine or hall, and is used since a lot of otaku seem to make shrines of their fave characters.

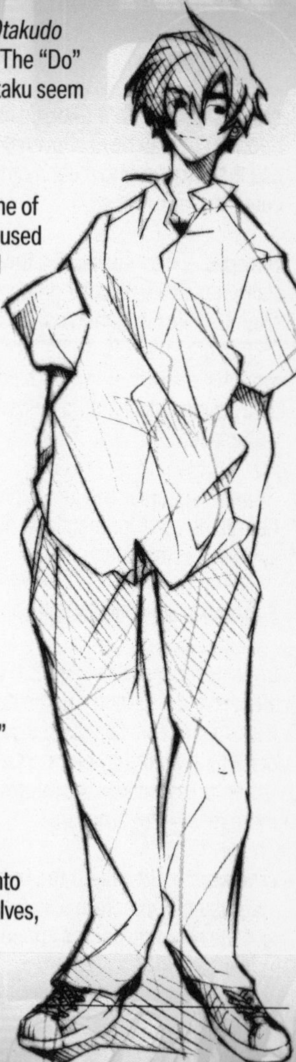

PAGE 5.2

Wanda Degitaru Doki Doki Dogi Okyan na Papico – "Wan" is one of the ways a dog barks in Japanese. (Bark Bark = Wan Wan.) It's used as a pun for the English word, "wonder." Doki Doki is the sound of your heart beating. Okyan means lively or active but is also a pun on how some smaller dogs (like Corgis) are thought to bark, "Kyan kyan." Meanwhile, Papiko is a pun on "Puppy-ko" or Puppy girl.

PAGE 5.3

"Akiba" is an abbreviation for Akihabara.

PAGE 10.1

Mano Takuro is a play on the words *"ma no otaku,"* which means "a true otaku."

PAGE 12.3

Plastic models are shortened to *"Puramo"* in Japanese. So he actually says that he's playing with puramo. Additionally, any plastic model reference after was translated from "puramo."

PAGE 45.6

Gashapon, or "capsule toy," is an onomatopoeia made up of two sounds: *"gacha"* for the turning of a crank on a toy vending machine, and *"pon"* for the sound of the toy capsule dropping into the receptacle. It is used to describe both the machines themselves, and any toy obtained from them.

PAGE 59.4

Little sister in Japanese is *"imouto."* So Sota tried to lie about the boxes belonging to his sister. When called on it, he made it sound as if Kenji had heard him wrong and that the boxes were actually filled with items from *Onono Imoko* instead.

PAGE 73.3
Around the time this comic was drawn, Tsuji Nozomi, famous for being tiny in both stature and brain power was part of Morning Musume. As for the back of his shirt, the Morning Musume members were at one point mainly 12-15 year olds. When members get too old they often are said to "graduate" to other singing groups.

PAGE 78.2
Hachioji is a city in Tokyo Prefecture.

PAGE 103
Manga Cave – The name of this bookstore was originally *"Manga no Ana,"* which is a play on the names of two existing Japanese manga store chains. Toranoana and Manga no Mori. Manga no Mori (literally: Manga Forest) is a manga specialty store. You can find other books there but no video games or DVDs.Toranoana (lit: the Tiger's Den/Cave) is known for selling and buying doujinshi and manga. However, like Manga no Ana, after a while they started selling games, DVDs, music and model kits. They even have a cat-maid café in one of their stores! Go check them out if you are in Japan... But, make sure to bring lots of money!!

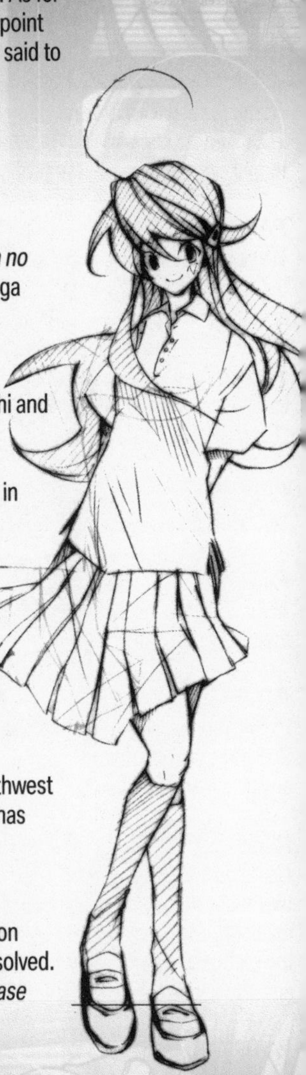

PAGE106.1
Taniya – This is another play on a Japanese brand. Tamiya, Inc is known worldwide for their model toys. They make everything from tanks and airplanes to radio controlled cars and train sets.

PAGE 110
Den-en-choufu is a very rich and exclusive neighborhood in Southwest Tokyo. Filled with boutiques and gourmet restaurants this place has some of the largest homes found in Tokyo City proper.

PAGE 127.3
Kindaichi refers to a creepy, gruesome or macabre sort of situation made famous by the crimes that the literary detective Kindaichi solved. Kindachi has been parodied in many manga such as *Kindaichi Case Files* and *Yoki, Kiku, Koto.*

PAGE 136.3
Doujin Shigeto's name is another of the series' many puns.
Doujin Shigeto = *DOUJINSHIgeto* = Doujinshi Get-o!

CREATOR'S COMMENTS

ゆめのよう…
"IT'S LIKE A DREAM..."

JIRO SUZUKI

SOTA-KUN NO AKIHABARA FUNTOHKI'S FINALLY IN BOOK FORM! IT'S LIKE I'M DREAMING.

I'D LIKE TO SAY A SPECIAL THANKS TO ALL MY FRIENDS, ACQUAINTANCES, AND FAMILY THAT LENT A HELPING HAND AND GAVE ME WORDS OF ENCOURAGEMENT. THANKS ALSO TO MY EDITOR WHO BROUGHT ME THIS FAR, AND TO THOSE WHO PICKED UP THIS BOOK! THANK YOU ALL SO VERY MUCH!

I'M GONNA GIVE IT MY VERY BEST! ★

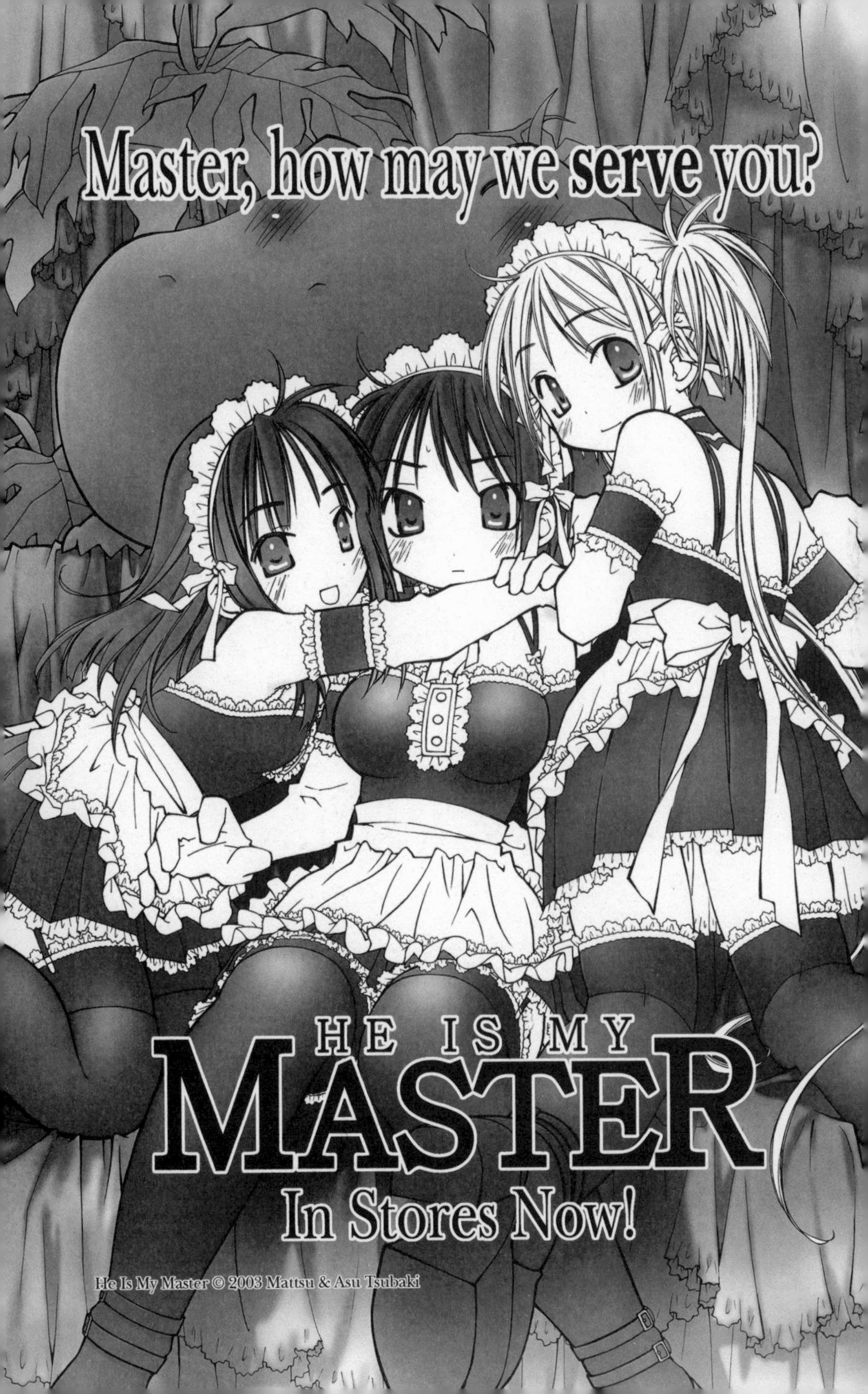

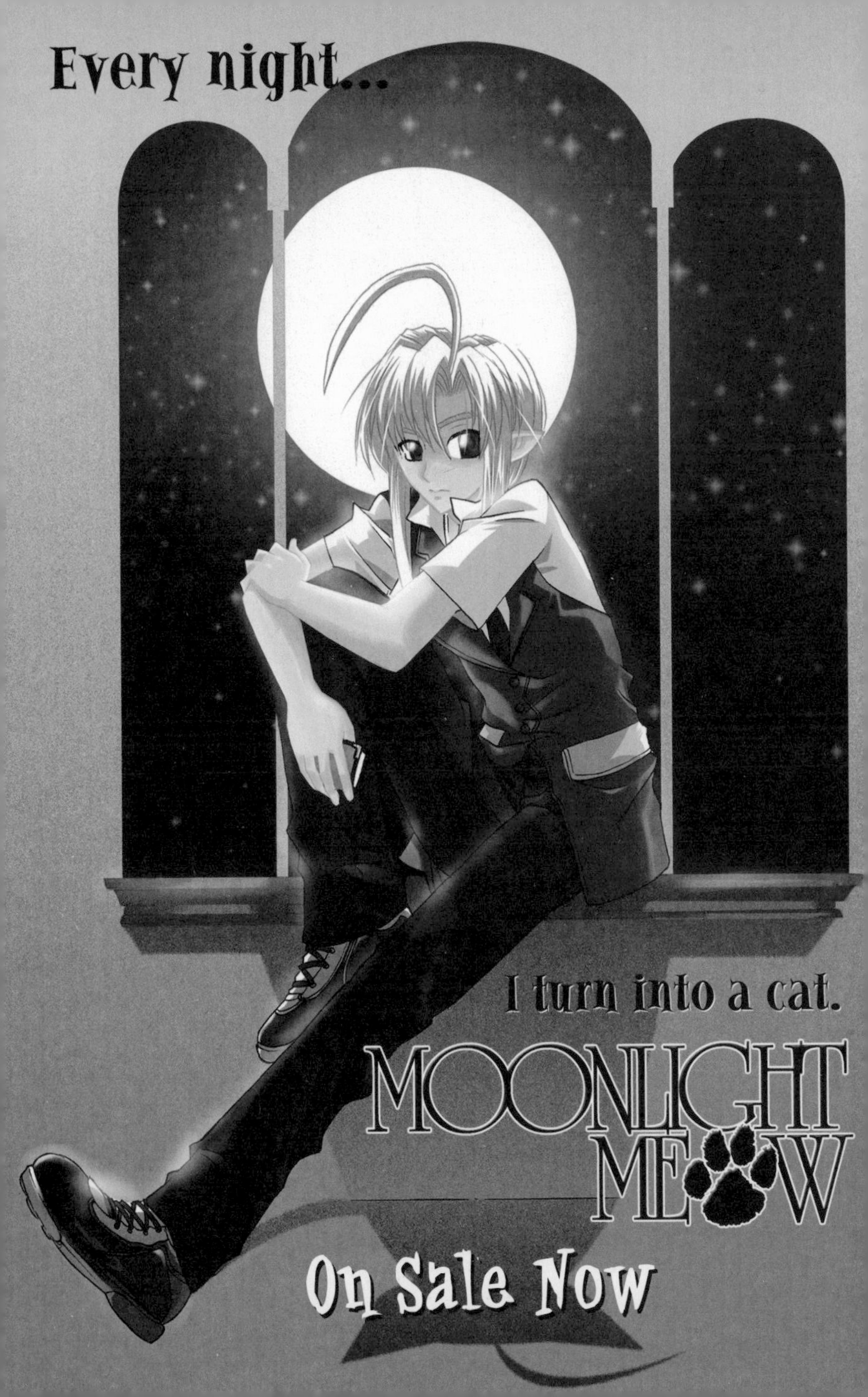
Every night...
I turn into a cat.
MOONLIGHT MEOW
On Sale Now

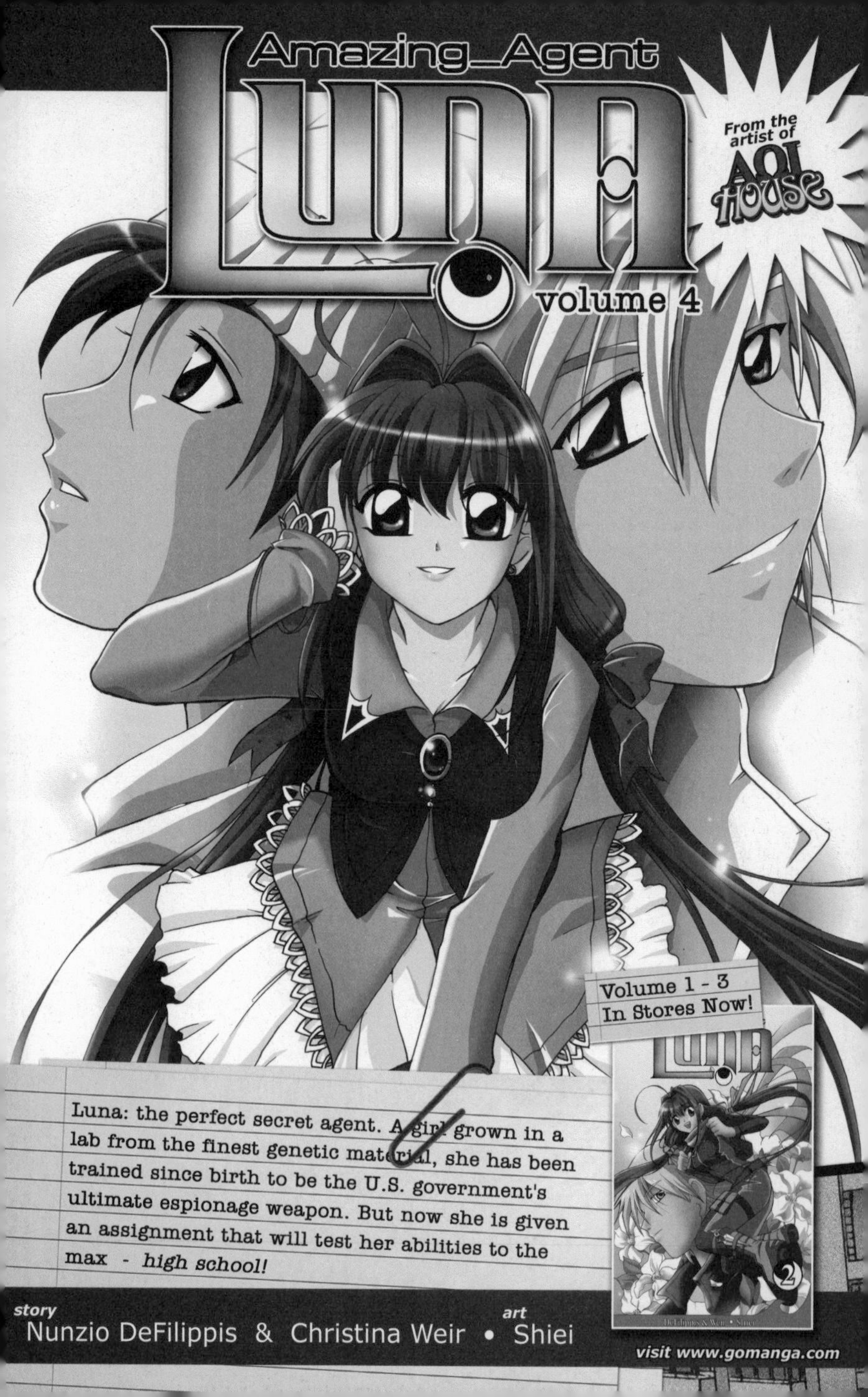
Amazing Agent
LUNA
volume 4
From the artist of
AOI HOUSE
Volume 1 - 3
In Stores Now!
Luna: the perfect secret agent. A girl grown in a lab from the finest genetic material, she has been trained since birth to be the U.S. government's ultimate espionage weapon. But now she is given an assignment that will test her abilities to the max - *high school!*
story
Nunzio DeFilippis & Christina Weir • Shiei
art
visit www.gomanga.com

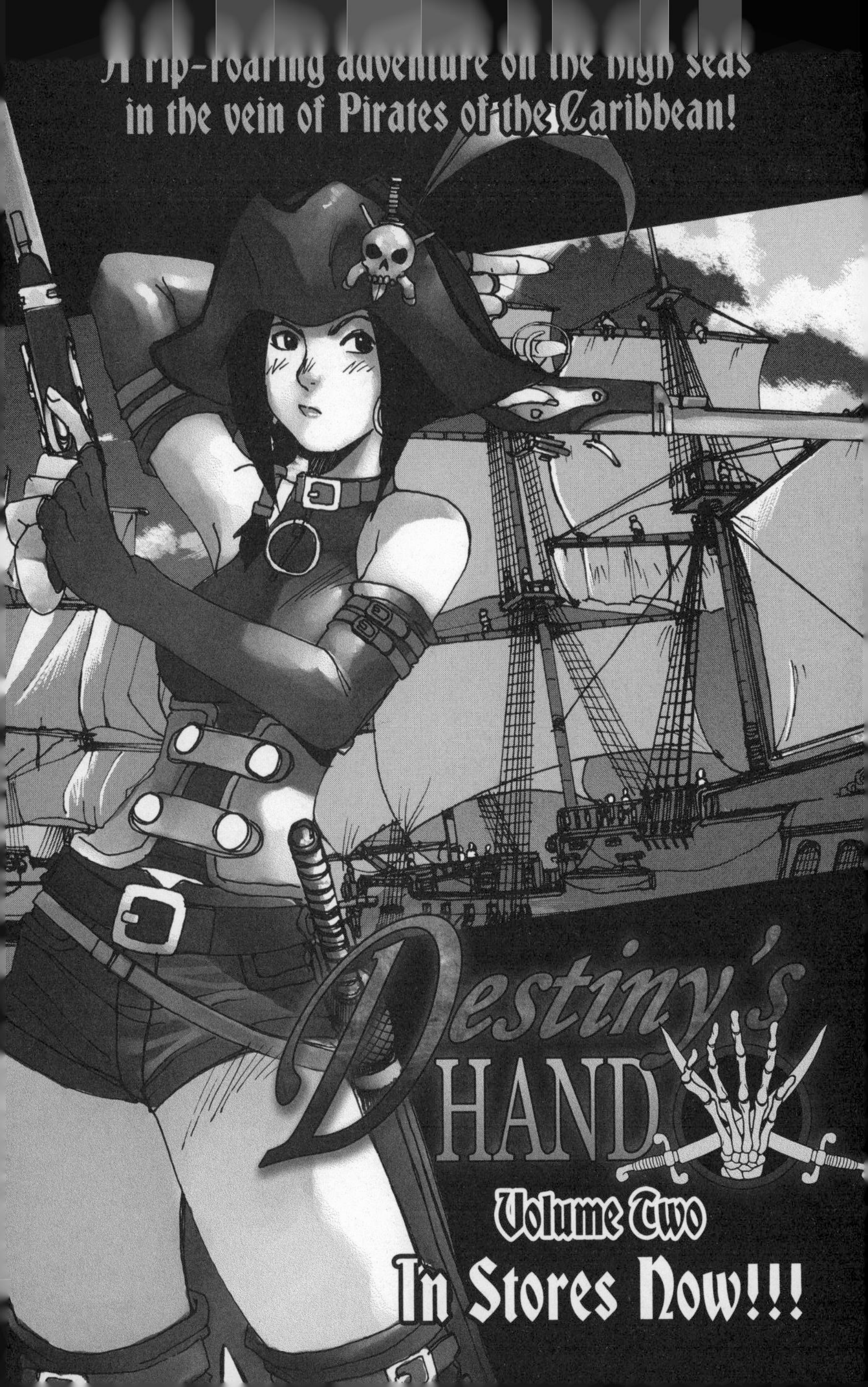
A rip-roaring adventure on the high seas
in the vein of Pirates of the Caribbean!
Destiny's
HAND
Volume Two
In Stores Now!!!

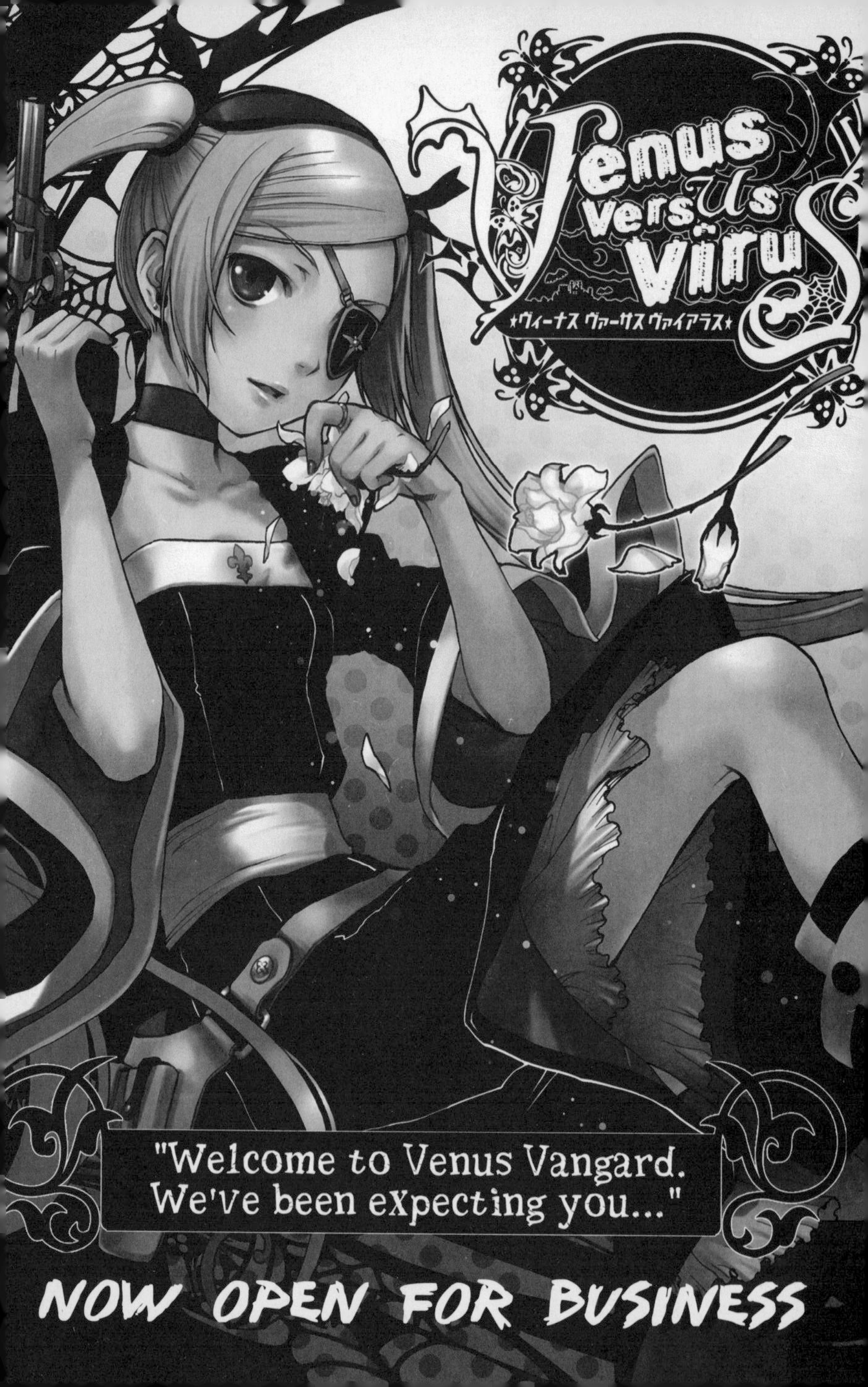

Venus Versus Virus
★ヴィーナス ヴァーサス ヴァイアラス★
"Welcome to Venus Vangard.
We've been expecting you..."
NOW OPEN FOR BUSINESS

Being a girl is harder than it looks...
Because just the other day, she...was a *he*.
The hit gender-bending manga series!
Kashimashi
~Girl Meets Girl~
In Stores Now.
Kashimashi © Satoru ... 2005

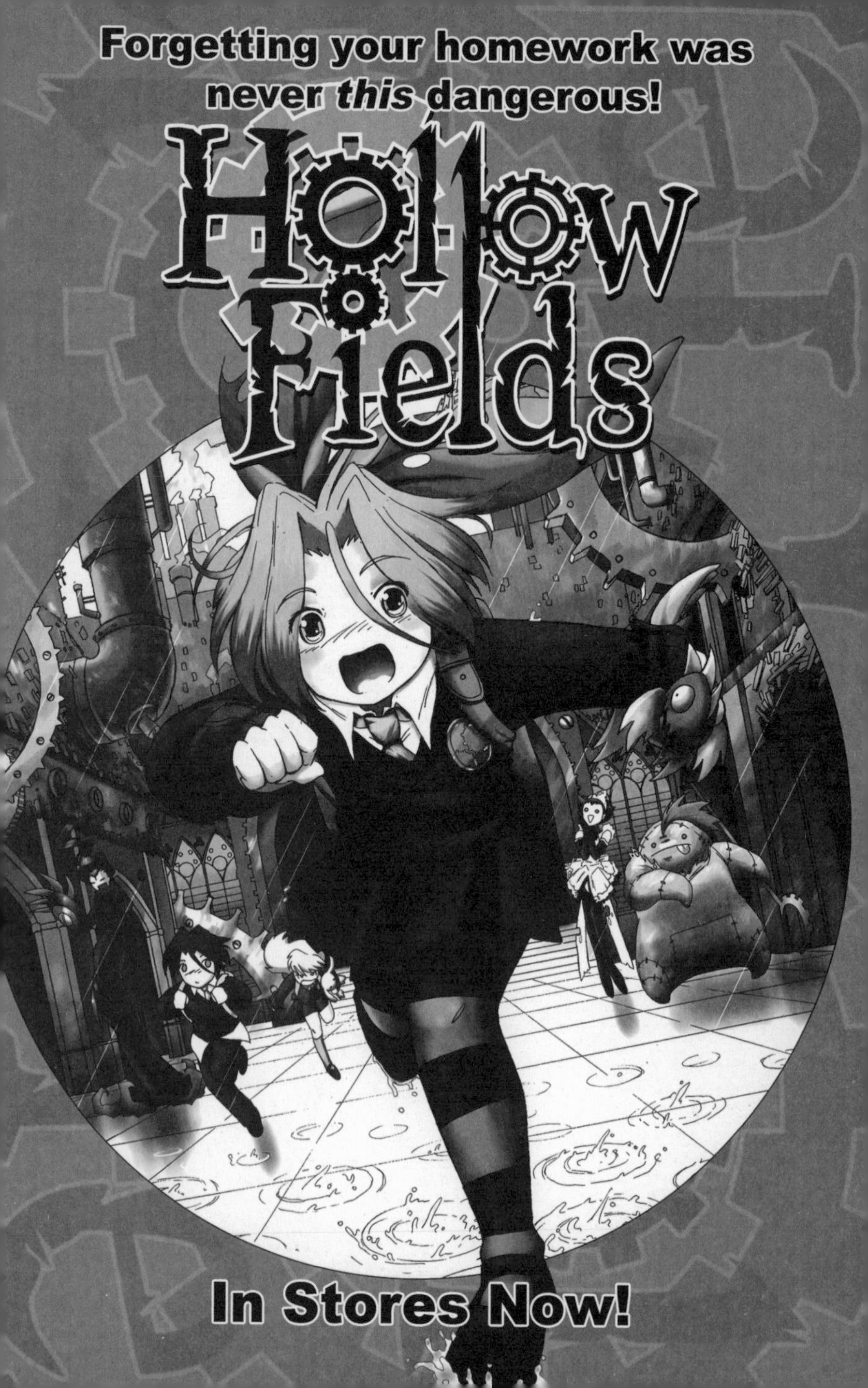
Forgetting your homework was never *this* dangerous!
Hollow Fields
In Stores Now!

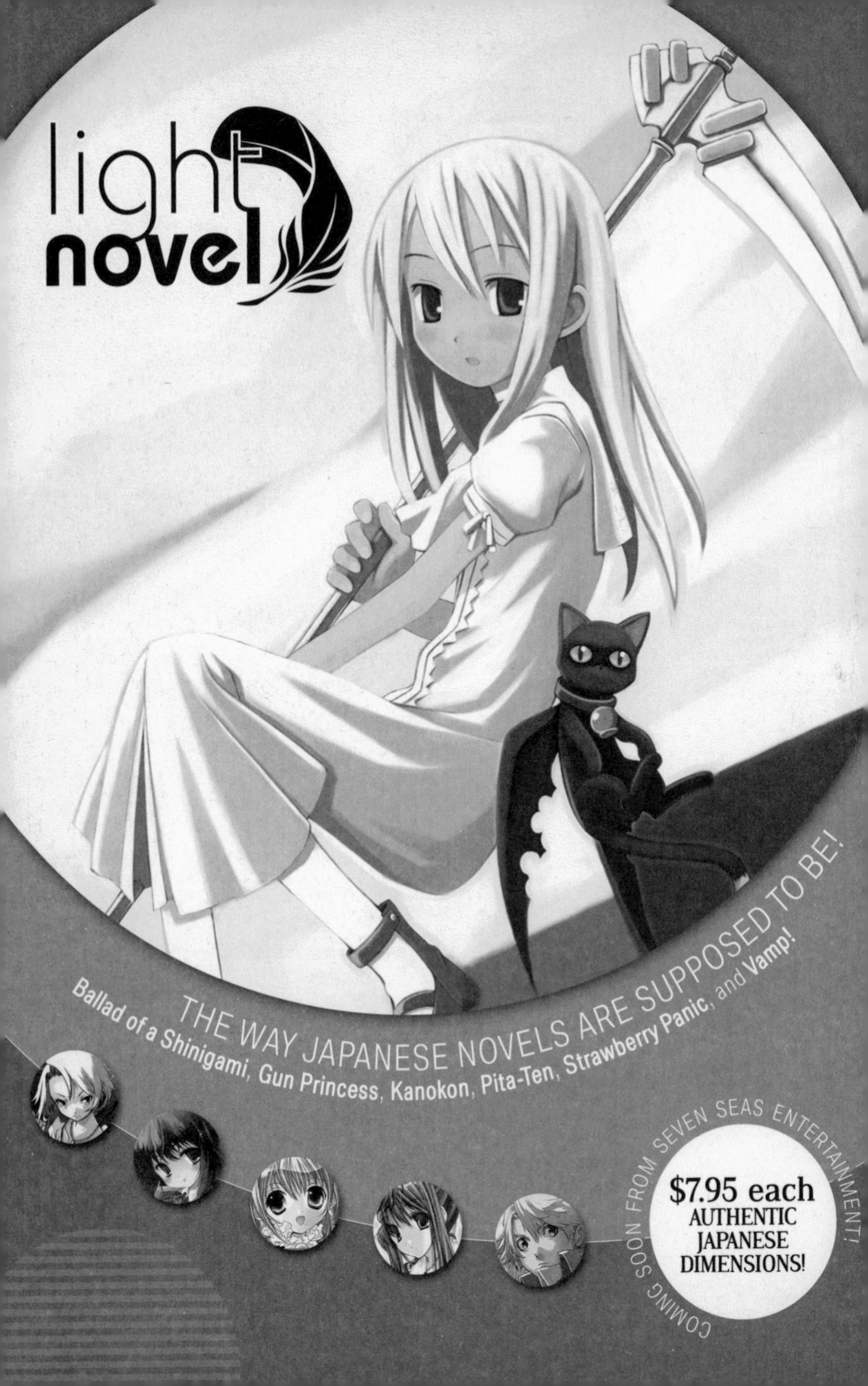
light novel
THE WAY JAPANESE NOVELS ARE SUPPOSED TO BE!
Ballad of a Shinigami, Gun Princess, Kanokon, Pita-Ten, Strawberry Panic, and Vamp!
COMING SOON FROM SEVEN SEAS ENTERTAINMENT!
$7.95 each
AUTHENTIC JAPANESE DIMENSIONS!

I, OTAKU
STRUGGLE IN AKIHABARA

Volume 1

Story & Art Jiro Suzuki

STAFF CREDITS

translation	**Nan Rymer**
adaptation	**Ed Chavez**
lettering	**Roland Amago**
retouch	**Cheese**
	Roland Amago
cover design	**Nicky Lim**
layout	**Bambi Eloriaga**
editor	**Adam Arnold**

publisher **Seven Seas Entertainment**

I,OTAKU VOL. 1
© 2003 Jiro Suzuki / SQUARE ENIX. All rights reserved.
First published in Japan in 2003 by SQUARE ENIX CO., LTD.
English translation rights arranged with SQUARE ENIX CO., LTD. and
Seven Seas Entertainment, LLC. through Tuttle-Mori Agency, Inc.

Visit us online at www.gomanga.com

ISBN: 978-1-933164-76-2

Printed in Canada

First printing: September 2007

10 9 8 7 6 5 4 3 2 1

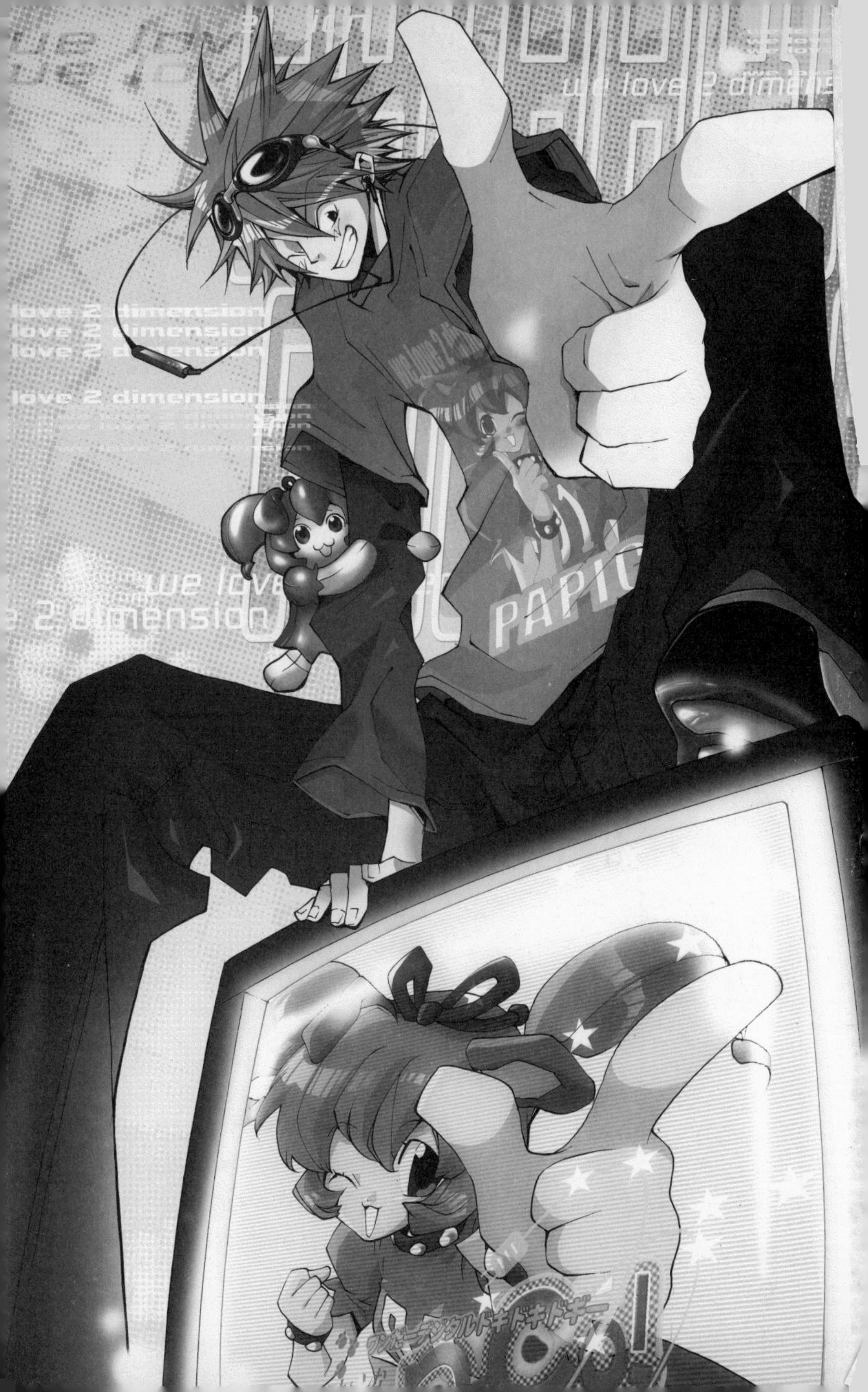
we love 2 dimension
love 2 dimension
love 2 dimension
love 2 dimension
love 2 dimension
we love
2 dimension
we love 2
PAPIC
ワンダーデジタルドキドキドギー

THE END

YOU'RE READING THE WRONG WAY

This is the last page of
I, OTAKU Volume 1.

This book reads from right to left, Japanese style. To read from the beginning, flip the book over to the other side, start with the top right panel, and take it from there.

If this is your first time reading manga, just follow the diagram. It may seem backwards at first, but you'll get used to it! Have fun!